FREE Test Taking Tips Video/DVD Offer

To better serve you, we created videos covering test taking tips that we want to give you for FREE. **These videos cover world-class tips that will help you succeed on your test.**

We just ask that you send us feedback about this product. Please let us know what you thought about it—whether good, bad, or indifferent.

To get your **FREE videos**, you can use the QR code below or email freevideos@studyguideteam.com with "Free Videos" in the subject line and the following information in the body of the email:

   a. The title of your product

   b. Your product rating on a scale of 1-5, with 5 being the highest

   c. Your feedback about the product

If you have any questions or concerns, please don't hesitate to contact us at info@studyguideteam.com.

Thank you!

ExCPT Study Guide 2025 and 2026
3 Practice Tests and ExCPT Exam Prep Book for Pharmacy Technicians [Includes Detailed Answer Explanations]

Lydia Morrison

Copyright © 2025 by TPB Publishing

All rights reserved. No part of this publication may be reproduced, distributed, or transmitted in any form or by any means, including photocopying, recording, or other electronic or mechanical methods, without the prior written permission of the publisher, except in the case of brief quotations embodied in critical reviews and certain other noncommercial uses permitted by copyright law.

Written and edited by TPB Publishing.

TPB Publishing is not associated with or endorsed by any official testing organization. TPB Publishing is a publisher of unofficial educational products. All test and organization names are trademarks of their respective owners. Content in this book is included for utilitarian purposes only and does not constitute an endorsement by TPB Publishing of any particular point of view.

Interested in buying more than 10 copies of our product? Contact us about bulk discounts:
bulkorders@studyguideteam.com

ISBN: 9781637759356

Table of Contents

Welcome --- *1*
   FREE Videos/DVD OFFER 1

Quick Overview --- *2*

Test-Taking Strategies --- *3*

Bonus Content --- *7*

Introduction to the ExCPT Exam --- *8*

Study Prep Plan for the ExCPT Exam --- *10*

Overview and Laws --- *15*
   Role, Scope of Practice, and General Duties 15
   Laws and Regulations 37
   Controlled Substances 49
   Practice Quiz 59
   Answer Explanations 60

Drugs and Drug Therapy --- *62*
   Drug Classification 62
   Frequently Prescribed Medications 84
   Practice Quiz 104
   Answer Explanations 105

Dispensing Process --- *106*
   Prescription and Medication Order Intake and Entry 106
   Preparing and Dispensing Prescriptions 131

Calculations 152

Sterile and Nonsterile Products, Compounding, Unit Dose, and Repackaging 185

Practice Quiz 210

Answer Explanations 211

Medication Safety and Quality Assurance ------------------ 212

Practice Quiz 229

Answer Explanations 230

ExCPT Practice Test #1 ------------------------------------- 231

Answer Explanations #1 ----------------------------------- 245

ExCPT Practice Test #2 ------------------------------------- 260

Answer Explanations #2 ----------------------------------- 275

ExCPT Practice Test #3 ------------------------------------- 290

Welcome

Dear Reader,

Welcome to your new Test Prep Books study guide! We are pleased that you chose us to help you prepare for your exam. There are many study options to choose from, and we appreciate you choosing us. Studying can be a daunting task, but we have designed a smart, effective study guide to help prepare you for what lies ahead.

Whether you're a parent helping your child learn and grow, a high school student working hard to get into your dream college, or a nursing student studying for a complex exam, we want to help give you the tools you need to succeed. We hope this study guide gives you the skills and the confidence to thrive, and we can't thank you enough for allowing us to be part of your journey.

In an effort to continue to improve our products, we welcome feedback from our customers. We look forward to hearing from you. Suggestions, success stories, and criticisms can all be communicated by emailing us at info@studyguideteam.com.

Sincerely,
Test Prep Books Team

FREE Videos/DVD OFFER

Doing well on your exam requires both knowing the test content and understanding how to use that knowledge to do well on the test. We offer completely FREE test taking tip videos. **These videos cover world-class tips that you can use to succeed on your test.**

To get your **FREE videos**, you can use the QR code below or email freevideos@studyguideteam.com with "Free Videos" in the subject line and the following information in the body of the email:

  a. The title of your product
  b. Your product rating on a scale of 1-5, with 5 being the highest
  c. Your feedback about the product

If you have any questions or concerns, please don't hesitate to contact us at info@studyguideteam.com.

Quick Overview

As you draw closer to taking your exam, effective preparation becomes more and more important. Thankfully, you have this study guide to help you get ready. Use this guide to help keep your studying on track and refer to it often.

This study guide contains several key sections that will help you be successful on your exam. The guide contains tips for what you should do the night before and the day of the test. Also included are test-taking tips. Knowing the right information is not always enough. Many well-prepared test takers struggle with exams. These tips will help equip you to accurately read, assess, and answer test questions.

A large part of the guide is devoted to showing you what content to expect on the exam and to helping you better understand that content. In this guide are practice test questions so that you can see how well you have grasped the content. Then, answer explanations are provided so that you can understand why you missed certain questions.

Don't try to cram the night before you take your exam. This is not a wise strategy for a few reasons. First, your retention of the information will be low. Your time would be better used by reviewing information you already know rather than trying to learn a lot of new information. Second, you will likely become stressed as you try to gain a large amount of knowledge in a short amount of time. Third, you will be depriving yourself of sleep. So be sure to go to bed at a reasonable time the night before. Being well-rested helps you focus and remain calm.

Be sure to eat a substantial breakfast the morning of the exam. If you are taking the exam in the afternoon, be sure to have a good lunch as well. Being hungry is distracting and can make it difficult to focus. You have hopefully spent lots of time preparing for the exam. Don't let an empty stomach get in the way of success!

When travelling to the testing center, leave earlier than needed. That way, you have a buffer in case you experience any delays. This will help you remain calm and will keep you from missing your appointment time at the testing center.

Be sure to pace yourself during the exam. Don't try to rush through the exam. There is no need to risk performing poorly on the exam just so you can leave the testing center early. Allow yourself to use all of the allotted time if needed.

Remain positive while taking the exam even if you feel like you are performing poorly. Thinking about the content you should have mastered will not help you perform better on the exam.

Once the exam is complete, take some time to relax. Even if you feel that you need to take the exam again, you will be well served by some down time before you begin studying again. It's often easier to convince yourself to study if you know that it will come with a reward!

Test-Taking Strategies

1. Predicting the Answer

When you feel confident in your preparation for a multiple-choice test, try predicting the answer before reading the answer choices. This is especially useful on questions that test objective factual knowledge. By predicting the answer before reading the available choices, you eliminate the possibility that you will be distracted or led astray by an incorrect answer choice. You will feel more confident in your selection if you read the question, predict the answer, and then find your prediction among the answer choices. After using this strategy, be sure to still read all of the answer choices carefully and completely. If you feel unprepared, you should not attempt to predict the answers. This would be a waste of time and an opportunity for your mind to wander in the wrong direction.

2. Reading the Whole Question

Too often, test takers scan a multiple-choice question, recognize a few familiar words, and immediately jump to the answer choices. Test authors are aware of this common impatience, and they will sometimes prey upon it. For instance, a test author might subtly turn the question into a negative, or he or she might redirect the focus of the question right at the end. The only way to avoid falling into these traps is to read the entirety of the question carefully before reading the answer choices.

3. Looking for Wrong Answers

Long and complicated multiple-choice questions can be intimidating. One way to simplify a difficult multiple-choice question is to eliminate all of the answer choices that are clearly wrong. In most sets of answers, there will be at least one selection that can be dismissed right away. If the test is administered on paper, the test taker could draw a line through it to indicate that it may be ignored; otherwise, the test taker will have to perform this operation mentally or on scratch paper. In either case, once the obviously incorrect answers have been eliminated, the remaining choices may be considered. Sometimes identifying the clearly wrong answers will give the test taker some information about the correct answer. For instance, if one of the remaining answer choices is a direct opposite of one of the eliminated answer choices, it may well be the correct answer. The opposite of obviously wrong is obviously right! Of course, this is not always the case. Some answers are obviously incorrect simply because they are irrelevant to the question being asked. Still, identifying and eliminating some incorrect answer choices is a good way to simplify a multiple-choice question.

4. Don't Overanalyze

Anxious test takers often overanalyze questions. When you are nervous, your brain will often run wild, causing you to make associations and discover clues that don't actually exist. If you feel that this may be a problem for you, do whatever you can to slow down during the test. Try taking a deep breath or counting to ten. As you read and consider the question, restrict yourself to the particular words used by the author. Avoid thought tangents about what the author *really* meant, or what he or she was *trying* to say. The only things that matter on a multiple-choice test are the words that are actually in the question. You must avoid reading too much into a multiple-choice question, or supposing that the writer meant something other than what he or she wrote.

5. No Need for Panic

It is wise to learn as many strategies as possible before taking a multiple-choice test, but it is likely that you will come across a few questions for which you simply don't know the answer. In this situation, avoid panicking. Because most multiple-choice tests include dozens of questions, the relative value of a single wrong answer is small. As much as possible, you should compartmentalize each question on a multiple-choice test. In other words, you should not allow your feelings about one question to affect your success on the others. When you find a question that you either don't understand or don't know how to answer, just take a deep breath and do your best. Read the entire question slowly and carefully. Try rephrasing the question a couple of different ways. Then, read all of the answer choices carefully. After eliminating obviously wrong answers, make a selection and move on to the next question.

6. Confusing Answer Choices

When working on a difficult multiple-choice question, there may be a tendency to focus on the answer choices that are the easiest to understand. Many people, whether consciously or not, gravitate to the answer choices that require the least concentration, knowledge, and memory. This is a mistake. When you come across an answer

choice that is confusing, you should give it extra attention. A question might be confusing because you do not know the subject matter to which it refers. If this is the case, don't eliminate the answer before you have affirmatively settled on another. When you come across an answer choice of this type, set it aside as you look at the remaining choices. If you can confidently assert that one of the other choices is correct, you can leave the confusing answer aside. Otherwise, you will need to take a moment to try to better understand the confusing answer choice. Rephrasing is one way to tease out the sense of a confusing answer choice.

7. Your First Instinct

Many people struggle with multiple-choice tests because they overthink the questions. If you have studied sufficiently for the test, you should be prepared to trust your first instinct once you have carefully and completely read the question and all of the answer choices. There is a great deal of research suggesting that the mind can come to the correct conclusion very quickly once it has obtained all of the relevant information. At times, it may seem to you as if your intuition is working faster even than your reasoning mind. This may in fact be true. The knowledge you obtain while studying may be retrieved from your subconscious before you have a chance to work out the associations that support it. Verify your instinct by working out the reasons that it should be trusted.

8. Key Words

Many test takers struggle with multiple-choice questions because they have poor reading comprehension skills. Quickly reading and understanding a multiple-choice question requires a mixture of skill and experience. To help with this, try jotting down a few key words and phrases on a piece of scrap paper. Doing this concentrates the process of reading and forces the mind to weigh the relative importance of the question's parts. In selecting words and phrases to write down, the test taker thinks about the question more deeply and carefully. This is especially true for multiple-choice questions that are preceded by a long prompt.

9. Subtle Negatives

One of the oldest tricks in the multiple-choice test writer's book is to subtly reverse the meaning of a question with a word like *not* or *except*. If you are not paying attention to each word in the question, you can easily be led astray by this trick. For instance, a common question format is, "Which of the following is...?" Obviously, if the question instead is, "Which of the following is not...?," then the answer will be quite different. Even worse, the test makers are aware of the potential for this mistake and will include one answer choice that would be correct if the question were not negated or reversed. A test taker who misses the reversal will find what he or she believes to be a correct answer and will be so confident that he or she will fail to reread the question and discover the original error. The only way to avoid this is to practice a wide variety of multiple-choice questions and to pay close attention to each and every word.

10. Reading Every Answer Choice

It may seem obvious, but you should always read every one of the answer choices! Too many test takers fall into the habit of scanning the question and assuming that they understand the question because they recognize a few key words. From there, they pick the first answer choice that answers the question they believe they have read. Test takers who read all of the answer choices might discover that one of the latter answer choices is actually *more* correct. Moreover, reading all of the answer choices can remind you of facts related to the question that can help you arrive at the correct answer. Sometimes, a misstatement or incorrect detail in one of the latter answer choices will trigger your memory of the subject and will enable you to find the right answer. Failing to read all of the answer choices is like not reading all of the items on a restaurant menu: you might miss out on the perfect choice.

11. Spot the Hedges

One of the keys to success on multiple-choice tests is paying close attention to every word. This is never truer than with words like *almost*, *most*, *some*, and *sometimes*. These words are called "hedges" because they indicate that a statement is not totally true or not true in every place and time. An absolute statement will contain no hedges, but in many subjects, the answers are not always straightforward or absolute. There are always exceptions to the rules

in these subjects. For this reason, you should favor those multiple-choice questions that contain hedging language. The presence of qualifying words indicates that the author is taking special care with his or her words, which is certainly important when composing the right answer. After all, there are many ways to be wrong, but there is only one way to be right! For this reason, it is wise to avoid answers that are absolute when taking a multiple-choice test. An absolute answer is one that says things are either all one way or all another. They often include words like *every*, *always*, *best*, and *never*. If you are taking a multiple-choice test in a subject that doesn't lend itself to absolute answers, be on your guard if you see any of these words.

12. Long Answers

In many subject areas, the answers are not simple. As already mentioned, the right answer often requires hedges. Another common feature of the answers to a complex or subjective question are qualifying clauses, which are groups of words that subtly modify the meaning of the sentence. If the question or answer choice describes a rule to which there are exceptions or the subject matter is complicated, ambiguous, or confusing, the correct answer will require many words in order to be expressed clearly and accurately. In essence, you should not be deterred by answer choices that seem excessively long. Oftentimes, the author of the text will not be able to write the correct answer without offering some qualifications and

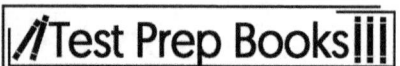

modifications. Your job is to read the answer choices thoroughly and completely and to select the one that most accurately and precisely answers the question.

13. Restating to Understand

Sometimes, a question on a multiple-choice test is difficult not because of what it asks but because of how it is written. If this is the case, restate the question or answer choice in different words. This process serves a couple of important purposes. First, it forces you to concentrate on the core of the question. In order to rephrase the question accurately, you have to understand it well. Rephrasing the question will concentrate your mind on the key words and ideas. Second, it will present the information to your mind in a fresh way. This process may trigger your memory and render some useful scrap of information picked up while studying.

14. True Statements

Sometimes an answer choice will be true in itself, but it does not answer the question. This is one of the main reasons why it is essential to read the question carefully and completely before proceeding to the answer choices. Too often, test takers skip ahead to the answer choices and look for true statements. Having found one of these, they are content to select it without reference to the question above. The savvy test taker will always read the entire question before turning to the answer choices. Then, having settled on a correct answer choice, he or she will refer to the original question and ensure that the selected answer is relevant. The mistake of choosing a correct-but-irrelevant answer choice is especially common on questions related to specific pieces of objective knowledge.

15. No Patterns

One of the more dangerous ideas that circulates about multiple-choice tests is that the correct answers tend to fall into patterns. These erroneous ideas range from a belief that B and C are the most common right answers, to the idea that an unprepared test-taker should answer "A-B-A-C-A-D-A-B-A." It cannot be emphasized enough that pattern-seeking of this type is exactly the WRONG way to approach a multiple-choice test. To begin with, it is highly unlikely that the test maker will plot the correct answers according to some predetermined pattern. The questions are scrambled and delivered in a random order. Furthermore, even if the test maker was following a pattern in the assignation of correct answers, there is no reason why the test taker would know which pattern he or she was using. Any attempt to discern a pattern in the answer choices is a waste of time and a distraction from the real work of taking the test. A test taker would be much better served by extra preparation before the test than by reliance on a pattern in the answers.

Bonus Content

We host multiple bonus items online, including all 3 practice tests in digital format. Scan the QR code or go to this link to access this content:

testprepbooks.com/bonus/excpt

The first time you access the tests, you will need to register as a "new user" and verify your email address.

If you have any issues, please email support@testprepbooks.com.

Introduction to the ExCPT Exam

Function of the Test

More and more employers are looking for certified pharmacy technicians to meet the evolving and growing needs of the pharmacy industry, particularly as pharmacy technicians are called upon to play an increasing role in ensuring the safety and efficacy of patient care. To meet that demand, the National Healthcareer Association (NHA) offers the Exam for the Certification of Pharmacy Technicians (ExCPT) to provide Certified Pharmacy Technician (CPhT) credentials to successful test-takers.

Test Administration

The eligibility requirements for the ExCPT exam consist of a high school diploma, GED, or other high school equivalency in addition to pharmacy technician experience through either a training program route or a work experience route. The training program route requires an ExCPT applicant to complete a program for training or educating pharmacy technicians within five years of the test application date. The work experience route requires an ExCPT applicant to have completed a minimum of 1200 hours of pharmacy-related work under supervision within a one year time period. This work experience must have occurred within three years of the test application date.

To apply, each applicant must create a free, online NHA account. This is where the applicant will submit their exam application.

Part of the application will include choosing a date for either an online or in-person test and paying the $125 exam fee. The online test will use live remote proctoring. In-person tests will take place either at the applicant's institution, if it is NHA approved, or at a PSI testing center.

Accommodations may be available for those with documented disabilities. Test-takers will need to submit the Accommodation Request form in order to be considered for accommodation.

Exam retakes are allowed after thirty days. To retake the exam, an applicant must login as a returning candidate, schedule the exam, and pay the $125 exam fee. The ExCPT exam may be retaken three times with thirty days between each attempt. For every retake after the third attempt, there is a one year waiting period.

Test Format

The ExCPT exam consists of 120 questions. One hundred questions are scored, while twenty unscored pretest questions are scattered throughout the exam. The test-taker will not know which questions are scored and which are unscored, although only the scored questions will count toward the final score.

Each question is multiple choice with four possible answer options. The test is primarily computer-based, although paper/pencil testing may be available at specific locations.

The test-taker will have two hours and ten minutes to complete the exam.

Introduction to the ExCPT Exam

The ExCPT exam has four main content areas, or domains. They are listed in the chart below, along with the number of questions for each content area:

Content Area	Number of Questions on the Exam
Overview and Laws	25 questions
Drugs and Drug Therapy	15 questions
Dispensing Process	45 questions
Medication Safety and Quality Assurance	15 questions
Pretest (unscored)	20 questions
Total	**120 questions**

Scoring

The ExCPT exam uses a scaled scoring method to ensure consistency across multiple forms of the test. A passing score is 390; possible scores range from 200 to 500.

A score report that includes the final exam score, pass/fail information, and diagnostic information of the test-taker's performance in each content area listed above will be provided in the test-taker's NHA account.

Computer-based tests taken at a test-taker's institution will provide preliminary score reports directly after completing the exam. Test-takers who take online exams or who take computer-based exams at PSI testing centers will receive official certification results via their NHA account page within two days of their test being scored. Test takers who opt for pencil/paper exams will receive their score reports within twenty-four hours of NHA receiving their answer sheets; please be advised that receipt of the answer sheets may take up to ten business days after completion of the exam.

If the test-taker achieves a passing score, they will be notified by email that they can print their certificate from their NHA account. Please note that a preliminary score report does not prove certification; the only documentation proving certification is the test-taker's formal certificate.

Expiration and Recertification

CPhT certification must be renewed every two years. To renew, the pharmacy technician must create an account or login to an existing account at NHANOW.com. Recertification consists of at least twenty hours of specifically pharmacy-technician practice continuing education, with one hour required to be in pharmacy law and one hour required to be in patient safety. In addition, there is a recertification fee of $55.

If a pharmacy technician's certification has expired within one year, they are eligible to be reinstated. Reinstatement will require the above continuing education hours, the recertification fee, and an additional reinstatement fee. If a pharmacy technician's certification expired more than one year ago, it will be necessary to retake the ExCPT exam, including paying the $125 exam fee.

Study Prep Plan for the ExCPT Exam

1 **Schedule** - Use one of our study schedules below or come up with one of your own.

2 **Relax** - Test anxiety can hurt even the best students. There are many ways to reduce stress. Find the one that works best for you.

3 **Execute** - Once you have a good plan in place, be sure to stick to it.

One Week Study Schedule

Day 1	Overview and Laws
Day 2	Drugs and Drug Therapy
Day 3	Prescription and Medication Order Intake and Entry
Day 4	Calculations
Day 5	Medication Safety and Quality Assurance
Day 6	Practice Test #1
Day 7	Take Your Exam!

Two Week Study Schedule

Day 1	Overview and Laws	Day 8	Calculating Individual and Total Daily Dosages
Day 2	Laws and Regulations	Day 9	Sterile and Nonsterile Products, Compounding...
Day 3	Drugs and Drug Therapy	Day 10	Medication Safety and Quality Assurance
Day 4	Frequently Prescribed Medications	Day 11	Practice Test #1
Day 5	Prescription and Medication Order...	Day 12	Practice Test #2
Day 6	Preparing and Dispensing Prescriptions	Day 13	Practice Test #3
Day 7	Calculations	Day 14	Take Your Exam!

Study Prep Plan for the ExCPT Exam

One Month Study Schedule						
	Day 1	Overview and Laws	Day 11	Processing Prescription Orders	Day 21	Medication Safety and Quality Assurance
	Day 2	Basic Medical Terminology...	Day 12	Preparing and Dispensing...	Day 22	Safety Strategies to Prevent Mix Ups
	Day 3	Identifying and Removing Expired...	Day 13	Labeling Medication Products	Day 23	Corrective Action after Detecting Potential...
	Day 4	Laws and Regulations	Day 14	Calculations	Day 24	Practice Test #1
	Day 5	Controlled Substances	Day 15	Calculating Individual and Total Daily Dosages	Day 25	Answer Explanations #1
	Day 6	Drugs and Drug Therapy	Day 16	Sterile and Nonsterile Compounding...	Day 26	Practice Test #2
	Day 7	Dosage Forms	Day 17	Basic Pharmacy Business Calculations	Day 27	Answer Explanations #2
	Day 8	Frequently Prescribed Medications	Day 18	Sterile and Nonsterile Products...	Day 28	Practice Test #3
	Day 9	Differentiating between...	Day 19	Compounding Non-Sterile Products	Day 29	Answer Explanations #3
	Day 10	Prescription and Medication Order...	Day 20	Maintaining Sterile and Nonsterile...	Day 30	Take Your Exam!

As you study for your test, we'd like to take the opportunity to remind you that you are capable of great things! With the right tools and dedication, you truly can do anything you set your mind to. The fact that you are holding this book right now shows how committed you are. In case no one has told you lately, you've got this! Our intention behind including this coloring page is to give you the chance to take some time to engage your creative side when you need a little brain-break from studying. As a company, we want to encourage people like you to achieve their dreams by providing good quality study materials for the tests and certifications that improve careers and change lives. As individuals, many of us have taken such tests in our careers, and we know how challenging this process can be. While we can't come alongside you and cheer you on personally, we can offer you the space to recall your purpose, reconnect with your passion, and refresh your brain through an artistic practice. We wish you every success, and happy studying!

Overview and Laws

Role, Scope of Practice, and General Duties

Tasks Performed by Pharmacy Technicians and Pharmacists

Role of the Pharmacy Technician

The primary role of a pharmacy technician is to assist a pharmacist with preparing medicine and providing it to patients. More specifically, they order, make, or locate the needed medication and then dispense, package, and label it. Their work is reviewed by the supervising pharmacist who confirms the accuracy of the final medication dispensed when compared to the original prescription. Their work may also include reviewing prescription orders; weighing, measuring, and mixing medications; maintaining patient records; and placing orders. A pharmacy technician's permitted activities are dictated by law; for instance, a pharmacy technician is not authorized to work in the absence of a pharmacist, and if they handle or dispense medication, it must be approved and supervised by a pharmacist. Pharmacy technicians can work in hospitals, drug stores, or grocery stores containing a pharmacy.

Role of the Pharmacist

There are certain activities in pharmacy operations that require pharmacist intervention in order to ensure safe and effective use of medications by patients. A pharmacist needs to utilize various resources, professional judgement, and/or consultation with the prescriber and patient to make a decision under those circumstances. Provided below are examples of situations where a technician should seek the pharmacist's attention for guidance and the appropriate intervention.

Verification of Prescriptions

There are several reasons why a pharmacist needs to verify a prescription before preparing and dispensing it. A prescription must be verified by a pharmacist to ensure that it is not fraudulent, the dosage is reasonable, it is being given to the correct patient, and more.

A pharmacist must complete the following steps to verify prescriptions properly. First, they must organize all items to be verified. This allows the pharmacist to identify prescriptions easily, fully understand the scope of each job, and work through all prescriptions for a single patient before moving to the prescriptions for the next patient. Second, they compare the prescriptions with the corresponding patient's medical records and decide whether they appear to be reasonable. This step enables them to identify errors such as incorrect or missing information from the prescriber. Third, they consider any interactions between the newly prescribed drug and other drugs the patient takes to make sure there are no duplicate prescriptions or undesirable drug interactions. This helps ensure the patient's safety because many drugs, when taken with certain other drugs, produce adverse effects. Finally, many pharmacists finish the verification process by ensuring that the drug in the vial matches its label and prescription and that the patient or insurance is being billed correctly.

Requirements for Counseling

The Omnibus Budget Reconciliation Act of 1990, often referred to as OBRA '90, established a legal requirement for all pharmacists within the United States to offer medication counseling to every patient. Pharmacists may be mandated to offer pharmaceutical counseling, but they are not required to provide counseling if a patient or their legal caregiver does not want it. The purposes of pharmaceutical counseling are to ensure that patients have access to the important information about their prescribed medication and to advise patients how to handle and take their medication properly.

Drug Utilization Review

A drug utilization review (**DUR**) is an authorized, systematic, and ongoing review about the prescribing, dispensing, and use of a medication in respect to a specific patient's condition(s). It incorporates a comprehensive review of the patient's health history and medication profile for the purpose of making an appropriate decision prior to dispensing a medication.

A pharmacist intervention in a DUR improves the quality of patient care by preventing adverse drug reactions and minimizing inappropriate drug therapies. Pharmacy software generally picks up on various issues that require a DUR intervention. When a DUR conflict arises, the pharmacist needs to use an appropriate intervention code to fill, or reject to fill, the prescription.

Here are some examples:

- **Drug-drug interactions**: patient taking two or more medications that could interact and alter the intended therapeutic effects and/or cause some adverse effects
- **Drug-disease interactions**: patient receives a prescription for a medication that is contraindicated in the patient's disease condition
- **Drug-patient precaution**: medication that could be inappropriate for a patient in respect to the patient's age, gender, allergies, pregnancy, or other factors
- Inappropriate treatment duration
- Medication overuse/misuse/abuse or under-utilization
- Drug dosage modification
- Formulary substitutions (e.g., therapeutic interchange, generic substitution)

Example Scenario for a DUR

A patient is on warfarin as a blood thinner for prevention of cardiovascular events. The patient receives a prescription for naproxen 500 mg (non-steroidal anti-inflammatory medication) for treatment of his tendinitis. This situation will result in a DUR conflict for drug-drug interaction requiring pharmacist intervention. The pharmacist needs to consult with the prescriber to change the therapy as naproxen could augment the effect of warfarin and cause internal hemorrhage (bleeding).

Over-the-Counter Recommendations

Patients often seek over-the-counter (OTC) recommendations for the treatment of minor ailments. However, the pharmacist should assess the patient's condition(s), including the disease and concurrent use of other medications, prior to giving any recommendation. Pharmacist intervention is crucial in OTC recommendations to ensure the patient's safety and benefit. Before recommending an OTC medication, a pharmacist should rule out any alarming symptoms that might require an emergency or physician intervention.

Example Scenario for OTC Recommendation

A patient comes to the pharmacy counter asking the technician for an OTC pain reliever for his neck and chest pain. When the pharmacist collects the patient's information, the description of his pain (pain radiating to the left side of the body) strongly resembles symptoms of ischemic heart disease. The patient should be immediately referred to a hospital without any OTC medication recommended.

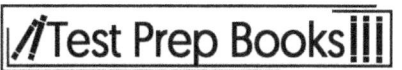

Overview and Laws

Post-Immunization Follow-Up

The vaccines commonly administered by pharmacists include pneumococcal for pneumonia, the herpes zoster series for shingles, and influenza for flu. Protocols govern which vaccines pharmacists may administer and the age groups they can administer vaccines to. Protocols also govern required licensing, training, and vaccine reporting procedures, which vary by state. Pharmacists are trained to recognize adverse reactions following immunizations, educate patients on potential side effects after receiving a vaccination, and report adverse reactions and side effects when they happen. Adverse vaccine reactions should be reported using the **Vaccine Adverse Event Reporting System (VAERS)**. VAERS operates under the guidance of the **Centers for Disease Control (CDC)** and the **Food and Drug Administration (FDA).** The CDC and FDA are responsible for the collection and surveillance of adverse event information across the United States.

Patient education is perhaps one of the most important responsibilities of a pharmacist regarding vaccinations. Pharmacists should understand current vaccination schedules in order to properly counsel patients on which vaccines are recommended and when to receive them. Vaccine schedules are important to make sure patients are fully protected. This is especially true of vaccines that are given in series. For example, the herpes zoster vaccine Shingrix is a series of two vaccines typically administered two to six months apart. Pharmacist follow-up will help to not only ensure that patients who receive the initial vaccine in the series also receive the second in the series but also ensure that the vaccines are administered within the recommended time frame.

Miscellaneous Interventions

There are certain other situations that require pharmacist intervention. Technicians should be advised to always seek the pharmacist's attention while dealing with these issues:

- **Formulary substitutions**: Therapeutic and generic substitutions often require an intervention by the pharmacist for the best treatment outcome. A pharmacist might contact the prescriber if drug-drug/drug-disease interactions or allergies warrant a therapeutic substitution.

- **Misuse/overuse**: Certain medications, including narcotics, controlled substances, stimulants, and psychotomimetic agents, may be misused or overused. A pharmacist should intervene appropriately to limit the use of those medications by the patient. The pharmacist can educate the patient and consult with the prescriber when he or she suspects medication overuse.

- **Missed doses**: Patients often seek advice regarding missed doses. The recommendations for a missed dose vary significantly for different medication types, including maintenance medications (e.g., for hypertension, diabetes), antibiotics, and oral contraceptives. A pharmacist can appropriately intervene in such situations to find solutions and offer the best advice to the patient.

- **Compliance**: Sometimes patients do not follow instructions for medication dosage (e.g., taking larger or smaller doses of medication than prescribed), length of time, and/or time of day to take their medication. They may also discontinue their treatment or take expired medications. Any of these scenarios should be brought to the attention of a pharmacist so they can consult with both the patient and the patient's doctor.

- **Forged prescriptions**: If a pharmacy technician has reason to believe that a prescription is a forgery, they must bring it to the attention of the pharmacist immediately.

Scope of Pharmacy Technician Practice

A pharmacy technician's scope of practice is broad and diverse yet much more limited than that of a pharmacist. The pharmacy technician's primary goal is to help the pharmacist to fulfill their responsibilities. This involves a wide range of tasks. For example, a pharmacy technician is licensed to communicate with insurance providers, healthcare providers, and patients. They may prepare and fill prescriptions, manage inventory, maintain the pharmacy

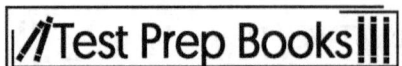

equipment, and prepare labels. Their work must be supervised or verified by a pharmacist. Additionally, pharmacy technicians are not licensed to give patients advice on prescription medications, over-the-counter drugs, or dietary supplements.

Pharmacy Operations and Process Flow

Pharmacies must provide prescribed medications to patients in a manner consistent with local and federal laws. Pharmacies are typically divided into two separate areas where processes occur: front-end and back-end. At the front-end, patients will give their prescription to a pharmacy technician or assistant. From there, the prescription is given to a pharmacist to fill in the back-end. The pharmacist must also verify that the prepared medications are accurate. At the front-end, the pharmacy technician or assistant collects payment either directly from the patient or by billing their insurance provider. Lastly, the patient receives their medication.

Pharmacy Practice Settings

Pharmacies most commonly exist in hospitals and stores, but they can also be found in many other settings. Those within hospitals are called in-patient pharmacies because they only serve patients within the hospital. Pharmacies within stores, as well as independent pharmacies that anyone can go to, are considered community pharmacies. Institutional pharmacies are part of a medical facility and only serve that facility's patients; however, they are not on the same premises as the medical institution. Like hospital pharmacies, a clinic pharmacy can be found within a medical clinic. This includes long-term care pharmacies that serve patients where they live, such as in a nursing home. Pharmacies within clinics enable pharmacists and pharmacy technicians to have close contact with prescribing physicians or physician assistants. Research pharmacies are typically found in facilities where pharmaceuticals are manufactured and other research institutes, such as universities. Research pharmacies discover and produce new drugs in laboratory settings. Regulatory pharmacies exist to test medications and ensure that they meet legal standards. Lastly, compounding pharmacies customize medication for each specific patient.

Maintaining Pharmacy Security

Pharmacy Security Measures

Pharmacies are federally required to utilize a variety of security measures to ensure that controlled substances do not get into the wrong hands and are not tampered with. First, pharmacies are required to be physically secured. For example, their doors must always remain closed, and unauthorized people should never be allowed to enter. Employees within a pharmacy may not access areas in which they are not authorized to work. A pharmacy must remain closed and locked whenever there is no pharmacist on duty. Additionally, many states require security cameras.

Various forms of paperwork track and monitor the stock of controlled substances. The ordering and receipt of controlled substances must be documented and verified by two individuals. If an order is incomplete or missing, the DEA must be contacted, and DEA Form 222 must be submitted.

Newer technology automatically matches prescriptions with patients' electronic health records to verify that they are receiving the correct prescriptions. Federal laws dictate that both controlled and non-controlled substances require prescriptions from an authorized medical professional before a pharmacist can dispense them. Electronic prescriptions are also utilized to prevent forged or stolen prescriptions. These require the patient to confirm their identity. Lastly, pharmacists are legally required to document the dispensing of drugs to ensure that the drug is adequately controlled.

Authorized Personnel, Access to Pharmacy Areas, Identification Requirements, and Level of Supervision

To secure controlled substances adequately, access to a pharmacy and specific areas within it must be limited to certain individuals. First, nobody is authorized to enter a pharmacy without a pharmacist's supervision; when no pharmacist is present, the pharmacy must be closed and locked. Given jurisdiction, adequate reason, and lawful permission (such as a warrant or subpoena), most law enforcement agents are permitted access to pharmacies and pharmaceutical records. Besides pharmacists, not many people are allowed to enter areas in which controlled substances are stored; those who are allowed must be supervised by a pharmacist. For example, intern pharmacists and pharmacy technicians are permitted within drug storage areas when the pharmacist approves and is present. Depending on the state's specific laws, a pharmacist is only allowed to supervise a specific number of pharmacy technicians at once. For example, in California, a pharmacist is permitted to supervise one pharmacy technician, but can supervise up to two pharmacy technicians when there is another pharmacist present. Authorization rules depend on the state in which the pharmacy practices.

Assisting Pharmacists in Medication Reconciliation

Medication Reconciliation

Purpose and Benefits

Medication reconciliation refers to the process of comparing medications that a patient is already taking with a newly ordered medication. The purpose of medication reconciliation is to ensure that a patient's medication information is accurately maintained and available for any relevant healthcare personnel or organization. Through medication reconciliation, safe and effective medication use is verified to keep patients safe and prevent possible substance abuse. Since its conception in the early 2000s, medication errors have decreased.

Pharmacy Technician's Role

Overall, medication reconciliation is the pharmacist's responsibility. However, pharmacy technicians can help in a couple of ways: they can obtain preadmission medication history, document a patient's compiled medication list, and collect all other relevant patient information from their various healthcare providers and other pharmacies. Completion of these tasks helps to resolve discrepancies in medication lists and can assist pharmacists' communication with prescribing physicians. The pharmacy technician's role in medication reconciliation is to assist the pharmacist and ideally prevent any medication discrepancies.

Medical Terminology

To understand medication reconciliation fully, knowledge of some medical terms is required. For example, omissions, duplications, dosing errors, and drug interactions are medication errors that are prevented by medication reconciliation. **Omissions** occur when a pharmacist fails to order or dispense a necessary drug. **Duplications** occur when prescribers order more than one medication for the same condition or when a patient has more than one prescription for the same medication. **Dosing errors** occur when an incorrect drug dose is prescribed or dispensed, which can result in ineffective medication or overdose. **Drug interactions** occur when one or more of a patient's medications react with one another to produce an undesirable—and often harmful—outcome for the patient.

Additionally, since medication reconciliation involves prescribed drugs, nutritional supplements, over-the-counter drugs, vaccines, and more, a pharmacy technician must be familiar with the differences between these terms. **Prescribed drugs** can only be dispensed to patients who have a prescription from an approved medical professional. **Nutritional supplements** are manufactured products that are added to a patient's diet to make up for nutrients that are undersupplied in the food they eat. **Over-the-counter drugs**, such as acetaminophen or ibuprofen, can be

obtained without a prescription. Lastly, **vaccines** are substances that are typically injected into a patient to stimulate the production of antibodies against a targeted disease-causing virus.

Communication Methods and Strategies

A pharmacy technician's duties relating to medication reconciliation are to make lists of patients' current medications along with those that have been ordered or prescribed to them and to provide the pharmacist with that information. Therefore, it is important for the pharmacy technician to communicate this information clearly. Additionally, it is the pharmacy technician's responsibility to communicate the newly compiled medication list to the patient and their caregivers. The pharmacy technician must communicate directly with physicians to provide them with current medication lists for their patients. Pharmacy technicians can confirm that medication information is accurate by asking patients in person for verification. They should also confirm the patient's identity by asking for their full name, birth date, and more to make sure they match the medication information that they have. Lastly, a pharmacy technician should compare the information provided by both the patient and physician with the patient's available medication history to ensure that there are no discrepancies. Many sources online, such as the American Society of Health System Pharmacists (ASHP), provide example scripts for patient interviews.

Assisting Pharmacists in Medication Therapy Management

Medication Therapy Management

Purpose and Benefits

Medication therapy management (MTM) is another tool that protects patient safety. MTM is a service provided by healthcare professionals to improve the safety and health outcomes of patients by helping them understand their specific medical conditions and medications. MTM optimizes the health outcomes of medications and detects potentially costly problems.

Through pharmacist-provided MTM, a patient receives a complete review of all prescribed medications, supplements, and over-the-counter medications they are taking. This is another step that pharmacies take to ensure proper medication use, no duplications, and avoidance of unnecessary medications. Additionally, MTM provides in-depth education on medications taken by or prescribed to patients. Lastly, it enables clear communication between patients, pharmacists, physicians, and other relevant healthcare professionals.

Pharmacy Technician's Role

Pharmacy technicians also play a role in providing MTM services. Typically, they monitor MTM databases along with each specific patient's adherence to taking their prescribed medications in the instructed manner. As they do this, pharmacy technicians should notify the pharmacist if a patient is late to refill their prescription or if they go through it at a faster rate than they should. The technician can flag the patient in the computer system so the pharmacist can identify the individual or contact them to set up a meeting and provide MTM if necessary.

Medical Terminology

Since the pharmacy technician's primary role is to monitor patient adherence to their medication regimens, they should know all abbreviations used by pharmacies to indicate how frequently a patient needs to take their medications. The letter *q* stands for the Latin word *quaque*, which means "every." Therefore, abbreviations beginning with *q* indicate the frequency of taking a medication. For example, qH means every hour, qAM means every morning, qD means every day, qMO means every month, etc. Other abbreviations important to MTM include but are not limited to:

- BID: two a day
- TID: three a day
- QID: four a day

- PRN: as needed
- AC: before a meal
- PC: after a meal
- STAT: immediately

Communication Methods and Strategies

It is the pharmacy technician's responsibility to ensure that patients take their medications with the correct frequency. Therefore, if a patient does not refill their prescription according to schedule, a pharmacy technician can assume that the patient is not taking their medication or is taking it at an incorrect rate; it is their responsibility to communicate this to the pharmacist by flagging non-adhering patients in the computer system.

Assisting Patients in Selecting Compliance Aids and Devices

Benefits of Compliance Aids and Devices

Compliance aids and devices are tools that can assist patients in taking their medications correctly. The most common example of a compliance aid is a container with seven wells that correspond to each day of the week. This allows patients to put their medications for each day into the corresponding well so that they don't have to reference their prescription information or doctor's notes every day. Instead, they can easily take the correct medication daily, and they only need to refer to the prescription information when the time comes to refill the container. Many pillbox compliance devices also indicate whether certain medications should be taken at specific times of day. For forgetful patients or medications that require a strict schedule, there are containers with digital timer caps that open when it's time to take a medication.

Advancements in technology offer a wide variety of devices and platforms to improve medication regimen adherence. For example, there are many medication apps for mobile devices with calendars and reminders to alert patients when they need their medications. Additionally, certain devices may improve medication adherence, such as automatic pill dispensers. Since it can be easy to forget what to take and when, especially if a patient has multiple prescriptions, these devices and others can help patients adhere to the instructions for taking their medications.

Communication Methods and Strategies

Pharmacists and pharmacy technicians may help patients select compliance aids. When a compliance aid is given to a patient, pharmacy technicians can conduct a technical check to ensure that it functions. Additionally, through conversation with their patients, pharmacy technicians can determine patients' needs based on age and lifestyle, enabling them to suggest better compliance aids. For example, they may suggest a simple pill case with large letters for an elderly patient with poor vision. The pharmacy technician can also assist the pharmacist by interviewing a patient's caretaker or family members to get a better idea of the patient's needs.

Basic Medical Terminology Commonly Used in the Pharmacy

A pharmacy technician should be able to communicate with other pharmacy staff so work can be completed efficiently and safely. To that end, a pharmacy technician must have knowledge of common medical terminology and abbreviations. **Medical terminology** is made up of *word parts*: roots, prefixes, and suffixes. These are combined to form medical words.

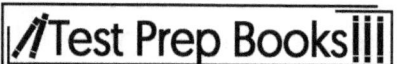

Overview and Laws

The following tables contain common word roots, prefixes, or suffixes (and their meanings) used in medical terminology:

Root	Meaning
cardi	Heart
gastr	Stomach
derm	Skin
arthr	Joint
pulmon	Lung
hem	Blood
gynec	woman, female
ped	Child
ren	Kidney
ophthalm	Eye
rhin	Nose
crani	Skull
cyst	urinary bladder
encephal	Brain
cephal	Head
aden	Gland
col	colon, large intestine
chondr	Cartilage
cyt	Cell
erythr	Red
leuk	White
electr	Electricity
onc	Tumor
oste	Bone
psych	Mind

Prefix	Meaning
tachy-	Fast
brady-	Slow
uni-	One
bi-	Two, both
tri-	Three

Prefix	Meaning
hyper-	Increased, above
hypo-	Decreased, below
inter-	Between
intra-	Within
retro-	Behind
dys-	Bad, painful, difficult, abnormal
aut-	Self
sub-	Below, under
trans-	Across, through

Suffix	Meaning
-logy	Study of
-logist	Specialist in the study of
-algia	Pain
-itis	Inflammation
-pathy	Disease
-stomy	Opening
-tomy	cutting into, incision
-ectomy	cutting out, removal, excision
-phasia	Speech
-emia	Blood condition
-phagia	Eat
-uria	Urine
-centesis	Surgical puncture to remove fluid
-scope	Instrument to visually examine
-scopy	Visual examination
-megaly	Enlargement
-oma	Tumor, mass
-gram	Record
-therapy	Treatment

Overview and Laws

Pharmacy technicians may come across medical abbreviations and acronyms in prescriptions, medical charts, and various forms of drug information. The following table contains common medical abbreviations and acronyms, along with their meanings:

Medical Abbreviation	Meaning
HIV	Human immunodeficiency virus
AIDS	Acquired immunodeficiency syndrome
BP	Blood pressure
HTN	Hypertension, high blood pressure
BM	Bowel movement
DM	Diabetes mellitus
FBS	fasting blood sugar
OA	Osteoarthritis
CAD	Coronary artery disease
RA	Rheumatoid arthritis
BPH	Benign prostatic hyperplasia
CVA	Cerebrovascular accident, stroke
DJD	Degenerative joint disease
GI	Gastrointestinal
COPD	Chronic obstructive pulmonary disease
CHF	Congestive heart failure
GERD	Gastroesophageal reflux disease
HR	Heart rate
P	Pulse
NKDA	No known drug allergies
RBC	Red blood cell
WBC	White blood cell
URI	Upper respiratory infection
UTI	Urinary tract infection
SOB	Shortness of breath
ECG	Electrocardiogram
EEG	Electroencephalogram
IBS	Irritable bowel syndrome
NPO	Nothing by mouth
STI	Sexually transmitted infection
PSA	Prostate specific antigen
ANA	Antinuclear antibody
NSAID	Nonsteroidal anti-inflammatory drug
CNS	Central nervous system
MS	Multiple sclerosis
CXR	Chest X-ray

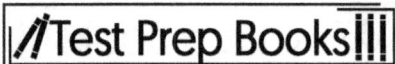

Many of these abbreviations are derived from Latin and may be used for routes of drug administration, dosage forms, weights, frequency of drug administration, volumes, names of drugs, and directions for compounding. Pharmacy abbreviations may be written in lower case or capital letters. They should be used with caution as misinterpretation can lead to medication error.

The following table contains common pharmacy abbreviations and their meanings:

Pharmacy Abbreviation	Meaning
tab	Tablet
cap	Capsule
oint	Ointment
g	Gram
mg	Milligram
mL	Milliliter
mcg	Microgram
U	Units
PO	By mouth
IV	Intravenous
BSA	Body surface area
mEq	Milliequivalent
IM	Intramuscular
SQ, SC	Subcutaneous
PRN	As needed
q	Every, each
cc	Cubic centimeter
gr	Grain
ac	Before meals
hs	Bedtime
bid	Twice a day
tid	Three times a day
QID	Four times a day
QS	Quantity sufficient
QD	Daily
QOD	Every other day
°	Hour
SL	Sublingual (under the tongue)
au	Both ears
ad	Right ear
as	Left ear
gtt	Drops
ou	Both eyes
os	Left eye

Overview and Laws

Pharmacy Abbreviation	Meaning
od	Right eye
amp	Ampule
atc	Around the clock
biw	Twice a week
tiw	Three times a week
wa	While awake
stat	Immediately

Drug Abbreviations

There are common abbreviations that are used for certain medications. The table below provides the abbreviations and the drug names for some of these medications:

Common Abbreviation	Medication
APAP	Acetaminophen
ASA	Aspirin
EE	Ethinylestradiol
Fe	Iron
HCTZ	Hydrochlorothiazide
INH	Isoniazid
MgSO4	Magnesium sulfate
MOM	Milk of magnesia
MVI	Multivitamin
NS	Normal saline
NTG	Nitroglycerin
PCN	Penicillin
PNV	Prenatal vitamins
SMZ/TMP	Sulfamethoxazole/trimethoprim
TAC	Triamcinolone
TCN	Tetracycline

Tailoring Communications to Different Audiences

Pharmacy technicians are often responsible for communicating between patients, the pharmacist, the patient's healthcare providers, insurance companies, and other pharmacy employees. One of their primary goals is to maintain patient satisfaction by being as available and helpful as possible. It is also helpful for pharmacy technicians to make sure that patients understand the instructions they receive from the pharmacists. When communicating with pharmacists, they must listen intently, follow instructions, and do whatever the pharmacist asks of them, whether that be providing verbal information, completing a task, or writing a report. It may also be beneficial for the pharmacy technician to write down the pharmacist's instructions before beginning a task. Additionally, pharmacy technicians are often responsible for calling insurance companies about billing and reaching out to physicians if they or the pharmacist discover an issue in the prescription. One particularly helpful communication

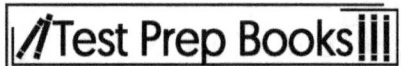

style is repetition, or closed-loop communication. In this strategy, the pharmacy technician repeats the instructions they received from the pharmacist and asks for confirmation that they understood correctly. Similarly, the technician may ask a patient to repeat the instructions they received from the pharmacist to confirm the accuracy of their understanding. This style of communication is helpful for avoiding errors and making sure that everyone is on the same page.

Interacting Professionally with Customers and Patients

As with any other job that involves talking directly with customers, pharmacy technicians should display excellent professionalism and customer service, which starts with being friendly and welcoming, whether in person or on the phone. Additionally, it can be beneficial to learn frequent patients' names and prepare their prescriptions in advance to limit lines and long wait times. Pharmacy technicians should also encourage patients to return expired medications. Lastly, but most importantly, a pharmacy technician must always be careful never to violate HIPAA law, which prohibits the sharing of a patient's medical information to anyone without their, or their caregiver's, permission.

Confirming the Completion of Final Product Verification

Role of the Pharmacy Technician
Before a medication is given to a patient, it must be thoroughly reviewed by the pharmacist, regardless of whether a technician filled the prescription for them or they did it themselves. However, a pharmacy technician can double check that a filled prescription matches the prescription itself. Any errors should be communicated to the pharmacist.

Role of the Pharmacist
The pharmacist must verify prescriptions before they are given to patients and offer counseling to patients in the form of medication therapy management. The pharmacist can delegate some aspects of these tasks to pharmacy technicians; however, it is their legal responsibility to verify prescriptions and offer medication counseling.

Assisting Pharmacists in Managing Inventory

Pharmacy Operations and Process Flow
For pharmacies to operate legally and provide the medications their patients need, they require meticulously managed inventory to ensure that vital materials are in stock, components haven't expired, orders are correct, and much more. Since pharmacists play an important role in direct patient care, they often do not have time to manage their pharmacy's inventory effectively. Therefore, pharmacy technicians can help manage the pharmacy's inventory. They can track trends in the amounts of products ordered to find efficient ways to bulk order, they can count inventory to determine what stock needs reordering and what isn't moving, and they can reach out to other pharmacies that might want products that are dead stock.

Drug Pricing Components
The bulk of a medication's final purchase price is the wholesale acquisition cost (WAC), which is the cost that the manufacturer charges. This price can be whatever the manufacturer desires without regulation, and it is typically marked up to 20% above the actual manufacturing cost. Distributors buy the drugs from manufacturers and typically pay less than the WAC due to various negotiations and incentives. Pharmacies then buy their drugs from the distributor after negotiating the price to keep it as low as possible. When the pharmacy sells medications, it will typically charge a dispensing fee that is included in the final price of the drug that the patient or their insurance will pay. The dispensing fee pays for the pharmacy's needs, including employee payroll.

Overview and Laws

Ordering and Inventory Management Methods

Inventory control may be utilized to provide pharmacy QA in a variety of fashions that include ensuring that needed medications are available to provide treatment, establishing parameters for the proper dispensing of medications, removing expired and short-dated medications from inventory, regularly checking for drug recalls and performing all pertinent follow-ups, and separating inventory to diminish the potential for picking the wrong drug. Properly trained pharmacy staff, meticulous attention to detail, and automation are crucial for successful and dependable inventory control. Most pharmacies have established minimum and maximum inventory levels for the medications they stock. This practice ensures that an adequate, but not excessive, amount of a particular medication is stocked on the shelves.

Many pharmacies use computerized systems to monitor inventory levels. When a maximum level of a medication is reached, the pharmacy knows not to exceed that quantity and will hold off on reorders. When a minimum level of a medication is reached, the pharmacy will reorder. Controlling inventory levels helps with order fulfillment and minimizes the potential for drugs expiring while in inventory. Computer systems capable of tracking National Drug Codes (NDCs), expiration dates, and lot numbers have added value and can help monitor for expired drugs and drug recalls as well as interface with pharmacy management software.

Pharmacy personnel often are required to remove drugs from stock for reasons such as being expired, being near their expiration date (short-dated), or being recalled. Proper inventory control and periodic manual checking of expiration dates helps to minimize the potential for dispensing expired medications. It also maximizes the usage of available stock before drugs become outdated. If an expiration date on a medication mentions

the month and year, the medication should be treated as expiring on the last day of the month. For example, a drug with an expiration date of 03/2025 should be treated as expiring on March 31, 2025.

PAR Levels

Periodic Automatic Replenishment (PAR) Levels refer to maximum and minimum quantity limits for specific items in a pharmacy's inventory. These limits are set for vital components in a pharmacy to ensure that there is always enough of the item in stock, but not so much that the medication will expire before it can be sold or take up too much space that could be better allotted to a different medication. When the stock of an item managed by PAR Levels approaches the minimum quantity, it should be reordered. When a stock approaches the maximum level, it should be noted that the item is being ordered too frequently. PAR Levels will vary from one pharmacy to another based on differences in patient needs.

Just-in-Time Ordering

Just-in-Time ordering (JIT) is an inventory management method that pharmacies use for items that rarely sell. This method involves only ordering an item when a patient needs it. It reduces costs by preventing unused inventory from sitting on the shelves and possibly expiring before a patient needs it.

Rotating Inventory

Rotating inventory is an inventory management technique used in every industry that deals with expiration dates or that values freshness. It involves using or selling older items before newer ones to make sure that older stock is purchased first and does not go to waste. Pharmacies do this by dispensing an older shipment of a medication before dispensing a newly arrived shipment. If there are shelves for over-the-counter drugs and compliance aids, new items will be stocked in the back of the shelf while older items will be moved to the front.

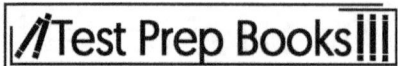

Fast Movers

Fast movers are items that sell constantly at a pharmacy and therefore must be regularly ordered, typically on a schedule. Some examples of fast movers typically include painkillers like acetaminophen and antibiotics like penicillin, but they may vary between pharmacies.

Storage of Medications

Pharmacy Operations and Process Flow

Temperature and humidity must be closely monitored in pharmacy storage rooms because many medications and vaccines have specific temperature and humidity requirements when in storage. Pharmacies must be able to store medications at various temperatures, and humidity must be kept low. If medication is stored at an incorrect temperature, then it can be ruined, which also wastes money.

Storage Requirements

Drug manufacturers determine specific storage conditions for the medications they produce. In addition, the drug manufacturer determines the type of container and temperature for storage of the medication.

Outside factors such as light, whether natural or artificial, can influence molecular changes in the active pharmaceutical ingredient (API) of a drug. Such changes can cause impurities in the drug that may not only harm the patient but can also lead to therapeutic failure. It is therefore imperative for pharmaceutical manufacturers to develop measures that can protect light sensitive drugs during all aspects of development and distribution of their products. Efforts to protect medications might include coating tablets in a light-resistant film that can block natural and artificial light exposure. Extended-release Verapamil tablets, for example, is a medication that is used for hypertension and is sensitive to both light and moisture. Applying a film coating to the tablet during the manufacturing process creates a seal around the tablet, preventing the degradation of the active ingredient by blocking light and moisture. Often these medications are packaged, stored, and dispensed in dark-colored amber bottles or vials in order to protect them from harmful light.

Prescription medications, as well as federally restricted over the counter (OTC) products, should be secured in the pharmacy, stored behind the counter, or locked in a cabinet that is accessible to pharmacy personnel only. Pseudoephedrine is the active ingredient in many OTC cold products, as well as the drug precursor for the illegal production of methamphetamine, a highly addictive stimulant. Federal law, mandated by the Combat Methamphetamine Epidemic Act, or CMEA, limits the sale of products containing ephedrine, pseudoephedrine, and phenylpropanolamine to 3.6 grams per day due to their abuse potential. Storage and access restrictions must be implemented by pharmacy staff to deter theft or the diversion of controlled drugs. The Drug Enforcement Administration (DEA) has issued minimum guideline requirements for the proper storage and access of controlled substances. Controlled substances must be stored in a cabinet or safe that can be securely locked per DEA regulations. It is also permitted to disperse controlled drugs amongst noncontrolled medications within the pharmacy. A safe or locked cabinet is typically reserved for storing Schedule II medications rather than Schedule III through V controlled drugs. The security of controlled drugs requires the thorough consideration of various factors including theft or diversion history, the physical location of the pharmacy, type of security system in place, the quantities of controlled drugs needing to be stored at a given time, and lastly, how many individuals have access to the drugs.

Storage Temperatures

Most medications may be stored safely at controlled room temperature. The United States Pharmacopeia has published the following standard parameters for medication storage:

Overview and Laws

- Freezer: Temperature maintained thermostatically between -13° and 14° Fahrenheit (-25° and -10° Celsius)
- Cold: Temperature not exceeding 46 °F (8 °C)
- Cool: Temperature between 46° and 59 °F (8° and 15 °C)
- Room temperature: Temperature prevailing in a working environment
- Controlled room temperature: Temperature maintained thermostatically between 68° and 77 °F (20° and 25 °C)
- Warm: Temperature between 86° and 104 °F (30° and 40 °C)
- Excessive heat: Temperature above 104 °F (40 °C)
- Protect from freezing: Freezing may lead to loss of potency or strength in a medication
- Dry place: Environment doesn't exceed 40% relative humidity

If the patient is to pick up medication from a community pharmacy, pharmacy staff should notify the patient of any special storage requirements. If the medication is being delivered by a pharmacy delivery service or mail-order pharmacy, special steps (e.g., ice packs and coolers) must be taken to ensure the medication is stored at appropriate temperatures.

Identifying and Removing Expired Products from Inventory

Pharmacy Operations and Process Flow

- Each pharmacy establishes policies regarding the process of pulling drugs that will expire.
- Expired drugs must be kept separate from in-date drugs.
- Both pharmacists and pharmacy technicians must be familiar with the institution's policies regarding out-of-date drugs.
- Should a drug pass its expiration date before or during the course of treatment, it should never be dispensed to a patient. Depending on the contract with pharmacies and hospitals, wholesalers and manufacturers will determine if a drug will be returned for partial or full credit. Properly rotating drugs and employing sound inventory management skills can reduce the incidence of expired drugs.
- Cytotoxic drugs must be destroyed in accordance with the biohazardous waste management protocol.
- Reconstituted or compounded medication cannot be returned to the manufacturer. Partially used bottles of medication are often (but not always) non-returnable.
- Controlled substances with DEA numbers can only be returned by institutions. Long-term facilities cannot return controlled substances to pharmacies because they do not have DEA numbers.
- Destruction of controlled substances involves notifying the DEA at least two weeks before destruction. Form 41 is used for expired controlled substances and must be on file at the pharmacy for at least 2 years after destruction.

Ordering and Inventory Management Methods

It is vital for pharmacy technicians to monitor products within the pharmacy regularly and remove any expired products. Expired products can lose efficacy, which means that they may not provide the patient with the correct strength of medication needed for their condition. In a worst-case scenario, expired medications can cause harm to patients. For further information on inventory management.

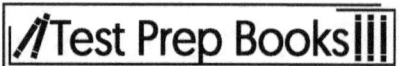

Identifying and Removing Recalled Products from Inventory

Pharmacy Operations and Process Flow
Medication Disposition

A drug recall can be opened by either the drug manufacturer or the Food and Drug Administration (FDA). The common causes for drug recall are serious adverse effects during post-marketing surveillance, formulation defects, formulation instability, lack of potency, packaging issues, delivery device (e.g., sprays or puffers) malfunctioning, and lack of good manufacturing practices. Poorly performed manufacturing practices involve a host of problems, such as unsanitary conditions for manufacturing a drug, which may constitute a recall.

Recalled Medication Processes

Six important steps are critical to the drug recall process:

- The manufacturer or wholesaler alerts the pharmacy/facility/institution via e-mail, mail, or fax about the reason for the recall. A recall notice contains the drug manufacturer's name, drug name, strength, package size, lot number or batch number, and expiration date.

- The pharmacy determines if the recalled medication is in stock. Physicians/clinics/institutions check to see if there are samples with that particular batch number in stock and then contact the respective company representative for return of the samples.

- The pharmacy contacts patients who have taken the drug. Should the customer have the recalled drug, it must be returned to the pharmacy for a refund or substitute.

- The drug manufacturer directs the pharmacy to follow disposition directions.

- Drugs that have been recalled are returned to the manufacturer and returned for credit.

- The physician is notified of the recall and asked for a new order, especially if the drug will not be available for an extended period of time.

Classes of Recalls and Required Actions

The FDA has several methods of intervening when it has been determined that a product poses a risk and should be taken off the market. The FDA can seize the product, obtain an injunction to halt production of the product, or issue a recall. A recall removes a product from the market. There are three classes of recalls (Class I, II, and III) that the Food and Drug Administration (FDA) uses to systematically address the severity of the recall:

- **Class I** is the most serious recall; drugs that fall under this class present risks for serious adverse health conditions or death.

- **Class II** is slightly less serious than Class I; drugs that fall under this class are unlikely to cause serious adverse health conditions or death, but the drugs can lead to temporary health problems.

- **Class III** is the least serious recall; this type is used when an FDA regulation has been violated but adverse health conditions are not likely to occur.

FDA Market Recalls are another type of warning issued for a drug, where minor violations need to be corrected or the drug needs to be removed from the market. Medical device recalls are part of FDA Medical Device Safety Alerts.

A **market withdrawal** is initiated when a product has an issue that would not be subject to legal action, and the manufacturer voluntarily removes the product. A **medical device safety alert** is issued when a medical device poses a substantial risk of harm. Pharmacies will receive notification when a product has been recalled either by letter or fax. When a pharmacy receives notification that a product has been recalled, the pharmacy must immediately cease distribution of the product. Any remaining stock of medication should be isolated from other medications. All patients who have received the product should be contacted. Medications should be returned to the pharmacy in exchange for a refund or substitution if available. The recall notification will include instructions for returning the product to the manufacturer as well as a response card to be returned that indicates that the pharmacy has followed instructions for administering the recall. A pharmacy representative should also notify prescribing physicians that medications have been recalled. While conducting a recall of medication, pharmacies must document the following things: the number of customers affected, the dates the customers were notified, the number of customers that responded to the notification, and the amount of medication that was returned as a result of the recall.

Ordering and Inventory Management Methods

Products can be recalled for a variety of reasons. Pharmacy technicians must remain aware of all current recalls and promptly remove recalled products from the pharmacy's inventory to avoid harm to patients. They must also contact any patients who have received recalled products so the products can be returned to the pharmacy for proper disposal.

Disposal Methods

In the past, expired medications were put in landfills or dumped down drains, but we now know that these actions can have negative consequences, such as fueling drug abuse or introducing harmful substances into the environment. In 2019, these irresponsible disposal practices were made illegal by the Environmental Protection Agency. Now, businesses known as reverse distributors will accept expired, damaged, or recalled medications from pharmacies at a cost. Another option is to go through waste management companies, which will put expired medications into proper containers that prevent them from interacting with other items. Through these methods, pharmacies can safely and responsibly remove stock that can no longer be dispensed responsibly. Additionally, the pharmacy can avoid getting fined for improper disposal of hazardous substances.

The process of removing recalled medications is much more complicated than simple disposal. The FDA requires that all recalled medications be tracked during the removal process to ensure that they are all accounted for and properly disposed of. When pharmacies are notified of a recall, they must check their inventory, find and remove the recalled item or product, then contact any patients who have received the recalled medication and ask them to return it. This enables the recalled medication to be removed from inventory and from patients so that it can be properly destroyed.

Disposal of Medications Based on Product-Specific Requirements

Pharmacy Operations and Process Flow

Pharmacy Waste

Pharmacy waste can be any chemically-manufactured good, vaccine, or allergenic used in the diagnosis, cure, mitigation, treatment, or prevention of disease or injury in humans or animals.

The following nine recommendations will minimize pharmacy waste:

- Make the best use of opened chemotherapy vials.
- Label medication for home use.
- Prime and flush intravenous lines with a saline (salt) solution.
- Check container sizes in relation to use.
- Substitute prepackaged unit dose liquids with specific oral syringes for patients.
- Get rid of stored controlled substances that are also hazardous waste.
- Use hard plastic buckets for delivering chemotherapeutic medication to hospitals.

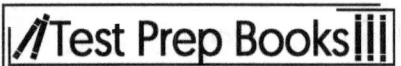

Overview and Laws

- Monitor dates on emergency syringes.
- Review inventory control to minimize expired medications.

The pharmaceutical waste generated during compounding should be appropriately handled and disposed. In the past, pharmacies used to destroy waste materials by incinerating them, washing them down a sink or toilet, or returning them to the sales representative/manufacturer. However, incineration pollutes the air, and dumping medications down a sink or toilet causes environmental pollution. Many medications are hydrophilic, biologically-active, and resistant to wastewater treatment. Therefore, disposal of pharmaceutical waste must comply with the corresponding state and federal regulations, as well as those regulations specified by the U.S. Environmental Protection Agency (EPA). A compounding pharmacy may contact a third party that has expertise in pharmaceutical waste collection, handling, and disposal.

There are three types of waste produced in a pharmacy:

- **Solid waste**: all solid, liquid, and gaseous waste
- **Hazardous waste**: any substance or combination of substances that could produce harmful effects on the health and safety of a person
- **Infectious waste**: blood, bodily fluids, blood products, sharps that are infectious, and waste from the laboratory

Waste receptacles are waste-specific. There is usually a specified container for biohazards and sharps (including infectious sharps); it is typically a red/dark orange receptacle that is labeled "bio-hazard."

For pharmaceuticals (expired or unused non-hazardous drugs), there are separate disposal containers (typically dark blue); these containers are appropriate for disposal of items such as antibiotics, IVs, and ibuprofen. For hazardous drugs, there are typically waste bags with the label **"Hazardous Drug Waste"**; these are leak-proof and come in a variety of colors, with the exception of white.

Pharmacy Waste Disposition
The following strategies pertain to waste disposal:

- Use hazardous waste labels to identify hazardous pharmacy waste.
- When not in use, keep containers covered.
- Limit quantity by allowing 3 days to dispose waste, once maximum capacity occurs.

Nonhazardous Waste
The proper disposal of pharmaceutical waste, including prescription medications, is regulated by the **Environmental Protection Agency (EPA)** under the guidelines set forth by the **Resource Conservation and Recovery Act, or RCRA**. The RCRA was enacted to prevent the improper disposal of unused hazardous medications. A medication that is not defined as hazardous under the RCRA is therefore categorized as nonhazardous. **Nonhazardous pharmaceutical waste** may include antibiotics, hormone medications, and OTC products. Despite being called nonhazardous pharmaceutical waste and not being classified as hazardous under the RCRA criteria, it does not mean it is not still harmful to the environment. Nonhazardous pharmaceutical waste should be processed by a DEA registered reverse distributor as such distributors are regulated and can ensure proper disposal methods are used. Reverse distributors are employed to retrieve unused and expired medications from the pharmacy to obtain manufacturer credit. Pharmaceutical medications that have expired or are considered unsaleable are called pharmaceutical waste. Once determined to be waste, the reverse distributor will process the waste according to regulations set by local environmental agencies as well as EPA guidelines. The EPA opposes the disposal of nonhazardous pharmaceutical waste in the sewer system. Preferred methods of disposal of nonhazardous pharmaceutical waste are incineration or a solid waste landfill. For patients who want to dispose of unwanted, unused, or expired medications at home, it

Overview and Laws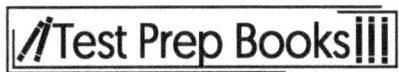

is recommended to put the loose medications in an undesirable substance such as coffee grounds or cat litter and place them in the trash.

Hazardous Waste

Pharmacies produce a variety of hazardous waste products, as defined by the Resource Conservation and Recovery Act (RCRA), that necessitate proper disposal. Some of these items include the following:

- Expired medications
- Incorrectly compounded medications
- Items that have been contaminated with bodily fluids
- Equipment (not machines, but attachable items) that can be disposed of that was used to dispense or make hazardous materials
- Chemotherapy drugs

There should be a designated bin for hazardous waste, specifically designed for such collection. The waste should be stored in the hazardous waste bin until it is picked up by an outside company for disposal.

Hazardous items should be handled with care and placed in bags that are marked with symbols identifying them as hazardous or biohazards.

There are outside companies that will come to the pharmacy to pick up hazardous waste that is generated.

Characteristics of Hazardous Waste	
Ignitability	Flashpoint of less than 60°C.
Corrosivity	pH of less than 2 or greater than 12.5.
Reactivity	When in contact with water, this substance is liable to explode, react violently, or release toxic gases.
Toxicity	Toxic at a concentration above the limit of a regulated substance.
K-list waste	Contains one or more corrosive, ignitable, reactive, or toxic substances.
P and U-list waste	Chemical matter that is commercially pure grade or technical grade, or a chemical formulation in which the chemical is the sole active ingredient.
Other	These substances are considered hazardous waste: Medications with more than one active ingredient All chemotherapy agents Medications with low LD50s* Endocrine disruptors All drugs on the P and U lists

*LD50 (lethal dose) is the quantity of a consumed substance that kills 50 percent of a test sample. Its unit is expressed in mg/kg or milligrams of substance per kilogram of body weight.

Disposal Methods

Medications need to be properly disposed; the FDA recommends the following to adhere to safe procedures:

- Medications should not be flushed down the toilet unless the package explicitly says to do so.
- Community take-back programs should be used if they are offered in the area.

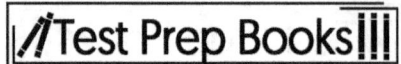

- The label should be destroyed or made illegible before the medication is thrown away.
- If medications are thrown in the garbage, the following should be done before doing so:
    - Medications should be removed from the original containers and mixed with a substance (coffee grounds or cat litter) and
    - Medications should be placed in a sealed bag or another empty container to avoid leakage.

Return to Stock
Most pharmacies have an inventory system that allows them to generate a daily report of prescriptions that have been filled but not picked up by a patient after a specific time frame. Prescriptions that were billed to insurance providers must be returned to stock and claims reversed. In addition, unclaimed medications tie up inventory of dispensable drugs that could be dispensed to other patients. It is recommended to pull unclaimed medications after fourteen days, reverse the insurance claim if applicable, and remove all protected health information such as patient name and address. Most computer systems will generate a return to stock label that includes the name of the drug, the **NDC**, or **national drug code**, and the product's expiration date.

DEA Take-Back Program
This program is a national event where pharmacies, community partners, and law enforcement agencies support collection sites where community members can return expired or unnecessary medications for proper disposal. After collection, the medications requiring disposal are retrieved by a local DEA representative. The main purpose of this program is to reduce the number of drugs that could possibly be used by unintended persons and to reduce risks to consumer safety by stopping the consumption of expired medication. Also, these events deter improper medication disposal and reduce possible environmental contamination.

Reverse Distribution
Pharmacies can dispose of unused or expired controlled substances by using a **reverse distributor**, which is a company that facilitates the movement of saleable and nonsaleable pharmaceutical goods. Reverse distributers operate in a regulated environment and are required to register with the DEA, which allows them to handle controlled substances.

Reverse distribution of **dispensable medications** usually involves the return of unopened overstock products. Dispensable medications processed by reverse distributers often are overstocked medications or medications sent to the pharmacy in error. These dispensable medications are deemed safe for redistribution within the pharmaceutical supply. Pharmacies may be able to receive credit for the return of dispensable medications.

Nondispensable medications include expired medications, medications that have been recalled, or medications that were delivered damaged. These medications are deemed pharmaceutical waste and are processed accordingly.

The controlled substances are transferred from the pharmacy to the reverse distributor where the drugs are evaluated to determine if credit can be given. The reverse distributor can also facilitate the return of controlled substances to a manufacturer for a credit. Upon transfer, a DEA Form 222 must be issued from the reverse distributor to the pharmacy when a Schedule II controlled substance is accepted. When Schedule III to V controlled substances are transferred, the pharmacy is responsible for recording the date of the transfer, the name of the medication, the dosage form, the dosage, and the quantity. If manufacturer credit cannot be given, the reverse distributor will dispose of the controlled substances according to DEA regulations. The reverse distributor must submit a DEA Form 41 to the DEA after the controlled substances have been destroyed.

Safety Data Sheets
Safety Data Sheets (SDS), formerly known as Material Safety Data Sheets (MSDS), are forms that contain information about hazardous materials and chemical compounds, including the name of the chemical and what

should be done in the case of a spill (i.e., precautions and procedures). SDS forms are available as physical forms or on computers. Each pharmacy is required by the Occupational Safety and Health Administration (OSHA) to make sure that the SDS forms can be readily accessed by all employees who work with hazardous chemicals and immediately accessible at all times, even in the case of an emergency such as a power outage.

There are sixteen sections to the SDS. Note that while Sections 12-15 are labeled non-mandatory and are not enforced by OSHA, they must be included to be compliant with the UN Globally Harmonized System of Classification and Labelling of Chemicals (GHS):

- Section 1: Identification
- Section 2: Hazard(s) Identification
- Section 3: Composition/Information on Ingredients
- Section 4: First-Aid Measures
- Section 5: Fire-Fighting Measures
- Section 6: Accidental Release Measures
- Section 7: Handling and Storage
- Section 8: Exposure Controls/Personal Protection
- Section 9: Physical and Chemical Properties
- Section 10: Stability and Reactivity
- Section 11: Toxicological Information
- Section 12: Ecological Information (non-mandatory)
- Section 13: Disposal Considerations (non-mandatory)
- Section 14: Transport Information (non-mandatory)
- Section 15: Regulatory Information (non-mandatory)
- Section 16: Other Information

The ingredients used in formulations should be handled cautiously in order to prevent contamination and degradation. Materials from the same container can be reused until they reach the expiration date labeled on the container. Staff should make sure to decrease exposure to the remaining content each time any material is withdrawn from the container.

The withdrawal of ingredients from the container should be performed by a trained individual who has expertise in handling the materials. If an ingredient is transferred from the original container to a different container, the new container should be labeled with the necessary information including name, supplier, lot number, and expiration date.

Accessing and Using References and Resources to Perform Job Duties

USP Standards

The United States Pharmacopeia (USP) is a non-profit scientific organization that is responsible for setting standards for the quality, strength, purity, and identity of a medicine. The USP standards are recognized in the federal Food, Drug, and Cosmetic Act. The USP establishes specific methods and procedures for preparing, formulating, and dispensing medications in a properly controlled manner. The USP produces informative resources on medications. For example, they create a manual that enables drug manufacturers to identify and verify drug substances. One of their most significant publications is a combination of two compendia, the United States Pharmacopeia (USP) and the National Formulary (NF), that together cover information on drug qualities and standards while also providing an enormous amount of information on medication and compounding standards for pharmacies.

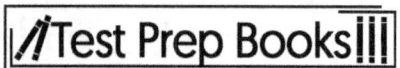

Orange Book
Orange Book is a reference to find drugs that have been approved and evaluated for therapeutic equivalence. The official name of the book is **Approved Drug Products with Therapeutic Equivalence Evaluations**, and it is now available online at the FDA's website. The purpose of the Orange Book is to make sure that only safe and effective medications are sold and used.

Red Book
The Red Book, created by a healthcare branch of IBM known as Micromedex, is a list of all FDA-approved drugs, their current prices, and descriptive information. The purpose of the Red Book is to make sure that pharmacists and other healthcare professionals have access to a comprehensive list of accurate medicine prices.

Clinical Information Sources
There are many resources available for pharmacies that provide information on medications and updated procedures. The Drug Facts and Comparisons book provides detailed information on thousands of drugs, including comparisons between similar medications. Micromedex is a database that includes a wide variety of literature regarding medications and their proper uses. Additionally, Micromedex published the Red Book that lists all current drug prices. Lexicomp is a database that provides information on drug interactions and allows pharmacists and other healthcare professionals to know which issues may arise when various medications are taken together. UpToDate is a web-based resource that provides new clinical information based on patient and medication information alongside references to other sources for medication information, medical calculators, and information on drug-to-drug interactions. It aids physicians in making medication decisions, and it allows pharmacy personnel to ensure that correct medications are being prescribed. There are many other resources available to find clinical information on drugs, but these sources are the most relevant and accessible for pharmacy personnel.

Ident-a-Drug
Ident-a-Drug is a reference book created to help identify unknown pills. Unidentified drugs can be dangerous. If a pill's identity is unknown, it cannot be safely and properly disposed. If a pharmacy receives an unknown drug, it can use *Ident-a-drug* to determine what the drug is. Additionally, there are similar web-based resources available to help with drug identification.

Handbook on Injectables
The Handbook on Injectables lists the procedures for the preparation of cytotoxic or hazardous drugs along with instructions for safe administration, spill clean-up, and waste management. Its goal is to reduce the risk of injectable drugs.

State Board of Pharmacy Regulations
Pharmacies and their personnel, including pharmacists and pharmacy technicians, are governed by the regulatory board of the state in which they practice. Each state has specific rules and regulations regarding the handling of medications and the management of personnel permissions within a pharmacy. All regulatory boards within the United Stated follow the rules set by federal organizations such as the FDA and EPA.

Poison Control Centers
Poison Control Centers are important resources for pharmacists. They are facilities that provide treatment and advice for anyone who has been exposed to a hazardous or poisonous substance or who has overdosed or otherwise improperly taken a medication or other pharmaceutical product. Pharmacists can use poison control as a resource if a patient experiences an adverse reaction to a medication or to advise in handling a spill of a hazardous substance. Additionally, pharmacists may work at poison control centers to become specialists in hazardous medication components.

Laws and Regulations

Complying with Federal Laws and Regulations Applicable to Pharmacy Practice

Reconciliation between State and Federal Laws and Regulations
Pharmacy laws and rules vary by state, and pharmacy law follows the strictest requirements if state and federal law differ.

HIPAA
The Health Insurance Portability and Accountability Act (HIPAA) was enacted in 1996 to provide nationwide protection of personal health information at hospitals and institutions, through the entirety of any research process, or with any associates who work closely with entities that are required to follow HIPAA regulations. Within the pharmacy practice, HIPAA regulations and policies are enforced to protect the patient's personal information in electronic, written, or oral form. Disclosing a patient's health information is a violation of HIPAA policies, and violators can incur fines up to $25,000 per category each year.

CMEA
The Combat Methamphetamine Epidemic Act (CMEA) of 2005 regulates certain non-prescription medications, specifically those including pseudoephedrine. Known to clear nasal congestion, pseudoephedrine can also be used in the illegal production of methamphetamine. The CMEA regulates daily and monthly maximum gram limits of pseudoephedrine allowed to be sold per driver's license. Only 3.6 grams are allowed per day and 9 grams per month. In addition to the gram limit, any product containing pseudoephedrine must be stored behind the counter or in a locked cabinet.

Drug Listing Act of 1972
The Drug Listing Act of 1972 added a requirement to the Federal Food, Drug, and Cosmetic Act that drug manufacturers must report all marketed products to the Food and Drug Administration; this includes human drugs, veterinary drugs, and medicated animal feed products. A proper product listing includes all information regarding the medication such as ingredients, dosage form, package information, and National Drug Code (NDC). The NDC is specific to the product, and alterations to any aspect of a properly listed drug will be required to obtain a new NDC.

Food and Drug Act of 1906
Prior to the Food and Drug Act of 1906, Upton Sinclair's *The Jungle* revealed how animal products were falsely labeled and sold to consumers. In response, there was a public outcry that caused the passing of the Meat Inspection Act. On the same day, President Roosevelt established the Food and Drug Administration (FDA) and passed the Food and Drug Act of 1906 because he believed that drugs should also be inspected to protect public health and safety. Pharmaceutical manufacturers go through various inspection processes to prove that their product aligns with their claims and can be marketed. The rigorous inspection process also instills confidence in the consumer that the product marketed is the product received.

OBRA '90
The Omnibus Budget Reconciliation Act of 1990 (OBRA '90) requires Medicaid patients to receive counseling on every prescription medication by a pharmacist for the state to receive federal Medicaid funding. Counseling became an important aspect in preventing drug-related events or reactions. Counseling services include, but are not limited to, technique demonstrations, review of side effects, and review of nonadherence effects.

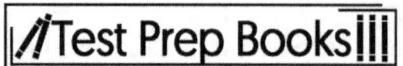

Durham-Humphrey Amendment

In 1951, President Truman added the Durham-Humphrey Amendment to the Federal Food, Drug, and Cosmetics Act. This amendment divided medications into two categories: prescription and non-prescription. Prior to the amendment, medical supervision and recommendation was not necessary to purchase drugs, but there were higher rates of drug-related illness and harm. Now, prescription medications must be prescribed by a medical professional and dispensed by an authorized healthcare professional, such as a pharmacist. Non-prescription medications are commonly known as over-the-counter or behind-the-counter drugs.

FD&C Act

The Federal Food, Drug, and Cosmetic (FD&C) Act was put in place in 1938 after over 100 people died from taking a medication that had traces of diethylene glycol. As technology and manufacturing have evolved over the years, the act continues to be amended to reflect current standards. This act gives the FDA supervision of the safety of the food, drug, and cosmetic industries.

There are ten sections, called subchapters, in the FD&C Act:

- Subchapter I – Short Title
- Subchapter II – Definitions
- Subchapter III – Prohibited Acts and Penalties
- Subchapter IV – Food
- Subchapter V – Drugs and Devices
- Subchapter VI – Cosmetics
- Subchapter VII – General Authority
- Subchapter VIII – Imports and Exports
- Subchapter IX – Tobacco Products
- Subchapter X – Miscellaneous

The act also covers issues such as adulteration, including bottled water, and homeopathic preparations.

DSCSA

The Drug Supply Chain Security Act (DSCSA), also known as Track and Trace, is a section in the Drug Quality and Security Act of 2013. It regulates the processing, packaging, and distributing of medications throughout the United States. The purpose of the act is to protect consumers by decreasing any chance of contamination or unwanted exposure throughout the shipping process. Any distributor or transporter of medications must be licensed per FDA standards, and they must renew their license annually.

Laws Related to Bioequivalence

The FDA regulates medications that claim bioequivalence to another. Bioequivalence is defined by an insignificant difference in pharmacologic properties, including absorption properties. If a manufacturer proves bioequivalence, they are authorized to apply for the abbreviated new drug application that allows them to bypass efficacy and quality study demonstrations.

PPPA

The Poison Prevention Packaging Act (PPPA), which called for specific medications and products to be placed in special packaging, was passed in 1970. Special packaging includes designs that prevent children under five years of age from opening it within a reasonable time but do not prevent adults from opening it. In a pharmacy, medications in vials must be sealed with child-resistant caps unless stated otherwise.

Kefauver-Harris Amendment

Prior to the Kefauver-Harris Amendment of 1962, drug manufacturers were not required to prove that their product was effective; they only had to list the correct ingredients on the label. Once the amendment was passed, manufacturers had to provide the FDA with proof of efficacy through the results of well-designed clinical trials. The FDA was given authority to perform retrospective analysis of the study to prove accuracy. In addition, the FDA established the new drug application that requires approval before a product can be marketed.

Orphan Drug Act

Passed in 1983, the Orphan Drug Act incentivized private companies and pharmaceutical manufacturers to research rare diseases in hopes of producing effective treatments. Prior to any incentives, only 38 products existed with the intent to treat rare cases, but within seven years of the act's passage, 370 treatments had been discovered, with 49 of them being approved. By 2002, the number of approved treatments for rare diseases increased to 232 and affected over 11 million patients.

Medicare Modernization Act

The Medicare Prescription Drug, Improvement, and Modernization Act of 2003 provided a prescription drug option to relieve financial burden for Medicare-eligible patients. Prior to this, only hospitals, managed care facilities, and physician services were covered under Medicare, and patients were forced to pay out-of-pocket costs or utilize private insurance companies to purchase medications. In addition to prescription coverage, the act also allowed for a redesign of Medicare parts B and C into Medicare Advantage.

CMS

The Centers for Medicare and Medicaid Services (CMS) is a federally run program that exists to provide a central place for resources and application forms regarding Medicare, Medicaid, and Children's Health Insurance services. CMS responsibilities also include expanding the Affordable Care Act, engaging with policymakers, and fostering innovation to advance and improve health outcomes.

Anabolic Steroid Act

The Anabolic Steroid Act was passed in 1990 to prevent illegal production and distribution of steroids in the United States. Testosterone was the most used steroid among men in the early 1900s for treating depression, increasing athletic endurance, and improving personal appearance. The act banned illegal steroid production, classified steroids in various controlled substance categories, and prevented the marketing and selling of precursor steroids over the counter. To this day, illegal smuggling of steroids is high due to lack of steroid regulation in countries like Mexico and several European countries.

Safe Handling and Disposal Practices for Hazardous Drugs (USP <800>)

USP <800> establishes standards, regulations, and policies that govern the packaging, distributing, and handling of hazardous drugs and substances. The standards include a list of hazardous drugs, defined by NIOSH; types of exposures; spill control procedures; and disposal methods. Disposal of hazardous material must comply with federal, state, and local standards. Any person expected to handle hazardous material is often required by their employer to receive training and is responsible for understanding the fundamental safety standards.

Laws Related to Non-Controlled Substances When Handling Refills and/or Partial Filling of Prescriptions

Non-controlled substances, as defined by the Federal Food, Drug, and Cosmetic Act, are valid for one year past the original prescription date and can be partially filled depending on insurance regulations and other circumstances. When transferring non-controlled substances between stores, there is no maximum number of transfers.

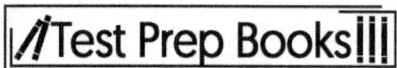

HIPAA Compliance

Communicating and Disclosing Information

It is extremely important to prevent HIPAA violations. There are many courses and certifications that can be taken or obtained to ensure that HIPAA policies are being maintained. When verbally disclosing personal information to a patient or caregiver, it's important to be in a private room and keep the voice volume low. When handling electronic personal information, it's important to have strong passwords, enable software protection, and never leave devices unattended. Disclosing a patient's health information to other healthcare providers should always be done in a professional manner. Health information should never be disclosed to unauthorized personnel.

Collection, Storage, and Disposal of Patient Information

Proper and efficient disposal of personal health information (PHI) is vital for adherence to HIPAA regulations and protection of patients' PHI. There are several disposal methods, including burning, shredding, or soaking in water and then grinding the remains. The goal is to make the document unreadable and impossible to reconstruct. When storing PHI electronically, it's important to have proper software protection programs, including encrypted passwords on all computers. If the PHI is a physical document, it should be stored in a locked area that is only accessible to authorized personnel.

Filling Prescriptions or Medication Orders

HIPAA

When filling electronic prescription orders, make sure that computers with patient information are not left unattended. When inputting orders, ensure that the patient's information on the prescription aligns with their information in the computer system.

CMEA

When a patient or customer purchases a product containing pseudoephedrine (whether at the pharmacy counter or the front register), they must show and scan an active driver's license. This procedure is designed to track recent purchases of pseudoephedrine and determine whether the current purchase would exceed the maximum gram limit. For example, 9 grams of pseudoephedrine can be purchased per month; if a patient purchased 5 grams two weeks ago and attempts to purchase another 5 grams within the same month, they would be denied. They would only be allowed to purchase up to 4 grams.

Drug Listing Act of 1972

Every medication has a specific NDC number that must be matched when filling the prescription order. Most pharmacies utilize an electronic system that allows the technician or pharmacist to scan the medication bottle and confirm that it matches the drug selected in the system for that patient. There may be options to bypass this, but it's not advised since each NDC matches a specific drug with FDA-approved ingredients, strength, dosage form, inactive ingredients, etc. Two bottles may look identical, but the mismatching NDC numbers reveal if they are different in some way.

Food and Drug Act of 1906

Recall that this act prohibits misbranded and adulterated medications. When compounding medications in a pharmacy, it's important to document all ingredients—active and inactive—and label the final product correctly to prevent violations with inspection agencies. Misbranding includes inaccurate labeling (e.g., claiming that the package contains 100 mL when there is only 90 mL). Adulteration includes adding unnecessary or harmful ingredients to change the drug's strength or quality for devious means, financial gain, or other unethical reasons.

OBRA '90
When filling a medication and running the order through insurance, it's important to determine whether the patient is covered under Medicaid. Under OBRA '90, the pharmacist is legally obligated to counsel Medicaid patients on every medication. The pharmacist must also complete a mandatory review of the medication list prior to filling each order. Each state has specific requirements, and pharmacists should be informed and kept up to date with changing policies.

Durham-Humphrey Amendment
Medication orders can be written for prescription and non-prescription drugs. Certain medications can be either prescription or non-prescription depending on their strength, and it's important to recognize the difference. In addition, it's important to understand that most insurance providers do not cover non-prescription medications, and this information should be relayed to the provider and patient.

FD&C Act
Under the Food, Drug, and Cosmetic Act of 1938, drugs must have adequate directions, and new medications must have pre-market approval that proves their safety to the FDA. Pharmaceutical manufacturers and researchers undergo stricter clinical trial regulations and must prove good manufacturing practices, per the FDA. This act applies to drugs, medical devices, food, and cosmetic products.

Laws Related to Bioequivalence
The Biologics Price Competition and Innovation Act of 2009 allows a manufacturer who proved bioequivalence to apply for the abbreviated new drug application, which allows them to bypass repeating efficacy and quality study demonstrations. It's important to identify when medications are bioequivalent to each other, and one way to verify this is by referring to the Purple Book. The Purple Book is run by the Center for Biologics Evaluation and Research and includes information regarding biological products and any bioequivalent, biosimilar, or other interchangeable products.

PPPA
The Poison Prevention Packaging Act requires that certain medications and products be placed in special packaging that prevents those under five years of age from opening it. In the pharmacy, unless stated otherwise, medications in vials must be sealed with child-resistant caps. When filling medications, it's important to note which patients are exempt from child-resistant caps (e.g., those with motor control issues). In addition, certain medications are exempt from the special packaging law under the PPPA, and the current list can be found at cpsc.gov.

Medicare Modernization Act
Through the Medicare Prescription Drug, Improvement, and Modernization Act of 2003, a prescription drug option became available to relieve financial burden for Medicare-eligible patients. In addition to prescription coverage, the act also allowed for a redesign of Medicare parts B and C into Medicare Advantage. This act allows more patients to fill medications at reasonable costs. Currently, this act has provided over 91% of Medicare beneficiaries with drug coverage.

CMS
As part of the Department of Health and Human Services, the Centers for Medicare and Medicaid Services (CMS) provides a central place for resources and application forms regarding Medicare, Medicaid, and Children's Health Insurance services. When filling prescriptions for patients covered under Medicare or Medicaid, pharmacists may need access to various forms (such as health insurance claim forms as well as forms related to CPAP devices for obstructive sleep apnea or the Retiree Drug Subsidy) that can be found at cms.gov.

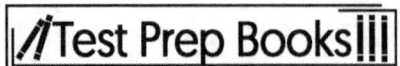

Anabolic Steroid Act

The Anabolic Steroid Act was passed in 1990 to prevent illegal production and distribution of steroids in the United States. "Stacking" steroids is common in those who misuse steroids with different dosage methods like oral and injectable, and it's important to recognize any change in a patient's medication history to prevent this.

Safe Handling and Disposal Practices for Hazardous Drugs

USP <800> establishes standards, regulations, and policies surrounding the packaging, distributing, and handling of hazardous drugs and substances. When filling prescription orders, it's important to recognize hazardous medications so that the proper protocols can be followed. In addition, disposal procedures for hazardous materials and drugs vary at the local, state, and federal levels, so it's crucial that any personnel filling and handling these materials remain current on all policies.

Refills and/or Partial Filling of Prescriptions

Non-controlled substances are valid for one year past the original date written and can be partially filled depending on insurance regulations or other special circumstances. When filling non-controlled substances, it's important to verify patient information, review prescription history, and pay attention to local, state, and federal updates on medication recalls. When transferring non-controlled substances between stores, there is no maximum number of transfers.

Organizations and Regulators Related to Pharmacy Practice

Pharmacies are regulated by various organizations like Occupational Safety and Health Administration (OSHA), The Joint Commission, and the FDA. When filling medication orders and administering vaccines, it's important to follow OSHA guidelines and procedures to prevent the spread of infectious disease or exposure to harmful substances, comply with workplace safety policies like hazard identification, promote educational training, and maintain open communication between employees and employers. The Joint Commission is a non-profit business that accredits healthcare institutions and facilities based on the organization's performance and ability to provide the safest health care with the highest quality and best value.

Handling Refills and/or Partial Filling of Prescriptions

HIPAA

Non-controlled substance prescriptions require the same handling, storage, disposal, and confidentiality measures as other prescriptions because they contain patient health information that must be protected. Violations include inputting the wrong prescription into a patient's profile, dispensing the wrong medication, or counseling inappropriately.

CMEA

Over-the-counter pseudoephedrine purchases are regulated by the federal government and limited to purchases of 3.6 grams per day and 9 grams per month. A provider can prescribe more than the daily or monthly limit if necessary, and this situation would not be regulated by the same laws as over-the-counter purchases. When prescribed, pseudoephedrine is labeled as a non-controlled medication. It can be partially filled and filled with refills.

Drug Listing Act of 1972

The NDC is specific to the product, and alterations to any aspect of a properly listed drug will be required to obtain a new NDC; therefore, medications should not be mixed. When filling a refill or partial order of a prescription, try to keep the same NDC to prevent confusion from the patient or other pharmacies.

Food and Drug Act of 1906
Recall that this act prohibits misbranded and adulterated medications. To maintain compliance, proper documentation of all ingredients used must be noted for the pharmacy, inspection agencies, and patient profiles. Therefore, when refilling a medication order, it's important to update the number of refills remaining and the expiration date on the bottle. If partially filling an order, the current quantity and remaining quantity should be noted to prevent misbranding violations.

OBRA '90
OBRA '90 requires that pharmacists provide counseling to Medicaid patients for all prescriptions (both controlled and non-controlled). In addition, the patient's medication history must be analyzed prior to filling new prescriptions, partial fills, or refills.

Durham-Humphrey Amendment
Recall that the Durham-Humphrey Amendment separated drugs into prescription and non-prescription categories. Prescription medications can be further classified into narcotic, controlled II-V, and non-controlled. All non-prescription medications are considered non-controlled. When filling non-controlled medications, there are important differences, including:

- The provider's DEA number does not need to be written on the prescription.
- There is an unlimited number of transfers, until the number of allowed refills is reached.
- Prescriptions can be partially filled for vacation, insurance, or financial reasons. Examples of each are listed below:
  - If a patient normally receives a 30-day supply of a medication but is leaving the country for 45 days, they can request a 45-day supply from their insurance provider.
  - If a patient's provider writes a 90-day prescription, but their insurance only covers 30-day supplies, then the prescription will be partially filled.
  - If a patient receives a 90-day supply of medication for $120 but can only afford $40, then the pharmacy will partially fill the medication for 30 days.

FD&C Act
Recall that this act requires producers of new drugs to provide adequate directions and pre-market safety approval to the FDA. This act applies to drugs, medical devices, food, and cosmetic products. When compounding or filling medications, it's important to label the vial with the correct directions given by the provider.

Laws Related to Bioequivalence
In some scenarios, the original prescribed medication needs to be changed. If the medication is a biologic product, then it's important to recognize the different options for replacement. Bioequivalent medications are neither clinically nor significantly different. Biosimilar medications have slight differences, and the prescription cannot be changed without a provider's approval. Generic medications are considered bioequivalent. The updated Purple Book is a helpful resource when differentiating between biosimilar and bioequivalent drugs.

PPPA
The Poison Prevention Packaging Act (PPPA) requires specific medications and products to be placed in special packaging. In the pharmacy, unless stated otherwise, medications in vials must be sealed with child-resistant caps. When refilling or partially filling an order, patients who request non-child-resistant caps must continue to receive them, and this should be documented.

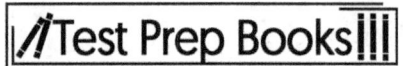

Medicare Modernization Act
This act created a prescription drug option to relieve the financial burden of patients eligible for Medicare services. Depending on the drug plan, the maximum day's supply can vary and must be considered when filling or partially filling medications.

CMS
This agency provides a central place for resources and application forms regarding Medicare, Medicaid, and Children's Health Insurance services. Medicare and Medicaid have differing plans for refilling and partially refilling orders; therefore, utilizing the CMS website can be beneficial for any overrides or forms.

Anabolic Steroid Act
Those who misuse steroids commonly "stack" them by using different dosage forms (e.g., oral and injectable) in the same time frame. "Plateauing" is also common and involves staggering or overlapping various steroids to prevent tolerance. To prevent this, it's important to recognize requests for changes in dosage form or requests for partial filling in a patient's medication history.

Safe Handling and Disposal Practices for Hazardous Drugs (USP <800>)
USP <800> dictates protocol about hazardous material and drugs. Any person handling hazardous material—directly or indirectly—is often required by their employer to receive training and is responsible for understanding fundamental safety standards. Pharmacists who fill or partially fill hazardous medication orders should follow proper protocols regarding transport, handling, disposal, and documentation.

Handling Refills and/or Partial Filling of Prescriptions
Non-controlled substances, as defined by the Federal Food, Drug, and Cosmetic Act, should not be filled if the pharmacist notices drug-drug interactions, allergies, or improper use. The pharmacist should appropriately notify the provider and patient. There are no protocols against partial fills of non-controlled substances. Controlled II substances can be partially filled, but the remaining prescription must be filled within 72 hours.

Organizations and Regulators Related to Pharmacy Practice
OSHA states that all prescription medications (whether filled or partially filled) must be documented and recorded according to local, state, and federal procedures. The FDA provides the Code of Federal Regulations that contains information on partially filling non-controlled and controlled substances.

Packaging Prescription Medications

FD&C Act
The Food, Drug, and Cosmetic Act mandated that all medications be accurately labeled with directions that the patient can easily understand. This includes proper labeling on all prescription packages, including vials, boxes, bottles, and other approved containers.

PPPA
The Poison Prevention Packaging Act (PPPA) mandates that specific medications and products be placed in special packaging. Unless stated otherwise, medications in the pharmacy must be sealed with child-resistant caps. This regulation also applies to dropper bottles, but it does not apply to medications designed for inhalation or topical application to the mouth or teeth.

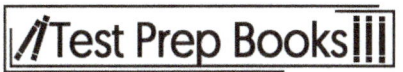

OSHA Regulations for Disposal of Sharps

OSHA has strict regulations about the disposal of sharps, which are devices that can puncture through skin. Failure to dispose of sharps properly can lead to unwanted contamination and exposure to blood-borne pathogens or other infectious diseases/organisms. Used sharps must be placed in a designated red and puncture-proof container that has a lid and is kept upright to prevent leakage of contaminated fluids. Unless they are reusable, full sharps containers can be disposed of at local hazardous waste collection sites, at some doctors' offices and fire/police stations, or in one's household trash, or, depending on the manufacturer, they can be sent back to them.

Monitoring and Reporting Fraud, Waste, and Abuse

CMEA

This act seeks to prevent illegal production of methamphetamine by limiting sales of pseudoephedrine, an over-the-counter nasal decongestant that can be used to produce methamphetamine. When purchasing the medication, an active driver's license must be scanned, a process which helps combat potential abuse. Since the maximum gram limit can be bypassed with a prescription, it's important for pharmacists to review medical charts prior to filling each order to identify potential fraud or abuse. If suspected, the pharmacist should follow the proper protocols per their employer and specific state regulations.

DSCSA

The Drug Quality and Security Act of 2013 contains the Drug Supply Chain Security Act (DSCSA) that regulates the processing, packaging, and distribution of medications throughout the United States. If any fraud, waste, or abuse is suspected during the transportation process, the issue should be reported according to proper company protocols and state-specific laws.

Medicare Modernization Act

This act created a prescription drug option to relieve the financial burden of patients eligible for Medicare services. Medicare is only available for those who are older than 65, disabled, suffering from end-stage renal disease, or living with Lou Gehrig's disease (also known as ALS). If a patient or provider is suspected of fraud regarding Medicare eligibility, they should be reported to the Inspector General's fraud hotline.

CMS

The Centers for Medicare and Medicaid Services (CMS) provides resources and application forms for Medicare, Medicaid, and Children's Health Insurance services. Their offered resources include a CMS online manual system that contains day-to-day operating policies, regulations, annual transmittals, models, and directives. The manual contains information regarding fraud, waste, and abuse related to Medicare and Medicaid eligibility and forms. Anyone who suspects fraud, waste, or abuse can report it using the manual's provided website, phone numbers, and emails.

Anabolic Steroid Act

"Stacking" and "plateauing" are forms of steroid abuse. If fraud, waste, or abuse is suspected, the pharmacist should follow local, state, and federal protocols to report the misuse.

Organizations and Regulators Related to Pharmacy Practice

Fraud, waste, and abuse within a healthcare facility can be reported to OSHA, The Joint Commission, or the FDA. OSHA regulates workplace safety, and suspected fraudulent activities should be reported to OSHA. The Joint Commission has a Code of Conduct manual that defines fraud, waste, and abuse, and it provides various sources for reporting suspected activity.

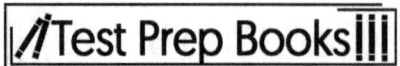

Federal Requirements for Record-Keeping and Retention Procedures

The pharmacy is required to maintain a log or file of dispensed prescriptions. Each prescription needs to be kept for a minimum of two years. The authorities or Board of Pharmacy need to be able to review and inspect the log or file of records at any time.

The log or records of dispensed medications should contain the following information:

- Date the medication was dispensed
- Details of the prescription: drug name, strength, and dosage form
- The patient's name
- The quantity of medication dispensed
- The patient's address

It is important to note that, for controlled substances, Schedule II medication prescriptions need to have their own file, and Schedule III-V prescriptions need to have their own separate file as well. Additional prescription medications that are not controlled substances may also have their own file. If Schedule III-V prescriptions are filed together with noncontrolled substances, then they should be stamped with a red C no less than an inch high.

HIPAA

All prescriptions, screening questionnaires, medical charts, and other personal information must be kept in secured areas, such as locked areas or computer systems with software encryption. Each state and company have designated timeframes regarding the retention of patient health information that can vary from one to twenty years. At any time, inspection agencies can request documentation from a pharmacy for a specific patient. Violation of record-keeping policies can result in heavy fines or termination.

CMEA

When a patient or customer decides to purchase a product containing pseudoephedrine, they will be required to show and scan an active driver's license and then sign a physical or electronic logbook. If the logbook is physical, the following information must be documented:

- Product name and strength
- Quantity sold
- Name and address of purchaser
- Date and time of sale

Records must be kept for at least two years, but stricter company or state policies may require them to be kept longer. Electronic logbooks are kept in a system called the National Precursor Log Exchange. The system tracks recent purchases of pseudoephedrine and evaluates whether the maximum gram limit has been met or would be exceeded by the current purchase.

Drug Listing Act of 1972

Each medication is designated by an individual national drug code (NDC), and every use of the code must be documented. In addition, when ordering medications, pharmacies must document their receipt physically or electronically, typically using the NDC numbers. It is important to maintain records of shipment and use for financial and accountability reasons.

Food and Drug Act of 1906

The Food and Drug Act of 1906 was one of the first laws enacted to prevent misbranded and adulterated drugs from appearing on the market. This act also created the FDA. It prevented manufacturers of drugs and food products from falsifying labels to ensure that the product consumed matches its label. In this process, companies must provide the FDA with proper documentation of the product's contents, which is then inspected for accuracy.

OBRA '90

OBRA '90 contains various provisions that allow pharmacists to review a patient's medication management therapy, including rebates, drug utilization reviews (DUR), and demonstration projects. Pharmaceutical systems often prompt pharmacists to review these provisions, and they must document their completion of the review through electronic signatures or unique identification codes. OBRA '90 requires documentation of patient information, including name, address, number, significant disease state history, and any relevant pharmacist notes. This documentation is essential for ensuring compliance, which allows continued Medicaid funding. Under this law, patients have the option to deny counseling; if this option is chosen, the pharmacist must document it.

Durham-Humphrey Amendment

When non-prescription medications are not covered by insurance companies and are too expensive, this information should be relayed to the provider and patient so that they can make necessary changes. The pharmacist should also document this information in the patient's chart. Non-prescription medication use reported by the patient should be noted in their chart to provide accurate assessment and diagnosis.

FD&C Act

The **FDA** was formed by the 1906 Pure Food and Drugs Act and received its name in 1930. The FDA's purpose is to provide oversight for the production and safety of food and drugs in the United States. The main goal of the FDA is to safeguard and advance public health by overseeing and modulating the production of the following products:

- Food products
- Prescription medications
- Over-the-counter medications
- Tobacco products
- Dietary supplements
- Biological drug products
- Vaccines
- Blood transfusions
- Medical devices
- Cosmetics

The President appoints the director of the FDA, who is also the Commissioner of Food and Drugs. The FDA can examine and implement laws related to food and drug safety through the Office of Criminal Investigations. A majority of the laws that are of interest to, and affect, the operations of the FDA are found in the Food, Drug, and Cosmetic Act.

The Food, Drug, and Cosmetic Act initiated FDA regulation of clinical trials, manufacturing processes, and other aspects of the pre-market drug approval process. Every step of the process must have clear and specific documentation to prove legal compliance. If a product is found to be adulterated or misbranded, this must be documented and reported to the proper personnel.

DSCSA

The Drug Quality and Security Act regulates the processing, packaging, and distributing of medications in the United States. Throughout the transport process, proper documentation is required by the personnel handling the medication to ensure that there was no tampering.

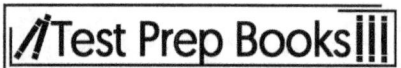

Laws Related to Bioequivalence
Remember that bioequivalent medications utilize the abbreviated new drug application that allows them to bypass repeating safety and efficacy studies. When conducting FDA-required studies, the original samples must be retained for at least five years for retesting at any given time.

PPPA
The Poison Prevention Packaging Act requires that certain medications and products be placed in special packaging for the protection of children. Unless stated otherwise, medications in vials must be sealed with child-resistant caps, and this must be documented in the patient's chart.

Kefauver-Harris Amendment
The Kefauver-Harris Amendment requires manufacturers to prove efficacy of their medications to the FDA through well-designed clinical trials. In addition, major observed side effects must be documented. All steps of the trials should be accurately documented and provided to the appropriate inspection agencies.

Orphan Drug Act
The Orphan Drug Act provides incentives for private companies and pharmaceutical manufacturers to research rare diseases. The FDA website provides updated information regarding drugs and devices for rare diseases, and this information can be used to research past, current, and upcoming orphan medication records.

Medicare Modernization Act
This act provides a prescription drug option to help relieve the financial burden of medications for patients eligible for Medicare services. Like all medication orders, records must be kept for the time frame required by company and state policies. The specific documents that must be kept for Medicare patients are listed below:

- Orders
- Certifications
- Referrals
- Prescriptions
- Requests for payments for Part A or B services, items, or drugs

CMS
The Centers for Medicare and Medicaid Services is a federal agency that provides resources and application forms regarding Medicare, Medicaid, and Children's Health Insurance services. The CMS has updated record schedules labeled "buckets 1-9" that can be found on the CMS website. For example, bucket 3 contains financial records and bucket 4 contains enrollment records. In addition, the CMS must notify the federal registrar of any changes in their record system and include "who, what, where, and why" explanations.

Anabolic Steroid Act
As previously mentioned, "stacking" or "plateauing" of steroids should be monitored. To prevent these practices, it's important to recognize requests for changes in dosage form or requests for partial filling. Proper record-keeping of steroid use in a patient's chart is important for monitoring proper use and potential misuse.

Safe Handling and Disposal Practices for Hazardous Drugs (USP <800>)
USP <800> establishes standards, regulations, and policies surrounding the packaging, distributing, and handling of hazardous drugs and substances. When transporting, ordering, and filling orders for hazardous drugs, records of each step should be documented and kept per company or state policies. Companies that require healthcare personnel to handle hazardous material should have specific protocols listed in their occupational safety plan.

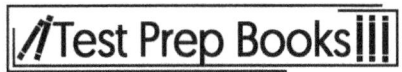

Handling Refills and/or Partial Filling of Prescriptions

Non-controlled substances have less documentation requirements compared to controlled substances; however, records of transfers and refills for both non-controlled and controlled substances must be documented and kept depending on state and company policies. For example, control II medications must be written on a special type of form/paper, which varies by state.

Organizations and Regulators Related to Pharmacy Practice

Records of OSHA workplace rights, training initiatives, and outreach programs should be documented for the U.S. Department of Labor. The FDA website contains the Code of Federal Regulations, which outlines the policies for all medications and record-keeping requirements. Such records must be readily available at the request of an inspection agency. All medication records must be kept for a minimum of one year per Title 21 Subchapter C in the Code of Federal Regulations.

Controlled Substances

In 1970, the U.S. Food and Drug Administration (FDA) released drug classifications, or drug schedules, under the Controlled Substance Act (CSA). The **drug schedules** arrange drugs into groups based on risk of abuse or harm. Under the CSA, drugs and other substances considered controlled substances are divided into five categories—Schedule I to Schedule V.

CSA

The Controlled Substance Act (**CSA**) was enacted in 1970 by the U.S. Congress as Title II of the Comprehensive Drug Abuse Prevention and Control Act. Through the CSA, every Federal law relating to the manufacture, regulation, and sale of certain controlled substances (narcotics as well) was made. Also, the CSA allowed for the creation of five controlled drug classes (Schedules I-V) and outlined the criteria for the medications in each class. Updates are made to the Act and the drug schedules to reflect up-to-date information and research.

DEA

The Drug Enforcement Administration (**DEA**) for controlled substances is a governmental agency set up in 1973 to implement laws around drug use and to fight drug trafficking. The Controlled Substances Act serves as the guiding document. This agency shares jurisdiction with the Federal Bureau of Investigation and with Immigrations and Customs Enforcement.

The DEA focuses on the following objectives:

- Instructing the public, especially through programs in the community targeted at youth, to lower the use of illegal and diverted drugs
- Supporting local and state law enforcement to assist in lowering drug-related crime and fighting/violence
- Disrupting origins and providers of illegal and diverted drugs on a local, national, and international level

Schedules of Controlled Substances and Drugs Within Them

Classification of controlled substances is based on currently accepted medical use for treatment and the likelihood of abuse or dependence on the drug:

- **Schedule I**: These substances have no currently accepted medical use, a lack of accepted safety for use under medical supervision, and a high potential for abuse. Examples include heroin, marijuana, lysergic acid diethylamide (LSD), peyote, and 3,4-methylenedioxymethamphetamine (ecstasy).

- **Schedule II/IIN**: Substances on this schedule have a high potential for abuse, which may lead to severe psychological or physical dependence. Examples include meperidine (Demerol®), hydromorphone (Dilaudid®), oxycodone (OxyContin®, Percocet®), methadone (Dolophine®), fentanyl (Duragesic®, Sublimaze®), morphine, opium, and codeine. Examples of Schedule IIN controlled substances include amphetamine (Adderall®, Dexedrine®), methylphenidate (Ritalin®), and methamphetamine (Desoxyn®).

- **Schedule III/IIIN**: These substances have less potential for abuse than substances in Schedules I or II, and abuse may lead to moderate or low physical dependence or high psychological dependence. Examples include combination medication products containing less than 15 mg of hydrocodone (Vicodin®) per dosage unit, products containing not more than 90 mg of codeine per dosage unit (Tylenol® with Codeine [Tylenol® #3]), and buprenorphine (Suboxone®). Examples of Schedule IIIN controlled substances include phendimetrazine, ketamine, benzphetamine (Didrex®), and anabolic steroids, such as testosterone.

- **Schedule IV**: Controlled substances on this schedule have a low potential for abuse relative to substances on Schedule III. Examples include carisoprodol (Soma®), clorazepate (Tranxene®), alprazolam (Xanax®), clonazepam (Klonopin®), midazolam (Versed®), lorazepam (Ativan®), diazepam (Valium®), triazolam (Halcion®), and temazepam (Restoril®).

- **Schedule V**: These substances have a low potential for abuse relative to substances on Schedule IV and consist primarily of preparations containing limited quantities of certain narcotics. Examples include cough preparations containing not more than 200 mg of codeine per 100 mL or per 100 g (Phenergan with Codeine, Robitussin® AC).

Exempt Narcotics

"Exempt narcotics," or Schedule V drugs, have a very low abuse risk and have safe, accepted medical uses in the US. Drugs that contain a limited amount of certain narcotics, such as codeine or cannabidiol (CBD), are considered "exempt narcotics" when they do not need a prescription to be purchased. An example is Robitussin AC, which has less than 200 mg/100 mL of codeine. Therefore, since the amount of codeine in the product is less than 200 mg/100 mL or 100 mg, it is a Schedule V drug instead of a Schedule II drug, which would be a drug that contains more than 200 mg/100 mL of codeine. This class also includes drugs that have opium preparations (100 mg/[100 mL or 100 g]), dihydrocodeine preparations (100mg/[100 mL or 100 g]), diphenoxylate preparations (2.5 mg/25 ug), and ethylmorphine preparations (100 mg/[100 mL or 100 g]). Rarely are these drugs abused, but because of their chemical makeup and inclusion of several highly controlled substances, they still can cause physical or psychological dependence, even in low amounts. Exempt narcotics mainly consist of cough suppressants (for example, Robitussin AC), antidiarrheals, and analgesics.

Verifying DEA Numbers

The type of registrant is identified by the first letter of the DEA number, and there are several different possible letters.

Overview and Laws

A	Used by older entities, last issued in 1985
B	Hospital or Clinic
C	Practitioners (physicians, dentists, veterinarians)
D	Teaching Institution
E	Manufacturer
F	Distributor
G	Researcher
H	Analytical Lab
J	Importer
K	Exporter
L	Reverse distributor (someone who collects unwanted or expired drugs to dispose of)
M	Mid-level practitioner (physician's assistants or nurse practitioners)
P, R, S, T, U	Narcotic treatment program
X	Suboxone or Subutex prescribing program

I, N, O, Q, V, W, Y, and Z are not valid DEA codes, so if any of these is the first letter of a DEA number on a prescription, it is a fake DEA number.

The formula is very specific for DEA numbers. In order to test the legitimacy of a DEA number, the following requirements must be met:

- DEA numbers have two letters accompanied by six numbers and a "check" number.
- The type of registrant is identified by the first letter in the DEA number as described in the table above.
- The second letter in the DEA number represents the first letter of the registrant's last name.
- The sum of the first, third, and fifth numbers is SUM1.
- The sum of the second, fourth, and sixth numbers is SUM2.
- SUM2 multiplied by two is PROD2.
- The last digit in the result of adding SUM1 and PROD2 should be the same as the check number.

Example: Dr. Pat Turner, a local physician, writes a prescription for Adderall 15 mg, and you need to verify his DEA number, which is CT8675300. Following the formula:

- The DEA number has two letters, six numbers, and the seventh "check" number.
- Pat Turner is a physician, so *C* is the correct first letter.
- *T* is for Turner, so the second letter is correct as well.
- The sum of the first, third, and fifth numbers (SUM1):
  - CT8675300 → 8+7+3=18
- The sum of the second, fourth, and sixth numbers (SUM2):
  - CT8675300 → 6+5+0=11
- Multiply the sum of the second, fourth, and sixth numbers (SUM2) by two to get PROD2:
  - $11 \times 2 = 22$

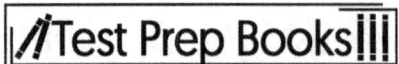

- Add SUM1 and PROD2. The last digit of this sum should be the same as the check number, which is the last digit of the DEA number:
    - $18 + 22 = 40$
    - The last digit of the sum above is 0
    - 0 matches the check number of the DEA number: CT8675300
- This is a valid DEA number.

Verifying on Intake That Required Information is on Prescriptions

CSA

Controlled (or scheduled) substances are chemicals, drugs, or substances that have a potential for abuse and are regulated under the Controlled Substances Act (CSA). The CSA is regulated and enforced by the Drug Enforcement Administration (DEA) under the federal government. It regulates every aspect of controlled substances, including the organization of drugs into schedules and the required DEA number from prescribers. The CSA also states what information is required on the prescriptions, when the prescription expires, how many refills are allowed, how controlled substance prescriptions can be transferred between pharmacies, and how the drugs themselves can be transferred between pharmacies.

Prescription Requirements for Controlled Substances

All controlled substance prescriptions must include all of the normal information required for any noncontrolled substance prescription plus additional information. A regular prescription must have the patient's name; patient's address (unless the patient's address is readily retrievable in the medication record); prescriber's name, address, and telephone number; drug name, drug strength, and quantity prescribed; directions for use; intended use of the drug; date of issuance for the prescription; and number of refills.

On a controlled substance prescription, the following additional information must be present: the patient's date of birth and the prescriber's DEA. Additionally, the patient's address must be on the prescription itself—unlike noncontrolled prescriptions, it is not sufficient for the patient's address to be only in the medication record.

Schedule II drugs require a written prescription with a manual signature from the prescriber or an electronic prescription with a pharmacy who meets the CSA requirements for receiving and dispensing controlled substances. For Schedules III–V, the prescription can be called in over the phone, as long as all of the necessary prescription requirements are collected over the phone (except for the manual signature from the prescriber; no manual signature is needed for these). The prescription label should also have a warning for Schedule II–IV drugs that states "Caution: Federal law prohibits the transfer of this drug to any person other than the patient for which it was prescribed."

Filling, Partial Filling, and Refilling Prescriptions

CSA

The Controlled Substances Act (CSA) regulates how prescriptions for controlled substances are filled, including partial fills and refills of controlled substances. It states that every person, institution, and pharmacy in the filling process has to be registered with the DEA before prescribing or dispensing a controlled substance. For example, the doctor prescribing the medication, the manufacturer of the medication, the distributor of the medication, the pharmacy, and the pharmacist must all be individually registered with the DEA. The patient does not need DEA licensure, as patients are considered the "ultimate users," which means they are the individual taking the medication and the controlled substance no longer needs to be tracked. Patients, however, are still subject to DEA-enforced laws on abuse and misuse.

Expiration Dates and Refills

For Schedule II controlled substances, the prescription is only good for thirty days from when it was first written. Schedule II drugs cannot be refilled and require a new prescription from the prescriber each time. For Schedule III–V controlled substances, the prescription cannot have more than five refills, and it cannot be filled after six months of the prescription's date of issuance. In these cases, the prescriber must be contacted to write a new prescription for the patient to use.

Refills can be made in three different ways: complete refills, partial refills, and emergency refills. A Schedule II prescription can still be partially filled and dispensed if the pharmacy does not have enough of the medication to completely fill the prescription. The rest of the prescription has to be filled in the next seventy-two hours; otherwise, a new prescription is required to fill the prescription further. However, there are slightly different procedures for Schedule II substances for terminally ill and long-term care facility (LTCF) patients. The pharmacist can partially fill the prescription, and they have to write "terminally ill" or "LTCF patient" on the prescription. The prescription is valid for sixty days after it is written, and it can be dispensed partially as many times as it needs to be without exceeding the prescription's total quantity. This is so that extra medications are not dispensed to a patient that may not need the whole prescription.

For Schedule III through V controlled substances, partial filling works similarly to the process for Schedule II terminally ill or LTCF partial fills. The prescription can be partially filled up to the original prescription's quantity, and it cannot be more than six months since the original prescription was written.

Emergency Filling Procedures

An emergency prescription occurs when a controlled substance is needed for immediate administration, but a prescription is not written for the medication because the prescriber is unable to write it. For example, the prescriber can call in a verbal order for a medication for the pharmacist to dispense immediately. An example of this type of emergency would be someone suddenly having a seizure in a hospital. Following this, the medical professional who administered and ordered the medication has to send in a written prescription for the controlled substance that was dispensed within the next seven days, and it should be written only for what was given during the emergency and nothing more.

Transferring Controlled Substances between Pharmacies

To transfer a Schedule II drug between pharmacies, the pharmacy receiving the medication has to file a DEA Form 222 in paper or electronically. This form is a "triplicate" form—the first copy is given to the pharmacy giving the drug, the second copy goes to the DEA, and the third copy is kept by the receiving pharmacy. To transfer a Schedule III–V drug between pharmacies, a form is not needed, but the drug name, dosage form, drug strength, quantity, and date transferred must be documented on paper and kept by the giving pharmacy.

Transferring Prescriptions for Controlled Substances between Pharmacies

Per the CSA, Schedule II prescriptions cannot be transferred. The patient has to contact the prescriber to send a new prescription to another pharmacy if the patient wishes to use another pharmacy. For Schedule III–V prescriptions, it was recently made legal to transfer a prescription once between pharmacies. For example, the patient can initially decide to fill their prescription at one pharmacy and then decide to change pharmacies. After this, a completely new prescription would be needed to transfer pharmacies again. However, if the pharmacies share a database, they may transfer the prescription as many times as they want. The transfer has to be communicated directly between two pharmacists and not technicians.

For Schedule III–V prescriptions that can be transferred, the transferring pharmacist has to write "VOID" on a written prescription or add the word "VOID" to the prescription record for electronic prescriptions. The name, address, and DEA number of the pharmacy must be noted as well as the date of the transfer and the name of the

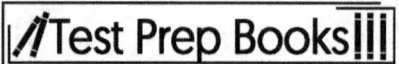

pharmacist who is transferring the prescription. The receiving pharmacist must write "transfer" on the prescription, and they must note the date of issuance of the original prescription, the original number of refills, the number of refills left, the locations of past refills, the date of original dispensing, the transferring pharmacy's name, the transferring pharmacy's address, the transferring pharmacy's DEA number, and the transferring pharmacist's name. In addition, if this was not the first transfer for this prescription, it must also have any other transferring pharmacies' names, addresses, and DEA numbers.

Appropriately Filing All Classes of Prescriptions

CSA

The Controlled Substances Act also outlines how to file records for controlled substances. This includes inventory, transfers of prescriptions, transfers of drugs, drug disposal, dispensing records, and shipments received.

DEA

All controlled substance records must be kept for two years in the pharmacy for the DEA to inspect and maintain. They must also be "readily retrievable," as defined by either an easy-to-access electronic record system or with important notes marked by an asterisk or red line to make those records visually separate from the rest of the records.

Separate from the CSA, the Combat Methamphetamine Epidemic Act of 2005 was written to limit the dispensing of medications containing ephedrine, pseudoephedrine, or phenylpropanolamine. A specific pharmacy cannot sell more than 9 grams of drugs containing these medications to one customer in thirty days, and a mail order or mobile pharmacy cannot sell more than 7.5 grams in thirty days. Examples of these medications include Sudafed, Allegra DM, and other common cold and cough medications that are sold behind the counter (BTC). A logbook must also be kept that states the product name, quantity sold, name and address of the customer, and date and time of the sale.

Filing Requirements

Very strict records must be kept for all controlled substances to prevent abuse of the system. Schedule II drug records are kept separately from the Schedule III–V records.

The required records must be kept on file: executed and unexecuted official order forms (DEA Form 222), power of attorney authorization, receipts and invoices for Schedules III–V, all inventory records, records of distribution of controlled substances, dispensing record, theft or significant loss reports (DEA Form 106), inventory of disposed controlled substances (DEA Form 41), records of transfers between pharmacies, DEA registration certificate, and self-certification certificate and logbook. If shipping or financial records are held at another location, the pharmacy must have written authorization to keep records offsite. Pharmacies also have the choice of organizing the records in two ways: the first way keeps Schedule II, Schedule III–V, and noncontrolled dispensing records separate, and the second way is to separate the Schedule II drugs and then have all other drugs filed in a manner that allows them to be readily retrievable.

Each state has slightly different laws for recordkeeping as far as tracking patient usage of controlled substances, but in most cases, a form of picture ID with an ID number, such as a driver's license, is needed, along with the person's name, birth date, address, and phone number. These should be noted in their chart or written down when dispensing the prescription to the patient.

Handling Schedule V and Regulated Non-Prescription Products

CSA

Schedule V drugs, also known as exempt narcotics, are regulated by the DEA as controlled substances under the CSA. Behind-the-counter (BTC) products are not listed under the CSA as controlled substances but are regulated by

Overview and Laws

the FDA and are kept behind the counter at the pharmacy. BTCs are usually over-the-counter (OTC) drugs, but they have some form of abuse potential and/or a monitoring program is in place, so they are placed behind the counter to limit patient access. An OTC is a drug that can be purchased without a prescription by a patient. Some exceptions include Schedule V drugs containing codeine, such as codeine-containing cough syrups, that are Schedule V controlled substances because of the codeine in the drug but are also considered BTC substances because a prescription is not always required. Examples of BTC drugs that can be purchased without a prescription include some codeine containing cough syrups (they can also be prescription medications), regular and NPH insulin, and pseudoephedrine (Sudafed). Various states have slightly different legislation around BTCs and their regulations, but these rules generally apply to all fifty states.

Filing Requirements
While their filing requirements are the same as Schedules III and IV, several BTC products, such as Sudafed, have Prescription Drug Monitoring Programs (PDMPs) that must be used at each purchase of a BTC medication.

Laws, Regulations, and Processes to Transfer Controlled Substances between Pharmacies
Schedule III–V medications follow the same process of transferring controlled substances between pharmacies. No form is needed, but the drug name, dosage form, drug strength, quantity, and date transferred must be documented on paper.

Laws, Regulations, and Processes to Transfer Prescriptions for Controlled Substances between Pharmacies
Prescriptions for Schedule III–V medications follow the same process of transferring prescriptions between pharmacies. The patient has to contact their provider to move the prescription over to the new pharmacy; the pharmacy cannot do that for the patient. It is then treated as a new prescription.

Ordering, Storing, and Maintaining Inventory of Controlled Substances

CSA
The CSA contains regulations for ordering, storing, and maintaining inventory of controlled substances.

DEA
The DEA tracks the creation, distribution, and purchase of controlled substances because of their potential for physical and psychological abuse and dependency risks. Keeping external, federal oversight on the controlled substances holds providers, manufacturers, distributors, pharmacies, and patients accountable for the use of these medications. The DEA also requires the medication packaging to display a symbol representing which schedule the drug is included in. The symbol does not have to be on the dispensed prescription, but it should be on the manufacturer's bottle, vial, box, etc. The symbols are provided below.

Schedule	Symbol
Schedule I	CI or C-I
Schedule II	CII or C-II
Schedule III	CIII or C-III
Schedule IV	CIV or C-IV
Schedule V	CV or C-V

DEA Forms
There are DEA forms that must be on file or used for certain procedures with controlled substances. DEA Form 222 is for the transfer of Schedule II controlled substances between pharmacies or from a manufacturer to a pharmacy.

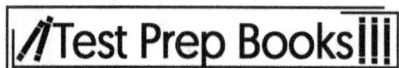

DEA Form 106 is for theft or significant loss. Significant loss is any form of loss of a controlled substance that has not been previously accounted for; for example, a bottle of pills is dropped in a puddle of water and therefore is not usable anymore. Another example would be when an inventory count reveals that some tablets are missing, and no theft has occurred. However, if this situation occurs, and the pharmacy is not sure if it was theft or loss, the form is the same, and the DEA will take the investigation from there. DEA Form 41 is used for a record of destroyed controlled substances. This form is usually used by reverse distributors who take back the drugs a pharmacy does not use after they expire and destroy the medications. These are the most common DEA forms used for controlled substances, and they must all be kept on file at the pharmacy for two years.

Procedures for Ordering, Receiving, Storing, and Disposing of Controlled Substances

Documentation Requirements for Receiving, Ordering, and Returning Controlled Substances

DEA Form 222 must be filled out, either electronically or on paper, by the pharmacy in order to transfer, order, or return Schedule II medications. Once filled out, the DEA Form 222 needs to be stored so that it can easily be accessed during an inspection if requested (this applies to both electronic and paper records). On the DEA Form 222, the date, the name of the medication ordered, and the amount are required.

There are several rules that need to be followed when filling out and filing the DEA Form 222:

- Do not make alterations to the form. If a mistake is made while filling out the form, a new form should be used.
- For triplicate paper versions (prior to October 30, 2021):
  - The blue copy of the form is kept by the recipient (the purchaser).
  - The green copy of the form is mailed to the local DEA office.
  - The brown copy of the form needs to be kept and filed at the supplying pharmacy for at least two years.
- For single-sheet forms (after October 30, 2021):
  - The recipient (the purchaser) must keep a paper or electronic copy for two years.
  - The supplier must keep the original form on record for two years.
  - The supplier can either report through the Automation of Reports and Consolidated Orders System (ARCOS) or they can send a paper or electronic copy of the original form to the DEA office.

Older copies of DEA Form 222 (in triplicate on carbon paper) were no longer acceptable after October 30, 2021, and the single-sheet form became the standard. The filing procedure with the single-sheet form is similar to the triplicate forms: the purchaser must keep a paper or electronic copy of the original for two years. The supplier must keep the original on record for two years. Suppliers who do not report through the **Automation of Reports and Consolidated Orders System (ARCOS)** must send a paper or electronic copy of the original to the DEA office.

Storing Controlled Substances

Per the CSA, controlled substances must be behind at least two different locks, and the same key or code cannot be used to open both locks. For example, the storage can be a safe in a locked room; or a keypad safe in a locked, keyed cabinet; or a safe with two locks. The substances have to stay locked during business hours, and the locks are only opened when it is necessary to fill a prescription. The safe has to be secured to the floor or in another way to the building. Only a select number of employees, such as the pharmacy manager and one other pharmacist, should have the keys and/or keycode to unlock the safe and/or the room. The safes are also generally time-delayed,

Overview and Laws

meaning they do not immediately open when the safe is unlocked. This is for security purposes, but the time delay is not a DEA requirement.

Transfer of Controlled Substances

Pharmacies are responsible for the physical transfer of controlled substances and for the precision of the inventory and records. For two years after the transfer, the pharmacy must keep the records immediately available for inspection by the DEA.

An outside firm may be hired by the pharmacy to take stock, pack, and coordinate the transfer of its controlled substances to another location (pharmacy, original supplier, or original manufacturer).

Depending on the schedule category of the substance, DEA Form 222 (Schedule II) or other written documentation (Schedule III or IV) containing the drug name, dosage form, strength, quantity, and the date of transfer is filled out.

Documentation Requirements for Loss/Theft of Controlled Substances

In the event of a loss or theft of any controlled substance at a pharmacy, the procedures outlined below must be carried out within one business day of discovering that theft or loss has occurred:

- Notify the local DEA Diversion Field Office in writing, as the theft of controlled substances is considered a criminal act and a source of deviation, which requires that the DEA be notified.

- It is not clearly required by federal law or policies, but it is important to also inform local law enforcement and state regulatory agencies.

- The DEA needs to be informed of the loss/theft precisely, without any intermediaries (i.e., other parts of the corporation); the notice needs to be signed by an authorized individual of the registrant.

- DEA Form 106 (Report of Theft or Loss of Controlled Substances) must be filled out by the pharmacy. This form will document what happened to lead to this situation and the amount of controlled substances involved. The following information should be included on the form:
    - Pharmacy name and address
    - DEA registration number
    - Local Police Department name and phone number (if contacted by the pharmacy)
    - Kind of theft (e.g., armed robbery, break-in, etc.)
    - Any identifying label features used on the containers (marks, symbols, or price codes)
    - Record of which controlled substances are missing, including the strength, dosage form, size of container, and National Drug code numbers

If the reported lost/stolen material is found after filing and notifying local authorities and the DEA, a written notification must be given to clear up why no Form 106 was filed after the initial notification.

Tracking Requirements for Perpetual Inventory of Controlled Substances

An initial inventory, a biennial inventory, and a newly scheduled controlled substance inventory are all required under Federal law in each pharmacy. These requirements, part of the Controlled Substances Act (CSA), are laid out in the Code of Federal Regulations (CFR). An initial inventory is a physical count of all the controlled substances in or under the control of the pharmacy at the time the inventory was taken, and this number is compared to what the inventory states should be in stock in the pharmacy. If the count does not add up, DEA Form 106 must be filled out and submitted to the DEA to prompt an investigation. If there are no controlled substances currently being kept, a zero must be recorded. This initial inventory must be completed every time an individual begins to distribute, dispense, or manufacture controlled substances. This could, for example, include the opening of a new pharmacy or a change in pharmacy owner or Pharmacist in Charge. A biennial inventory is done every two years and follows the same process as the initial inventory. It has to be done within two years of either the initial inventory date or of the date of the last biennial inventory. The newly scheduled controlled substance inventory is done when a drug that was not previously controlled becomes a controlled substance, or when a substance changes schedules within the controlled substances scheduling. Any newly controlled substance must be included in future biennial inventories that occur after the newly scheduled controlled substance inventory.

However, even though the CSA and the CFR only state that a pharmacy needs an initial, biennial, and newly controlled substance inventory count, most pharmacies count much more frequently, even daily, to ensure they have the correct amount of controlled substances and that no theft or loss has occurred. The requirements for these inventories vary from state to state. One method of inventory called perpetual inventory uses computer systems to keep an accurate count of all controlled and non-controlled prescription medications on hand at all times. The perpetual inventory is periodically reconciled with a physical count of the medications, although again, the specifics of the reconciliation may vary from state to state.

Diversion and Prescription Monitoring Programs

Prescription drug monitoring programs (PDMPs) differ from state to state, but they have the same basic foundation. They are electronic databases that track the controlled prescriptions dispensed at a pharmacy. They can survey a patient's usage of controlled substances across all pharmacies, which helps prevent abuse of the controlled substances system. For example, if a patient filled a prescription for Xanax at one pharmacy for thirty days, and then they tried to fill the same prescription at a different pharmacy three days later, the PDMP system would show an alert to the second pharmacy that they cannot fill this medication because it is too soon. It can also help patients keep track of how many times they have filled a certain prescription and make it easier to transfer to a different pharmacy as needed. However, some states do not require timely updates of the PDMP, so sometimes the records will not always be the most accurate or up to date.

The DEA has a division named the Diversion Control Division that is tasked with preventing, detecting, and investigating illegal uses of controlled substances. They also oversee the legal distribution of controlled substances for legitimate purposes. In this context, diversion is defined as the illegal use of legal controlled substances by ordering in a legitimate way and redirecting the drugs to an illegal source. For example, a pharmacist selling extra inventory of morphine to a drug dealer, a physician prescribing for themselves under different names to exceed limits, or any pharmacy employee falsifying records to cover up stolen controlled substances would all be considered diversions of controlled substances. The Diversion Control Division has the right to investigate any claims regarding diverted controlled substances.

Practice Quiz

1. Which of the following resources for pharmacists lists the accurate prices of medications?
    a. *The Orange Book*
    b. *The Red Book*
    c. *Handbook on Injectables*
    d. *Ident-A-Drug*

2. In the year 2019, what action was made illegal for pharmacies and is now regulated by the EPA?
    a. Failing to require electronic prescriptions
    b. Using drug components that are harmful for the environment
    c. Disposing of medications down a drain
    d. Failing to offer medicinal counseling for patients

3. A patient comes in with a prescription for acetaminophen/codeine 1,000 mg/60 mg from Kevin Kirk, NP, DEA Number MK1928303. Is this a valid DEA number?
    a. Yes, everything is correct.
    b. No, the letters are correct, but the numbers are not.
    c. No, the numbers are correct, but the letters are not.
    d. No, both the numbers, and the letters are wrong.

4. Which DEA number is valid?
    a. GR1893402 for Dr. Ralph, a researcher
    b. MY9143239 for Ms. Young, a PA
    c. CZ3128965 for Dr. Oliphant, a physician
    d. AT1532666 for Dr. Tate, a hospitalist

5. Which prescription does NOT need a DEA number on it?
    a. Trazadone 100 mg daily
    b. Lyrica 300 mg daily
    c. Clonazepam 1 mg twice daily
    d. Alprazolam 5 mg as needed

See answers on the next page.

Answer Explanations

1. B: *The Red Book* is a publication of the Micromedex branch of IBM that provides a summary of drugs and their accurate prices. Choice *A*, *The Orange Book*, is incorrect because it is a reference book created by the FDA that lists all FDA-approved medications. Choice *C*, *Handbook on Injectables*, is incorrect because it is a reference book made by the American Society of Health-System Pharmacists that provides quick information on injectable drugs. Choice *D*, *Ident-A-Drug*, is incorrect because it is a resource that can be used for identifying unknown pills.

2. C: "Disposing of medications down a drain" is the correct answer. In 2019, The Resource Conservation and Recovery Act for hazardous waste pharmaceuticals ruled that disposal of hazardous pharmaceutical waste down drains into the sewer is prohibited. Choice *A*, failing to require electronic prescriptions, is incorrect because not all states require e-prescriptions. Most states do mandate e-prescriptions, but some states like Alaska, Oregon, Idaho, and a few others have no such mandate. Choice *B*, using drug components that are harmful for the environment, is incorrect because many pharmaceuticals require harmful components and do not have safer alternatives. Choice *D*, failing to offer medicinal counseling for patients, is incorrect because it was prohibited by the Omnibus Budget Reconciliation Act of 1990.

3. B: The DEA number has two letters, six numbers, and then the seventh "check" number. Kevin is a nurse practitioner (NP), so M is a correct first letter. K is for Kirk, so the second letter is correct as well.

- The sum of the first, third, and fifth numbers:
    - MK1928303 → 1+2+3 = 6
- The sum of the second, fourth, and sixth numbers:
    - MK1928303 → 9+8+0 =17
- Multiply the sum of the second, fourth, and sixth numbers by 2.
    - 17 x 2 = 34
- Add the first sum and the product of the second sum and 2, and the last digit of this sum should be the same as the last number on the DEA number.
    - 6+34=40, MK1928303

This is an invalid DEA number because the last number is 3; it would be 0 if it were a valid DEA number. Therefore, the correct answer is Choice *B* because the letters are correct, but the numbers are wrong.

4. B: The DEA number for Ms. Young, PA, is MY9143239. This DEA number has two letters, six numbers, and then the seventh "check" number. She is a physician's assistant (PA), so *M* is a correct first letter. Her name is Young, so the second letter, *Y*, is correct as well.

- The sum of the first, third, and fifth numbers:
    - MY9143239 → 9+4+2=15
- The sum of the second, fourth, and sixth numbers:
    - MY9143239 → 1+3+3=7
- Multiply the sum of the second, fourth, and sixth numbers by 2.
    - 7 x 2 = 14

Overview and Laws

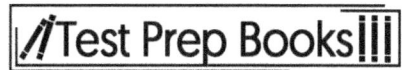

- Add the first sum and the product of the second sum and 2, and the last digit of this sum should be the same as the last number on the DEA number.
    - 15+14=29, MY9143239

This is a valid DEA number because it follows the formula. Therefore, Choice *B* is correct.

For Choice *A*, GR1893402 for Dr. Ralph, a researcher:

- The sum of the first, third, and fifth numbers:
    - GR1893402 → 1+9+4=14
- The sum of the second, fourth, and sixth numbers:
    - GR1893402 → 8+3+0=11
- Multiply the sum of the second, fourth, and sixth numbers by 2.
    - 11 x 2 = 22
- Add the first sum and the product of the second sum and 2, and the last digit of this sum should be the same as the last number on the DEA number.
    - 14+22=36, GR1893402

This is an invalid DEA number because the last number is 2, when it would be 6 if it was a valid DEA number. This makes Choice *A* incorrect.

Choice *C*, CZ3128965, is the DEA number for Dr. Oliphant, a physician. The number has two letters, six numbers, and then the seventh "check" number. She is a physician, so *C* is a correct first letter. Her name is Oliphant, so the second letter should be *O*, not *Z*, which makes the DEA number invalid. Therefore, Choice *C* is incorrect.

Choice *D*, AT1532666, is the DEA number for Dr. Tate, a hospitalist. The number has two letters, six numbers, and then the seventh "check" number. She is a hospitalist, a practitioner, so the first letter should be *C*, not *A*. The letter *A* is not a letter for any DEA prescriber, so this is not a valid DEA number, and therefore Choice *D* is incorrect.

5. A: Only controlled prescriptions require the DEA number of the prescriber. Choice *A* is correct because trazadone is not a controlled substance, so a DEA number from the prescriber is not needed to fill the prescription. Choice *B*, Lyrica (pregabalin); Choice *C*, clonazepam (Klonopin); and Choice *D*, alprazolam (Xanax) are all controlled substances and would require a prescriber's DEA number on the prescription. Therefore, Choices *B*, *C*, and *D* are incorrect.

Drugs and Drug Therapy

Drug Classification

Therapeutic Classes of Drugs

Drug Classes

It is important to recognize that drugs with a similar therapeutic effect might have different mechanisms/modes of action. For example, ACE inhibitors (e.g., ramipril), calcium channel blockers (e.g., amlodipine), and antihypertensive agents have similar therapeutic effects, but their mechanisms of action are different. When filling a prescription, it is important to understand how a drug works. Not only does knowledge about the pharmacology of a medicine help to identify possible drug interactions, but it also helps to facilitate patients' understanding of why medications are prescribed for them.

Analgesics

Analgesics are medications used to treat acute and chronic pain. It is important to note the difference between analgesics and anesthetics. Analgesics provide pain relief and partial loss of physical sensation without loss of consciousness, whereas anesthetics provide pain relief through complete loss of physical sensation, with or without consciousness. Analgesics can treat a wide variety of pain categories including headaches, arthritis or joint pain, menstrual cramps, muscle soreness, and even pain associated with cancer. They are available in a variety of forms including tablets, capsules, creams, ointments, suppositories, and liquids.

There are two categories of analgesics: opioid analgesics, which require a prescription from an authorized provider, and non-opioid analgesics, which are commonly prescribed or sold over the counter in local drug stores. Opioids, also known as narcotics or opiates, interact with opioid receptors located on the nerve cells of the brain and block pain signal transmissions to the rest of the body while also increasing the sensation of pleasure. Opioids can be natural, semi-synthetic, or synthetic. Natural opiates are chemical moieties, found in plants such as opium seeds (*Papaver somniferum*), that make up morphine and codeine. Semi-synthetic opiates, such as hydrocodone, oxycodone, and hydromorphone, are human-made medications derived from natural opiates. Synthetic opioids are entirely human-made and include medications like fentanyl, methadone, and tramadol.

Opiates are highly regulated at the local, state, and federal level due to the high occurrence of addiction and abuse. They are known to carry high physical dependence addiction rates because over time, and with increased use and dosage, a person can develop a tolerance that requires them to increase the dose or combine medications to experience the same type of pain relief. This is because usage decreases production of the body's natural painkilling neurotransmitters, called endorphins. Increasing the opioid dose and combining medications are common causes of death associated with this class of drugs. Additionally, patients may try various dosage forms like injection, crushing the tablets to snort them up the nose, or smoking the crushed-up medication. Using different forms of the drug increases the risk of addiction even more. Since opiates typically require a provider-written prescription every one to three months, patients who cannot get a prescription often resort to illegal means of obtaining pain medications, such as stealing prescriptions from other people. This can increase their risk of ingesting laced medications, which are drugs containing additional substances that are not intended to be taken with the original medication. In a clinical setting, opioids are prescribed to prevent severe pain, such as after a surgery or due to chronic disease, or to prevent diarrhea since a known side-effect of opioids is constipation. Other side effects include drowsiness, a sense of euphoria, vomiting, and slowed breathing.

Non-opioid analgesics target the cyclooxygenase enzyme and inhibit its action to prevent production of prostaglandins that are known to play a large role in increasing sensitivity to pain and in creating signs of inflammation, pain, and fever. There are two categories of non-opioid analgesics: prescription and non-prescription medications. Prescription non-opioid analgesics can be non-controlled or controlled. Non-controlled non-opioid prescription analgesics include medications such as duloxetine, amitriptyline, and celecoxib. Controlled non-opioid prescription analgesics include pregabalin and gabapentin (a controlled medication in some states). Over-the-counter non-opioid analgesics are less addictive than opioids and include drugs like ibuprofen, naproxen, acetaminophen, and aspirin.

Even though analgesics can be purchased without a provider's oversight, they can still be abused and cause clinical damage to a patient. When taking ibuprofen over the counter, the maximum dose is 1,200 mg dosed at 200 to 400 mg by mouth every four to six hours as needed for pain. Common short-term side effects (meaning they should only last while the medication is in the body) include heartburn, nausea, vomiting, and headaches. A long-term side effect of non-opioid analgesics is stomach bleeding and ulcers. These effects are not common but can be induced with excessive use. Since prostaglandin production is inhibited, the stomach's line of defense against gastric acid is mostly eliminated. The acid can attack and damage the stomach lining, which causes open sores (ulcers) to form.

Dermatologics

Dermatologic medications are formulations (typically topical) that are applied to the various areas of the skin, including intravaginally or rectally, to prevent and/or treat specific or broad skin disorders. These types of medications come in a variety of dosage forms including ointments, pastes, creams, gels, lotions, powders, shampoos, patches, and suppositories. Dermatological dosage forms can be medicated or non-medicated. Non-medicated topical formulations are used for their physical properties as protectants or lubricants. Topical medications are typically local (designed to affect a specific spot) rather than systemic (designed to affect the whole body), but systemic absorption is not unheard of. Most topical medications are applied to the skin, which means they must penetrate the stratum corneous layer to reach the epidermis to have clinical effect. In this case, the skin is considered the target organ.

The stratum corneum is the major skin barrier to drug absorption rates because it is twenty layers thick. It is known as the rate-limiting step. When a drug is placed on the skin, there are several methods it can use to get through the stratum corneum including transport between cells, transport within hair follicles and sweat glands, transport within cells, and stripping. Stripping is an abrasive method that consists of physical removal of the stratum corneum to make greater pathways into the skin.

There is only a certain selection of molecules that can penetrate the skin, such as those that are small, lipophilic (preferring fat), potent, and nonirritating. However, transdermal patches do not need to possess the same characteristics. Although these patches are applied on the skin, the skin is not the target organ. The skin has mechanisms that allow the drug to pass through all its layers (stratum corneous, epidermis, adipose tissue, dermis) and into the blood vessels where it will have a systemic effect. The goal of transdermal medications is to provide a steady release of drug through the skin to keep a consistent concentration of the drug in the blood supply. The most common transdermal patches are nicotine and fentanyl patches for smoking cessation and pain relief, respectively.

Drug classes that may be used as dermatologic medications include the following:

- Antipsoriatics: These drugs treat psoriasis, a type of disorder that causes excessive flaking of the skin.

- Antihistamines: This type of drug is often used to treat, or provide relief from, allergic reactions on the skin like poison ivy, bug bites, or other allergen exposure.

- Acne agents: These are often used to prevent or minimize sebaceous gland activity that can cause whiteheads, blackheads, hyperpigmentation, and scarring.

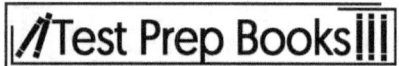

- Anti-infectives: This includes antibiotics, antifungals, and antivirals. Antibiotics inhibit bacterial infections, and antifungals can be used for athlete's foot and nail fungal infections. Antivirals are used to treat virus-based infections.

- Antineoplastics: These drugs are used to treat malignant tumors. The two types of tumors are malignant (cancerous) and benign (non-cancerous).

- Non-steroidal anti-inflammatories (NSAIDs): There is only one topical non-steroidal anti-inflammatory on the market, which is diclofenac (Voltaren®). It is indicated for relief of joint pain caused by arthritis.

- Anti-pruritic: These drugs are used to stop itching.

The following dermatological products are used for cosmetic and general health purposes:

- Vitamin A, C, or D
- Wet wraps
- Soap
- Shampoos
- Insect repellants
- Facial cleansers
- Sunscreen

Topical medications prescribed for pregnant people should be used with caution, as some drugs are able to reach systemic circulation and thus fetal circulation. Those who are breastfeeding should also be aware of possible issues with topical medications because they can end up in the breast milk and get into the infant's blood supply. The area of application, age of the patient, and history of previous skin disorders and conditions can all affect topical drug absorption rate and, thus, its intended clinical effect.

Medications Acting on the Nervous System

Antidepressants and Anxiolytics

Antidepressants are used to treat different mood disorders including depression, anxiety, phobias, and obsessive-compulsive disorder (OCD). Treatment for depression includes various medications, in addition to cognitive behavioral therapy (e.g., counseling).

The following are some of the symptoms frequently observed with depression:

- Difficulty concentrating
- Decreased interest or no interest in activities that used to be enjoyable
- Fatigue or lack of energy
- Sense of worthlessness or hopelessness
- Difficulty sleeping
- Changes in appetite
- Suicidal thoughts

Antidepressants exert their therapeutic effects by modulating the release or action of various neurotransmitters in the brain. **Neurotransmitters** are chemical messengers that transmit signals from one neuron to another. The common side effects of antidepressants are serotonin syndrome (headache, agitation, tremor, hallucination, tachycardia, hyperthermia, shivering, and sweating), sexual dysfunction, weight changes, gastric acidity, diarrhea, sleep disturbances, and suicidal ideation.

Drugs and Drug Therapy

Commonly prescribed antidepressant medications include:

- Sertraline
- Fluoxetine
- Paroxetine
- Citalopram
- Escitalopram
- Venlafaxine
- Desvenlafaxine
- Duloxetine
- Trazodone
- Bupropion
- Amitriptyline
- Nortriptyline

Benzodiazepines are a class of medications used for the short-term treatment of anxiety. They are often combined with antidepressants during initial treatment to increase treatment compliance. Benzodiazepines have the potential for significant physical dependence and withdrawal symptoms. These drugs can be used as sedatives and hypnotics and are also utilized as an add-on therapy with anti-convulsant medications. Benzodiazepines are often used to treat symptoms from alcohol withdrawal. The majority of benzodiazepines are labeled as Class IV controlled substances. The common side effects of these medications include physical dependence, sedation, drowsiness, dizziness, and lack of coordination.

The following are commonly prescribed benzodiazepines:

- Diazepam
- Lorazepam
- Clonazepam
- Alprazolam
- Midazolam
- Temazepam

Antipsychotics

Antipsychotics are used to treat psychosis, including schizophrenia and bipolar disorder. Psychosis is often characterized by a cluster of symptoms including delusions (false beliefs), paranoia (fear or anxiety), hallucinations, and disordered thoughts. The most common side effects of antipsychotics are dyskinesia (movement disorder), loss of libido or sex drive, gynecomastia (breast enlargement) in males, weight gain, heart diseases (QT prolongation), and metabolic disorders including type 2 diabetes.

The following are examples of commonly prescribed antipsychotics:

- Chlorpromazine
- Fluphenazine
- Haloperidol
- Aripiprazole
- Olanzapine
- Risperidone
- Ziprasidone
- Clozapine

Stimulant Medications

Stimulant medications are also called sympathomimetic agents, as they work by augmenting the sympathetic neurotransmitter activity (e.g., epinephrine and norepinephrine). These drugs are often used during emergencies to treat cardiac arrest and shock. Stimulant medications are also commonly used to treat attention-deficit hyperactivity disorder (ADHD). The common side effects of such medications include irritability, weight loss, insomnia, dizziness, agitation, headache, abdominal pain, tachycardia, growth retardation, hypertension, cardiovascular disturbances, and death.

The following are examples of sympathomimetic drugs that are used in the treatment of ADHD:

- Methylphenidate
- Dextroamphetamine
- Lisdexamfetamine
- Mixed salts of amphetamine
- Atomoxetine

Anticonvulsant Medications

Anticonvulsants are also called antiepileptic or anti-seizure medications. They are used in the treatment of epileptic seizures. They suppress excessive firing of neurons and therefore prevent the initiation and spread of seizures. This class of medications is often used to stabilize mood in bipolar disorder or for the treatment of neuropathic pain. The common side effects are dizziness, sedation, weight gain, hepatotoxicity, hair loss, blood disorders, etc. Anticonvulsants are teratogenic and can cause significant harm to a fetus and result in birth defects. Therefore, female patients on anticonvulsant therapy should consult with their physicians before planning pregnancy.

The common medications in this class include the following:

- Carbamazepine
- Oxcarbazepine
- Phenytoin
- Valproic acid
- Divalproex
- Levetiracetam
- Lamotrigine
- Topiramate
- Clobazam

Medications Acting on the Cardiovascular System

Lipid-Lowering Medications

Lipid-lowering medications are used for the treatment of high blood lipids (**hyperlipidemia**), including high cholesterol (**hypercholesterolemia**) and high triglycerides (**hypertriglyceridemia**). Although a patient with hypercholesterolemia typically will not experience symptoms, the condition leads to the accumulation of fatty deposits in the blood vessels and liver, called atherosclerotic plaques. As time progresses, the deposits slow, impede, or block the flow of blood through the vessels. When blood flow is compromised to the heart muscle, ischemic heart disease can result. If the blood flow to the brain decreases, there is a possibility of ischemic stroke. Compromised blood supply in peripheral tissues and limbs can cause the development of peripheral vascular diseases (PVD). Lifestyle changes, such as a healthy diet and regular exercise, can significantly reduce the risk of hypercholesterolemia, even in the presence of predisposing genetic risk factors. Total cholesterol is determined from two components: **high-density lipoprotein (HDL) cholesterol**, considered the "good" cholesterol, and **low-**

density lipoprotein (LDL) cholesterol, considered the "bad" cholesterol. Although it is helpful to keep a lower total cholesterol level for health and reduced disease risk, it is more critical to keep the ratio of HDL to LDL elevated.

Examples of lipid-lowering agents include:

- Statins: pravastatin, simvastatin, atorvastatin, rosuvastatin
- Cholesterol absorptions inhibitors: ezetimibe, cholestyramine, colestipol
- Fibrates: Gemfibrozil, fenofibrate

Antihypertensive Medications

Antihypertensive medications are used to treat high blood pressure. Although hypertensive individuals generally do not have symptoms, some people experience headaches, blurred vision, and dizziness. When high blood pressure is left untreated, it can lead to different clinical conditions including coronary artery disease, heart failure, kidney failure, or stroke. There are two values that comprise a blood pressure measure. The top number is the systolic pressure (the pressure on the arterial walls when the heart muscle contracts) and the bottom number is the diastolic pressure (the pressure on the arterial walls when the heart muscle relaxes). Normal, healthy blood pressure in adults should be a systolic reading less than 120 mmHg and a diastolic pressure less than 80 mmHg.

There are three stages of high blood pressure, as outlined below:

- Prehypertension is characterized by systolic pressure between 120-139 mmHg and diastolic pressure between 80-89 mmHg
- Stage 1 hypertension is characterized by systolic pressure between 140-159 mmHg and diastolic pressure between 90-99 mmHg
- Stage 2 hypertension is characterized by systolic pressure of 160 mmHg and higher and diastolic pressure of 100 mmHg and higher

ACE Inhibitors (ACEIs)

"ACE inhibitors," or angiotensin-converting enzyme inhibitors, are used to treat hypertension and cardiovascular diseases. The most common side effect of ACE inhibitors is a chronic dry cough, which, in many cases, is so annoying for a patient that it results in switching the medication to a different class. Other frequent side effects are low blood pressure (hypotension), dizziness, fatigue, headache, and hyperkalemia (increased blood potassium levels).

Examples of some ACE Inhibitors include:

- Ramipril
- Enalapril
- Lisinopril
- Captopril
- Quinapril
- Perindopril

Angiotensin Receptor Blockers (ARBs)

ARBs have similar therapeutic effects as ACE Inhibitors; however, they tend to have better compliance, due to their lower incidence of persistent cough. They block the effect of angiotensin at the receptor site and are widely used for hypertension and cardiovascular disease. The common side effects are hypotension, fatigue, dizziness, headache, and hyperkalemia.

Examples of ARBs include:

- Losartan
- Irbesartan
- Valsartan
- Candesartan
- Telmisartan
- Olmesartan

Calcium Channel Blockers (CCBs)
CCBs work by decreasing calcium entry through calcium channels. By regulating the movement of calcium, contraction of vascular smooth muscle is controlled, which causes blood vessels to dilate. This reduces blood pressure and workload on the heart, so this type of medication is used to treat hypertension and angina and to control heart rate. Common side effects of CCBs include dizziness, flushing of the face, headache, edema (swelling), tachycardia (fast heart rate), bradycardia (slow heart rate), and constipation. In combination with other medications that treat hypertension, calcium channel blocker toxicity is possible. Combinations, like verapamil with beta-blockers, can lead to severe bradycardia.

The following are examples of common calcium channel blockers:

- Amlodipine
- Nifedipine
- Felodipine
- Verapamil
- Diltiazem

Beta Blockers
Beta blockers are an important class of antihypertensive medications and are widely used to treat hypertension and cardiovascular disease. Some of them are also used to treat migraines, agitation, and anxiety. The side effects of beta blockers include hypotension, dizziness, bradycardia, headache, bronchoconstriction (trouble breathing), and fatigue.

Commonly prescribed beta blockers include:

- Atenolol
- Metoprolol
- Propranolol
- Sotalol
- Nadolol
- Carvedilol
- Labetalol

Vasodilators
Vasodilators cause blood vessels to dilate, lowering resistance to flow and reducing the workload on the heart. Vasodilators are used to treat hypertension, angina, and heart failure. The common side effects associated with their use include lightheadedness, dizziness, low blood pressure, flushing, reflex tachycardia, and headache. Vasodilators should not be combined with medications for erectile dysfunction, as this interaction can cause a fatal drop in blood pressure.

Drugs and Drug Therapy

Examples of common vasodilators include:

- Nitroglycerin (available as sublingual tablets, sprays, patches, and extended-release capsules)
- Isosorbide mononitrate
- Isosorbide dinitrate
- Hydralazine
- Minoxidil (limited use)

Alpha-1 Receptor Blockers

Alpha-blockers decrease the norepinephrine-induced vascular contraction, causing relaxation of blood vessels and a resultant reduction in blood pressure. This type of medication is used to treat high blood pressure and benign prostatic hyperplasia (BPH). The common side effects of this class of medications include hypotension, dizziness, headache, tachycardia, weakness, and nausea.

Examples of alpha blockers include:

- Prazosin
- Doxazosin
- Terazosin
- Tamsulosin (primarily used to treat BPH)
- Alfuzosin (primarily used to treat BPH)

Diuretics

Diuretics are used alone and in combination with other medications to treat hypertension. They are often used to eliminate excess body fluid to treat swelling/edema. Diuretics inhibit the absorption of sodium in renal tubules, resulting in increased elimination of salt and water. This action increases urine output, decreases blood volume, and lowers blood pressure. Side effects of diuretics include hypotension, dizziness, hypokalemia, dehydration, hyperglycemia, polyuria (frequent or excessive urination), fatigue, syncope (fainting), and tinnitus (ringing in ears).

Examples of commonly prescribed diuretics include:

- Furosemide
- Bumetanide
- Hydrochlorothiazide
- Spironolactone
- Amiloride
- Triamterene

Medications Acting on the Respiratory System

Antiasthmatics

Antiasthmatics are used to prevent and treat the acute symptoms of asthma, which is a disease characterized by wheezing, cough, chest tightness, and shortness of breath. Acute asthma can be life-threatening and needs to be treated promptly. **Asthma** is caused by inflammation and constriction of the airways, which results in difficulty breathing. Acute asthma may be exacerbated by certain triggering factors including environmental allergens, certain medications (e.g., aspirin), stress or exercise, smoke, and lung infections. It is important to avoid the triggering factors to prevent acute symptoms. The common side effects of antiasthmatics are cough, hoarseness, decreased bone mineral density, growth retardation in children, mouth thrush, agitation, tachycardia, and a transient increase in blood pressure.

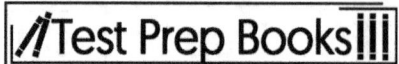

There are two categories to asthma medications that can be used alone or in combination:

- Bronchodilators (dilate the airway to ease breathing)
  - Salbutamol
  - Formoterol (generally used in combination with inhaled corticosteroids)
  - Salmeterol (generally used in combination with inhaled corticosteroids)
- Anti-inflammatory agents
  - Fluticasone (inhaled corticosteroid)
  - Budesonide (inhaled corticosteroid)
  - Beclomethasone (inhaled corticosteroid)
  - Montelukast
  - Zafirlukast

COPD Medications

Chronic Obstructive Pulmonary Disease (**COPD**) is an obstructive airway disease that is characterized by coughing, wheezing, shortness of breath, and sputum production. COPD is a progressive disease that worsens over time. COPD is a combination of two common conditions: chronic bronchitis and emphysema. **Chronic bronchitis** is the inflammation of the smooth lining of bronchial tubes. These tubes are responsible for carrying air to the alveoli, which are the air sacs in the lungs responsible for gaseous exchange between the lungs and blood. **Emphysema** results from alveolar damage, reducing the ability for healthy gas exchange. These two pathologies cause breathing difficulties in patients with COPD. The contributing factors for the development of COPD include smoking, environmental pollutions, and genetic risk factors. The side effects of COPD medications are similar to that of antiasthmatics.

The medications commonly used to treat COPD include the following:

- Bronchodilators (dilate the airway to ease breathing)
  - Salbutamol
  - Formoterol (generally used in combination with inhaled corticosteroids)
  - Salmeterol (generally used in combination with inhaled corticosteroids)
- Anti-inflammatory agents
  - Ipratropium (Atrovent)
  - Tiotropium (Spiriva)
  - Fluticasone
  - Budesonide

Medications Acting on the Digestive System

Gastric acid neutralizers/suppressants either neutralize stomach acid or decrease acid production, and therefore, provide relief of symptoms associated with hyperacidity. They are also used to treat gastroesophageal reflux disease, or GERD. In **GERD**, the lower esophageal sphincter does not close properly, which causes the contents of the stomach to back up into the esophagus. This leads to irritation, which is why the common symptoms of GERD include heartburn, coughing, nausea, difficulty swallowing, and a strained voice. There are many factors that can cause or exacerbate GERD including obesity, pregnancy, eating a large meal, acidic foods, a hiatal hernia, and smoking. Lifestyle modifications such as avoiding trigger foods, losing weight (if obesity is a component), decreasing meal size, and trying not to lie down immediately after eating can reduce symptoms.

The medications used to treat hyperacidity in stomach include the following:

- Antacids (e.g., calcium carbonate)
- Ranitidine

- Famotidine
- Omeprazole
- Esomeprazole
- Lansoprazole
- Rabeprazole
- Pantoprazole

Medications Acting on the Endocrine System

Anti-Diabetic Medications

Anti-diabetic medications are used to treat diabetes, which is a chronic metabolic disease in which the body cannot properly regulate blood sugar levels. This dysregulation is caused by either inadequate or absent insulin production from the pancreas (type 1 diabetes) or inadequate action of insulin in peripheral tissues (insulin resistance in type 2 diabetes). Type 1 diabetes usually occurs in early childhood and is typically treated with insulin injections or medications. Type 2 diabetes generally develops later in adolescence or adulthood and is related to poor diet, lack of physical activity, and obesity. Diabetes often does not to cause daily symptoms, but symptoms do arise when blood sugar is either too high (from inadequate control) or too low (from inappropriate dosing of hypoglycemic (antidiabetic) agents, including insulin). A few of the symptoms of diabetes include increased thirst and hunger, fatigue, blurred vision, a tingling sensation in the feet, and frequent urination.

Examples of some antidiabetic medications include:

- Insulin
- Metformin
- Acarbose
- Gliclazide, glyburide, glimepiride
- Rosiglitazone, pioglitazone
- Sitagliptin, saxagliptin

The most effective way of treating type 2 diabetes is to combine both drug and non-drug therapies. As a part of the treatment, drug therapy can stimulate the pancreas to produce more insulin or help the body better use the insulin produced by the pancreas. As part of the non-drug therapy, counseling is necessary to help patients understand the important diet and lifestyle modifications. Patients with type 2 diabetes should try to decrease their consumption of processed foods, simple carbohydrates and refined sugars, and overall caloric intake, while increasing physical activity. These interventions help to decrease the requirement of antidiabetic medications and prevent long-term diabetes-related complications.

Female Hormones

Hormonal medications are generally used as oral contraceptives to prevent pregnancy. Female hormonal medications are also used to treat premenstrual symptoms (PMS), post-menopausal symptoms, acne, and endometriosis. They are also used as emergency contraceptives to prevent unwanted and accidental pregnancy. **Oral contraceptives** can provide hormones (estrogen and/or progestin), which suppress the egg maturation and ovulation process. Additionally, hormonal contraceptives prevent the endometrium from thickening in preparation to hold the fertilized egg. A mucus barrier is created by progestin, which stops the sperm from migrating to the fallopian tubes and fertilizing the egg. There are many side effects associated with oral contraceptives, including increasing the risk of fatal blood clots, especially in women older than 35 or in women who smoke. More common and less severe side effects include:

- Nausea and stomach upset
- Headache

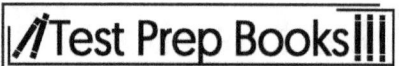

- Weight gain
- Spotting between periods
- Mood changes
- Lighter periods
- Aching or swollen breasts

More serious side effects that need immediate emergency care include:

- Chest pain
- Blurred vision
- Stomach pain
- Severe headaches

Examples of some commercially available brands of contraceptive include:

- Yasmin
- Ortho Tri-Cyclen
- TriNessa
- Sprintec
- Ovcon
- Plan B (emergency contraceptive)

Medications Acting on the Immune System

Antivirals

Antivirals are used to fight viruses in the body, by either stopping replication or blocking the function of a viral protein. They are used to treat HIV, herpes, hepatitis B and C, and influenza, among other viruses. Vaccines are also available to prevent some viral infections. Side effects of antivirals include headache, nausea, blood abnormalities including anemia and neutropenia (low neutrophil count), dizziness, cough, runny or stuff nose, etc.

Some examples of disease-specific antivirals include:

- Acyclovir, valaciclovir (Valtrex): Herpes simplex, herpes zoster, and herpes B
- Ritonavir, indinavir, darunavir: Protease inhibitor for HIV
- Tenofovir (Viread): Hepatitis B and HIV infection
- Interferon: Hepatitis C
- Oseltamivir (Tamiflu): Influenza

Antibiotics

Antibiotics are antimicrobial agents that are used for treatment and prevention of bacterial infections. The mechanism of action of an antibiotic involves either killing bacteria or inhibiting their growth. Antibiotics are not effective against viruses, and therefore, they should not be used to treat viral infections. Antibiotics are often prescribed based on the result of a bacterial culture to ascertain which class of antibiotic(s) the respective strain will respond to. The common side effects of antibiotics include allergies, hypersensitivity reactions or anaphylaxis, stomach upset, diarrhea, candida (fungal) infections, and bacterial resistance (superinfection, in which a strain of bacteria develops resistance to a broad classes of antibiotics).

Commonly prescribed antibiotics include:

- Penicillin V
- Amoxicillin (with or without clavulanic acid)

- Ampicillin
- Cloxacillin
- Cephalexin
- Cefuroxime
- Cefixime
- Tetracycline
- Doxycycline
- Minocycline
- Gentamicin
- Tobramycin
- Ciprofloxacin
- Levofloxacin
- Erythromycin
- Azithromycin
- Clarithromycin
- Clindamycin

Antimetabolites

Antimetabolites are used to treat diseases including severe psoriasis, rheumatoid arthritis, and several types of cancer (breast, lung, lymphoma, and leukemia). The most commonly used medication of this class is methotrexate, which suppresses the growth of abnormal cells and the action of the immune system. Methotrexate is widely used to treat rheumatoid arthritis. This medication is typically prescribed as a once-a-week dose, and it should not be prescribed for daily dosing because overdosing can be lethal. Pharmacists should be alerted to any prescriptions for daily methotrexate, as the doctor must be contacted to confirm and correct the dosing.

The following are the potential side effects of methotrexate:

- Dizziness
- Drowsiness
- Headache
- Swollen gums
- Increased susceptibility to infections
- Hair loss
- Confusion
- Weakness

Steroids

Steroids are used to treat allergies, asthma, rashes, swelling, and inflammation. These medications are available in different forms, such as oral tablets, nasal sprays, eye drops, topical creams and ointments, inhalants, and injections. The common side effects of steroids include insulin resistance and diabetes, osteoporosis, depression, hypertension, edema, glaucoma, etc.

The following are examples of commonly prescribed corticosteroids:

- Prednisone
- Hydrocortisone
- Fluticasone
- Triamcinolone
- Mometasone

- Budesonide
- Fluocinolone
- Betamethasone
- Dexamethasone

Drug Class Abbreviations

Common drug class abbreviations are listed below:

- **ACE Inhibitor**: angiotensin converting enzyme inhibitor
- **ARB**: angiotensin receptor blocker
- **CCB**: calcium channel blocker
- **NDRI**: norepinephrine dopamine reuptake inhibitor
- **NSAID**: non-steroidal anti-inflammatory drug
- **PPI**: proton pump inhibitor
- **SARI**: serotonin agonist and reuptake inhibitor
- **SNRI**: serotonin norepinephrine reuptake inhibitor
- **SSRI**: selective serotonin reuptake inhibitor
- **TCA**: tricyclic antidepressant
- **TeCA**: tetracyclic antidepressant

Dosage Forms

A **pharmaceutical dosage form** is a formulation type in which the active ingredient(s) (with excipients) is manufactured to be administered to patients. There are different types of pharmaceutical dosage forms, some of which are described below.

Tablets

Tablets are the most common oral dosage form. Tablets can be made from firmly condensing powder into the desired shape. Tablets are often coated to mask a bad taste and/or smell of a medication. There are also more complex types of tablets that are designed by using special polymers, which release the medication from the tablet core in a controlled pattern, often in slow-release formulations.

Capsules

Capsules consist of a hard or soft shell with powder or liquid ingredients inside. Most capsules are made from gelatin, a collagen by-product of an animal protein. Other capsule shells contain plant-based polysaccharides such as carrageenan, modified starch, and cellulose.

Liquid Formulations

Liquid formulations are primarily of two categories: elixirs and suspensions. An **elixir** is a clear liquid solution in which active ingredients are mixed in a liquid carrier (or formulation vehicle); shaking is not required to mix the ingredients. In **suspensions**, medication is suspended in a liquid carrier. It is essential to shake suspensions before administration, as some ingredients often collect at the bottom as sediment. Sometimes a suspension is supplied as a dry powder, which needs to be mixed with the appropriate volume of distilled water before being dispensed to the patient.

Suppositories

Suppositories are solid dosage forms that are inserted into body cavities, including the rectum, vagina, and urethra, where they melt and provide local or systemic effects. Due to local administration, suppositories show fewer side

Drugs and Drug Therapy

effects compared to orally-administered medications. Suppositories also provide greater absorption of the medication, as they bypass the first pass metabolism in the liver.

Injectables

An **injectable** is a pharmaceutical dosage form that follows the parenteral route to administer a medication locally or systemically. An injectable is manufactured in an aseptic environment and must be sterile in nature. Examples of some types of injectable routes are intravenous, intradermal, subcutaneous, intramuscular, intraperitoneal, intrathecal, intracardiac, epidural, etc.

Ointments and Creams

Both **ointments** and **creams** are considered semisolid dosage forms along with gels, pastes, and solidified emulsions. Semisolid dosage forms are those that can retain their shape until force is applied to them, at which point they become easily deformed. Of all the semisolid dosage forms, ointments and creams are the most common, but they are used in different situations. For example, creams are best used on dry skin or wet, weeping lesions, whereas ointments are preferred on normal to oily skin types and dry, thick lesions.

The biggest difference between creams and ointments is the amount of oil and water they contain. Creams contain more water, which makes for a smoother application, whereas ointments contain more oil, which causes a greasy look after it has been applied. They can both be used for topical application on various sites including the skin, eyes, nose, rectum, and vagina, and both can produce local and systemic effects. Ointments are composed of an ointment base and the active drug. The four common bases for ointments are oleaginous, absorption, water-removable, and water-soluble. Oleaginous bases are greasy and keep moisture from escaping; petrolatum is a common example. Absorption bases absorb water without major changes in consistency and include hydrophilic petrolatum and lanolin. Water-removable bases are easily washed away with water. They are sometimes also called oil-in-water emulsions and include products like vanishing cream. Water-soluble bases are greaseless, like polyethylene glycol ointments. Ointments are best used when occlusive protection is required or when treating areas with high friction, like the inner thighs. Occlusive protections, or dressings, are used when an airtight and watertight application is needed for a wound to protect it from external pathogens, air, or fluids.

Creams have a spreadable consistency and "creamy" appearance due to their ability to reflect light. Examples include vanishing cream and cold cream. Most patients prefer creams over ointments because they are easier to apply and remove. Both ointments and creams have similar methods of preparation, including incorporation and fusion. These preparations differ in the order of active and inactive ingredients added, but both include two separate portions, lipid and aqueous, that are heated separately and then combined. Depending on their purpose, creams and ointments are packaged in various containers including jars, tubes, syringes, and vaginal or rectal tubes with special applicator tips.

Controlled-Release and Immediate-Release Tablets

Active ingredients in medications are designed to target a specific area of the body, but oral medications must have a method of ensuring the drug reaches the stomach versus the small intestine versus the colon. Since most controlled-release and immediate-release medications are in tablet or capsule form, that will be the dosage method discussed here.

Controlled-Release Tablets

Controlled-release tablets, also known as extended-release or delayed-release, are designed to release the active ingredient either over an extended period or when the tablet comes in contact with a specific type of fluid. One way to ensure specific timing is through the outer coating on the tablet. Enteric-coated tablets are compressed with a polymer that prevents it from dissolving in acidic conditions, like in the stomach. Instead, the outer coating dissolves in a more basic environment, like in the small intestine.

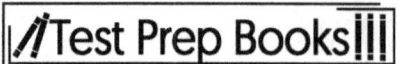

Another way to ensure slow release of a medication is its placement in the body. For example, buccal tablets are designed to be placed between the cheek and gingiva and dissolve slowly so that the drug can be slowly absorbed through the oral mucosa and into the blood. These tablets are not meant to be chewed or swallowed because their purpose is to bypass first-pass metabolism (avoid stomach absorption). Another example is vaginal tablets used as an antibacterial, antifungal, or steroid medication. Once inserted, they dissolve very slowly. Disintegrating agents, commonly used in immediate-release dosage forms, are avoided to keep this type of tablet intact and prevent it from being dissolved too soon. Medicated lozenges are another method to ensure controlled, slow delivery of a medication as they are intended to dissolve slowly in the mouth to exert a local effect, like treating pain caused by a sore throat.

Most injectable medications are immediate release, but many intramuscular or subcutaneous injections may have a controlled-release formulation, like insulin. Insulin is divided into rapid-acting, regular-acting, intermediate-acting, and long-acting forms. The variation is caused by changes in the amino acid sequences that do or do not allow for the formation of insulin hexamers. Insulin is active when in the monomeric or dimeric form, but in the hexamer form, the insulin must be broken down into monomeric or dimeric forms to be active. Long-acting insulin, when injected, readily forms hexamers; over the course of fifteen to thirty hours, the hexamer is slowly dissolved into the active ingredient, ensuring constant insulin action.

Immediate-Release Tablets

Most medications are formulated as **immediate release** and are intended to begin releasing the drug as soon as they come in contact with a disintegrating fluid. Most immediate-release tablets contain many excipients (inactive ingredients), like disintegrating agents that aid in the breakup of the tablet and allow for the rapid release of the active ingredients. There are three mechanisms for disintegrating agents. The swelling mechanism occurs when the disintegrating agents come in contact with an aqueous fluid and expand to the point where the tablet falls apart. These agents include sodium starch glycolate, pregelatinized starch, and croscarmellose. The wicking mechanism occurs when disintegrating agents create pores in the tablet that draw liquid through and rupture the inter-particulate bonds inside, causing the tablet to fall apart. The last mechanism is deformation and occurs when starch grains are compressed into the tablet and expel energy once in contact with water. Immediate-release tablets are produced in a variety of ways including being compressed, molded, freeze-dried, and 3D printed. The molded method includes hypodermic tablets and injections, which are made from water-soluble ingredients and are only used for medications that require rapid drug availability.

Freeze-dried or lyophilized tablets are a form of orally dissolving tablet (ODT) that rapidly disperse when placed in the mouth (not swallowed) and do not require water. Another delivery method for immediate-release tablets includes placing the medication beneath the tongue. These are known as sublingual tablets, which are designed to dissolve rapidly and avoid first-pass metabolism. The sublingual epithelium is much thinner than other areas in the mouth, like the cheek. Sublingual administration has a shorter absorption period than buccal administration. All intravenous injections are immediate release, as they are injected directly into the bloodstream.

Dosage Abbreviations

The list below shows the different dosage abbreviations and their meanings:

- **cap** = capsule
- **tab** = tablet
- **gtt** = drop
- **i, ii, iii, iv** = 1, 2, 3, 4 (quantities are often identified with roman numerals on prescriptions)
- **mg** = milligrams
- **mL** = milliliter
- **tbsp** = tablespoon (15 mL)

Drugs and Drug Therapy

- **tsp** = teaspoon (5 mL)
- **ss** = one-half
- **mcg** or **ug** = microgram

Note that *ug* is not being used as much anymore, as it is confused with *mg*. If unsure, pharmacy technicians should check with the prescriber.

Routes of Administration

There are different routes of administration for medications including the following:

- **Oral**: by mouth in the form of oral tablets, capsules, liquid preparations (elixirs and suspensions)
- **Nasal**: sprays or drips into the nose
- **Intravenous (IV)**: goes through the veins and must be liquid
- **Intramuscular (IM)**: goes into the muscle and must be liquid
- **Subcutaneous**: usually an injection under the skin
- **Epidural**: may be infused into epidural space in the spinal cord
- **Transdermal route**: medication is absorbed through the skin via patches and creams
- **Rectal**: these usually are suppositories and some cream medications administered at the rectum
- **Sublingual**: medications are held under the tongue
- **Inhalation route**: many sprays and nebulizer solutions are inhaled into the lungs
- **Ocular route**: into the eye, usually in the form of solutions and suspensions
- **Aural**: into the ear, usually in the form of solutions and suspensions

Total parenteral nutrition is used in situations where a patient cannot orally ingest food or digest food through the stomach and intestines. In such cases, total parental nutrition is essential to maintain patient nourishment and to prevent wasting or malnutrition.

The clinical conditions requiring total parenteral nutrition include the following:

- Any cause of malnourishment
- Failure of liver or kidneys
- Short bowel syndrome
- Severe burns
- Enterocutaneous fistulas
- Sepsis
- Chemotherapy and radiation
- Neonates
- Conditions requiring full bowel rest, such as pancreatitis, ulcerative colitis, or Crohn's disease

Common abbreviations for administration of medications include:

- **au** = both ears
- **as** = left ear
- **ad** = right ear
- **ou** = both eyes
- **od** = right eye
- **os** = left eye
- **po** = by mouth
- **c** = with

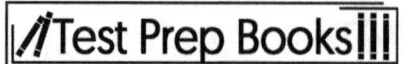

- **sl** = sublingual (under tongue)
- **top** = topically (apply to skin)

Common Prescription/Legend Medications and Their Indications

Indications for Frequently Prescribed Medications

An indication is a disease state that a drug is approved to treat or prevent. Common indications and brief descriptions of each are listed below:

- Asthma: The narrowing of the airways.

- Aortic disease: A heart valve disease that causes problems keeping blood flowing from the heart to the rest of the body.

- Benign prostatic hyperplasia: Prostate gland enlargement most often found in men.

- Chronic kidney disease: Gradual destruction of kidney function.

- Coronary heart disease: Conditions affecting the arteries that directly supply the heart with blood, oxygen, and nutrients.

- Depression: A mood disorder that causes consistent feelings of anguish, sadness, and negativity. It is often caused by environmental factors but may also occur due to a depletion of serotonin, norepinephrine, and/or dopamine.

- Diabetes: Type 1 is an autoimmune disease that causes destruction of beta cells in the pancreas that results in a complete deficiency of insulin. Type 2 is a genetic and environmental disease that causes insulin resistance. Both types result in an increase in blood glucose levels that can be an implication for many other disease states.

- Hypertension: High blood pressure.

- Infections: Can be bacterial, fungal, or viral.

- Insomnia: An inability to fall asleep.

- Muscle spasms: Involuntary contractions and tightening of muscles, the cause of which is unknown but may be related to lack of blood supply to a certain area.

- Peripheral artery disease: Narrowing of the blood vessels in the lower extremities that cause a decreased supply of blood in that area.

- Seizures: An uncontrollable electrical disturbance in various areas of the brain that can cause abnormal activity such as jerking, shaking, or stiffening of the body.

- Stroke: Lack of blood flow to the brain caused by trauma, infection, or clots.

- Tachycardia: Fast heart rate.

Basic Body Systems and Disease States

Cardiovascular

A variety of conditions can cause disease or damage to the heart or blood vessels, including the following:

- Coronary heart disease: The wall of the heart is lined with arteries that supply the heart with blood and oxygen. These are known as coronary arteries. When the coronary arteries are blocked by plaque or foreign substances or become damaged, they are unable to give the heart enough blood and oxygen to pump efficiently.

- Stroke: Strokes are caused by a lack of blood and oxygen to the brain. If this loss of blood and oxygen persists for too long, brain damage is the result.

- Peripheral arterial disease (PAD): The term peripheral refers to areas that are away from the center of the body, like legs, feet, or arms. In PAD, the peripheral arteries, usually those in the legs, are blocked or damaged and prevent adequate blood flow to those peripheral areas, thus causing pain.

- Aortic disease: The aorta is the biggest vessel in the body and is responsible for transporting oxygenated blood from the heart to the rest of the body. If the aortic wall becomes damaged, there can be consequences to the whole body due to the lack of blood and oxygen supply.

Endocrine

The endocrine system includes a variety of organs (e.g., pancreas, ovaries) and glands (e.g., thyroid, pituitary, adrenal) that play a role in hormonal regulation, sleep, mood, metabolism, and more. Different endocrine diseases result in different bodily consequences depending on the location of the disease. For example, adrenal insufficiency, called Addison's disease, occurs when the body does not make enough cortisol and aldosterone, resulting in muscle weakness, low mood, and weight loss due to a loss of appetite.

Digestive

The digestive system begins in the mouth and travels down to the anus. A variety of diseases can affect this system, including diseases of the mouth like cavities, thrush, and canker sores; diseases of the stomach like heart burn and irritable bowel syndrome; diseases of the intestines like Crohn's disease or ulcerative colitis; and diseases of the anus like hemorrhoids and anal fistulas.

Respiratory

The lungs regulate the intake of oxygen and exhalation of carbon dioxide. Diseases that affect the respiratory system include asthma, chronic pulmonary obstructive disorder (COPD), and bronchiolitis.

Excretory

This system is composed of the kidney, ureters, and urinary bladder and is responsible for elimination of unnecessary biological components like body fluids, microorganisms, and cellular waste products. Disease states that affect this system include chronic kidney disease, urinary tract infections, and glomerulonephritis.

Lymphatic

The lymphatic system is a system of tubules that span the entire body to aid the immune system in fighting infections. Diseases within the lymphatic system are rarer than in other body systems but can include conditions like Gorham's disease, lymphedema, and filariasis.

Nervous

The nervous system comprises two parts: the central nervous system, which includes the brain and spinal cord, and the peripheral nervous system, or the nerves that extend from the spinal cord throughout the body. Conditions affecting these systems include Alzheimer's disease, cerebral palsy, epilepsy, and Parkinson's disease.

Skeletal

This system includes the bones, joints, and cartilage that make up the backbone of the body. Diseases of the skeletal system include osteoporosis, scoliosis, rheumatoid arthritis, and gout.

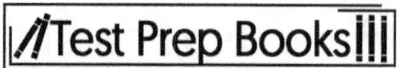

Drugs and Drug Therapy

Prescription/Legend Medications and Their Indications

Various classes of drugs are listed below along with their indications and examples of the specific medications used for treatment:

- Alpha blockers or alpha antagonists: Medications like doxazosin and prazosin inhibit alpha receptor stimulation to treat a variety of conditions including benign prostatic hyperplasia, hypertension, and migraines.

- Antiarrhythmics: These medications help control heartbeat irregularities by slowing the heart rate. Some of these medications can be classified as follows:
    - Class I: Flecainide and propafenone are sodium channel blockers used to slow electrical impulses.
    - Class II: Metoprolol and propranolol are beta blockers that slow down the heart rate and are used for conditions that cause fast heart beats or tachycardia.
    - Class III: Amiodarone and sotalol are potassium channel blockers that help slow electrical impulses.
    - Class IV: Diltiazem and verapamil are non-dihydropyridine calcium channel blockers that are used to slow the heart rate and contractility.

- Antibiotics: These can help prevent or treat bacterial, fungal, or parasitic infections. Some medications can treat a wide variety of pathogenic organisms, whereas others are only able to treat a few specific pathogens. Amoxicillin, cephalexin, ciprofloxacin, and doxycycline are all common antibiotics.

- Anticoagulants: These drugs prevent blood from clotting. Rivaroxaban, dabigatran, and apixaban are common anticoagulants used in various conditions including atrial fibrillation, coronary artery disease, and venous thromboembolism.

- Anticonvulsants: Medications like carbamazepine and lamotrigine prevent epileptic seizures.

- Antidepressants: These are medications that help improve mood. There are two common categories.
    - Tricyclics: Amitriptyline and doxepin are common drugs in this category.
    - Serotonin selective reuptake inhibitors (SSRIs): Examples include citalopram and escitalopram.

- Beta blockers: These medications treat fast heart rate abnormalities. Most beta blocker medication names end in the suffix "-lol," like metoprolol or bisoprolol.

- Bronchodilators: This type of medication dilates the bronchial tubes in the lungs to treat narrowing caused by muscle spasms. Drugs like salmeterol, vilanterol, and tiotropium are bronchodilators.

- Central nervous system (CNS) depressants: These medications target the central nervous system to reduce stimulation and include drugs like diazepam, clonazepam, and alprazolam.

- Diuretics: This type of medication increases the production of urine by the renal system to eliminate excessive fluid from the body that can be caused by various conditions like hypernatremia (increased sodium concentration) or peripheral edema. They can help decrease fluid accumulation in the tissues caused by retention issues involving the heart, kidneys, and liver. Diuretic medications include furosemide, torsemide, and bumetanide.

- Muscle relaxants: This class of medication decreases disorders that cause muscle spasm, such as backaches. The most common are carisoprodol, cyclobenzaprine, and methocarbamol.

- Sleeping medications: The two main classes of sleep-inducing medications include benzodiazepines and barbiturates. In low doses, both classes have a sedative effect and help make patients sleepy or calm them down. In higher doses, they are effective at inducing complete sleep. Benzodiazepines are used more widely than barbiturates because they are safer with fewer side effects, but most importantly, they have a lower incidence of causing addiction and physical dependance.
- Thrombolytics: These medications help break down active blood clots. Alteplase, reteplase, and tenecteplase are common thrombolytics used in conditions such as acute ischemic stroke, pulmonary embolism, and ST-elevation myocardial infarction.

OTC Products and Their Indications

Basic Body Systems and Disease States

Cardiovascular
A variety of conditions that cause disease or damage to the heart or blood vessels have symptoms that can be relieved with over-the-counter medications. When arteries in the heart or other areas have large clots that block blood and oxygen flow, blood-thinning medications can be taken to prevent rupturing of those clots. Rupturing can damage blood vessel walls but can also cause parts of the clot in peripheral areas to travel to the heart or brain and impair oxygen supply.

Endocrine
The endocrine system is made up of a variety of organs and glands that aid in hormonal regulation, sleep, mood, metabolism, and more. Sleep disturbances and fever are common disease states treated with over-the-counter medications.

Digestive
The digestive system includes many diseases of the stomach like heartburn, which is caused by an increase of stomach acid that travels through the esophagus, resulting in a burning sensation in the chest. The main over-the-counter treatment for heartburn neutralizes stomach acid and can be used for rapid relief or long-term prevention. Hemorrhoids are a common self-treatable condition of the digestive system that uses corticosteroid-based wipes, creams, or ointments to minimize inflammation and pain in the rectal area.

Respiratory
The lungs are responsible for oxygen and carbon dioxide regulation, which are altered in various respiratory disease states including asthma, allergies, nasal congestion, and cough. In asthma, wheezing and chest tightness are caused by the narrowing of airway vessels. Allergies can be triggered by various environmental conditions. Nasal congestion, also known as a stuffy nose, is caused by increased fluids in the nasal tissues that cause them to become swollen and plugged. Coughing is the body's attempt to get rid of an irritating factor in the airways due to a foreign object, mucus, or other irritants.

Excretory
The elimination of unnecessary biological components is important for our body to maintain homeostasis, and conditions that affect the body's ability to regulate this function can result in various symptoms. For example, vaginal yeast infections and lower urinary tract infections alter vaginal pH and are considered common conditions that require over-the-counter medications for symptom relief. Vaginal infections are a type of fungal infection that causes itching and discharge. Although these infections can go away on their own, over-the-counter treatments such as creams, ointments, or vaginal suppositories can help treat the symptoms. Lower urinary tract infections require antibiotics to treat, but over-the-counter medications can provide relief for common symptoms like burning when urinating.

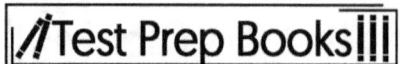

Lymphatic
Most diseases within the lymphatic system are rare, and most diagnoses require prescriptions. However, swollen lymph nodes, which are a part of the lymphatic system, are a common side effect of an infection that can be treated with over-the-counter drugs to relieve pain and swelling.

Skeletal
This system includes the bones, joints, and cartilage that provide structure to the body. Issues with this system are responsible for a large amount of over-the-counter medication purchases. Self-treatable disease states that affect the skeletal system include pain in various parts of the body like the back, head, joints, and feet.

OTC Medications and Their Indications
Categories of OTC (over-the-counter) medications are listed below along with their indications and examples of specific medications used for treatment:

- Antacids: Medications like aluminum hydroxide, magnesium carbonate, and sodium bicarbonate prevent or slow down heartburn. They are basic (pH) medications that help counteract the buildup of stomach acid.

- Antiemetics: Medications like bismuth subsalicylate and Dramamine® can prevent or treat nausea and vomiting.

- Antifungals: Medications like miconazole and clotrimazole are used to treat fungal infections that can occur in the hair, skin, nails, or mucous membranes.

- Antihistamines: Medications like loratadine, cetirizine, and diphenhydramine are used to prevent production or binding of histamine. There are two major types: drowsy and non-drowsy.

- Anti-inflammatories: These medications decrease inflammation symptoms including redness, heat, swelling, and increased blood flow. These are among the top-sold over-the-counter medications and include ibuprofen, naproxen, diclofenac, and aspirin.

- Antipyretics: These medications reduce fever and include acetaminophen, ibuprofen, and naproxen.

- Expectorants: These medications are intended to increase the flow of saliva and promote the cough reflex to eliminate bacteria-filled phlegm from the lower respiratory tract. The only over-the-counter medication in this category is guaifenesin.

- Laxatives: Medications of this type stimulate bowel movements to increase frequency or to make stool easier to pass. There are several categories of laxatives:
    - Bulk laxatives: Medications like Metamucil and Benefiber increase the bulk of bowel contents.
    - Stimulant laxatives: Medications like bisacodyl and senna increase movement in the gut.
    - Stool-softeners: Medications like docusate sodium or docusate calcium lubricate the fecal matter to help facilitate elimination.

- Vitamins: Vitamins are essential for various enzymatic reactions in our body. Some vitamins, like D and K, can be made in the body. However, some vitamins that are not made in the body are nonetheless necessary for survival. An adequate diet with fruits, vegetables, and protein can provide sufficient levels of the vitamins that humans don't make, but these vitamins can also be obtained in pill form for those whose diets are insufficient or who have digestive tract or liver disorders. These vitamins include the following:
    - Vitamin A for eye health

- - - Vitamin C for boosting immunity
    - Vitamin D for bone health
    - Vitamin E is an important antioxidant
    - Vitamin K for blood clot formation

- Cough suppressants: Medications that treat cough include two main types: those that change the consistency or production of phlegm like mucolytics and expectorants, and those that suppress the coughing reflex, such as codeine, antihistamines, and dextromethorphan.

- Decongestants: These medications decrease the swelling of the mucosal membranes that line the nose. The main mechanism of relieving stuffiness in the nasal cavity is through the constriction of blood vessels. In the nasal cavity, alpha receptors line the vascular smooth muscle wall. When stimulated, they activate various biological pathways that increase calcium influx, causing constriction. Decongestants act to stimulate the alpha receptors in the nasal cavity to cause constriction. For example, phenylephrine, oxymetazoline, and pseudoephedrine are alpha-receptor activators.

BTC Products and Their Indications

Basic Body Systems and Disease States
Cardiovascular
A variety of conditions can cause disease or damage to the heart or blood vessels. Diabetes is the most common disease state that offers BTC (behind-the-counter) medication therapy. Diabetic patients experience an increased blood sugar content that, over time, can damage the vessels and nerves that control the heart. Most commonly, the high blood sugar increases blood pressure and causes the heart to work harder than normal. In chronic conditions that cause the heart to work very hard, the muscle surrounding the heart will become thicker and stiffer. Common symptoms include shortness of breath, chest pain, and problems with controlling heart rhythm.

Endocrine
In diabetes, the pancreatic beta cells are affected. This causes a decrease in insulin production or response, which increases blood sugar levels.

Digestive
The most common disease that affects this body system and can be treated with BTC medications is diabetes. Many oral medications must first be metabolized in the liver or intestine, which causes a decrease in the amount of active drug available. Once a medication has traveled through the hepatic portal vein to the liver, it can reach the body's systemic circulation where it can perform its effect. Insulin, on the other hand, is injected intramuscularly or into subcutaneous tissue and can skip first-pass metabolism.

Respiratory
Disease states that affect the upper respiratory system include sinus congestion, sinus pressure, and allergies. Inhaled medications include nasal and pulmonary drug delivery that can provide a rapid onset of action, a pain-free method of administration, and a reduction in systemic side effects. Depending on the severity of the pulmonary disease state, the penetration, deposition, and absorption of drugs into the lungs can be affected. For example, narrowing in the airways caused by inflammation, excess mucus, or bronchial constriction will produce increased central airway deposition.

Excretory
One of the disease states that affects this system is diabetes. The high blood sugar content must be excreted through the urinary bladder, which causes high glucose levels in the kidney and urine and can create more problems in other organs of the excretory system.

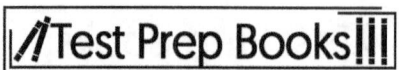

BTC Medications and Their Indications

BTC (behind-the-counter) medications are available for purchase without a prescription but require intervention from either a pharmacist or regulatory agency. Medications in this category are considered dangerous without proper intervention and are in this group to prevent abuse or unintentional misuse. In the United States, there are currently only two behind-the-counter medications available, specific insulins and pseudoephedrine.

Novolin N and Humulin R are both available for BTC purchase for the purpose of lowering blood glucose levels in patients with diabetes. Novolin N, also known as Humulin N, and Humulin R, also known as Novolin R, are both indicated for glycemic control for patients with type 1 or type 2 diabetes. Novolin N is also known as neutral protamine Hagedorn (NPH) and is an intermediate- to long-acting medication. Once injected, the protamine is gradually degraded and the active insulin is released and can act on its target cells. It can last up to sixteen hours. Humulin R is also known as regular insulin, as it is typically injected thirty to forty-five minutes prior to a meal. Once inside, the hexamer will begin to dissolve and will show effects after thirty minutes. The major side effects of all insulins include hypoglycemia, weight gain, and lipodystrophy. Hypoglycemia includes symptoms such as confusion, tachycardia (fast heart rate), and sweating. Most of the weight gain will be seen in stomach fat. Lipodystrophy is caused when insulin is injected into the same area repeatedly and causes more fat to present, ultimately leading to the destruction of fat at that site.

Pseudoephedrine is an adrenergic agonist with a variety of mechanisms that work to increase the body's natural norepinephrine levels. This in turn leads to mucosal edema, reduction of sinus vessel engorgement, and the narrowing of vessels that line the nasal airways. Pseudoephedrine is indicated for temporary relief of nasal congestion in patients who are over four years old. Pseudoephedrine has a variety of side effects including elevated blood pressure, arrythmias, insomnia, tremors, and anxiety. This medication should be used with caution by patients with hypertension, coronary heart disease, diabetes, and ischemic heart disease. Overdose can cause central nervous system depression, collapse, and coma. Purchase of this medication is limited by the local, state, and federal government through the Combat Methamphetamine Epidemic Act of 2005, which limits each person with an active driver's license to 3.6 grams per day and 9 grams per month. This is due to illegal production of methamphetamine using products containing pseudoephedrine.

Frequently Prescribed Medications

One of the most crucial abilities for any person working in pharmacy is the quick recognition and comprehension of the brands of each generic being discussed, for ease of identifying their classes and indications. This is so that when talking to a patient, side effects can be distinguished from adverse reactions requiring greater care; contraindications can be identified before the prescription is intaken, filled, or dispensed; and potential interactions between the drug and other drugs, food, and OTC medications can be addressed and counseled on. Additionally, this helps to ensure that parenteral and compounded medications can be mixed, handled, stored, and administered safely and that common prophylactic and preventive measures against infectious disease, such as vaccines and immunizations, can be taken to ensure the best health outcomes for the patient.

Brand and Generic Names of Commonly Used Prescription Medications

Each medication, upon submission for patent and drug use, will be given a generic, common-use name. This is to distinguish the medication from the brand it is sold under. For example, Bayer and Tylenol are brands most associated with aspirin and acetaminophen (APAP), but similar products are also sold, which may risk confusion with the intended medication, such as different strengths or formulations of aspirin or Tylenol PM, which includes diphenhydramine as well as APAP. Referring to generic medications is ideal to reduce confusion and lower the possibility of medication errors.

Drugs and Drug Therapy

Generic drugs are subjected to a similar review process as brand-name drugs to ensure safety, efficacy, and quality. Generally, **generic drugs** are copies of the brand-name drug and allow more affordable access to treatment and care. Pharmacy technicians should be familiar with the major therapeutic classifications of medications and should be able to match brand names of medications with the corresponding generic names.

Drug Topics Top 200 Medications

Several versions of a top 200 commonly prescribed medications list have been compiled and are updated as new medications are released. Some of those medications are found OTC, including non-steroidal anti-inflammatory drugs (NSAIDs) such as ibuprofen (Advil) and naproxen (Aleve), antihistamines such as cetirizine (Zyrtec) and fexofenadine (Allegra), proton pump inhibitors (PPIs) such as omeprazole (Prilosec) and pantoprazole (Protonix), and laxatives such as polyethylene glycol (PEG) (Miralax®) and bisacodyl (Dulcolax®). The prescription medications contain the same drug as those found OTC but require a prescription to be billed to insurance. In addition, they may be sold at a higher strength with a prescription (OTC ibuprofen's strength is 200 mg, whereas prescription strengths may range up to 800 mg) or in delayed-release formulations, such as pantoprazole and omeprazole.

The following table lists many generic medications and their common brands, including some that are part of the Drug Topics Top 200 Medications list. Although some questions on the test may directly ask to identify a drug's brand, generic, or class from a list of answers, many questions will require the test-taker to use this ability in tandem with other skills from the exam outline, so familiarity with these drugs is key.

Brand Name	Generic Name	Class of Medication (Treatment of)
Medications Acting on the Nervous System		
Desyrel®	Trazodone	SARI (depression)
Celexa®	Citalopram	SSRI (anxiety and depression)
Lexapro®	Escitalopram	SSRI (anxiety and depression)
Prozac®	Fluoxetine	SSRI (anxiety and depression)
Paxil®	Paroxetine	SSRI (anxiety and depression)
Zoloft®	Sertraline	SSRI (anxiety and depression)
Effexor®	Venlafaxine	SNRI (anxiety and depression)
Cymbalta®	Duloxetine	SNRI (anxiety and depression)
Wellbutrin®	Bupropion	NDRI (anxiety and depression)
Elavil®	Amitriptyline	TCA (anxiety and depression)
Remeron	Mirtazapine	TeCA (anxiety and depression)
Buspar®	Buspirone	Anxiolytic (anxiety)
Atarax®	Hydroxyzine	Antihistamine (anxiety)
Seroquel®	Quetiapine	Anti-psychotic (schizophrenia, bipolar disorder)
Risperdal®	Risperidone	Anti-psychotic (schizophrenia, bipolar disorder)
Zyprexa®	Olanzapine	Anti-psychotic (schizophrenia, bipolar disorder)
Abilify®	Aripiprazole	Anti-psychotic (schizophrenia, bipolar disorder)
Geodon®	Ziprasidone	Anti-psychotic (schizophrenia, bipolar disorder)
Topamax®	Topiramate	Anticonvulsant (seizure, migraine)
Dilantin®	Phenytoin	Anticonvulsant (seizure)
Keppra®	Levetiracetam	Anticonvulsant (seizure)
Depakote®	Divalproex, valproic acid	Anticonvulsant (seizure)
Tegretol®	Carbamazepine	Anticonvulsant (seizure)

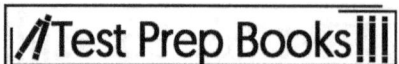

Drugs and Drug Therapy

Brand Name	Generic Name	Class of Medication (Treatment of)
Trileptal®	Oxcarbazepine	Anticonvulsant (seizure)
Lamictal®	Lamotrigine	Anticonvulsant (seizure)
Neurontin®	Gabapentin	Anticonvulsant (seizure, neuropathic pain)
Lyrica®	Pregabalin	Anticonvulsant (seizure, neuropathic pain)
Aricept®	Donepezil	Cognition enhancer (Alzheimer disease)
Namenda®	Memantine	Cognition enhancer (Alzheimer disease)
Requip®	Ropinirole	Dopamine agonist (Parkinson's disease)
Mirapex®	Pramipexole	Dopamine agonist (Parkinson's disease)
Sinemet®	Levodopa/carbidopa	Dopamine agonist (Parkinson's disease)
Ambien®	Zolpidem	Sedative (insomnia)
Lunesta®	Eszopiclone	Sedative (insomnia)
Restoril®	Temazepam	Sedative (insomnia)
Ativan®	Lorazepam	Sedative (anxiety, seizure)
Xanax®	Alprazolam	Sedative (anxiety)
Klonopin®	Clonazepam	Sedative (anxiety)
Valium®	Diazepam	Sedative (anxiety)
Catapres®	Clonidine	Sedative (hypertension)
Strattera®	Atomoxetine	SNRI (ADHD)
Ritalin®	Methylphenidate	Stimulant (ADHD)
Concerta®	Methylphenidate	Stimulant (ADHD)
Dexedrine®	Dextroamphetamine	Stimulant (ADHD)
Adderall®	Mixed salt of amphetamine	Stimulant (ADHD)
Vyvanse®	Lisdexamfetamine	Stimulant (ADHD)
Intuniv®	Guanfacine	Stimulant (ADHD)
Tenex®	Guanfacine	Stimulant (ADHD)
Provigil®	Modafinil	Stimulant (sleep disorder)
Maxalt®	Rizatriptan	Triptan (migraine)
Imitrex®	Sumatriptan	Triptan (migraine)
Medications Acting on the Cardiovascular System		
Zestril®	Lisinopril	ACE inhibitor (hypertension)
Zestoretic®	Lisinopril/HCTZ	ACE inhibitor & diuretic (hypertension)
Altace®	Ramipril	ACE inhibitor (hypertension)
Altace® HCT	Ramipril/HCTZ	ACE inhibitor & diuretic (hypertension)
Vasotec®	Enalapril	ACE inhibitor (hypertension)
Diovan®	Valsartan	ARB (hypertension)
Diovan® HCT	Valsartan/HCTZ	ARB & diuretic (hypertension)
Cozaar®	Losartan	ARB (hypertension)
Hyzaar®	Losartan/HCTZ	ARB & diuretic (hypertension)
Avapro®	Irbesartan	ARB (hypertension)
Avalide®	Irbesartan/HCTZ	ARB & diuretic (hypertension)
Atacand®	Candesartan	ARB (hypertension)
Atacand® Plus	Candesartan/HCTZ	ARB & diuretic (hypertension)
Micardis®	Telmisartan	ARB (hypertension)

Drugs and Drug Therapy

Brand Name	Generic Name	Class of Medication (Treatment of)
Micardis® Plus	Telmisartan/HCTZ	ARB & diuretic (hypertension)
Benicar®	Olmesartan	ARB (hypertension)
Benicar® HCT	Olmesartan/HCTZ	ARB & diuretic (hypertension)
Tenormin®	Atenolol	Beta-blocker (hypertension)
Inderal®	Propranolol	Beta-blocker (hypertension)
Toprol®	Metoprolol	Beta-blocker (hypertension)
Coreg®	Carvedilol	Beta-blocker (hypertension)
Bystolic®	Nebivolol	Beta-blocker (hypertension)
Norvasc®	Amlodipine	CCB (hypertension)
Lotrel®	Amlodipine/benazepril	CCB & ACEI (hypertension)
Cardizem®	Diltiazem	CCB (hypertension)
Adalat®	Nifedipine	CCB (hypertension)
Verelan®	Verapamil	CCB (hypertension)
Lasix®	Furosemide	Diuretic (CHF)
Microzide®	HCTZ	Diuretic (hypertension, CHF)
Aldactone	Spironolactone	Diuretic (CHF)
Zocor®	Simvastatin	Statin (hyperlipidemia)
Lipitor®	Atorvastatin	Statin (hyperlipidemia)
Crestor®	Rosuvastatin	Statin (hyperlipidemia)
Pravachol®	Pravastatin	Statin (hyperlipidemia)
Altoprev®	Lovastatin	Statin (hyperlipidemia)
Zetia®	Ezetimibe	Absorption inhibitor (hyperlipidemia)
Vytorin®	Ezetimibe/simvastatin	Absorption inhibitor & statin (hyperlipidemia)
Tricor®	Fenofibrate	Fibrate (hyperlipidemia)
Lopid®	Gemfibrozil	Fibrate (hyperlipidemia)
Nitrostat	Nitroglycerin	Nitrate (coronary artery disease)
Plavix®	Clopidogrel	Blood thinner (blood clot)
Coumadin®	Warfarin	Blood thinner (blood clot)
Xarelto®	Rivaroxaban	Blood thinner (blood clot)
Eliquis®	Apixaban	Blood thinner (blood clot)
Lanoxin®	Digoxin	Glycoside (heart failure)
Digitek®	Digoxin	Glycoside (heart failure)
Klor-Con®	Potassium	Potassium supplement (hypokalemia)
Medications Acting on the Respiratory System		
Singulair®	Montelukast	Anti-inflammatory (asthma)
Nasonex®	Mometasone	Steroid (asthma, allergy)
Flovent®	Fluticasone	Steroid (asthma, COPD, allergy)
Qvar®	Beclometasone	Steroid (asthma)
Deltasone®	Prednisone	Steroid (asthma, autoimmune disorders)
Medrol®	Methylprednisolone	Steroid (asthma, allergy, inflammation)
Cortef®	Hydrocortisone	Steroid (asthma, COPD)
Ventolin®	Albuterol	Bronchodilator (asthma)
Combivent®	Albuterol/ipratropium	Bronchodilator (asthma, COPD)

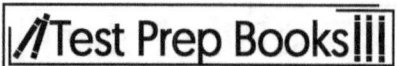

Brand Name	Generic Name	Class of Medication (Treatment of)
Spiriva®	Tiotropium	Bronchodilator (COPD)
Rhinocort®	Budesonide	Steroid (nasal allergy)
Pulmicort®	Budesonide	Steroid (asthma, COPD)
Advair®	Fluticasone/salmeterol	Steroid & bronchodilator (asthma, COPD)
Symbicort®	Budesonide/formoterol	Steroid & bronchodilator (asthma, COPD)
Zonatuss®	Benzonatate	Local anesthetic (cough)
Medications Acting on the Digestive System		
Prilosec®	Omeprazole	PPI (GERD)
Nexium®	Esomeprazole	PPI (GERD)
Prevacid®	Lansoprazole	PPI (GERD)
Protonix®	Pantoprazole	PPI (GERD)
AcipHex®	Rabeprazole	PPI (GERD)
Pepcid®	Famotidine	PPI (GERD)
Zofran®	Ondansetron	Antiemetic (nausea and vomiting)
Anzemet®	Dolasetron	Antiemetic (nausea and vomiting)
Aloxi®	Palonosetron	Antiemetic (nausea and vomiting)
Motilium®	Domperidone	Antiemetic (nausea and vomiting)
Compro®	Prochlorperazine	Antiemetic (nausea and vomiting, migraine)
Bonine®	Meclizine	Antiemetic (nausea and vomiting, vertigo)
Colace®	Docusate	Stool softener (constipation)
Medications Acting on the Urinary System		
Flomax®	Tamsulosin	Urinary retainer (BPH)
Propecia®	Finasteride	Urinary retainer (BPH)
Cardura®	Doxazosin	Urinary retainer (BPH)
Detrol®	Tolterodine	Bladder relaxant (urinary incontinence)
Viagra®	Sildenafil	Vasodilator (erectile dysfunction)
Cialis®	Tadalafil	Vasodilator (erectile dysfunction)
Levitra®	Vardenafil	Vasodilator (erectile dysfunction)
Medications Acting on the Endocrine System		
Glucophage®	Metformin	Anti-diabetic (type 2 diabetes)
Glucotrol®	Glipizide	Anti-diabetic (type 2 diabetes)
Actos®	Pioglitazone	Anti-diabetic (type 2 diabetes)
Januvia®	Sitagliptin	Anti-diabetic (type 2 diabetes)
Janumet®	Sitagliptin/metformin	Anti-diabetic (type 2 diabetes)
Amaryl®	Glimepiride	Anti-diabetic (type 2 diabetes)
Lantus®	Insulin glargine	Anti-diabetic (type 1 and type 2 diabetes)
Humalog®	Insulin lispro	Anti-diabetic (type 1 and type 2 diabetes)
Byetta®	Exenatide	Anti-diabetic (type 2 diabetes)
Synthroid®	Levothyroxine	Hormone (hypothyroidism)
Levoxyl®	Levothyroxine	Hormone (hypothyroidism)
Premarin®	conjugated estrogens	Hormone (postmenopausal symptoms)
Yuvafem®	Estradiol	Hormone (postmenopausal symptoms)
Previfem®	Norgestimate/EE	Hormone (postmenopausal symptoms)

Drugs and Drug Therapy

Brand Name	Generic Name	Class of Medication (Treatment of)
Yasmin®	Drospirenone/EE	Hormone (postmenopausal symptoms)
Plan B®	Levonorgestrel/EE	Hormone (postmenopausal symptoms)
Norlyda	Norethindrone	Hormone (menstrual disorders)
Medications Acting on the Immune System		
Amoxil®	Amoxicillin	Antibiotic (infections)
Zithromax®	Azithromycin	Antibiotic (infections)
Vibramycin®	Doxycycline	Antibiotic (infections)
Levaquin®	Levofloxacin	Antibiotic (infections)
Omnicef®	Cefdinir	Antibiotic (infections)
Avelox®	Moxifloxacin	Antibiotic (infections)
Biaxin®	Clarithromycin	Antibiotic (infections)
Flagyl®	Metronidazole	Antibiotic (infections)
Clindagel®	Clindamycin	Antibiotic (infections)
Bactrim®	SMZ/TMP	Antibiotic (infections)
Neosporin®	Neomycin/polymyxin B/ bacitracin	Antibiotic (skin infections)
Ciprodex®	Ciprofloxacin/dexamethasone	Antibiotic/steroid (ear infection)
TobraDex®	Tobramycin/dexamethasone	Antibiotic/steroid (eye infection)
Valtrex®	Valacyclovir	Anti-viral (herpes)
Viread®	Tenofovir	Anti-viral (hepatitis B, HIV)
Lamisil®	Terbinafine	Anti-fungal
Medications Acting on the Muscular and Skeletal System		
Fosamax®	Alendronate	Bone density modifier (osteoporosis)
Actonel®	Risedronate	Bone density modifier (osteoporosis)
Boniva®	Ibandronate	Bone density modifier (osteoporosis)
Evista®	Raloxifene	Estrogen modulator (osteoporosis)
Skelaxin®	Metaxalone	Muscle relaxant (musculoskeletal conditions)
Fexmid®	Cyclobenzaprine	Muscle relaxant (musculoskeletal conditions)
Zyloprim®	Allopurinol	Xanthine oxidase inhibitor (gout)
Uloric®	Febuxostat	Xanthine oxidase inhibitor (gout)
Lidoderm®	Lidocaine	Anesthetic (pain)
Vicodin®	Hydrocodone/acetaminophen	Opioid/NSAID (pain)
Oxycontin®	Oxycodone	Opioid (pain)
Percocet®	Oxycodone/acetaminophen	Opioid/NSAID (pain)
Ultram®	Tramadol	Opioid (pain)
Statex®	Morphine	Opioid (pain)
Advil®	Ibuprofen	NSAID (pain)
Bayer®	Aspirin	NSAID (pain)
Celebrex®	Celecoxib	NSAID (pain)
Mobic®	Meloxicam	NSAID (pain)
Aleve®	Naproxen	NSAID (pain)
Cambia®	Diclofenac	NSAID (pain)
Medications Acting on the Eyes		

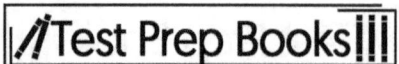

Brand Name	Generic Name	Class of Medication (Treatment of)
Xalatan®	Latanoprost	Anti-glaucoma (increased intraocular pressure)
Lumigan®	Bimatoprost	Anti-glaucoma (increased intraocular pressure)
Travatan®	Travoprost	Anti-glaucoma (increased intraocular pressure)
Cosopt®	Dorzolamide/timolol	Anti-glaucoma (increased intraocular pressure)
Alphagan®	Brimonidine	Anti-glaucoma (increased intraocular pressure)
Claritin®	Loratadine	Antihistamine (allergy)
Zyrtec®	Cetirizine	Antihistamine (allergy)
Allegra®	Fexofenadine	Antihistamine (allergy)
Flonase®	Fluticasone	Antihistamine (allergy)
Astelin®	Azelastine	Antihistamine (allergy)
Patanol®	Olopatadine	Antihistamine (eye allergies)

Abbreviation key: **ADHD**: attention-deficit hyperactivity disorder, **ACEI**: angiotensin converting enzyme inhibitor, **ARB**: angiotensin receptor blocker, **CCB**: calcium channel blocker, **CHF**: congestive heart failure, **GERD**: gastroesophageal reflux disease, **NDRI**: norepinephrine dopamine reuptake inhibitor, **NSAID**: non-steroidal anti-inflammatory drug, **PPI**: proton pump inhibitor, **SARI**: serotonin agonist and reuptake inhibitor, **SNRI**: serotonin norepinephrine reuptake inhibitor, **SSRI**: selective serotonin reuptake inhibitor, **TCA**: tricyclic antidepressant, **TeCA**: tetracyclic antidepressant.

Therapeutic Equivalence

When substituting one medication for another, it is vitally important to understand various types of medication equivalence. There are certain parameters (bioavailability, dosage form, active ingredients, safety profile, and clinical efficacy) that need to be identical or nearly identical to ensure that a specific medication and the reference medication are equivalent. The extent that one medication can be substituted for another depends on which type of equivalence (bio, pharmaceutical, and therapeutic) has been established. Therefore, pharmacy technicians must understand the different types of equivalence.

Pharmaceutical Equivalents

Pharmaceutical equivalents refer to two or more medications that have equal quantities/strength of the identical active ingredients in the same dosage form and with the same route of administration. The active ingredients in pharmaceutical equivalent formulations should meet the official compendia (e.g., USP and NF) standard on identity, purity, strength, and quality. Pharmaceutical equivalent formulations, however, may vary in shape, scoring configuration, packaging, excipients (preservatives, colors, and flavors), labeling, and date of expiration.

Pharmaceutical Alternatives

Pharmaceutical alternatives refer to medications that have the same therapeutic moiety (structure), but are formulated as different salts, esters, or complexes. They might have different strengths and dosage forms. For example, tetracycline 250 mg formulated as hydrochloride and phosphate salts are pharmaceutical alternatives. Generally, different dosage forms and strengths of a single medication by a single manufacturer are pharmaceutical alternatives. The extended-release formulations and the standard/immediate release formulations are, therefore, pharmaceutical alternatives, as they carry the same active ingredient.

Bioequivalents

Bioequivalents refer to two or more pharmaceutically-comparable products that demonstrate equivalent bioavailability when tested under similar experimental conditions. The rate and extent of absorption of bioequivalent products should be identical. Bioequivalence of two or more formulations is determined by comparing the rate and extent of absorption of those formulations with that of the reference standard formulation.

Drugs and Drug Therapy

Therapeutic Equivalents

Therapeutic equivalents refer to two or more pharmaceutical products that provide identical clinical effect, safety, and efficacy. Therapeutic equivalents should meet the following criteria:

- They should have identical safety and efficacy.
- They should be pharmaceutically-equivalent.
- They should be bioequivalent.
- They should be adequately labeled.
- They should be manufactured in accordance with the standards of Current Good Manufacturing Practice (cGMP).

Bioavailability

Bioavailability is a function of the rate and extent of absorption of a drug from a formulation. It is the fraction of a drug that reaches the blood circulation after administration. The bioavailability following an intravenous administration is 100%, since the medication is completely available in circulation.

The following are parameters that measure bioavailability on a concentration-time curve:

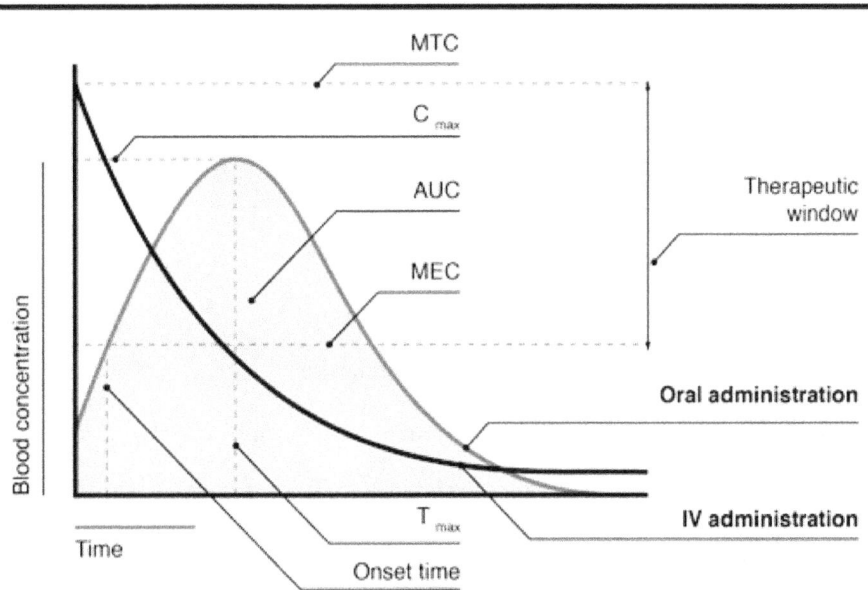

- **C_{max}**: The peak blood concentration of the medication
- **T_{max}**: The time to reach the peak blood concentration of the medication; indicative of the rate of absorption of a drug from a formulation
- **MEC**: The minimum effective concentration (i.e., the minimum drug concentration required to exhibit the therapeutic effect)
- **MTC**: The maximum therapeutic concentration at which the greatest therapeutic effect of a drug is achieved

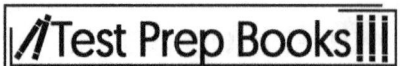

Drugs and Drug Therapy

- **Therapeutic window**: The range of drug concentrations between which the desired therapeutic effect is obtained without any significant toxicity
- **AUC**: The area under the concentration-time curve; refers to the amount of the drug absorbed in the system following administration. It is the principal index of the bioavailability of a drug from a dosage form.

Below are explanations of two types of bioavailability:

- **Absolute bioavailability**: This refers to the comparison between the bioavailability of a drug following a non-intravenous route (e.g., oral, rectal, sublingual, subcutaneous, transdermal, etc.) of administration and the bioavailability of the same drug following intravenous administration. It is measured by the ratio of AUC from the non-IV route to that of the IV route. So, % absolute bioavailability is:

$$F_{abs} = \frac{AUC_{PO}}{D_{PO}} \times \frac{D_{IV}}{AUC_{IV}} \times 100$$

Where, AUC_{PO} = AUC from oral administration

AUC_{IV} = AUC from intravenous administration

D_{PO} = dose of oral formulation

D_{IV} = dose of intravenous formulation

- **Relative bioavailability**: This refers to the comparison of the bioavailability of a drug from one dosage form (e.g., tablet or capsule) to the bioavailability of the same drug from a reference dosage form (e.g., syrup or suspension). When the reference formulation is an IV dosage form, it also indicates absolute bioavailability. So, % relative bioavailability is:

$$F_{rel} = \frac{AUC_A}{D_A} \times \frac{D_B}{AUC_B} \times 100$$

Where, AUC_A = AUC from formulation A (test formulation)

AUC_B = AUC from formulation B (reference standard)

D_A = dose of formulation A (test formulation)

D_B = dose of formulation B (reference standard)

Narrow Therapeutic Index Medications

The efficacy and safety of a drug are determined quantitatively by comparing the amount of the drug needed to achieve a specific therapeutic goal and the amount at which toxicity occurs. The therapeutic index, or TI, compares the concentration of a drug in the blood at levels considered to be effective and at levels that are toxic. The therapeutic index is equal to the ratio of the toxic dose, or TD, for fifty percent of subjects and the effective dose, or ED, for fifty percent of subjects.

$$TI = \frac{Toxic\ Dose}{Effective\ Dose} = TD_{50}/ED_{50}$$

Generally, a medication with a high therapeutic index has a broader margin of safety and does not require close monitoring by a physician. For example, simvastatin, a statin medication, is used to reduce cholesterol and is

Drugs and Drug Therapy

available in strengths ranging from 5 mg to 80 mg. Statins require minimal monitoring, such as annual bloodwork for cholesterol screening. Simvastatin, like many medications, can have adverse effects, but overall, it is considered safe because of its broad therapeutic range.

Medications with a low therapeutic index are referred to as narrow therapeutic index drugs. Narrow therapeutic index, or NTI, medications have a small window between being effective and lethal. Some NTIs can have significant drug and dietary interactions which can complicate dosing. Examples of narrow therapeutic index medications include the anticoagulant warfarin, thyroid medications such as levothyroxine, transplant rejection medications like cyclosporine, and the anticonvulsant phenytoin, to name a few. Narrow therapeutic medications require close monitoring of a patient by the physician to ensure its use does not result in therapeutic failure, serious injury, or death. **Vancomycin** is a narrow therapeutic antibiotic medication that is used to treat serious bacterial infections like Methicillin-resistant Staphylococcus aureus (MRSA). The antibiotic vancomycin is typically delivered via intravenous infusions when treating these types of bacterial infections and requires extensive monitoring to ensure efficacy. To effectively inhibit bacterial growth, vancomycin must hit a peak blood concentration followed by a low concentration called a trough. Dosing is repeated until a steady state, or the balance between infusion and elimination of the medication in the body, is achieved. A trough level is drawn, usually before the fourth dose in the course is administered, as this is when the drug is at its lowest concentration in the bloodstream. Vancomycin is cleared from the body by the kidneys; therefore, kidney function must also be monitored to ensure adequate elimination from the body. Renal impairment may allow for the buildup of the medication in the body, possibly leading to irreversible nephrotoxicity. Vancomycin is most effective at a specific and steady concentration in the bloodstream; it is vital to monitor the patient's level to determine adjustments in dosing.

The blood thinner warfarin is another example of a narrow therapeutic index medication. **Warfarin** is an anticoagulant used to prevent the formation of blood clots in the body. Achieving the correct dose of Warfarin can be challenging because of its narrow therapeutic range. Further complicating warfarin dosing is the fact that it interacts with other medication, dietary supplements, and some foods. A patient taking a blood thinner should avoid taking nonsteroidal anti-inflammatory drugs (NSAIDS) like aspirin or ibuprofen, or dietary supplements such as garlic, as these can increase bleeding. In some foods like leafy greens, which are rich in Vitamin K, warfarin acts to slow down the process of clotting factor production by blocking Vitamin K.

Vitamin K is a fat-soluble vitamin which is necessary to produce clotting factors like the protein prothrombin. A dose too low can allow for clot formation resulting in stroke, embolism, or heart attack. A dose too high can cause uncontrolled bleeding in the body. Warfarin patients require close monitoring by performing a PT/INR test to determine how quickly the blood is clotting. **Development of the International Normalized Ratio (INR)** helped to standardize these test results and account for any laboratory variations that may affect test results. The INR values range from zero to five with the standard therapeutic target INR for a patient taking warfarin being between two and three. A low INR value can put the patient at risk of clot formation, whereas a higher INR value can put the patient at risk for excessive bleeding.

Anticonvulsants are considered narrow therapeutic index medications and are used to minimize seizure activity in patients with seizure disorders such as epilepsy. Determining the correct therapeutic dose requires the patient to self-monitor any medication side effects they experience in addition to monitoring seizure activity, such as how frequently seizures occur or the duration of the seizure. In addition, bloodwork must be monitored to ensure organ function is within range and blood concentration of medication is at a steady state.

Generic Substitution

Generic substitution refers to filling a prescription with a generic, therapeutically-equivalent formulation instead of an original brand name formulation. For example, the generic form of Lipitor® is Atorvastatin; both have the same clinical efficacy and safety for treating high cholesterol. Dispensing generic Atorvastatin for a prescription written

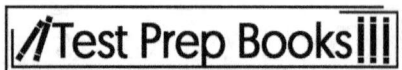

for Lipitor® is an example of generic substitution. There are different laws in each state for filling prescriptions with generic substitutions; therefore, it is important to know and abide by the laws in the state of employment.

Generally, generic medications are less expensive for patients. Prescribers may deem the brand name medically necessary and order "dispense as written" or "no substitution" to prevent generic substitutions. It is also important to check the therapeutic index of a drug before substituting with a generic medication. Drugs with a narrow therapeutic index should be cautiously dispensed as generics, as minute changes in bioavailability can impose significant toxicity. Examples of such drugs include levothyroxine, lithium, warfarin, phenytoin, and digoxin.

Therapeutic Substitutions
Therapeutic substitution can be done in two different forms: substitution of an equally potent drug from within the same class or substitution of a drug from a different class of drugs with a different mechanism of action but with the same pharmacologic effect and similar potency. An example of the first type of substitution is dispensing enalapril for lisinopril, which is substitution of an ACE inhibitor with another ACE inhibitor. An example of the second type of substitution is giving enalapril in place of amlodipine, which is substituting a calcium channel blocker with an ACE inhibitor, where both drugs have similar antihypertensive effect but different modes of action. The frequency of therapeutic substitutions is low in community pharmacies and is more likely to happen in hospitals or federal facilities. It is imperative to make sure that these types of substitutions are discussed with the prescriber before making the substitution.

There are several consequences of therapeutic substitutions:

- Either over- or under-treating the patient
- The unfavorable effects either get better or worse
- There could be different adverse effects
- The cost of the prescription could be higher or lower for the patient

Differentiating between Side Effects and Adverse Drug Reactions

Effects and Side-Effects of Pharmacotherapy
It is important to be able to distinguish side effects from adverse drug reactions (ADRs). A good understanding of common class side effects and the hallmark symptoms of allergic reactions and intolerances improves the counsel given to a patient on whether something they are experiencing is a typical side effect, an adverse reaction of concern, or something unrelated to their medications.

Common Side Effects
Some regularly noted side effects are quite serious, such as severe skin sensitivity to light in the case of tetracyclines or acute tendon rupture in the case of fluoroquinolone antibiotics. These are well-documented potential side effects and should be counseled to the patient upon dispensation, but their severity may allow them to be treated as an ADR. In this way, the distinction between side effects and ADRs breaks down; all side effects are technically ADRs, as they cause injury or discomfort through the direct action of the drug even with proper and advised doses and use. For the purposes of this exam, consider ADRs to include both severe side effects and unexpected reactions due to medication use, such as allergies, hypersensitivities, and intolerances.

Patients may be intolerant of a medication for many reasons, but it is chiefly a personal decision for the patient on whether they can suffer through the side effects to benefit from the positive effects. Severe, recurrent side effects will lower the ability and willpower of a patient to continue taking the drug. The exception to this should be hypersensitivities and allergies, which may progress to become more severe with repeated administrations of the drug.

A hypersensitivity is an overreaction by the patient's immune system upon exposure to an antigen, of which an allergy is a subtype (Type I). Most true drug hypersensitivities are allergies, but others affect different parts of the immune system and are not classified as such. Examples include drug reaction with eosinophilia and systemic symptoms (DRESS) syndrome, toxic epidermal necrolysis (TEN) syndrome, and Stevens-Johnson syndrome. Both allergies and general hypersensitivities are patient-specific and cannot be predicted except through trial and error.

Hallmark symptoms of an allergy include nausea/vomiting, diarrhea, eye watering, sweating, tachycardia, urticaria (hives), dermatitis (rash) and skin peeling, inflammation, eyelid and lip swelling, shortness of breath, and anaphylaxis. Anaphylaxis is a suite of potentially lethal symptoms with sudden onset, which can include throat swelling and struggling to breathe, hypotension and dizziness, and loss of consciousness in addition to milder allergy symptoms. Epinephrine may be administered to reduce symptoms, but emergency services should be called to ensure optimal outcomes.

When triaging a patient's side effects for allergy or emergency, these should be distinguished from common gastrointestinal (GI) side effects such as the diarrhea associated with antibiotics, as these are more related to the elimination of gut flora rather than a patient-specific allergy and unrelated topical allergens that may have caused local reddening and inflammation similar to poison ivy reactions or hay fever allergy.

The following table lists some classes of medications and side effects commonly associated with them. This list is not exhaustive, but side effects tend to be class-dependent (such as angiotensin-converting enzyme [ACE] inhibitors causing dry cough or antihistamines causing drowsiness), and individual lists are published for each drug product in their package insert. Some medications may cause suites of side effects; an example is anticholinergic drugs causing decreased salivation, lacrimation, urination, and defecation (SLUD). Some entries such as clindamycin are of singular drugs, which may be part of a larger class of drugs found elsewhere; in this case, although antibiotics cause the general side effect of diarrhea, clindamycin was included by itself to draw attention to its unique association to *Clostridium difficile*–induced diarrhea, which is of serious concern due to the infection's difficulty to treat and the severity of the associated diarrhea and dehydration.

Class	Side Effects
Stimulants (attention-deficit/hyperactivity disorder [ADHD])	Insomnia, Hypertension, Appetite loss
Anti-Alzheimer's	Anti-SLUD, Dizziness
Anti-Parkinson's	Orthostatic hypotension, Dyskinesia, Extrapyramidal symptoms
Antipsychotics	Anti-SLUD, Weight gain, Sedation, Tardive dyskinesia
Antidepressants	SLUD or Anti-SLUD, Insomnia or Sedation, Suicidal ideation, Sexual dysfunction, Serotonin syndrome
Selective serotonin reuptake inhibitors (SSRIs)	Impotence, Erectile dysfunction
Serotonin and norepinephrine reuptake inhibitors (SNRIs)	Insomnia, Hypertension, Sweating
Tricyclic antidepressants (TCAs)	Sedation, Arrhythmia
Benzodiazepines (BZDs)	Sedation, Ataxia, Abnormal behavior
Anti-Migraine	Dysgeusia, Dizziness
Anti-Epileptics	Asthenia, Sedation
Muscle relaxants	Dizziness, Sedation, Asthenia
Estrogens	Blood clots, Nausea, Vaginitis
Thyroid replacement	Hyperthyroidism, Hypertension, Insomnia, Arrhythmia

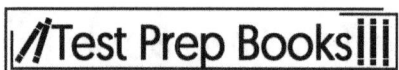

Drugs and Drug Therapy

Class	Side Effects
Anti-Thyroid	Hypothyroidism, Hypotension, Sedation
Antibiotics	Diarrhea, Nausea
Beta-Lactams	Rash
Bactrim	Skin photosensitivity
Tetracyclines	Skin photosensitivity, Teeth discoloration
Macrolides	Arrhythmia
Clindamycin	*C. difficile*–induced colitis
Fluoroquinolones	Arrhythmia, Tendon rupture
Antifungals	Nausea, Headache, Arrhythmia
Antivirals	Nausea
Anti-Nausea	Arrhythmia, Sedation
Laxatives	Diarrhea
Humira	Injection site pain, Headache, Blood clot
Hydroxychloroquine	Arrhythmia
Methotrexate	Photosensitivity, Increased liver enzymes
Steroids	Opportunistic infection, Hyperglycemia, Hypertension
Opioids	Respiratory depression, Constipation, Nausea, Arrhythmia, Sedation
NSAIDs	Indigestion, Nausea, Bleeding
Tramadol	Nausea, Arrhythmia, Sedation
Bladder agents	Hypotension, Dizziness
Phenazopyridine	Reddish-orange urine
Diuretics	Electrolyte imbalances, Insomnia, Diuresis
ACE inhibitors	Dry cough, Hypotension, Headache
Angiotensin receptor blockers (ARBs)	Angioedema, Hypotension
Beta-Blockers	Bradycardia, Hypotension, Dyspnea
Calcium channel blockers (CCBs)	Edema, Hypotension
Digoxin	Arrhythmia, Dizziness
Nitrates	Headache, Flushing, Dizziness
Anticoagulants	Bruising, Bleeding
Warfarin	Purple toe syndrome
Anti-Cholesterols	Increased liver enzymes, Muscle pain, Rhabdomyolysis
Statins	Myalgia, Arthralgia
Antidiabetics	Hypoglycemia, Weight gain
Insulins	Hypoglycemia, Weight gain, Hypokalemia
Sodium-glucose cotransporter-2 (SGLT-2) inhibitors	Urinary infection, Diabetic ketoacidosis (DKA), Increased urination
Glucagon-like peptide 1 (GLP-1) analogues	Weight loss
Metformin	Metabolic acidosis, Diarrhea
Albuterol	Tachycardia, Nervousness
Steroidal bronchodilators	Candidiasis, Xerostomia
Antihistamines	Sedation, Dizziness
PPIs	Osteoporosis, Nausea, Electrolyte imbalance
Latanoprost	Blurred vision, Burning sensation in eyes

Drugs and Drug Therapy

Class	Side Effects
Phosphodiesterase 5 (PDE-5) inhibitors	Priapism, Headaches
Potassium	Hyperkalemia, Dysgeusia, Nausea
Phentermine	Agitation, Insomnia, Tachycardia
Anti-Osteoporosis	Bone pain, Esophageal erosion, Nausea

Adverse Drug Reactions

An adverse drug reaction is a reaction that is undesirable, yet happens even when a medication is taken according to its standard dosing. Adverse drug reactions can manifest with the first dosing of the medication or can develop over time. They can happen in a limited area of the body (locally) or can affect the whole body (systemic). An intervention is needed in cases of serious adverse drug reactions that can cause injury and fatality.

The different types of adverse reactions to medications are as follows:

- Compounded pharmacologic effects that include tolerance and side effects
- Peculiar and unpredictable effects (idiosyncratic drug reaction, which could be life-threatening)
- Chronic effects
- Delayed effects
- Effects at the end of treatment
- Treatment failure
- Genetic reactions

Allergies

Symptoms

The following are symptoms that indicate an allergy to a medication:

- Hives
- Skin redness and rashes or other types of reactions
- Swelling in the face, throat, tongue or other area of the body
- Difficulty breathing, wheezing, or chest tightness
- Irregular or rapid heartbeat

Severe forms of these reactions can indicate an **anaphylactic reaction**, which is life-threatening and requires immediate emergency treatment. **Emergency Medical Services (911)** should be contacted right away in cases of suspected anaphylactic reactions to any substance. It is common for patients to confuse allergic reactions and adverse events. Therefore, it is important for the pharmacy staff to ask about the symptoms a patient experiences so that the reaction can be categorized correctly.

Foods and Excipients

There are some medications and supplements that contain food-based ingredients, and therefore, precautions need to be taken when prescribing such substances to a patient with food allergies. The coatings of medications, for example, can have excipients such as lactose, maltodextrin, and other starches that can cause allergic reactions in a person susceptible to those ingredients. Other medications, including Prometrium® (a hormone medication), contain peanut oil so patients with peanut allergies should avoid such formulations. Some calcium products and omega-3 supplements are derived from shellfish; hence, a person with a seafood allergy may need to avoid these supplements. Patients with dietary restrictions, such as celiac disease or gluten intolerance, should avoid capsules made with gluten fillers or gelatin. If there are any questions about the ingredients, it is best to contact the manufacturer.

Differentiating between Contraindications and Drug Interactions

Drug Interactions

Drug interaction refers to the alteration in pharmacology (absorption, distribution, metabolism, elimination, efficacy, side effects, etc.) of a medication by various factors including disease conditions, prescription and OTC medications, and foods or nutritional supplements. These interactions may result in either an augmentation or decrease in the efficacy and/or toxicity of the respective medication. Drug interaction should be carefully reviewed in order to avoid serious life-threatening conditions.

Contraindications are factors that would make using a particular medication or treatment potentially harmful to the patient.

Examples of different types of drug interactions and contraindications and examples within each type are described below.

Drug-Disease Interactions

NSAIDS and Peptic Ulcers

NSAIDs including aspirin, ibuprofen, naproxen, and indomethacin can cause stomach irritation and can aggravate peptic ulcer symptoms. Therefore, NSAIDs should not be used by patients with peptic ulcers or GERD. If NSAIDs are used by patients with hyperacidity, gastro-protective agents, such as proton pumps inhibitors (e.g., omeprazole, pantoprazole, lansoprazole, etc.), should also be used.

Diuretics and Diabetes

Diuretics are used to treat hypertension and edema. Hydrochlorothiazide is a commonly prescribed diuretic that can cause glucose intolerance and hyperglycemia. Therefore, if a patient with type 2 diabetes is prescribed a diuretic, blood sugar control becomes difficult, so routine monitoring of blood sugar is required. If blood sugar is not properly controlled, dose adjustments of the anti-diabetic medication or alternative diuretics should be considered.

Drug-Drug Interactions

Warfarin and NSAIDs

Warfarin is a commonly prescribed blood thinner, indicated to prevent blood clots in various cardiovascular diseases. Patients on warfarin should not take other prescription/OTC/herbal medications without consulting with their prescriber and pharmacist. For example, commonly available OTC NSAIDs can cause an increase in the blood-thinning effect of warfarin and result in internal hemorrhage.

The following medications can interact with warfarin:

- Aspirin
- Acetaminophen (at high doses)
- Ibuprofen
- Naproxen
- Celecoxib
- Diclofenac
- Indomethacin
- Piroxicam

Oral Contraceptives and Antibiotics

Antibiotics can decrease the effect of hormonal oral contraceptives and cause accidental pregnancy. Non-hormonal back-up methods, such as condoms, should be used while a woman taking an oral contraceptive is prescribed an antibiotic. Other medications that can affect the efficacy of oral contraceptives include anti-fungals, a few anti-seizure medications, certain HIV medications, and a few herbal preparations, like St. John's Wort.

Nitroglycerin and Erectile Dysfunction Medications

Nitroglycerin is a vasodilator that is often used to treat episodes of angina. To prevent recurring angina, the extended-release capsules of nitroglycerin are taken daily, whereas in cases of non-frequent occurrence, sublingual tablets or sprays can be used. Medications to treat erectile dysfunctions, such as sildenafil, tadalafil, and vardenafil, should not be taken with nitroglycerin. These medications augment the vasodilatory effect of nitroglycerin and can lead to irreversible hypotension and fatality. Emergency care should be sought immediately if this combination accidentally happens. The symptoms of hypotension include dizziness, fainting, and cold, clammy skin.

Drug-Food and Drug-Nutrient Interactions

Statins and Grapefruit Juice

Statins (e.g., pravastatin, simvastatin, atorvastatin, and rosuvastatin) are used to treat hypocholesteremia. Patients taking this medication should avoid drinking grapefruit juice or consuming large amounts of grapefruit because this juice decreases the metabolism of statins, resulting in a buildup of statins in the body. The risk of serious side effects is increased when statin buildup occurs, with possible resultant muscle or liver damage. Pharmacists should counsel patients about avoiding grapefruit juice while on statins. Although increasing statin dosage may seem to benefit the patient, the liver can only process so much. Accumulation of a statin in the body can cause muscle damage, pain, and rhabdomyolysis—a serious and potentially lethal side effect. In rhabdomyolysis, the skeletal muscle is rapidly catabolized. Patients taking statins should undergo routine blood tests and notify their doctors immediately about symptoms of muscle pain or fatigue. Undetected and unmanaged rhabdomyolysis can result in death.

MAOIs and Tyramine

Monoamine oxidase inhibitors (MAOIs) are used to treat chronic depression that does not respond to other medications or treatments. Due to side effects and drug interactions, MAOIs are not commonly prescribed. Examples of MAOIs are phenelzine (Nardil®), selegiline (Emsam®), and tranylcypromine (Parnate®). MAOIs can cause serotonin syndrome. There are many medications and foods that can lead to severe side effects when combined with MAOIs. Foods like wine, cheese, certain meats, and pickled foods carry tyramine, which leads to spikes in blood pressure if co-administered with MAOIs.

Drug-OTC Interactions

Antihypertensives and Decongestants

Pseudoephedrine and **phenylephrine** are used as decongestants in different OTC cough and cold medications. These medications have sympathomimetic effects and can cause elevated blood pressure. Therefore, if a decongestant medication is taken by patients on antihypertensive medication, it reduces the blood pressure control of the antihypertensive agent. Hypertensive patients should avoid taking OTC medications containing sympathomimetic agents.

Antihistamines and Sedatives

OTC **antihistamines**, such as diphenhydramine and chlorpheniramine, are used to treat various allergic conditions. Antihistamines can cause sedation and drowsiness, which can potentiate the side effects of sedatives and hypnotics. Patients taking sedatives—such as diazepam, lorazepam, alprazolam, and midazolam—should be cautious when taking an OTC antihistamine.

Drug-Laboratory Interactions

Treatment with certain medications can affect laboratory results. For example, the blood or urine sample collected from a patient taking an antibiotic for one infection might yield a false antibiotic sensitivity or culture report for a second infection. The lab work should, therefore, be scheduled after the wash-out period of the first antibiotic.

Polypharmacy

Polypharmacy occurs when a patient takes multiple medications to treat different medical conditions. This happens mostly in elderly patients who are being treated for several medical conditions. Polypharmacy can cause serious drug interactions. Polypharmacy also tends to happen when a patient sees multiple doctors to treat separate conditions. Pharmacy technicians can help to prevent adverse consequences of polypharmacy by alerting pharmacists to drug interactions.

Therapeutic Contraindications Associated with Medications

Alcohol

Alcohol should be avoided while patients are on prescription medications. Consumption of alcohol with medications can cause nausea, vomiting, fainting, loss of coordination, or extreme drowsiness. More severe reactions can lead to heart problems, internal bleeding, and difficulty breathing. Certain medications, when combined with alcohol, can cause toxicity. As alcohol is a strong CNS depressant, combining it with other depressants, like benzodiazepines or sleeping medications, can be dangerous and can cause respiratory failure. If alcohol is combined with a high dose of acetaminophen, there is potential for serious liver damage. Additionally, if alcohol is consumed while taking metronidazole, the patient can experience significant side effects including nausea, vomiting, abdominal pain, cramps, facial redness, headache, tachycardia, and liver damage.

Age

Age has a significant effect on the pharmacology of medications. Maturation during childhood causes various changes in body composition, accompanying growth and development. Therefore, newborns, infants, children, and adolescents often do not receive full adult dosages. As mentioned, medication doses should be appropriately calculated based on the age and weight of the child. There are many medications that are not approved by the FDA for children and yet are used "off label." Unexpected reactions can happen when medications are not studied in pediatric populations. For example, tetracycline is contraindicated in children because it can bind with the calcium in bones, modify bone cartilage, and cause growth retardation. Generally, if a physician prescribes a medication that is not approved for use in children, pharmacy technicians should consult with the pharmacist, who will rely on their professional judgment about how to proceed (i.e., dispense the medication or talk with the physician).

In elderly adults, there can also be significant changes in pharmacokinetics and pharmacodynamics of a medication. Geriatric populations often have comorbid conditions, including cardiovascular disease, diabetes, and renal insufficiencies. Aging can decrease the body's clearance of a medication, resulting in buildup and manifesting in unwanted effects. Routine blood work and dose adjustments may be necessary in the geriatric population.

OTC Medications

Some OTC medications impose significant risks with certain disease conditions. A few OTC medications can lead to an increase in blood pressure, so these may be contraindicated in patients with hypertension. The following medications are known to cause problems for patients with hypertension:

- NSAIDS (ibuprofen and naproxen)
- Decongestants like pseudoephedrine
- Migraine formulations with caffeine

Patients with high blood pressure should talk to a pharmacist or a physician before taking OTC medications or herbal supplements.

Pregnancy

During pregnancy, medications should be prescribed carefully, to prevent harm to the developing fetus. For some medications, there might not be enough data available regarding safety during pregnancy, and therefore, they must be used cautiously after weighing the benefits versus the risks. Many medications are contraindicated during pregnancy, as they have teratogenic effects and can cause birth defects. If a patient is on a teratogenic medication prior to pregnancy, the medication should be stopped upon conception. A few examples of medications that are contraindicated in pregnancy include ACE inhibitors (e.g., ramipril, enalapril, lisinopril, etc.), ARBs (e.g., losartan, candesartan, irbesartan, etc.), isotretinoin, tetracycline antibiotics, hormonal therapies, and immunosuppressants (e.g., methotrexate).

Physical Interactions and Incompatibilities in the Preparation of Compounded and Parenteral Medications

Some patients are unable to swallow foods and must be fed intravenously through a parenteral solution. This may include a dextrose solution for sugar, an amino acid solution for protein, a lipid emulsion for fat, electrolytes, trace elements, vitamins, and/or drugs. Along with following a sterile procedure and aseptic technique, some of these inclusions may precipitate or chelate, so caution is necessary. Typically, electrolytes and trace elements are added to the three bags of dextrose, amino acids, and lipids; the dextrose is mixed with the amino acids; and then the lipids are added. Following this, vitamins or drugs may be added as well. The most important order to follow is the separation of phosphate and calcium addition, as these two will combine and immediately precipitate out of the solution. Phosphate is typically added near the beginning of the admixture preparation so that the other electrolytes (sodium and potassium) may associate with the phosphate and lower the chance for calcium phosphate to form.

In the case that a patient is unable to swallow a medication, there are several intravenous (IV) solutions that may be used to administer a drug. Common solutions include 0.9% normal saline (NS), dextrose 5% in water (D5W), and lactated Ringer's (LR). LR contains sodium, potassium, calcium, chloride, and lactate; as such, if a medication such as Cipro, which chelates in calcium, is added to the bag, it will form clumps, clog up the tube, and may cause lethal clots upon administration.

In a similar fashion, some medications are not as easily soluble in some IV solutions, whereas other medications lose stability much faster in others. When compounding an IV drip, it is important to use the IV solution indicated by the manufacturer. This also applies to the plastic that makes up the bag, as some medications may leach into the material and reduce the overall amount administered, or materials of the plastic in the bag may leach into the solution and contaminate the IV. For example, polyvinyl chloride (PVC) bags using the plasticizer di-2-ethylhexylphthalate (DEHP) have been shown to allow the plasticizer to seep into solutions made using the stabilizers Tween 20 and Tween 80. Additional information may be found in a resource of drug stability such as *Trissel's Stability of Compounded Formulations*.

Some medications are more stable in their powder form but are either for pediatric patients who cannot swallow pills or for topical application as a cream or paste. Most pediatric oral antibiotics and the methylphenidate suspension Quillivant® come this way and must be reconstituted by mixing with a certain amount of distilled water as directed by the manufacturer's instructions. Other medications contain their own solution liquid in the packaging with their own directions for mixing prior to dispensation, such as the oral First-Omeprazole and the topical clindamycin/benzoyl peroxide gel. This is also the preferred packaging method for certain vaccines—namely, Shingrix (zoster recombinant vaccine [ZRV]), Varivax® (VAR), Menveo, M-M-R II, Vaxchora®, and the Pfizer and Moderna coronavirus disease 2019 (COVID-19) vaccines. When reconstituting medications administered via

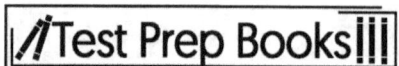

injection, proper sterile protocol must be followed according to training, and each powder must be mixed only with its corresponding diluent according to the manufacturer's instructions. As with all reconstituted medications, the final product should be examined for any discoloration and particulates or clumps in the solution. Most vaccines should be colorless and semi-transparent, but VAR, Shingrix, and M-M-R II notably form pale yellow solutions once reconstituted. Oral PPI medications such as First-Lansoprazole and First-Omeprazole tend to be flavored with strawberry extract and colored using red food dye.

Common Vaccines and Immunization Schedules

There are several immunizations available to the general public via outpatient nurses and pharmacies. Chief among them target influenza, COVID-19, tetanus, pneumonia, hepatitis A (HepA) and hepatitis B (HepB), and zoster virus (shingles).

There are many brands of flu immunizations, and each has its own place in therapy. Most patients will require a simple quadrivalent vaccine (IIV4), protecting against two A strains (H1N1, H3N2) and two B strains (Yamagata, Victoria); examples include Afluria, Fluarix, and Fluzone® (when high-dose [HD] is not noted, Fluzone refers to the typical adult dose). Some vaccines have a higher dose or are adjuvanted specifically for use in patients older than sixty-five; these include Fluzone High-Dose (Fluzone HD), Fluad®, and Flublok®. If these are unavailable, another flu vaccine would also be okay to give, although it may produce fewer antibodies. In addition, patients who have mild oral egg allergies may receive any of the flu shots, but those with severe allergies should receive it in a controlled medical setting or receive non-egg-based vaccines, including Flublok and Flucelvax. Finally, there is one live flu vaccine (FluMist®, a live attenuated influenza vaccine [LAIV]), which is indicated for ages two through forty-nine and is dispensed as a nasal spray.

There are four COVID-19 vaccines available to the American public: one each from Pfizer, Moderna, Janssen, and Novavax, as shown in the chart below. Janssen is the only one that requires a single dose, whereas the others require two for full efficacy. For the two-dose series, it is recommended that the primary dosing series be completed with the same manufacturer throughout, but the Centers for Disease Control and Prevention (CDC) considers patients with two doses of different manufacturers to still be fully vaccinated. Boosters may be given eight weeks after the primary series has been completed or the most recent dose has been given; the newer bivalent Pfizer and Moderna are preferred for the booster regardless of which manufacturer was used in the primary series, but if these are unavailable, monovalent Novavax or Janssen may be used.

Manufacturer	Brand	Type	Dosing
Pfizer	Comirnaty	Messenger RNA (mRNA)	Primary series: 2 doses between 21 days and 8 weeks apart
Moderna	Spikevax	mRNA	Primary series: 2 doses between 28 days and 8 weeks apart
Novavax	Nuvaxovid, Covovax	Subunit	Primary series: 2 doses between 21 days and 8 weeks apart
Janssen	Jcovden	Viral vector	Primary series: 1 dose

The most common tetanus vaccine given in the outpatient pharmacy is Tdap (Adacel®, Boostrix), which also provides protection against diphtheria and pertussis (whooping cough). Other formulations such as tetanus and diphtheria (Td) (Tenivac®, Tdvax®) may lack the protection against pertussis or give a stronger immune response to diphtheria as in the pediatric diphtheria, tetanus, and pertussis (Dtap) (Daptacel®, Infanrix®). In unvaccinated individuals, one dose of Tdap should be given, followed by one dose of Td or Tdap every ten years thereafter as booster doses. In addition, one dose of Tdap should be given during each pregnancy, regardless of previous immunization history. A dose of Td or Tdap may be given to vaccinated individuals for minor wound care as

Drugs and Drug Therapy

prophylaxis against tetanus infection if it has been ten years since their last vaccination (or five years for larger wounds).

Three pneumonia vaccines are available on the market: Vaxneuvance® (15-valent pneumococcal conjugate vaccine [PCV15]), Prevnar (PCV20), and Pneumovax (pneumococcal polysaccharide vaccine [PPSV23]). With the recent addition of PCV15 to the market and the recent reformulation of Prevnar from PCV13 to PCV20, the CDC has recommended two viable dosing schedules: either one dose of PCV15 followed a year later by one dose of PPSV23 or a single dose of PCV20. Most patients will receive pneumonia vaccines only when they're older than sixty-five, but pneumonia vaccines are also indicated for patients suffering from chronic conditions, including alcoholism, organ disease/failure, immunosuppression, and cancer. A more detailed recommendation list may be found on the CDC website.

Vaccinations against both HepA (Havrix®, Vaqta®) and HepB (Engerix-B®, Recombivax HB®, HEPLISAV-B) exist in addition to a combination product that protects against both (Twinrix®). However, hepatitis C (HepC) currently has no vaccine available. Each of the available hepatitis vaccines requires multiple doses. Typically, HepA vaccines require two doses, whereas HepB vaccines require three, but Heplisav-B® only requires two, and because the HepA-HepB combination product includes the original HepB formulation, it needs three doses as well. As with other vaccines, an extra dose of each may be required in immunocompromised patients, or one less dose may be required if being administered as catch-up doses.

The M-M-R II is a multiple-target vaccine that protects against measles, mumps, and rubella (German measles), given as a single dose to adults who have no evidence of past immunity or vaccination. VAR is a two-dose vaccine that protects against varicella (chickenpox) and may be administered in adults if they have not received immunization through the regular pediatric schedule. Because infection with varicella may cause shingles later in life, the ZRV, Shingrix, is indicated in adults older than fifty. It is a two-dose series administered two months apart and is an improvement on the recently discontinued Zostavax; Shingrix demonstrated prevention rates greater than 90 percent and was contrasted against the prevention rates of Zostavax, which approached 60 percent.

Other potential vaccines include rabies, dengue fever, inactivated poliovirus vaccine (IPV) (polio), MenB (Bexsero, which protects against meningitis B), Japanese encephalitis, cholera, and yellow fever, but these are not carried at all pharmacies due to their specificity, and larger 24-hour pharmacies or regional health centers are likeliest to source them.

The CDC has also published guidance for immunization in some special populations, such as pregnant patients and patients with sickle cell or asplenia, end-stage renal disease (ESRD) (including patients undergoing hemodialysis [HD]), human immunodeficiency virus (HIV), or immunocompromised conditions and chronic health susceptibilities such as heart, lung, and liver conditions. For example, because live vaccines (MMR, VAR, LAIV) may cause severe illness in patients with weak immune systems, they are contraindicated in pregnant, immunocompromised, and HIV patients. They are also cautioned against using while a patient is sick or has recently had a different live vaccine, although multiple live vaccines may be given at the same appointment.

The exam chiefly focuses on outpatient immunizations; these tend to be for the adult population. Most infant and child vaccination regimens are given by the pediatrician, but outpatient pharmacies do serve as a source for the annual influenza and novel COVID-19 shots. Pharmacies may also administer catch-up vaccinations for multi-dose series such as HepA, HepB, IPV, MMR, VAR, and Tdap for pediatric patients. In addition, Gardasil (human papillomavirus [HPV]) may be administered as a two-dose series starting at age nine, and Menactra® and Menveo (MenACWY) both may be given as a two-dose series starting at age eleven or as a single dose for first-year college students and new military recruits. In each case, the pharmacist's ability to administer these vaccinations may still require a physician's prescription unless allowed via state standing order.

Practice Quiz

1. Which drug class is correctly paired with the system on which it works?
    a. Statins and the nervous system
    b. Antipruritics and the gastrointestinal system
    c. Antibiotics and the musculoskeletal system
    d. Steroids and the immune system

2. Which of the following definitions describes a capsule?
    a. An oral dosage form that is a firmly condensed powder pressed into a desired shape
    b. An oral dosage form that uses a shell to hold powder or liquid ingredients inside
    c. A rectally, vaginally, or urethrally inserted dosage form that melts to provide systemic effects
    d. A semisolid dosage form that is applied topically

3. Which of these are NOT considered to influence pharmacokinetics?
    a. Allergies
    b. Genetic factors
    c. Age
    d. Dosage form

4. Which of these generic and brand names are paired correctly?
    a. Zolpidem and Xanax
    b. Lisinopril and Altace
    c. Pregabalin and Lyrica
    d. Rosuvastatin and Lipitor

5. Which medication is most likely to cause sedation?
    a. Stimulants
    b. Thyroid replacement medications
    c. Statins
    d. Benzodiazepines

See answers on the next page.

Answer Explanations

1. D: Choice *D* is the correct answer; steroids are commonly prescribed to help with infections. Statins lower lipid levels in the cardiovascular system, antipruritics are anti-itch medications that help with the dermatological system, and antibiotics work on the immune system to also fight infections. While some medications are used for many different reasons, especially steroids, this is the only correct pairing presented here.

2. B: Choice *B* is the correct answer; capsules are encased in a shell and filled with the medication to be taken whole as a pill. Choice *A* is the definition of a tablet, Choice *C* is the definition of a suppository, and Choice *D* is the definition of an ointment or cream.

3. A: Choice *A* is the correct answer. The other answer choices are commonly known as affecting pharmacokinetic factors, while allergies are not a major discussion in the pharmacokinetic profile of a medication.

4. C: Choice *C* is the correct pairing. Zolpidem's brand name is Ambien, and Xanax's generic name is alprazolam. Lisinopril has three brand names—Prinivil, Qbrelis®, and Zestril—and Altace's generic name is ramipril. Rosuvastatin's brand name is Crestor, and Lipitor's generic name is atorvastatin.

5. D: Choice *D* is correct; benzodiazepines are infamous for causing sedation, and sometimes that is the main goal when a doctor prescribes it. Stimulants and thyroid replacement medications can cause the opposite (insomnia), and statins are not supposed to affect a patient's sleep either way.

Dispensing Process

Prescription and Medication Order Intake and Entry

During the order-entry and prescription-filling process, a pharmacy technician may be required to carry out a broad array of tasks, such as:

- Accepting new prescriptions
- Receiving prescription refills
- Asking prescribers for refill authorizations
- Gathering patient data
- Initiating and maintaining an electronic patient profile
- Entering pertinent information into the pharmacy management software system
- Interpreting prescriptions
- Billing prescriptions to third-party pharmacy benefit providers
- Counting and pouring medications
- Labeling prescription containers
- Returning medication stock to pharmacy shelves
- Repackaging medications
- Preparing unit dose medications

Under no circumstances should pharmacy technicians provide medical advice to patients. It is essential for pharmacy technicians to maintain current awareness of medications and healthcare information. This equips them to be better able to recognize possible mistakes and other issues so they can notify the pharmacist.

Every pharmacy should have a standardized book outlining their particular policies and procedures, including a **mission statement** stating the goals and purpose of an organization. A book of policies and procedures is mandatory per regulatory and professional bodies (e.g., the American Pharmacists Association [APhA], the Joint Commission, and the American Society of Health System Pharmacists [ASHP]). Manuals for policies and procedures may be used as reference tools as well as for the promotion of workplace safety.

Analyzing Prescription or Medication Orders for Completeness and Obtaining Missing Information

Required Components of Prescriptions

Legend drugs are those that require a prescription. The following information is required to be on prescription labels as mandated by the Food, Drug, and Cosmetic Act:

- The name and address of the pharmacy dispensing the medication
- The prescription number
- The date the prescription was filled
- The last date for refills
- The name of the prescriber
- The patient's name
- The instructions for use
- Any precautions or things to not take while on the medication

A prescription should include the following information:

- **Date written**: Prescriptions for non-controlled substances may be honored for up to one year after they are written.
- **Prescriber information**: Includes full name and title, office address, office telephone and fax number, and, if applicable, National Provider Identifier (NPI) number and medical registration/license number.
- **Patient information**: Includes full name and home address and, if applicable, weight, height, and allergies.
- **Inscription**: Includes name of medication, strength of medication, dosage form, and quantity to dispense.
- **Subscription**: Instructions to pharmacist
- **Number of refills**
- **Drug Enforcement Administration (DEA) number**: Only required for prescriptions for controlled substances.
- **Signature of prescriber**

There are several types of prescription medication orders: STAT, ASAP, PRN, and standing. **STAT** refers to a medication order that must be filled within 15 minutes of receiving it in a hospital. **ASAP** refers to a medication order that doesn't have the priority of a STAT order but needs to be processed as soon as possible. **PRN** refers to a medication order that may be filled or administered per patient request, but there are parameters set forth by the prescriber. **Standing** refers to a medication order that a patient receives at regularly scheduled intervals (e.g., one capsule every 6 hours).

Understanding Leading and Trailing Zeros

A decimal point could be misplaced and lead to misinterpretation. The following strategies should be followed to avoid errors:

- **Leading zero**: A decimal point (a dose less than 1) should never be left "naked" and should carry a leading zero. It is often missed in fax prescriptions due to "fax noise." For example, without a leading zero, .5 mg of haloperidol could be misinterpreted as 5 mg and cause overdosing.
- **Trailing zero**: A whole number should never be followed by a decimal point and a trailing zero. For example, with a trailing zero, 1.0 mg warfarin could be misinterpreted as 10 mg and cause ten-fold overdosing.

Abnormal Doses

It is important for pharmacy technicians and pharmacists to understand the normal dosing for a medication in order to better identify abnormal dosing regimens. A prescription with directions that do not reflect the typical dosing regimen for the drug being prescribed could be due to an off-label or unapproved use of the medication. **Off label use** of a medication is when a medication is used to address a specific health issue that it was not initially approved to treat. It is therefore best to consult with the prescribing practitioner to clarify if it is simply off-label usage or a serious medication error. Abnormal dosing patterns are seen often with the blood thinner Warfarin, where patients might take different strengths of the medication on different days of the week. It is best to evaluate the written order for irregularities, for example, recognition of an adult dose of the NSAID Prednisone that is written for a small child. Prescription errors related to abnormal dosing of a medication can be avoided with attention to detail and some due diligence.

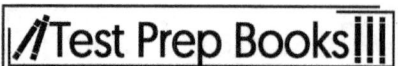

Types and Formats of Prescription and Medication Orders

Per federal law, a pharmacy may receive a prescription order via one of the following methods:

- Written: The patient hands the original prescription to a pharmacy technician.
- Telephone: Also called a verbal order
  - If the original prescription is not for a Schedule II controlled substance, it may be telephoned in by prescribers or their representatives (e.g., a nurse).
  - The patient may call in a refill for a prescription.
- Electronic or E-prescription: Transmitted electronically
- Fax

It is becoming common practice for Medicaid, Medicare, and private insurers to track prescriptions using a prescription origin code (POC). The codes are usually entered into the pharmacy management software system and signify the following:

- 0 = Unknown (e.g., a transferred prescription)
- 1 = Written prescription
- 2 = Telephone prescription
- 3 = Electronic prescription
- 4 = Fax prescription

Providers with Prescribing Authority

Prescriptive authority allows a healthcare professional to write prescriptions for medications, and this capability can be classified according to the drug class. For example, some providers are capable of prescribing controlled medications, whereas others are only authorized to prescribe non-controlled medications. Each state has its own laws regarding prescribing authority and collaborative practice agreements that allow pharmacists to provide additional patient care responsibilities outside their scope of practice. For example, with provider agreement, pharmacists can prescribe, initiate, modify, or stop treatments, tests, and procedures.

Prescription medications can be classified as controlled II-V and non-controlled. All non-prescription medications are considered non-controlled. Controlled medications are regulated differently than non-controlled medications including, but not limited to, refill quantity, transfer laws, and who can prescribe. This is because controlled medications, when compared to non-controlled classes, are characterized by increased strength, increased adverse event frequency or intensity, and increased addictive properties. Because of this, only trained healthcare providers are capable of prescribing controlled II-V medications. Additionally, medications are classified according to therapeutic use or indication, and this can limit a provider's prescriptive authority as well. For example, a veterinarian can only prescribe medications that have a proven benefit and use in animals.

The categories of prescriptive authority are described below:

- Doctor of Medicine (MD): This is the most common healthcare provider with the broadest spectrum of prescribing power. MDs have an allopathic, or conventional, approach to treating and/or diagnosing conditions.
- Doctor of Osteopathic Medicine (DO): They have the same prescriptive authority as MDs; however, DOs take a more holistic approach, which means they are taught to use non-conventional methods to treat and/or diagnose varying conditions.
- Physician Assistant (PA): They may prescribe all medication classes under the supervision of a physician.

- Nurse Practitioner (NP): They may prescribe all medication classes under the supervision of a physician.
- Veterinarian: They can prescribe all medication classes that are approved for animal use.
- Dentist (DDS): Dentists, including all specialties within dentistry, can only prescribe medications used to treat mouth-related diseases. They can prescribe non-controlled and controlled medications.
- Doctor of Podiatric Medicine (DPM): These physicians can prescribe all medication classes related to treating conditions of the feet, legs, and nearby structures.
- Optometrist (OD): These eye specialists can prescribe only non-controlled and controlled medication intended to treat eye-related diseases.
- Certified Registered Nurse Practitioner (CRNP): They must have a collaborative practice agreement and apply to their state's board of nursing. They may or may not have authority to prescribe controlled medications, depending on the specific agreement.
- Certified Midwife: They are licensed to prescribe all medication classes relating to hormonal regulation, birth preparation, etc.
- Psychiatrist: They are authorized to prescribe all medication classes related to treating psychological disorders.
- Pharmacist: Under a collaborative practice agreement, they can prescribe medications that the provider authorizes, depending on the specialty. For example, an oncologist may authorize an oncology pharmacist to prescribe cancer medications, but they would not be able to prescribe medications for a foot infection unless they had an additional collaborative practice agreement with another physician or podiatrist.

National Provider Identifier

The National Provider Identifier (NPI) is a unique and specific set of numbers that identify a healthcare professional and their prescribing authority. It is required by the Health Insurance Portability and Accountability Act (HIPAA) and is utilized to find providers in various electronic healthcare systems and administrative and financial situations. There are two types of NPI categories: NPIs for individual providers and NPIs for organizational providers. For example, a branch of CVS will have its own store NPI. In terms of prescriptions, NPIs are required to be documented on all Medicare part D claims. Generally, NPIs are written on all prescriptions because it provides an easy method for finding a provider in the system, and providers are hesitant to put their DEA number on prescriptions for non-controlled medications.

SIG Codes and Pharmacy Abbreviations

Signature codes, or SIG codes, are utilized in the pharmacy as a shorthand for common medical terms. SIG codes can be used to describe dosage form, frequency, route of administration, measurements, and times. For example, *Take 1 tab PO TID AC for HTN* in longhand will read, *Take one tablet by mouth three times a day before meals for hypertension*. This system is utilized to save time for both the provider and the pharmacist; however, unclear handwriting can lead to mistakes. SIG codes should always be verified if they are unclear.

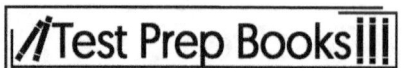

Error-Prone Abbreviations

Some abbreviations could be misinterpreted and cause medication dispensing errors. According to the Institute for Safe Medication Practices, it is recommended that pharmacies minimize the use of the following abbreviations in prescriptions, labels, and medication administration records:

Abbreviations for Doses/Measurement Units			
Abbreviation	**Intended Meaning**	**Misinterpretation**	**Best Practice**
cc	Cubic centimeters	Mistaken as u (units)	Use mL
IU**	International unit(s)	Mistaken as IV (intravenous) or the number 10	Use unit(s) (International units can be expressed as units alone)
l	Liter	Lowercase letter l mistaken as the number 1	Use L (UPPERCASE) for liter
ml	Milliliter		Use mL (lowercase m, UPPERCASE L) for milliliter
MM or M	Million	Mistaken as thousand	Use million
M or K	Thousand	Mistaken as million. M has been used to abbreviate both million and thousand (M is the Roman numeral for thousand)	Use thousand
Ng or ng	Nanogram	Mistaken as mg. Mistaken as nasogastric	Use nanogram or nanog
U or u**	Unit(s)	Mistaken as zero or the number 4, causing a 10-fold overdose or greater (e.g., 4U seen as 40 or 4u seen as 44). Mistaken as cc, leading to administering volume instead of units (e.g., 4u seen as 4cc)	Use unit(s)
µg	Microgram	Mistaken as mg	Use mcg

Abbreviations for Route of Administration			
Abbreviation	**Intended Meaning**	**Misinterpretation**	**Best Practice**
AD, AS, AU	Right ear, left ear, each ear	Mistaken as OD, OS, OU (right eye, left eye, each eye)	Use right ear, left ear, or each ear
IN	Intranasal	Mistaken as IM or IV	Use NAS (all UPPERCASE letters) or intranasal
IT	Intrathecal	Mistaken as intratracheal, intratumor, intratympanic, or	Use intrathecal

Dispensing Process

Abbreviations for Route of Administration			
Abbreviation	Intended Meaning	Misinterpretation	Best Practice
		inhalation therapy	
OD, OS, OU	Right eye, left eye, each eye	Mistaken as AD, AS, AU (right ear, left ear, each ear)	Use right eye, left eye, or each eye
Per os	By mouth, orally	The os was mistaken as left eye (OS, oculus sinister)	Use PO, by mouth, or orally
SC, SQ, sq, or sub q	Subcutaneous(ly)	SC and sc mistaken as SL or sl (sublingual) SQ mistaken as "5 every" The q in sub q has been mistaken as "every"	Use SUBQ (all UPPERCASE letters, without spaces or periods between letters) or subcutaneous(ly)

Abbreviations for Frequency/Instructions for Use			
Abbreviation	Intended Meaning	Misinterpretation	Best Practice
HS	Half-strength	Mistaken as bedtime	Use half-strength
Hs	At bedtime, hours of sleep	Mistaken as half-strength	Use HS (all UPPERCASE letters) for bedtime
o.d. or OD	Once daily	Mistaken as right eye (OD, oculus dexter), leading to oral liquid medications administered in the eye	Use daily
Q.D., QD, q.d., or qd**	Every day	Mistaken as QID, especially if the period after the q or the tail of a handwritten q is misunderstood as the letter i	Use daily
Qhs	Nightly at bedtime	Mistaken as qhr (every hour)	Use nightly or HS for bedtime
Qn	Nightly or at bedtime	Mistaken as qh (every hour)	Use nightly or HS for bedtime
Q.O.D., QOD, q.o.d., or qod**	Every other day	Mistaken as qd (daily) or QID (four times daily), especially if the "o" is poorly written	Use every other day
q1d	Daily	Mistaken as QID (four times daily)	Use daily
q6PM, etc.	Every evening at 6 PM	Mistaken as every 6 hours	Use daily at 6 PM or 6 PM daily
SSRI SSI	Sliding scale regular insulin Sliding scale insulin	Mistaken as selective-serotonin reuptake inhibitor Mistaken as Strong Solution of Iodine (Lugol's)	Use sliding scale (insulin)
TIW or tiw	3 times a week	Mistaken as 3 times a day or twice in a week	Use 3 times weekly

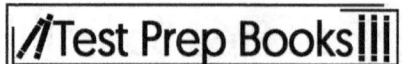

Abbreviations for Frequency/Instructions for Use			
Abbreviation	Intended Meaning	Misinterpretation	Best Practice
BIW or biw	2 times a week	Mistaken as 2 times a day	Use 2 times weekly
UD	As directed (ut dictum)	Mistaken as unit dose (e.g., an order for "dilTIAZem infusion UD" was mistakenly administered as a unit [bolus] dose)	Use as directed

Miscellaneous Abbreviations Associated with Medication Use			
Abbreviation	Intended Meaning	Misinterpretation	Best Practice
BBA BGB	Baby boy A (twin) Baby girl B (twin)	B in BBA mistaken as twin B rather than gender (boy) B at end of BGB mistaken as gender (boy) not twin B	When assigning identifiers to newborns, use the mother's last name, the baby's gender (boy or girl), and a distinguishing identifier for all multiples (e.g., Smith girl A, Smith girl B)
D/C	Discharge or discontinue	Premature discontinuation of medications when D/C (intended to mean discharge) on a medication list was misinterpreted as discontinued	Use discharge and discontinue or stop
IJ	Injection	Mistaken as IV or intrajugular	Use injection
OJ	Orange juice	Mistaken as OD or OS (right or left eye); drugs meant to be diluted in orange juice may be given in the eye	Use orange juice
Period following abbreviations (e.g., mg., mL.)†	mg or mL	Unnecessary period mistaken as the number 1, especially if written poorly	Use mg, mL, etc., without a terminal period

Dispensing Process

Drug Name Abbreviations

To prevent confusion, avoid abbreviating drug names entirely. Exceptions may be made for multi-ingredient drug formulations, including vitamins, when there are electronic drug name field space constraints; however, drug name abbreviations should NEVER be used for any medications on the *ISMP List of High-Alert Medications* (in acute care settings, community/ambulatory settings, and long-term care settings). Examples of drug name abbreviations involved in serious medication errors include:

Abbreviation	Intended Meaning	Misinterpretation	Best Practice
Antiretroviral medications (e.g., DOR, TAF, TDF)	DOR: doravirine TAF: tenofovir alafenamide TDF: tenofovir disoproxil fumarate	DOR: Dovato® (dolutegravir and lamiVUDine) TAF: tenofovir disoproxil fumarate TDF: tenofovir alafenamide	Use complete drug names
APAP	Acetaminophen	Not recognized as acetaminophen	Use complete drug name
ARA A	Vidarabine	Mistaken as cytarabine ("ARA C")	Use complete drug name
AT II and AT III	AT II: angiotensin II (Giapreza®) AT III: antithrombin III (Thrombate III®)	AT II (angiotensin II) mistaken as AT III (antithrombin III) AT III (antithrombin III) mistaken as AT II (angiotensin II)	Use complete drug name
AZT	Zidovudine (Retrovir)	Mistaken as azithromycin, azaTHIOprine, or aztreonam	Use complete drug name
CPZ	Compazine (prochlorperazine)	Mistaken as chlorpromazine	Use complete drug name
DTO	Diluted tincture of opium or deodorized tincture of opium (Paregoric)	Mistaken as tincture of opium	Use complete drug name
HCT	Hydrocortisone	Mistaken as hydrochlorothiazide	Use complete drug name
HCTZ	HydroCHLOROthiazide	Mistaken as hydrocortisone (e.g., seen as HCT250 mg)	Use complete drug name
MgSO4**	Magnesium sulfate	Mistaken as morphine sulfate	Use complete drug name
MS, MSO4**	Morphine sulfate	Mistaken as magnesium sulfate	Use complete drug name
MTX	Methotrexate	Mistaken as mitoXANTRONE	Use complete drug name
Na at the beginning of a drug name (e.g., Na bicarbonate)	Sodium bicarbonate	Mistaken as no bicarbonate	Use complete drug name
NoAC	Novel/new oral anticoagulant	Mistaken as no anticoagulant	Use complete drug name
OXY	Oxytocin	Mistaken as oxyCODONE,	Use complete drug

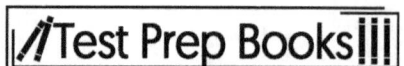

Dispensing Process

Drug Name Abbreviations

To prevent confusion, avoid abbreviating drug names entirely. Exceptions may be made for multi-ingredient drug formulations, including vitamins, when there are electronic drug name field space constraints; however, drug name abbreviations should NEVER be used for any medications on the *ISMP List of High-Alert Medications* (in acute care settings, community/ambulatory settings, and long-term care settings). Examples of drug name abbreviations involved in serious medication errors include:

Abbreviation	Intended Meaning	Misinterpretation	Best Practice
		Oxy**CONTIN**	name
PCA	Procainamide	Mistaken as patient-controlled analgesia	Use complete drug name
PIT	Pitocin (oxytocin)	Mistaken as Pitressin®, a discontinued brand of vasopressin still referred to as PIT	Use complete drug name
PNV	Prenatal vitamins	Mistaken as penicillin VK	Use complete drug name
PTU	Propylthiouracil	Mistaken as Purinethol® (mercaptopurine)	Use complete drug name
T3	Tylenol with codeine No. 3	Mistaken as liothyronine, which is sometimes referred to as T3	Use complete drug name
TAC or tac	Triamcinolone or tacrolimus	Mistaken as tetracaine, Adrenalin, and cocaine; or as Taxotere, Adriamycin, and cyclophosphamide	Use complete drug name Avoid drug regimen or protocol acronyms that may have a dual meaning or may be confused with other common acronyms, even if defined in an order set
TNK	TNKase	Mistaken as TPA	Use complete drug name
TPA or tPA	Tissue plasminogen activator, Activase (alteplase)	Mistaken as TNK (TNKase, tenecteplase), TXA (tranexamic acid), or less often as another tissue plasminogen activator, Retavase® (reteplase)	Use complete drug name
TXA	Tranexamic acid	Mistaken as TPA (tissue plasminogen activator)	Use complete drug name
ZnSO4	Zinc sulfate	Mistaken as morphine sulfate	Use complete drug name

Dispensing Process

\multicolumn{4}{c}{Stemmed/Coined Drug Names}
Abbreviation/Drug Name	Intended Meaning	Misinterpretation	Best Practice
Nitro drip	Nitroglycerin infusion	Mistaken as nitroprusside infusion	Use complete drug name
IV vanc	Intravenous vancomycin	Mistaken as Invanz®	Use complete drug name
Levo	Levofloxacin	Mistaken as Levophed® (norepinephrine)	Use complete drug name
Neo	Neo-Synephrine, a well-known but discontinued brand of phenylephrine	Mistaken as neostigmine	Use complete drug name
Coined names for compounded products (e.g., magic mouthwash, banana bag, GI cocktail, half and half, pink lady)	Specific ingredients compounded together	Mistaken ingredients	Use complete drug/product names for all ingredients. Coined names for compounded products should only be used if the contents are standardized and readily available for reference to prescribers, pharmacists, and nurses
Number embedded in drug name (not part of the official name) (e.g., 5-fluorouracil, 6-mercaptopurine)	Fluorouracil Mercaptopurine	Embedded number mistaken as the dose or number of tablets/capsules to be administered	Use complete drug names, without an embedded number if the number is not part of the official drug name

\multicolumn{4}{c}{Dose Designations and Other Information}
Abbreviation	Intended Meaning	Misinterpretation	Best Practice
1/2 tablet	Half tablet	1 or 2 tablets	Use text (half tablet) or reduced font-size fractions (½ tablet)
Doses expressed as Roman numerals (e.g., V)	5	Mistaken as the designated letter (e.g., the letter V) or the wrong numeral (e.g., 10 instead of 5)	Use only Arabic numerals (e.g., 1, 2, 3) to express doses
Lack of a leading zero before a decimal point	0.5 mg	Mistaken as 5 mg if the decimal point is not seen	Use a leading zero before a decimal point when the dose is less

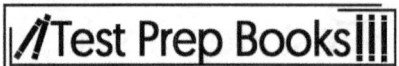

Dispensing Process

Dose Designations and Other Information			
Abbreviation	Intended Meaning	Misinterpretation	Best Practice
(e.g., .5 mg)**			than one measurement unit
Trailing zero after a decimal point (e.g., 1.0 mg)**	1 mg	Mistaken as 10 mg if the decimal point is not seen	Do not use trailing zeros for doses expressed in whole numbers
Ratio expression of a strength of a single-entity injectable drug product (e.g., **EPINEPH**rine 1:1,000; 1:10,000; 1:100,000)	1:1,000: contains 1 mg/mL 1:10,000: contains 0.1 mg/mL 1:100,000: contains 0.01 mg/mL	Mistaken as the wrong strength	Express the strength in terms of quantity per total volume (e.g., **EPINEPH**rine 1 mg per 10 mL) **Exception:** combination local anesthetics (e.g., lidocaine 1% and **EPINEPH**rine 1:100,000)
Drug name and dose run together (problematic for drug names that end in the letter l [e.g., propranolol20 mg; **TEG**retol300 mg])	propranolol 20 mg **TEG**retol® 300 mg	Mistaken as propranolol 120 mg Mistaken as **TEG**retol 1300 mg	Place adequate space between the drug name, dose, and unit of measure
Numerical dose and unit of measure run together (e.g., 10mg, 10Units)	10 mg 10 mL	The m in mg, or U in Units, has been mistaken as one or two zeros when flush against the dose (e.g., 10mg, 10Units), risking a 10- to 100-fold overdose	Place adequate space between the dose and unit of measure
Large doses without properly placed commas (e.g., 100000 units; 1000000 units)	100,000 units 1,000,000 units	100000 has been mistaken as 10,000 or 1,000,000 1000000 has been mistaken as 100,000	Use commas for dosing units at or above 1,000 or use words such as 100 thousand or 1 million to improve readability **Note:** Use commas to separate digits only in the US; commas are used in place of decimal points in some other countries

Symbols

Abbreviation	Intended Meaning	Misinterpretation	Best Practice
ʒ or ₥†	Dram / Minim	Symbol for dram mistaken as the number 3 / Symbol for minim mistaken as mL	Use the metric system
x1	Administer once	Administer for 1 day	Use explicit words (e.g., for 1 dose)
> and <	More than and less than	Mistaken as opposite of intended / Mistakenly have used the incorrect symbol / < mistaken as the number 4 when handwritten (e.g., <10 misread as 40)	Use more than or less than
↑ and ↓†	Increase and decrease	Mistaken as opposite of intended / Mistakenly have used the incorrect symbol / ↑ mistaken as the letter T, leading to misinterpretation as the start of a drug name, or mistaken as the numbers 4 or 7	Use increase and decrease
/ (slash mark)†	Separates two doses or indicates per	Mistaken as the number 1 (e.g., 25 units/10 units misread as 25 units and 110 units)	Use per rather than a slash mark to separate doses
@†	At	Mistaken as the number 2	Use at
&†	And	Mistaken as the number 2	Use and
+†	Plus or and	Mistaken as the number 4	Use plus, and, or in addition to
°	Hour	Mistaken as a zero (e.g., q2° seen as q20)	Use hr, h, or hour
Φ or ∅†	Zero, null sign	Mistaken as the numbers 4, 6, 8, and 9	Use 0 or zero, or describe intent using whole words
#	Pound(s)	Mistaken as a number sign	Use the metric system (kg or g) rather than pounds. Use lb if referring to pounds

Apothecary or Household Abbreviations			
Explicit apothecary or household measurements may **ONLY** be safely used to express the directions for mixing dry ingredients to prepare topical products (e.g., dissolve 2 capfuls of granules per gallon of warm water to prepare a magnesium sulfate soaking aid). Otherwise, metric system measurements should be used.			
Abbreviation	Intended Meaning	Misinterpretation	Best Practice
gr	Grain(s)	Mistaken as gram	Use the metric system (e.g., mcg, g)
dr	Dram(s)	Mistaken as doctor	Use the metric system (e.g., mL)
min	Minim(s)	Mistaken as minutes	Use the metric system (e.g., mL)
oz	Ounce(s)	Mistaken as zero or 02	Use the metric system (e.g., mL)
tsp	Teaspoon(s)	Mistaken as tablespoon(s)	Use the metric system (e.g., mL)
tbsp or Tbsp	Tablespoon(s)	Mistaken as teaspoon(s)	Use the metric system (e.g., mL)

Common Abbreviations with Contradictory Meanings		
Abbreviation	Contradictory Meanings	Best Practice
B	Breast, brain, or bladder	Use breast, brain, or bladder
C	Cerebral, coronary, or carotid	Use cerebral, coronary, or carotid
D or d	Day or dose (e.g., parameter-based dosing formulas using D or d [mg/kg/d] could be interpreted as either day or dose [mg/kg/day or mg/kg/dose]; or x3d could be interpreted as either 3 days or 3 doses)	Use day or dose
H	Hand or hip	Use hand or hip
I	Impaired or improvement	Use impaired or improvement
L	Liver or lung	Use liver or lung
N	No or normal	Use no or normal
P	Pancreas, prostate, preeclampsia, or psychosis	Use pancreas, prostate, preeclampsia, or psychosis
S	Special or standard	Use special or standard
SS or ss	Single strength, sliding scale (insulin), signs and symptoms, or ½ (apothecary) SS has also been mistaken as the number 55	Use single strength, sliding scale, signs and symptoms, or one-half or ½

** On The Joint Commission's **"Do Not Use"** list
† Relevant mostly in handwritten medication information

Processing Prescription Orders

Types and Formats of Prescription and Medication Orders

There are a variety of methods by which prescription orders can be relayed to the pharmacy. While most methods are suitable for non-controlled medications, some methods are prohibited for controlled medications. Regardless of the method of communication, all prescription orders must include the patient's name and date of birth, provider's name, date, medication name, dose, frequency, route of administration, and directions for use. See below for the types of communication methods that are utilized, information that needs to be specifically documented, and when each method can and cannot be used:

- Telephone: This can be utilized for non-controlled and controlled (CIII-V) medications, however the prescriber's DEA number and the patient's address must also be documented. Schedule II medications cannot be prescribed via this method.

- Fax/Facsimile: This method is utilized less frequently today, but it can be utilized to prescribe all medications including CII.

- Electronic: This is a preferred system for all prescribed medications.

- Computerized physician order entry: This is a preferred system for all prescribed medications.

- Written: This is the most commonly used method for prescription ordering. It can be used for all medication classes but can also be associated with the most errors as handwriting may be difficult to read.

Providers with Prescribing Authority

It is the pharmacist's responsibility to verify all prescription orders that are being processed including proper documentation, clear instructions, and provider-specific information. This also includes verifying that the prescribed medication is within the prescriber's scope of practice. For example, a veterinarian cannot prescribe medications for humans. It's important to note that all prescribers can utilize all methods of communication for ordering prescriptions.

Patient Profile Components

The patient profile must stay updated within the pharmacy and provider's office, especially since it is utilized every time a prescription order is processed. It is particularly important to have the patient's current address, since it is required for a controlled prescription order and needs to match the patient's profile; the patient's allergy information (to verify the drug will not produce any adverse effects); and their insurance details so the order can be properly paid for.

Types of Formularies

Formularies are utilized by various insurance companies to inform patients and healthcare professionals what medications are covered or how to get certain medications covered. When processing prescriptions, most pharmacies utilize an electronic system that will provide immediate feedback on whether a prescription is covered. It is important to know the types of formularies so the pharmacy team can inform the patient and provider about next steps if the medication is not covered:

- Open formulary: Not often used because it states that the payer, or insurance company, will pay for all prescriptions unless they are used for cosmetic purposes or can be purchased over the counter.

- Closed formulary: A specific set of medications are covered, and if a medication is not on the formulary, the patient or provider will not be reimbursed if the drug is purchased.

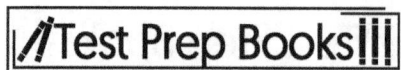

Drug Utilization Reviews

Drug utilization review (DUR) is a verification step utilized by pharmacies, providers, and insurance companies to help prevent medication errors. In the pharmacy, DURs are utilized when processing all prescriptions. If an error occurs, the prescription process cannot continue until it's been resolved. Examples of DURs include:

- Therapeutic duplication: In most cases, a patient should not have an active prescription for two medications within the same class, like two statin medications used for lowering cholesterol. The only way to continue is to verify with the provider which statin the patient should be on and then to make inactive the incorrect order while informing the patient of the change.

- Drug allergy: If a patient has a known penicillin drug allergy and an order comes through to process a prescription for amoxicillin-clavulanate, a DUR will appear and will either require the medication to be changed or the patient profile to be updated (in the case that the allergy was entered incorrectly).

- Drug-drug interactions: This is a common DUR and is critical in catching errors for patients who take numerous medications. One example would be having an active prescription for both an anti-diarrheal and a diarrheal medication.

- Abuse: There are retrospective DURs that help providers and pharmacists become aware of a potential abuse situation by determining if the patient has filled the highly addictive medication recently, at different pharmacies, or more than a certain number of times in the last year.

Processing Prescription Refill Authorization Requests from Prescribers

Providers with Prescribing Authority

All providers are authorized to include refills on their prescription orders if deemed appropriate, depending on the medication class. However, if no refills are intended or only a certain number of refills are allowed within a set amount of time, the prescriber must indicate that on the prescription.

Allowable Refills Based on Prescription Drug Type and Drug Class

The number of allowable refills is set by the federal government and cannot be changed depending on the state:

- Non-Controlled Prescriptions: These can technically have an unlimited number of refills. However, non-controlled medication orders are only valid for one year, so most 30-day prescription orders have twelve refills to provide a one-year supply.

- Controlled III-V Prescriptions: These medications can have a maximum of five refills and cannot be refilled more than six months after the date the prescription was written. This means a thirty-day tramadol prescription order can be filled six times in total or a ninety-day order filled two times in total.

- Controlled II Prescription: No refills are allowed, and a new prescription must be written each time. However, the prescription can be written for either a thirty-day or ninety-day supply.

Obtaining Information for Patient Profiles from Patients

Patient Profile Components

Demographics

Adding information to a patient's demographics is important for medication and disease-related decisions, and the information should be as accurate and detailed as possible. This includes all non-clinical information like their full name, date of birth, current address, contact information (phone number, email, fax number, etc.), age, biological sex, ethnicity, and insurance information. It can also include patient occupation, marital status, etc. This information can be used to verify that the correct patient has been selected when processing a prescription order.

Patient's Medical History

To prevent possible adverse effects with medications, the following information should be included in a patient's medical history:

- All prescription medications, OTC drugs, and dietary supplements taken by the patient
- Chronic and acute medical conditions
- Patterns of prescription compliance
- Allergies to substances, medications, and foods
- Possible interactions that have previously occurred (drug-drug, drug-food, drug-disease etc.)

With access to a patient's medical history, the pharmacist can determine whether there are any risks to the patient. Certain medications may be contraindicated with particular medical conditions or health concerns. Allergies or prior adverse reactions to one medication may also indicate an allergy risk with other medications in the same class. A complete medical history helps the pharmacist prevent drug interactions and serious clinical consequences.

Components Required to Process a Third-Party Claim

When a patient has insurance, key components on their insurance card are utilized or required to process the medication order through the insurance company:

- BIN: The Bank Identification Number is the number that identifies the provider themselves and does not involve a financial institution. Examples include United Healthcare, Aetna, and Blue Cross Blue Shield. These will all have a specific number that identifies them and differentiates them from other companies.

- PCN: The Processor Control Number identifies the specific pharmacy benefit manager associated with the patient's insurance company and is often known as a secondary identifier number. Within each insurance company, a patient can choose from various plans that are associated with a specific pharmacy benefit manager, and the PCN helps make sure that the right plan is utilized when processing the prescription in order to determine copays, formulary coverage, etc.

- Group: Most patients have insurance coverage through an employer, and the group number is specific to that employer. The employers are also capable of picking specific plans, coverages, and prices for the employee's insurance.

- Person code: The person code is not always consistent but can have connotations such as 01 (primary card holder), 02 (spouse), and 03–09 (dependents).

Types of Coverage

Various types of medical coverage are offered to patients depending on work status, age, and other factors. Depending on this coverage, the cost of a medication can also vary for the patient. The types of coverage are as follows:

- Medicare: Medicare is a federally run program offered to those who are older than 65, those who are younger than 65 and disabled, and anyone with end-stage renal disease.

- Medicaid: Medicaid is a state-funded program that is not offered in all states and has different requirements and coverages within each available state. Coverage can cover all persons over the age of 18 who earn under a set income, like in California, or can cover only low-income children/families, seniors, or disabled persons.

- Workers' Compensation: If a patient is injured at work, their employer may offer workers' compensation to help cover the medical costs. Considerable documentation must be included on the prescription, including ICD codes (diagnosis codes) and the fact that the order is related to a workers' compensation claim.

- HMO/PPO: A Health Maintenance Organization plan is a stricter insurance plan that only allows the patient to see a specific set of providers. However, they often are less expensive plans compared to a PPO, or Preferred Provider Organization plan, which allows more flexibility in utilizing various providers, including those that are out-of-network.

- Patient assistance programs: Various programs are offered for patients who don't have insurance or whose treatment is not covered under their plan. These programs can be sourced from pharmaceutical or insurance companies, government agencies, and non-profit organizations. They can be utilized to cover the entire cost of the medication or a portion of the cost, and they can be used multiple times or only once.

Entering and Maintaining Electronic Patient Profiles

In the pharmacy, it is good practice to keep a patient profile updated regarding demographic information, such as the patient's address, and clinical information, such as allergies, recent drug adverse events, and an updated medication list. Medication reconciliation is an important responsibility of the pharmacist and includes verifying all active and inactive medications for the patient. This helps prevent future DUR rejections, confusion, and other unwanted effects. Each pharmacy will have a specific program for entering prescriptions and patient information, and new pharmacists or pharmacy technicians will be trained to use it. In busier situations, performing a full medication reconciliation may not be plausible, but in most cases, the prescription will also contain new and updated information that should be entered into the pharmacy system immediately. For example, if a new medication for a newly diagnosed disease state is ordered for a patient who has a new address, the pharmacist or pharmacy technician should make sure to enter the new address and then the new disease state in the patient's history of acute and chronic conditions.

Identifying and Inputting Third-Party Payer Identifier Numbers

Components Required to Process a Third-Party Claim

A typical prescription insurance card will have the BIN, PCN, group number, and ID number clearly listed out for easy interpretation and will look something like the card below. Prescription savings programs will also have cards with a similar layout so the identification process is easy for the pharmacy team.

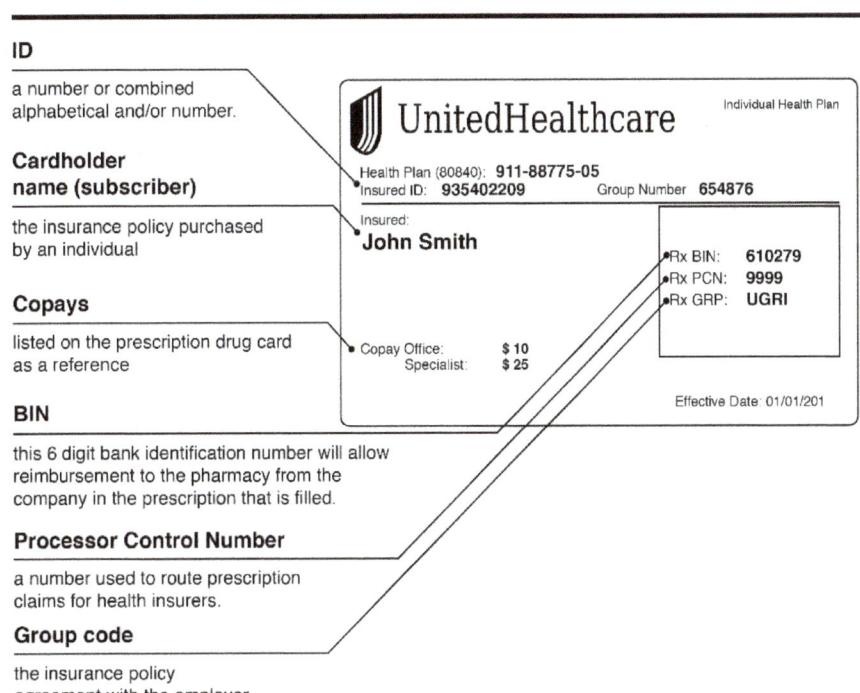

Coordination of Benefits

When the patient's profile is updated, some pharmacy systems can search for active insurance coverage. If more than one insurance company pops up, it's important to reach out to the patient and ask them which insurance is their primary insurance and which is their secondary insurance so that claims can be processed for the primary plan first and then the secondary insurance plan can be processed for the remaining amount due.

Types of Coverage

Medicare part D patients, Medicaid patients, and patients with an HMO/PPO plan will each have a specific prescription card that will have all the same information as a private insurance card, including BIN, PCN, group, and ID numbers. Workers' compensation claims will have unique ID, BIN, PCN, and group numbers that will be provided to the patient and will need to be indicated in the pharmacy system as a workers' compensation plan. When a patient signs up for a patient assistance program, they will also have a unique set of numbers. If the program allows multiple uses, patients may bring the pharmacy a different set of numbers each time, which means that it's important for pharmacy technicians to delete the old numbers as the new ones come in.

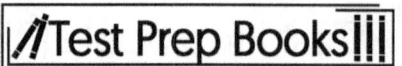

Processing Third-Party Prescriptions

Components Required to Process a Third-Party Claim

When processing third party prescriptions, the only way to process the claim correctly under the patient's plan is to input the proper components of their insurance such as BIN, PCN, group number, and person code. It is possible to utilize either BIN or PCN when finding the initial plan in the system, but all the information should be input correctly and then verified. If a patient hands over a card that does not have a BIN or PCN number, this typically indicates that the card is only for medical office use and that they should have received a separate prescription card with the proper information required for processing prescriptions.

Coordination of Benefits

Coordination of benefits is important when processing prescriptions because things need to be done in a specific order to allow the patient to pay the minimal cost for the prescriptions or medical services. However, in the pharmacy it may not be obvious which insurance should be billed first. Therefore, if two active insurances are in the patient profile, it is best practice to contact the patient to verify which insurance is the primary plan and which is the secondary plan. Some rejections may state *bill primary first*, which indicates to the pharmacy team that the claim must be processed under the other insurance first or that the patient should be contacted to get the other plan's information.

Types of Formularies

When it comes to processing prescriptions, it's impossible to know the formularies for all the insurance plans. The electronic pharmacy system is built for "real-time claims" to help determine whether there needs to be a change in medications or if everything is covered. Open formularies typically won't have any problems because they cover most medications. Most issues arise with closed formularies when processing prescriptions, and these can be resolved without intervention or with patient or provider intervention.

Types of Third-Party Rejections

Most pharmacies have real-time databases that allow them to process prescriptions and find out immediately whether the insurance covers them. If the insurance does not reject the medication, then it is covered and does not need any alteration. However, insurances can reject the medication for a variety of reasons, including duplicate therapy (such as two cholesterol drugs within the same drug class), high dose (more than what is clinically approved), required prior authorization (the insurance just needs more information from the prescriber as to why this specific drug or equipment was prescribed), and incorrect diagnosis code (often required by Medicare).

Tiered Copays

Tiered copays often come in three categories, although some insurance companies use four or even five tiers. While the tier systems can vary from company to company, the following are examples of what might be included in each tier for the various types of tiered insurance plans.

In a three-tier system. Tier 1 includes all generic medications, Tier 2 includes brand name medications, and Tier 3 includes high-cost drugs. Under a four-tier system, Tier 1 usually includes only preferred generic drugs, although some systems may include both low-cost generic drugs and low-cost prescription drugs in this tier. Tier 2 includes more expensive, generally nonpreferred generic drugs as well as preferred brand name drugs, both of which have a higher cost than Tier 1 drugs. Tier 3 includes high-cost drugs, usually brand name and often with a cheaper generic version available. Tier 4 includes the most expensive drugs that are usually brand name and frequently known as specialty drugs. In a five-tier system, Tier 1 is preferred drugs, which are usually low-cost generics. Tier 2 includes drugs that are often generic and low cost but that are not preferred. Tier 3 includes both preferred brand name drugs and possibly some generic drugs that are higher cost than in the previous tiers. Tier 4 includes both nonpreferred brand-name drugs and the most expensive generic drugs. Tier 5 includes the most expensive drugs or specialty drugs.

Unless stated otherwise, most medication orders are for the generic version, but if a prescriber indicates *brand name only* for a high-cost medication, the insurance company may reject the prescription and require the prescriber to provide an explanation for why they chose a high-cost, brand-name medication rather than a cheaper, generic version.

Communicating About Prescription Coverage

Appropriate Responses to Electronic Alerts

A variety of electronic alerts can occur when processing prescriptions, and some may be able to be resolved without intervention from the provider or the patient, such as in situations where the insurance only covers a thirty-day supply rather than a ninety-day supply. However, some situations will require either provider or patient intervention, such as in the example of a non-covered medication. When this occurs, it's important to inform the patient about the situation and explain to them why the medication was not covered. This can be because the insurance requires step-therapy, meaning the provider must prescribe a different medication first and then if that medication fails, the insurance will cover the originally prescribed medication. In this scenario, the pharmacy team is responsible for informing the prescriber of the rejection and asking them to change the medication, but if the prescriber deems the original medication necessary, they can submit a prior authorization to get it covered for the patient. The patient should be informed in every step of this process so they know when they can expect to receive their medication.

Coordination of Benefits

In some cases, patients will have more than one insurance company, and when a prescription needs to be filled, the insurance companies have a specific preference for who pays first and who covers the remaining bill. This is known as the coordination of benefits. This system is for families that have two income-earning parents that have their own insurance that allows them to have nearly full coverage for medical and prescription costs.

Types of Third-Party Rejections

Most insurance companies need additional information or clarification from the pharmacy when processing prescriptions:

- Duplicate therapy: If the insurance company notices two active prescriptions for two medications in the same drug class, they will reject the prescription order and require the pharmacy to address the duplication, usually through inactivation of one of the orders. This can also occur if a patient filled the same medication prescription at two different pharmacies.

- High dose: For each medication, there is a maximum dose allowed for human consumption and these values are placed within the insurance company database to catch a potential error in prescription or prescriber entry. These rejections can be overridden, but it must be documented by the pharmacy after confirming with the prescriber that this dose was intended.

- Prior Authorization: Some medications are not covered and will require the prescriber to fill out a prior authorization form to inform the insurance company why that specific medication is required and not the one that the insurance company normally covers. The pharmacy will get this rejection and is responsible for relaying it to the prescriber's office.

- Missing diagnosis code: For Medicare patients, most prescriptions require an ICD-10 code that informs the insurance company what the indication for the prescriptions is. For example, in patients with diabetes, the ICD-10 code for diabetes mellitus without complication is E11.9.

Tiered Copays

Certain plans within the insurance company will have tiered copays for a patient that determine how much the patient will pay in certain situations. The situations can be in-network/PCP visits, out-of-network visits, ER/Urgent care visits, or specialist visits, and there are also tiered copays specific to medications. For example, under a three-tier system, Tier 1 would include generic drugs, Tier 2 would include brand-name drugs, and Tier 3 would include high-cost drugs.

Depending on insurance preference or previous patient medication history, there can be a rejection for a Tier 3 drug because certain Tier 1 and then Tier 2 medications must be tried first. Some insurance companies may also use four- or five-tier systems.

Types of Coverage

Medicare
Only patients with Medicare part D have prescription insurance and will have a specific prescription card indicating that. If the patient has a Medicare part A or B card, it's important to inform them that medications will not be covered, and they may need to utilize a prescription discount service, like GoodRx, or a patient assistance program.

Medicaid
Medicaid insurance is similar to private insurance companies in that the types of drugs covered and the cost will depend on the patient-specific plan.

Workers' Compensation
Workers' compensation will only cover medical and prescription expenses directly related to a specific workers' compensation claim, and patients and pharmacists may not submit an insurance claim for medications or expenses not directly related to the workers' compensation claim.

HMO/PPO
HMOs and PPOs can limit their coverage to specific pharmacies, and if there is a rejection for "pharmacy not covered," it's important to let the patient know that their medication is covered by the insurance, just not at the specific pharmacy. Depending on the medication class, the pharmacy can transfer the order to a covered pharmacy or have the prescriber send in a new order.

Patient Assistance Programs
It is important to let the patient know that patient assistance programs are not for patients who have insurance that covers the medication but who want the program to take care of the copay. These programs are essential for patients who are underinsured or don't have insurance, and the pharmacy staff is the best resource for these patients. It is also important to let patients know that coverage may be for one-time use and that there may be a lengthy process to sign-up for it.

Drug Utilization Reviews

In retail pharmacies, systems for DURs can pop-up when trying to check-out the patient's prescription, and they require pharmacist intervention before continuing. For example, if a medication strength was changed, the pharmacist may need to confirm with the patient that they are aware of the change and will properly discard the old prescription.

Translating Prescriber's Directions

Types and Formats of Prescription and Medication Orders

Over the phone, prescribers will not typically utilize SIG codes and would rather state all the directions fully. If they do use any form of shorthand, the pharmacists receiving the order may utilize SIG codes when writing it down but will need to put it into layman's terms when entering it into the computer. If a prescriber utilizes the fax machine or a written prescription, all information written on the prescription must be entered in without codes. For example, if a prescription states *for HTN*, that information is not just for the pharmacy but is also for the patient. Electronic and computerized methods for entry can help eliminate any handwriting misinterpretation but can still be written in code, so make sure to translate for the patient.

Allowable Refills Based on Prescription Drug Type and Drug Class

If a prescriber writes ten refills for a controlled medication, it's important to relay to the patient that the maximum number of refills for CIII-CV medications is five and that all remaining refills will be voided. Additionally, if a prescriber writes refills for a CII medication, the patient should be informed that there are no refills allowed for this class of drugs and that they will need a new order each time.

DAW Codes and Their Uses

As patients are not fluent in healthcare abbreviations, it's important for pharmacists and pharmacy technicians to translate the codes into something that they can understand. Listed below are the DAW codes and how a pharmacy staff member may relay their meanings to a patient:

- DAW 0: "The doctor is okay with you taking either the generic version of the medication or the brand-name version, and it does not matter which manufacturer it comes from."

- DAW 1: "The doctor would like you to only take the brand-name medication because it would work better for you."

- DAW 2: "Your doctor is okay with the generic or the brand-name medication, but you prefer the brand name, therefore we have to relay that to your insurance company."

- DAW 3: "The doctor and you are okay with both the generic or the brand-name version; however, as the pharmacist, we have to dispense the brand-name medication, and this code tells your insurance that we are doing that."

- DAW 4: "This tells your insurance that all of us (doctor, pharmacist, and patient) are okay with the generic version; however, the pharmacy only has the brand-name version in stock, and that is why we are dispensing it."

- DAW 5: "This code is for all situations where we have to dispense the brand-name medication for other situations not having to do with preference or stock."

- DAW 6: "This means the brand-name version was dispensed for undefined reasons; it is known as an all-purpose override code."

- DAW 7: "This means that all parties allow generic substitution, but the current state you live in requires that the pharmacy dispense the brand-name medication."

- DAW 8: "This means that all parties allow generic substitution; however, no generic exists currently, so the pharmacy must dispense the brand-name medication."

- DAW 9: "This code is used to override other insurance rejections not related to preference, stock, or law."

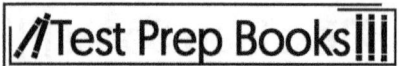

Interpreting Abbreviations

Purpose and Use of SIG Codes and Pharmacy Abbreviations

SIG codes are important to recognize and properly translate for accurate prescription entry, but there is also a list of SIG codes that are recommended to be avoided due to high potential in misreading. This can be found on the ISMP (Institute for Safe Medication Practices) website.

Examples of authorized SIG codes:

- BID: Twice a day
- TID: Three times a day
- QID: Four times a day
- PO: By mouth
- A.C: Before meals
- B.C: After meals
- QAM: Every morning
- TBSP: Tablespoon
- PRN: As needed

Institute for Safe Medication Practices Error-Prone Abbreviations List

Examples of error-prone SIG codes and what to use instead:

- cc is often used for cubic centimeters but is mistaken for u (units) and instead should be written as mL.

- AD refers to right ear, AS refers to left ear, and AU refers to both ears, but these are mistaken for OD (right eye), OS (left eye), and OU (both eyes), so instead they should just be written out.

- IT is often used for intrathecal but can be interpreted as intratracheal, intratumor, etc., and should instead just be written out.

- QD is often used to indicate that a medication is for daily use, but depending on the handwriting, it can be viewed as QID which means four times a day. So, it's best practice to write out daily or every day.

- IN refers to intranasal but can be mistaken as IM or IV and should be written out instead or written as NAS.

Entering Prescription Information into the Computer

When receiving a new prescription, whether written or via telephone, fax, or electronic methods, multiple pieces of information need to be entered into the computer correctly. The first step is finding the correct patient by searching for their name, date of birth, and address. This is why it's important to keep the patient's address updated. The second step is entering the prescription, starting with drug name, dose, instructions, indication (if listed), and ICD codes (if listed). When entering the instructions, make sure to spell out the full sentence if it was originally written in SIG code. For example, the prescription could say *1T BID PO x 14D*, but in the computer it should be written as *Take 1 tablet twice a day by mouth for 14 days*. Some computer systems can automatically translate SIG codes, and in those cases, the correct translation needs to be verified. The next step is processing the insurance information if it is not already in the computer. Lastly, process the prescriptions and check the system for any DURs or rejections.

Dispensing Process

Using Correct DAW Codes

DAW Codes and Their Uses

DAW (dispense as written) codes are written by the prescriber to inform the pharmacy whether the medication listed can be switched to a generic, but they are also utilized by the pharmacy to inform the insurance company why a medication brand was dispensed:

- DAW 0: This means that the provider has not indicated that the drug needs to be anything specific, and the pharmacy can choose any manufacturer that is in stock or preferred by the patient's insurance company.

- DAW 1: This means that substitution by the pharmacy is unauthorized per the prescriber. Most times, the prescription is written for the brand-name medication, and DAW 1 indicates that the pharmacy may not switch to the generic version. This can be for a variety of reasons including patient preference, allergies, etc.

- DAW 2: This means that the provider allows substitution, but the patient prefers the brand-name medication. This may or may not be covered by their insurance.

- DAW 3: This means that the provider and the patient allow substitution, but the pharmacist chooses the specific product dispensed.

- DAW 4: This means that substitution is allowed by all parties; however, the generic drug was not in stock, so the brand-name drug was dispensed.

- DAW 5: This means that for a reason not listed above, the brand-name medication was dispensed instead of the generic.

- DAW 6: This is for any override and can be used in various situations.

- DAW 7: This means that in some states, laws require the brand name to be dispensed for a certain indication.

- DAW 8: This means all parties allow substitution, but there is no substitution available, therefore the brand-name medication is dispensed.

- DAW 9: This is for all other situations not listed above.

Responding to Electronic Alerts While Processing a Prescription

Appropriate Responses to Electronic Alerts

Most electronic alerts within the pharmacy will require provider or patient intervention. For example, the pharmacy systems can alert for potential drug-drug interactions, high dose alerts, and drug-allergy interactions. When these alerts occur, it's important for the pharmacist to address the problem either by contacting the prescriber for verification or contacting the patient for things like confirming an allergy. It is important to follow through with provider and patient interaction during the process of resolving the alert so that the patient can get the correct medication therapy in a timely manner.

Types of Third-Party Rejections

Most third-party rejections will require prescriber intervention to resolve the alert, depending on what it is. For example, duplicate therapy alerts can be verified through the prescriber or the patient and can be resolved by a phone call to either party clarifying which medication should be active and which one should be inactive. High dose alerts will require a call to the provider to clarify whether it was intentional or a mistake. Prior authorization can only be completed by the prescriber, and then, once approved, they will let the pharmacy know to reprocess the claim. Diagnosis codes are often required for patients covered under Medicare, and they can be obtained easily through calling the prescriber office and getting the code that indicates the purpose of the prescription.

Drug Utilization Reviews and Drug Utilization Evaluations

Drug utilization reviews are a common electronic alert system utilized by pharmacies to catch potential drug or allergy interactions, high dose alerts, providers prescribing outside of their scope of practice (such as a veterinarian prescribing a medication for a human patient), and incorrect route of administration. This method helps pharmacists prevent liability issues and supports the patient care process.

DME Prescriptions

Coordination of Benefits

For patients who have both Medicare and a private insurance plan, it does not matter who pays first, there just needs to be a contractual agreement made between the two. This may be established without patient intervention or may need to be set up by the patient, and this information needs to be relayed to the pharmacy so the correct insurance is billed first. If the preferred insurance company is not billed first, then this can cause problems for the patient and possibly cost them more money. This is especially important when it comes to processing durable medical equipment (DME) claims because Medicare Part B is the portion that covers almost all DME, and they may need to process the claim through Medicare first in this case rather than the private insurance company to ensure that the DME is covered correctly.

Types of Coverage

Medicare is one of the best insurances when it comes to covering durable medical equipment because it covers a wide range of equipment such as blood sugar meters, crutches, walkers, nebulizers, and more. Medicare Part B is the specific plan that covers medically necessary durable medical equipment, whereas Medicare Part D is utilized to cover the medication costs. When processing a prescription for durable medical equipment, an insurance company that does not cover the equipment will notify the pharmacy, and the patient may need to be referred to specific DME suppliers. Workers' compensation claims cover all medical expenses related to the accident, and if the patient requires DME, then it should be covered. HMOs can vary on DME coverage and can be very specific to the plan and medical indication; however, the insurance may only cover DME from a specific supplier.

DME

Durable medical equipment (DME) is utilized by patients who may need daily or extended-use assistance, depending on their disease/condition, and it is defined as a medically necessary supply that has continuous use. DME includes oxygen equipment; mobility aids like wheelchairs, crutches, and walkers; meters for measuring blood sugar or blood pressure; and continuous glucose monitors used to show periodic blood sugar levels. Specific companies specialize in durable medical equipment supply, demonstration, and set up, and these may be the better option for patients who are just starting to require DME and need experts in the field to guide them in proper use. Some retail pharmacies carry basic durable medical equipment like crutches, blood pressure and blood sugar monitors, and continuous glucose monitors. These can be covered by the insurance, but they may require ICD-10 codes to process the claims, and the amount that can be purchased within a certain time interval may be limited. For example, blood pressure monitors may be covered by the insurance once every two years, or crutches may be covered once every five years. However, the prescriber can submit prior authorizations to get specific equipment covered.

Preparing and Dispensing Prescriptions

Dispensing Process

Proper product validation uses National Drug Codes (NDCs), barcode scanning, and visual inspection/verification. The pharmacy technician should make a habit of checking the NDC in the pharmacy management software system against the product being dispensed. The practice not only decreases pharmacy error but may also help avoid billing fraud. Many pharmacies use barcode scanning systems to provide another opportunity to reconcile the NDC in the computer with the one on the stock medication bottle containing the drug to be dispensed. Lastly, visual inspection is the oldest and most common form of verification. A registered pharmacist (RPh) traditionally carries out the validation, but some states allow pharmacy technicians to perform the task.

Visual inspection should verify the following:

- Accurate interpretation of the original prescription to the prescription label
- Accurate patient information on the product
- Appropriate packaging has been used
- Correct drug is being dispensed

After the medication has been filled and checked, it's ready for the patient to pick up. All new patients at a pharmacy should be given a copy of the **Health Insurance Portability and Accountability Act of 1996 (HIPAA)** notice of privacy practices. Pharmacy technicians must be sure to document the receipt of the notice by the patient. Per the **Omnibus Budget Reconciliation Act of 1990 (OBRA '90)**, the pharmacist is required to offer medication counseling. The pharmacy technician may also feel compelled to offer medication counseling. If a patient would like to see the pharmacist for medication counseling, the request should be noted in the pharmacy management software system. The pharmacist should make a valid attempt at providing privacy during patient counseling sessions, and this may be achieved through a simple privacy screen or a dedicated room.

Medications That Require Special Handling Procedures

When being prescribed, processed, and stored, certain medicines require additional oversight for reasons such as temperature and humidity considerations or a drug's abuse potential or extreme toxicity. Temperature-regulated medications and controlled substances require climate control and chain of custody, but these problems are solved with refrigeration and documentation. The prescription process for controlled substance is covered in another section, but certain nonprescription drugs can be diverted into illicit substance manufacturing, indicating the need for a new category of specially handled drugs.

CMEA

The Drug Enforcement Administration is responsible for ensuring pharmacies abide by the federal regulations covered in the **Combat Methamphetamine Epidemic Act (CMEA)**. Federal regulations state that all asthma and cold products containing the chemical ingredients ephedrine, pseudoephedrine, and phenylpropanolamine be kept secured behind the pharmacy counter or in a locked cabinet. The provisions in the CMEA restrict the total number of packages or grams a person can purchase of products containing these ingredients to 3.6 grams per day and no more than 9 grams in a thirty-day period. A purchaser must show a form of state or federal photo identification to purchase any product with the restricted chemical. The pharmacy is required to document the customer's name, address, date and time of sale, product name, quantity sold, and signature. The information from the sale of these products must be recorded electronically or in a physical logbook, and it must be readily accessible if requested by state or federal regulatory agencies.

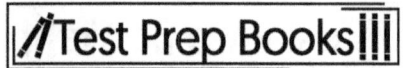

Dispensing Process

REMS Program

For medications with serious risks that may outweigh their benefits, the FDA may require a **Risk Evaluation and Mitigation Strategy (REMS)**. The FDA's evaluation of a medication to determine whether a REMS is necessary considers several factors including serious risks, potential and known adverse effects of the drug within the afflicted population, and the seriousness of the condition being treated. The FDA also considers the size of the population expected to use the medication, the expected duration of treatment, the beneficial expectation of the drug, as well as other factors. It is the responsibility of the drug manufacturer to develop and implement the REMS for their drugs. The iPledge program is an example of a REMS program for acne medications that contain isotretinoin. Isotretinoin is contraindicated in pregnancy and can cause serious birth defects. The REMS outlines the requirements of the prescriber, patient, and pharmacy to ensure safe and effective use. To obtain a prescription for isotretinoin, females who can bear children must register with the iPledge program and verify with a urine or blood test performed by a certified laboratory that they are not currently pregnant. The physician is required to counsel patients regarding the risks associated with the medication as well as document which two forms of contraception the patient is taking and enter the information into the iPledge system. Once the information is entered in iPledge, including the results of a second pregnancy test, the patient has seven days to obtain the medication from the pharmacy. The pharmacy must also register with iPledge to be able to verify that all patient requirements have been met. This requires entering the patient's iPledge ID and documenting the Risk Management Authorization (RMA) number on the prescription as well as the date it must be picked up by. If, however, the patient does not pick up the medication, then the RMA must be reversed in the iPledge system and the drug returned to stock.

Considerations for Handling Hazardous Drugs (USP <800>)

Most drugs that require special handling are explicitly hazardous and are regulated under federal code USP <800>. The FDA defines hazardous drugs as all non-radiotherapeutic drugs approved for human use and are considered to be a carcinogenic, developmental, reproductive, genotoxic, or otherwise toxic hazard. This essentially includes any FDA-approved non-nuclear drug that may induce cancer, harm the reproductive health of a parent or child, or cause organ failure at low doses. USP <800> also applies to any drug whose package insert specifies Manufacturer Special Handling Information (MSHI), which instructs workers on protective equipment to wear, precautions to be followed, safe handling procedures for storage and spillage of the material.

The National Institute for Occupational Safety and Health (NIOSH) has arranged hazardous drugs into two groups: those that are designated as carcinogenic or whose manufacturers specify MSHI, and those that do not. In this sense, *hazardous* refers to any drug that presents an occupational risk towards any worker or technician who may handle, prepare, or package the medication. Care must be taken to maximize safety and minimize exposure, especially among healthcare workers who are breastfeeding, pregnant, or able to conceive.

Personal protective equipment (PPE) is vital in protecting against accidental exposure when handling hazardous drugs. Personnel should use double chemotherapy gloves to handle all hazardous materials, except when counting or administering intact, coated tablets and capsules. A protective gown should be worn along with eye and face protection when handling liquids and powders. Masks and respiratory protection should be worn when working with hazardous substances that can aerosolize or form respiratory droplets.

Ventilation and mechanical engineering controls may also be used to avoid accidental inhalation events. Vented hoods like a Class II Biological Safety Cabinet (BSC) or a Compounding Aseptic Containment Isolator (CACI) are usually standard for compounding pharmacies and should be used when working with hazardous materials. For medication transport, a closed system drug-transfer device (CSTD) may be used to minimize the amount of time that the hazardous drug spends in contact with or in proximity to workers and passers-by.

Most antineoplastics and oncotherapeutics are hazardous since they directly interfere with normal cellular function and division, and their concentrated cytotoxicity tends to severely damage the organs that metabolize and excrete

Dispensing Process

them. As mentioned previously, some cancer medications require routine lab tests to ensure that the affected organ remains viable (e.g., an ECG for doxorubicin or audiograms and kidney function tests for cisplatin).

Antineoplastics in NIOSH's carcinogenic category (e.g., fluorouracil and topotecan) tend to interfere more directly with the transcription process, while hedgehog pathway inhibitors (e.g., vismodegib and EGFR-inhibitors like erlotinib) are less likely to cause cancer. Other medications included in NIOSH's carcinogenic category include chloramphenicol; dexrazoxane; estrogen-containing contraceptives; lenalidomide; thalidomide; the immunosuppressants azathioprine and cyclosporine; and the antiretrovirals cidofovir, ganciclovir, and valganciclovir.

Non-carcinogenic hazardous drugs generally fall into the following categories: hormones, hormone modulators, antiepileptics, and immunosuppressants. Some drugs do not fit easily into these categories (e.g., cabergoline, colchicine, dihydroergotamine, lomitapide, paroxetine, warfarin, and ziprasidone), but the majority are categorized in the table below. Not all immunosuppressants, antiretrovirals, BZDs, and azoles are hazardous, but they provide useful categories with which to group the medications.

Hormones	Antiepileptics	Antiretrovirals
medroxyprogesterone	carbamazepine	abacavir
methyltestosterone	divalproex	entecavir
oxytocin	eslicarbazepine	nevirapine
progesterone	fosphenytoin	zidovudine
testosterone	oxcarbazepine	**Retinoids**
Hormone Modulators	phenytoin	acitretin
cetrorelix	topiramate	alitretinoin
clomiphene	valproate	isotretinoin
dinoprostone	vigabatrin	tretinoin
exenatide	zonisamide	**Benzodiazepines**
ganirelix	**Immunosuppressants**	clobazam
liraglutide	leflunomide	clonazepam
methimazole	mycophenolate	temazepam
mifepristone	sirolimus	**Antifungals**
misoprostol	tacrolimus	fluconazole
nafarelin	teriflunomide	voriconazole
ospemifene	**Antihypertensives**	**Bisphosphonates**
pasireotide	ambrisentan	pamidronate
peginesatide	bosentan	zoledronate
plerixafor	dronedarone	**5α-reductase Inhibitors**
propylthiouracil	macitentan	dutasteride
raloxifene	riociguat	finasteride
spironolactone		

Automated Dispensing Machines

Role and Benefits in the Pharmacy

Automation of pharmacies has increased both pharmacy productivity and efficiency with fewer medication errors. Automation to improve these processes may include barcode scanners, automated filling cabinets (e.g., ScriptPro or Omnicell®), and electronic pill counters. **Barcodes** are used to detect a drug's dosage form and strength.

The following are advantages to using barcodes:

- Because the barcode is portable, it can be used during prescription filling and examining at any location. The handheld device scans the NDC number on the barcode of the patient's label or receipt and confirms it with the scanned NDC number of the barcode on the stock medication container from which the prescription was filled.
- The nurse can scan the barcode on the patient's wristband before administering a drug in a hospital. Directly after, the software compares information with the doctor's request to ensure that the correct drug and dosage were dispensed to the right patient at the right time.
- This system establishes greater relations with the patient and care provider.

The following are disadvantages to using barcodes:

- Not all drugs are linked or barcoded to the dose.
- Not every medicine has a barcode, as there are numerous dosage types.
- Installation of barcoding is costly.

In pharmacy practice, **robotics** encompasses a centralized system of using barcode technology. It contains a chain of computers working cohesively. In this system of conveyors, robots are capable of choosing drugs from a patient's file, as well as putting the medicine in the right drawer for the given patient.

Pharmacies are increasingly using drug distribution systems that rely on **automated dispensing systems**. These systems serve as storage, dispensing, and charging (as in retail) hubs in a pharmacy. Automated dispensing systems simplify inventory control tracking, save time, and reduce medication errors. These automated systems are commonly implemented in hospital pharmacies and may be either decentralized or centralized.

A **decentralized distribution system** is housed in patient care areas, which is supposed to reduce or eliminate system management issues, such as poor recordkeeping and diversion of narcotics. This is done by use of automated dispensing cabinets (ADCs) located in care units. Advantages of a decentralized system include the ability to document medication waste, dispense and return medications, and generate reports. Decentralized systems can also reduce the time it takes to receive ordered medications.

A **centralized distribution system** is used to improve the manual unit-dose cart filling process. With this system, medications are distributed from a central location, instead of from several dispensing systems. The pharmacy technician usually hand-delivers medications to the patient care units in a centralized system. The automated centralized systems help reduce errors in filling medication carts and may require less equipment and fewer staff to maintain it, due to having a single location. One disadvantage of centralized automated dispensing systems is the inability to stock all dosage forms of a medication.

Automated dispensing systems used in decentralized medication management include:

- **Pyxis MedStation™ system**: Barcode scanning ensures accurate dispensing of medications. Active alerts are also included to provide added safety precautions. It is considered one of the industry standards.
- **Cubie™ system**: Allows a nurse to access and remove only one medication at a time. The system reduces the risk of a nurse selecting a medication from the wrong pocket.
- **Pyxis™ anesthesia system**: Provides ease of access to medications needed by anesthesia practitioners by providing visibility to medication inventory. The system has biometric access and an array of drawer types.
- **Pyxis™ CII Safe**: Monitors and tracks the refilling of controlled substance inventory within a hospital.

Selecting Appropriate Medication Product

Prescription Interpretation

After intake, the pharmacy staff is obligated to understand and fill the patient's prescription. Prescription interpretation requires knowledge of medical abbreviations and may also require calculations to ensure that the proper quantity of medication is dispensed.

Prescription interpretation is ideal when the following elements are provided:

- Name, strength, dosage form, and quantity of medication to be dispensed
- Route of administration
- Frequency of administration
- Indication of whether a generic medication may be dispensed
- Number of refills: In the event that the prescriber does not indicate the number of refills, it is assumed that no refills will be permitted.
- If doubt exists when interpreting a particular prescription, a pharmacist should be asked to clarify.
- If the pharmacist cannot clarify, the prescriber should be contacted for clarification.

Expiration Dates

For many pharmaceutical drugs, stability studies are performed to validate the potency, efficacy, and safety of a drug. Stability studies involve products placed in controlled experimental conditions and followed by analytical laboratory testing to determine the expiration date of a drug. Some drugs are assigned a month or year expiration date, but drugs typically have a 12- to 60-month expiration date provided by the manufacturer.

Lot Numbers

To identify a product that has been manufactured, a lot number is assigned. A **lot number** helps track the product in the event of a recall. Lot numbers are usually assigned to a large batch of a product and placed on the retail packaging. This makes the product easier to track and trace back to its origin, even as it gets distributed nationwide.

NDC Number Components

The **Drug Listing Act of 1972** implemented the **National Drug Code** or **NDC** as a 10-digit number, which distinguishes each and every medication used by humans. When one breaks down the 10-digit NDC number, each segment correlates specifically to the drug as follows:

- The labeler code is the first segment and refers to the manufacturer who produced the drug.
- The product code is the second segment and refers to the drug's strength and dosage form.
- The packaging code is the third segment and refers to the package size and type.

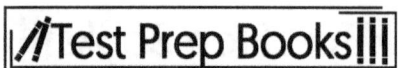

It is important to note that in order to avoid possible mix-ups and to prevent health hazards to patients, reassignment of an NDC number to a drug is prohibited.

Sample NDC Number

Labeler
Roerig

Product code
Zoloft
50mg

Package code
100 tablets

NDC 0049 - 4900 - 66

Distinction between Prescription (Legend), OTC, and BTC Medications

While many medications require a prescription from a healthcare provider in order to be dispensed to the patient, there are two other categories of mediations that can be purchased without a prescription. Some medications are available "**over the counter**," or **OTC**, without a prescription. OTC medications are still regulated by the FDA, as the manufacturing and sales of these medications are regulated under the Federal Food, Drug, and Cosmetic Act. There are some medications that are classified as OTC, yet, due to federal or local laws, require pharmacy staff to intervene with patients buying the medication. These are called "**behind the counter**," or **BTC**, medications, and the patient needs to sign a ledger before the sale can be completed. Examples include medications with pseudoephedrine.

It is important to cross-check the ingredients of OTC and BTC medications to prevent duplication of treatment, especially those intended to treat coughs, colds, and flu. Two medications that pose a risk for overdose are acetaminophen and dextromethorphan, which are commonly used in cough and cold preparations such as Theraflu and Nyquil. Moreover, OTC sleep aids often have identical ingredients to those found in antihistamines. It is, therefore, important to check the ingredients in OTC medications to prevent duplicate therapies. The pharmacist should help patients pick appropriate OTC and BTC medications and counsel them accordingly.

While some medications are either OTC or BTC or prescription-only, several are found both behind and over the counter. For some (e.g., acetaminophen, aspirin, and loratadine), there is not much difference between the OTC and prescription formulations. Others may be found in a different formulation or in an extended-release pill; for example, fluticasone is available OTC as a nasal spray (Flonase) and as a prescription-only oral inhaler (Flovent). Another example is prescription fluoride toothpastes which have a strength nearly five times as strong as those found OTC.

Many OTC and BTC medications have similar names and ingredients, and many are sold as combination products. Be aware of suffixes that indicate drugs like DM (dextromethorphan), PM (diphenhydramine), -D (pseudoephedrine), AC (codeine), and PE (phenylephrine). Additionally, be cognizant of the differences between the rapid-acting Rx-only

Humalog (insulin lispro) and Novolog (insulin aspart), the short-acting BTC Humulin-R and Novolin-R, and the intermediate-acting BTC Humulin and Novolin.

Before filling a prescription, take care to match the ordered drug name and strength with the information on the stock bottle and give special note to previously mentioned safety strategies that prevent simple mistakes (such as the tall man lettering found on sound-alike, look-alike drugs). Additionally, while most pharmacies require redundant barcode scans as fail safes, the NDC and lot number should be examined to ensure parity between the ordered drug and the stock bottle. Since each product section of the NDC is determined by each manufacturer independently, it is the least likely to be duplicated when comparing two random medications; therefore, it is best for a quick check. Both the manufacturer and package size sections of the NDC must also be correct to bill properly and to minimize errors.

Finally, each stock bottle should be examined to ensure that it has not passed the expiration date. Ideally, the lot number should also be checked against a list of recent recalls before filling a medication, but this is likely self-corrected through normal pharmacy workflow. The lot number should be recorded in certain situations (e.g., when marking the results of a point-of-care test, recording relevant data for an immunization, and filling out a compounded drug worksheet).

Counting, Measuring, and Pouring Medication into Appropriate Containers

Packaging Requirements

All medication leaving a pharmacy—whether inpatient or outpatient—must be packaged. Ideally, medication packaging should be sufficient enough to do the following:

- Protect against all adverse external environmental factors that could alter characteristics of a medication (e.g., light, moisture, temperature, and oxygen variables)
- Protect against physical/mechanical damage
- Protect against biological damage
- Provide identification and correct information for drugs

Types of raw materials used in medication packaging include cardboard, paper, glass, plastic, rubber, and metal (e.g., aluminum and stainless steel). The use of these raw materials generates a significant amount of waste. Methods of disposal of uncontaminated medication packaging include recycling, incineration (burning), and placement in landfills. Cardboard, paper, glass, and metal are best disposed via recycling. Plastics and rubber are best disposed via incineration.

In general, packaging should maintain the stability of the medication while furnishing needed safety to patients and others who have to access the medication (e.g., caregivers and nurses).

Light Resistance

Medication packaging must have adequate light resistance. Currently, there are more than 200 medications that are sensitive to light. For example, when nitroprusside is exposed to direct sunlight, it changes into cyanide (a poison). The chemical composition of other medications may be altered by exposure to direct sunlight. As a result, many medications are dispensed in amber-colored containers. Common light-sensitive medications include doxycycline (Vibramycin®), linezolid (Zyvox®), acetazolamide (Diamox®), and zolmitriptan (Zomig®).

Child Resistance

In clinical trials, the implementation of child-resistant packaging has proven effective in reducing child mortality from oral prescription-drug intoxication. The three most common child-resistant closures are the "squeeze-turn," the "push-turn," and a combination lock. Most medication containers that are considered child-resistant require two hands to open. This requirement may cause difficulty for elderly individuals.

Containers and Container Materials

Medication packaging requires many different types of containers. The following is a list of containers used in medication packaging:

- **Round vials** for capsules or tablets
- **Wide-mouth bottles** for bulk powders or large quantities of capsules, tablets, and high-viscosity (thick) liquids
- **Prescription bottles** for low-viscosity (thin) liquids
- **Applicator bottles** to apply liquid medications to the skin
- **Dropper bottles** for otic, ophthalmic, nasal, or oral liquids requiring administration by dropper
- **Hinged-lid** or **slide boxes** for dispensing powders or suppositories
- **Ointment jars** and **collapsible tubes** to dispense semi-solid medications

The following is a list of container classifications:

- **Tamper-evident packaging** refers to a sealed container with medication intended for ophthalmic or otic use—a broken seal is evidence of tampering.
- A **well-closed container** protects the medication from loss under normal conditions.
- A **light-resistant container** protects the medication from direct sunlight.
- A **tight container** prevents contamination by solids, liquids, or vapors.
- A **hermetic container** is unable to be penetrated by gas or air.
- A **single-dose container** refers to a single-unit container intended for parenteral (non-oral) administration.
- A **single-unit container** holds one dose of medication.
- A **unit-of-use container** holds a specific quantity of medication that's ready to be dispensed but not yet labeled.
- A **unit-dose container** is a single-dose container for which the intended use is other than parenteral.
- A **multiple-unit container** allows for multiple withdrawals of a medication without affecting the quality, strength, or purity of the remainder.
- A **multiple-dose container** is a multiple-unit container intended for parenteral administration.

Other vehicles for the packaging of pharmaceuticals may include:

- **Ampules**: Single-dose containers sealed by fusion that can only be opened by breaking
- **Bags**: Containers composed of flexible surfaces with closed bottoms and sides that can be sealed
- **Blisters**: Multi-dose containers composed of two layers, with one layer constructed to hold single doses
- **Bottles**: Container with a neck and a flat bottom

- **Cartridges**: Containers to hold solid or liquid dosage forms (e.g., prefilled syringes)
- **Gas cylinders**: Containers capable of holding compressed, dissolved, or liquefied gas, and outfitted to regulate the flow of gas
- **Injection needles**: Hollow needles with locking hubs intended to administer liquid dosage forms
- **Injection syringes**: Syringes with or without fixed needles and freely movable pistons
- **Pressurized containers**: Containers capable of holding compressed, dissolved, or liquefied gas, and outfitted to produce the spontaneous, controlled release of a gas
- **Strips**: Multi-dose containers composed of two layers with perforations that holds single doses of solid or semi-solid dosage forms
- **Tubes**: Multi-dose containers made of collapsible material for release of semi-solid dosage forms released through a nozzle when package is squeezed
- **Vials**: Single- and multi-dose containers for parenteral medications containing an overseal and stopper

In May 1992, the United States Food and Drug Administration specified 11 technologies capable of fulfilling the definition of tamper-evident packaging. The list encompasses blister and bubble packs, film wrappers, heat-shrunk wrappers or bands, bottles equipped with inner-mouth seals, plastic packs or paper foil, breakable cap-ring systems, sealed tubes, tape seals. plastic blind-end heat-sealed tubes, sealed cartons, all metal and composite cans, and aerosol containers.

A variety of plastics, including *polyvinyl chloride* (PVC), have been used in the last 50 years as materials for medication packaging. Plastics are an affordable option, keeping the majority of medications intact and uncontaminated. Plastics are unbreakable, light, and collapsible, which are significant advantages over glass. The main use of plastics is as material for bags for *parenteral solutions* (e.g., IV solutions).

Some medications may be able to bond with the PVC in containers, which may alter the structure and eventually harm the efficacy of a medication. In these scenarios, glass is a great alternative because it is *inert* (nonreactive). For example, sublingual nitroglycerin should not be exposed at length to traditional PVC medication containers. Many pharmacists will dispense this medication in glass vials.

Metal is also used as a raw material in medication packaging. Metal is strong, impervious to gases, and shatterproof. Metal may be included in the structure of tubes, cans, blister packs, and pressurized containers (e.g., gas and aerosol cylinders). Aluminum and stainless steel are the predominant metals used in medication packaging.

Keeping Medication in Original Packaging

For most medications, the original manufacturer's packaging suffices. In repackaging medications, pharmacy technicians should always be sure to consult the manufacturer's guidelines to determine whether light-resistant packaging is required.

Some medications are supplied in dose packs for easy distribution (as with Z-Paks or sumatriptan), for ease of use, or to provide administration instructions (as with Paxlovid, Tamiflu, Eliquis starter packs, Medrol Dosepaks, and most oral contraceptives). Others are reconstituted with distilled water in their original packaging (e.g., pediatric antibiotics and Quillivant), while others come as an ointment or cream in a tube or tub. Others like nitroglycerin are shipped in special amber glass bottles for photoprotection. In these cases, the original packaging is often used to reduce assembly time and prevent excess waste.

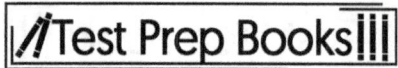

Some medications are sold in unit-size containers that are impossible to separate, such as ProAir Respiclick® and Advair Diskus inhalers. In this case, the medication's packaging cannot be broken, so the prescription must be filled in quantities of whole inhalers.

Some medications come in boxes of unit-dose forms (e.g., Lovenox syringes, NuvaRings, and single-dose lidocaine vials), while others are shipped in both single-dose packets and larger bottles (e.g., GlycoLax® and cholestyramine powder). Boxes of unit-dose packets may be sold as-is or repackaged if fewer packets are needed. Powder from multi-dose bottles should remain in the original packaging unless the pharmacy is equipped to measure and package precise amounts.

While some pharmacies prefer not to break down bottles of OTC medications like cetirizine or Senokot to simplify stock management, there are no legal stipulations that prevent a pharmacy from filling a prescription with the appropriate drug, regardless of whether the medication was manufactured with the intent of being sold OTC.

Some drug products are sensitive to ambient moisture or are particularly fragile, so they should be dispensed in their original containers per manufacturer guidance. This may include typical tablets and capsules (e.g., Effient®, NitroStat®, and Pradaxa), chewable and ODT medications (e.g., chewable montelukast, Nurtec® ODT, and Zofran ODT), liquids (e.g., Kaletra® and Trileptal), and injectables (e.g., Humira, Ozempic, and Repatha).

Handling Hazardous Drugs (USP <800>)

Counting tablets and handling medication bottles indicate minimal hazard, but technicians may incur a higher risk of accidental exposure when working with powders and liquids. Tasks such as compounding with powders, cutting or crushing tablets, admixing solutions for drips, and dealing with residue from bottles require extensive preparation and multiple steps and provide ample opportunities to aerosolize the drug and possibly inhale or absorb the drug via mucus membranes. The potential for dispersal and contamination of hazardous powders is the rationale against stocking hazardous drugs in dispensary units or using automated mechanical counters with them.

Some hazardous drugs and controlled substances are distributed in the containers intended for end users. These include the narcotics Belbuca®, Belsomra®, and Suboxone as well as the antiretroviral therapies Biktarvy®, Descovy®, and Truvada. These medications are particularly fragile and already come packaged in 30-day supplies, so it is typically unnecessary and inadvisable to repackage these products.

Selecting Appropriate Prescription Vials, Caps, Bottles, and Other Supplies

Administering certain medications may require specific medical equipment or supplies, including syringes, spacers, various diabetic supplies, alcohol swabs, and sharps containers. These additional supplies may be required for proper administration or use. For example, prescription sets for diabetic testing supplies should be processed by the same manufacturer, and quantities of testing strips and lancets should be double checked to ensure that the patient will have enough for the intended prescription lifetime. For nebulized medications like albuterol and budesonide solutions, patients must understand that these breathing treatments are not substitutes for rescue inhalers and that they require a special machine for use. Some prescriptions are written with the assumption that the patient already has the necessary nebulizer, tubing, and mask; sometimes, prescriptions can be unclear about which form was requested, so verifying the patient's expectations can help determine whether they need a nebulized medication or a handheld inhaler. Along with pediatric spacers for inhalers, nebulizer masks should fit the face correctly. These are sold in various sizes for the best administration and highest efficacy.

As previously discussed, the PPPA requires that prescription and OTC drugs be sold in child-resistant containers. However, there are several exceptions, including OTC products that contain instant-release powdered or effervescent aspirin, acetaminophen, and iron as well as prescription medications like sublingual nitroglycerin, instant-release isosorbide dinitrate, hormones including OCs and HRT, and extremely viscous hydrocarbon liquids.

Child-resistant caps may be removed per patient request, and many outpatient pharmacies dispense reversible caps to minimize inventory; however, the FDA discourages this because it increases the risk of accidental child poisoning. Patients may also ask for a duplicate labeled bottle for school or extracurricular purposes, which may be dispensed with a nonresistant cap if and only if the other bottle's cap is child-resistant.

Generally, oral liquids should be combined by starting with the most viscous ingredient with the largest quantity and then incorporating successive ingredients with agitation in between each addition to ensure proper mixing. To reduce spillage risk and allow for enough empty space to properly mix the liquids, choose a container that is comfortably larger than the recipe's total volume. Some automated dispensing systems, recipes, and protocols may instruct technicians to use certain vial or bottle sizes for convenience. These suggestions may be approximated through either averaged trials or technical equations based on the pill's dimensions and the container's dead space; however, these vary by manufacturer and are not standard.

Syringes

Pharmacies dispense two general types of syringes: oral/topical syringes and injectable syringes. **Oral/topical syringes** are perfect for precise dosing of oral or topical medications and have a safety feature that doesn't allow the attachment of needles. **Injectable syringes** are available in a wide assortment of sizes with numerous needle options. Historically, prescribers have been responsible for writing prescriptions for syringes and needles needed by patients. However, pharmacy staff may still have to determine the appropriate number of syringes and needles to dispense. In many states, patients are permitted to request syringes without prescriptions, although most insurance carriers don't cover syringes.

Several dimensions can describe syringes and needles: volume, needle length, and needle gauge. The syringe's volume refers to its maximum capacity; typical sizes are 0.3 mL, 0.5 mL, and 1.0 mL. The markings on insulin syringes' barrels may indicate units other than mL; this assumes a U-100 insulin and represents a conversion of 10 units to 0.1 mL. While there are specially marked syringes for use with U-500 insulin, there are no vial formulations of U-200 and U-300 insulins. The most common insulin syringe is of the U-100 variety.

The required needle length is heavily dependent on the medication's route of administration. Therefore, the length of all needles and syringes (regardless of BTC status) should be checked and directions given to the patient prior to sale. Insulin injections should be given subcutaneously, so these needles should be 1/2" or 5/8". Injections of medroxyprogesterone and testosterone should be given intramuscularly, so they require a longer needle length, preferably 1.5". Overweight patients may request 1" needles to inject insulin since they have larger fat deposits, and thinner patients may request 5/8" or 1" needles for IM injections to avoid hitting the bone or going too deep.

The gauge of the needle indicates the width of the needle's bore. Lower gauge numbers (15-25 G) indicate a larger bore and are preferred when drawing up viscous liquid from a pressurized vial like testosterone, while higher gauge numbers (27-33 G) indicate a smaller bore and are preferred for thin liquids and insulin injections. Due to injection pain associated with thick needles, some hormone replacement patients choose to draw up the testosterone using a lower gauge 15 G needle before swapping it with a higher gauge 25 G needle for injection.

Spacers

Albuterol inhalation aerosol, a medication often prescribed for asthma, is dispensed in a canister that requires an inhaler or puffer to administer. The medication is best administered by modifying the inhaler with a device called a spacer. A **spacer** is an elongated closed tube that attaches to the inhaler on one end and has a mouthpiece on the other. Pediatric patients may require a **breathing mask**, which can be attached to the spacer. The medication is sprayed into the spacer, keeping the aerosol contained, while the patient breathes it in. Spacers are an easy and effective way to ensure that the medication is being inhaled into the lungs, which increases the likelihood of patient adherence, rather than being deposited in the mouth or on the tongue.

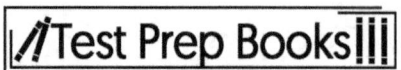

Diabetic Supplies

Diabetic patients who are dependent on insulin require specialized medical supplies to safely administer medications. Insulin syringes are used to draw insulin from medication vials for administration. The most common insulin syringes are U-100 syringes, meaning a 1-milliliter insulin syringe will deliver up to one hundred units of insulin (the most common concentration of insulin). The **gauge of an insulin syringe** refers to the diameter or thickness of the needle and ranges from a 28 G to a 31 G. The larger the gauge, the smaller the diameter of the needle. Prefilled insulin pens are disposable pens containing up to 300 units of insulin. An insulin pen requires **pen needles**, which are attached to the end of the insulin pen. The pen is then dialed to the desired dose, and the insulin is injected. Patients should use **alcohol swabs** to wipe the rubber seal or stopper on vials and insulin pens as well as the site of injection to prevent contamination. Lastly, it is important for diabetic patients to have a **sharps container** to safely dispose of insulin syringes after each use.

PPPA

The **Poison Prevention Packaging Act (PPPA) of 1970** requires all prescription medications and controlled substances to be dispensed in vials with child-resistant caps. The purpose of the Act was to combat and decrease these poisonings. The **Consumer Products Safety Commission** was empowered by the Act to develop rules about packaging for products that would be applied in households with young children. As a result of the Act, the development and mandatory use of child-resistant caps was instituted, as well as regular safety tests for caps, to ensure standards are met to keep children safe.

Exceptions to the legislation are few and may include a request by patient or physician not to receive the safety caps for oral contraceptives and select emergency sublingual (under the tongue) cardiovascular medications (e.g., nitroglycerin sublingually to treat angina associated with heart disease). If a patient or physician requests not to receive child-resistant caps, make sure that the back of the prescription is signed indicating the request for a non-child resistant container. The request should also be noted in the pharmacy management software system.

Medications dispensed or administered in inpatient environments (e.g., hospitals, long-term care facilities, and nursing homes) are also exempt from the child-resistant packaging legislation. A pharmacist's failure to abide by the PPPA could result in prosecution and imprisonment for no longer than one year, or payment of a fine of no more than $1,000, or both.

Labeling Medication Products

Medications Kept in Original Packaging

When labeling OTC medications dispensed in their original packaging, opaque labels should be placed on empty areas or over advertising images to preserve as much of the original labeling as possible. Take care not to obscure the medication's generic and brand names, NDC, lot number, expiration date, and barcodes because these confirm the drug's identity, manufacturer, batch, and sell-by date to ensure safe and effective use. Instructions on proper handling and disposal should also not be obscured.

Patient Prescription Label Components

Every label for a prescription medication or insulin must contain the following information:

- The proprietary (generic) name of the drug
- The established (brand) name of the drug if there is one
- The packer, manufacturer, or distributor of the drug
- An identifying lot or control number

Dispensing Process

- Adequate directions for use, including indication; the quantity or dose to be given by age or weight; potential preparation prior to use; and the frequency, timing, and route of administration
- A complete statement of all ingredients

These elements must be prominent and conspicuous. The label should include no misleading comparisons to other brands or products.

Most of the above information is pertinent to the normal use of the medication, including its name, purpose, and instructions for use. This is followed by several headings that indicate interactions, side effects, and circumstances in which the drug may be too dangerous to use. The last part of the label includes academic information about how the drug works, how it is supplied, and what kinds of studies are available to support its use.

Normal Use	Warnings	Academic and Reference
Product Names Indications and Usage Dosage and Administration Use in Specific Populations Patient Counseling Information	Boxed Warning Contraindications Warnings and Precautions Adverse Reactions Drug Interactions Drug Abuse and Dependence Overdosage	Dosage Forms and Strengths Description Clinical Pharmacology Nonclinical Toxicology Clinical studies References Supplier Information/Storage and Handling

Label Placement

It is important to attach the label as close as possible to the drug vehicle itself (e.g., labeling a tube of fluoride toothpaste rather than its original box or labeling each box of albuterol nebules individually rather than the large plastic bag holding them all). For particularly small packages, the label may need to be flagged or folded back onto itself to reduce the adhesive area to the appropriate size.

Additionally, the barcodes for all drug products should be clearly marked, and the white space surrounding them should be wide enough to make them legible for the scanner. These barcodes must indicate the NDC of the drug product, and they are required for all medications except physician drug samples, allergenic extracts, IUDs, medical gases, radiopharmaceuticals, and low-density polyethylene fill-and-seal containers.

Labels for Different Types and Classes of Drugs

The FDA requires that certain qualifications and declarations be included on the drug label. For example, if a product contains certain allergens like the dyes FD&C Yellow Nos. 5 and 6 or sensitivity agents like sulfites, this must be declared on the label. Additionally, if a product contains the artificial food sweetener aspartame, which metabolizes to the amino acid phenylalanine and cannot be broken down in patients with phenylketonuria, potentially leading to convulsions and neurological damage, this must be declared on the label. OTC labels must also refrain from the use of nonspecific words like *infant* in favor of a specific age in months or years. All antibiotic labels must contain language noting that they are not meant to treat viruses; they should only be used to treat bacterial infections, and the full course should be taken to ensure effectiveness of treatment and to prevent antibiotic resistance.

Many requirements for OTC labels are the same as those for prescription labels: the active ingredient and its net quantity, the purpose or class of the medication, the medication's intended use or indication, the directions for use, and a contact number for questions and concerns. Avenue of use (topically, ophthalmically, otically, orally, rectally, or vaginally) should be explicitly stated. The label must also include the product's common side effects, a description of an allergic response, and instructions about when to stop taking the medication and seek help.

OTC labels must also contain warnings and cautionary statements that act as substitutes for a pharmacist consult. For example, products containing aspirin must warn about the potential for Reye's syndrome; nonoxynol contraceptives must warn that they cannot protect against STDs; common painkillers must include their potential to induce liver toxicity or gastrointestinal bleeding; NSAIDs must note that they should not be used in the third trimester of pregnancy; and certain cold medications must note that their products may cause a sore throat via postnasal drip. OTC medications must declare their contraindications and instruct patients to consult their physicians for certain disease states and ages. Additionally, the contents of electrolytes and minerals like sodium, potassium, calcium, magnesium, and sodium phosphate must be disclosed.

These labeling requirements do not pertain to products that are used in the course of law enforcement, chemical analysis, or physical testing, nor do they apply to any products used in the legal practice of pharmacy, chemistry, medicine, or research not involving clinical use.

Auxiliary Labels

Purpose

Auxiliary labels are meant to remind patients of routine warnings and alerts. They are usually small, colored stickers applied to a medication container, and they communicate important warnings using a handful of words and a monotone image.

These labels are common in hospitals where reminders can be useful when delivering multiple scheduled medications or where the route of administration is not immediately evident. For example, many IV antibiotics must be administered multiple times per day at specific intervals to maintain bactericidal levels long enough to reduce the infection, and some bagged solutions should only be given through a peripherally inserted central catheter (PICC) or central venous catheter (CVC) rather than a normal peripheral IV drip.

Auxiliary labels may also be useful in outpatient settings, especially if the medication is administered by a caregiver/guardian or if the patient has poor memory or concentration. In these cases, AM/PM, HS (at bedtime), and PRN (as needed) stickers may be applied as reminders of dose timing; additionally, clarification of the administration route (e.g., external, rectal, or oral use only) may be helpful. Some auxiliary labels may indicate storage directions (e.g., refrigerated, frozen, kept at room temperature, kept in an amber vial away from light) or additional instructions on how to take the medication (e.g., take with/without food/water, crush/do not crush, shake well/do not shake, do not take with grapefruit juice, do not take with alcohol or other sedating medications). Other labels may warn of common side effects, especially those that may affect alertness or consciousness, such as drowsiness, dizziness, and confusion. Sedatives and antidepressants may cause suicidal ideation, so these should have a warning label as well.

Some auxiliary labels may indicate the drug's contents. This may be done in the presence of common drug allergens like beta-lactams or sulfa antibiotics; in the case of hormones and abortifacient medications that should be handled with care in women of childbearing age; or in the case of federally controlled substances, which require a label explicitly notifying the reader that the law prohibits drug transfer to anyone for whom it was not prescribed.

Labels for Different Types and Classes of Drugs

Some oral medications come in formulations that should not be broken or crushed (DNC). Some medications should not be broken because the pill itself is designed to provide a long-acting release (to reduce the number of doses per day) or a controlled release (in the case of abusable narcotics or to prevent an upset stomach from iron or metformin). The names of many non-crushable formulations contain abbreviations that describe how the medication is released; these include CD (controlled delivery), CR (controlled release), DR (delayed release), EC (enteric-coated), ER (extended release), HS (bedtime dosing), LA (long-acting), MR (modified release), PM (bedtime dosing), SA (sustained action), SR (sustained released), and XR (extra or extended release).

Suppositories are also considered DNC; however, the more pressing concern for any medication that must be inserted is to ensure that the patient unwraps the drug from its protective covering and places it in the correct location. Meanwhile, some oral medications are non-crushable because they can become toxic when released too early; for example, if a patient chews Tessalon Perles, the liquid inside the capsule will numb the mouth and throat, causing obstruction of breathing and potential asphyxiation.

Printed Patient Information Leaflets and Required Medication Guides

Purpose of REMS Programs

Risk Evaluation and Mitigation Strategy (REMS) programs are designed to preclude foreseeable medication interactions and to prevent serious adverse events. The risks associated with medications in REMS programs are similar to contraindications because, without a mitigation strategy in place, these types of medications present such severe problems that they likely cannot be used safely; however, through robust monitoring, these risks can be surveilled and managed much earlier, thus improving the patient's quality of life.

Many of these programs are intended to prevent administration of certain drugs in pregnant patients or in patients who practice unprotected intercourse because several of the medications included in the program are teratogenic and could cause severe malformation in a developing fetus. Other REMS programs may monitor blood levels of ions or blood cells to prevent potentially lethal electrolyte imbalances, anemias, and other blood dyscrasias. Consider the following examples:

- Thalidomide: The program S.T.E.P.S. (System for Thalidomide Education and Prescribing Safety) is used for patients that are prescribed thalidomide. Mandatory counseling, pregnancy testing (if applicable), and registration are required before patients can receive their first prescription. Continued regular pregnancy screenings and counseling are required for patients before refills can be dispensed.

- Isotretinoin: The iPledge program is used to confine isotretinoin drug distribution. Before patients can receive their first prescription, they must register for the program, undergo pregnancy testing (if applicable), choose two types of birth control, and promise to keep all scheduled appointments. In order to refill subsequent prescriptions, female patients need to take monthly pregnancy tests, use the iPledge system to describe their methods of birth control, and answer questions about the iPledge program.

- Clozapine: This prescription medication requires using a program to track the patient's white blood cell count and the absolute neutrophil count. There are different programs through each manufacturer; any of these programs are acceptable, as long as the pharmacist and prescriber can have access to the files to see how the patient is reacting to the medication.

Prescriptions that Require Federal Medication Guides

Federal Medication Guides (MGs) are mandated by the FDA for medications that are too complicated to use safely and effectively without additional instruction or that have a low benefits-to-cost ratio in terms of potential adverse effects.

The full list of MGs may be found on the FDA's website. Generally speaking, the list is grouped into controlled medications (e.g., BZDs, opioids, narcotics, stimulants), NSAIDs (excluding aspirin), PPIs (e.g., esomeprazole, omeprazole, pantoprazole, rabeprazole), reconstitutable PEG-and-electrolyte laxatives like Golytely®, FQNs (e.g., ciprofloxacin, levofloxacin, moxifloxacin), DPP-4 inhibitors (e.g., alogliptin, saxagliptin, sitagliptin), TZDs (e.g., pioglitazone, rosiglitazone), anticoagulants (e.g., apixaban, dabigatran, rivaroxaban, warfarin), seizure medications (e.g., carbamazepine divalproex, gabapentin, lamotrigine, levetiracetam), serotonin modulators (e.g., duloxetine, nortriptyline, quetiapine, selegiline, varenicline), some hormone modulators (e.g., anti-estrogen agents like tamoxifen, anti-osteoporotic agents like alendronate, and testosterone), immunosuppressants and inhaled steroids

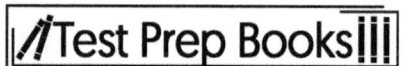

Dispensing Process

(e.g., mycophenolate, sirolimus, tacrolimus, formoterol), numerous HIV and oncological drugs, and a handful of others such as acitretin, desmopressin, epoetin alfa, isotretinoin, metoclopramide, montelukast, and pancrelipase.

Differences between Medication Guides and Product Package Inserts

Several types of printed information may be distributed to patients or used by healthcare workers to answer questions or address concerns related to medications. Package Inserts (**PIs**) are fairly technical and are predominantly used as reference materials for healthcare providers. Patient Package Inserts (**PPIs**) are patient-friendly versions of PIs that answer most questions that patients might have about their medications. Medication Guides (**MGs**) provide general guidance for patients on specific medications that may be dangerous to take without supervision. Instructions for Use (**IFUs**) are detailed explanations on how to safely and effectively administer medications in tandem with an unfamiliar device or delivery mechanism.

Package Inserts

Package Inserts (PIs), also called Product Package Inserts, are written for every medication and supplied to the FDA. They are designed to answer fundamental questions about the medication and its use as well as potential precautions. Typically, PIs are used only by pharmacists or prescribers when researching specialized information concerning the drug, such as its pharmacological class, method of action (MOA), pharmacodynamics (PD) and how the drug acts on the body, pharmacokinetics (PK) and how the body metabolizes and disposes of the drug, toxicology, storage and handling information, and clinical studies and references.

While PIs exist for every drug, most do not find their way to patients. Since PIs are predominantly for providers, patients do not usually receive them.

Written Patient Information

Written patient information refers to any written information about a prescription medication that is provided to the patient and falls under one of the following three categories:

- Patient Package Insert (PPI)
- Medication Guide (MG)
- Instructions for Use (IFU)

The written patient information addresses various issues that are specific to the medication regarding its safe and effective use. It also discusses special directions and precautions that help to avoid medication-induced adverse events. Not all medications have written patient information. Patients can ask their healthcare provider or pharmacist for details about their prescriptions.

PPI

Like PIs, Patient Package Inserts (PPIs) are written for every medication and supplied to the FDA, but they are written for the average patient, so they are less technical and easier to understand than PIs. PPIs are developed and submitted voluntarily to the FDA by the manufacturer and are approved by the FDA.

Also like PIs, PPIs generally do not find their way to patients. PPIs are not legally mandated except in two medication classes: oral contraceptives (OCs) and estrogen-containing drugs. In these cases, a PPI must be dispensed with every prescription filled, regardless of prior use or refill status. The FDA warrants the safe and effective use of these products by requiring that patients be fully informed about the benefits and risks associated with the uses of these medications. In other circumstances, it is neither illegal nor mandatory to dispense a PPI to a patient, even though manufacturers do voluntarily submit PPIs for other medications to the FDA for approval.

Dispensing Process

MG

Like PPIs, Medication Guides (MGs) aim to be patient-friendly; unlike PPIs, MGs attempt to address concerns of which the patient would otherwise be unaware and to prevent undue risk or accident resulting from ignorance or recklessness.

Specifically, MGs are paper handouts that contain FDA-approved information about specific drugs and drug classes. They are provided in order to help patients avoid adverse events. The manufacturer of the medication develops the MG, and the FDA approves it. The FDA requires that MGs be supplied to patients receiving certain prescribed drugs and biological products. MGs help patients prevent serious adverse effects and make informed decisions (by providing information about serious side effects of a product). They also help patients adhere to the product's directions to ensure the product's effectiveness.

IFU

Instructions for Use (IFU) refers to written patient information that is produced by the manufacturer and approved by the FDA. They are provided to ensure proper use of certain medications with complicated dosing instructions.

IFUs may also be included by the manufacturer to aid with patients' self-administration of medications. These instructions might cover preparation and administration of a drug (e.g., how to hold, inhale, and wash medications from a dry-powder inhaler; how to insert and use an enema; or how to identify a seizure and administer a diazepam rectal gel). IFUs may also instruct patients how to handle, store, and dispose of the medication (e.g., how to administer and dispose of topical hormones and nitroglycerin ointments or how to safely store, use, and discard the hypodermic needles associated with insulin).

The chart below indicates which pieces of information are relevant to each type of patient information.

	PI	MG	IFU
Brand and generic name	X	X	X
Controlled substance schedule	X	X	X
Indication and usage	X	X	X
Dosage and administration, missed doses	X	X	X
Overdosage	X	X	
Contraindications	X	X	
Boxed warnings	X	X	
Warnings and precautions	X	X	
Adverse reactions	X	X	
Drug interactions	X	X	
Special populations (prenatal, nursing, pediatric, geriatric)	X	X	
Drug abuse and dependence	X	X	
Dosage forms and strengths	X		X
Visual image of the drug product			X
Active ingredients' pharmacological classes	X		
Clinical pharmacology (MOA, PD, PK)	X		
Nonclinical toxicology (carcinogenesis, mutagenesis, effects on fertility, animal toxicology)	X		
Relevant clinical studies	X		
References	X		
Patient information	X		
Supply, storage, and handling information	X		X

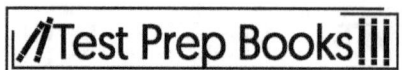

Dispensing Process

	PI	MG	IFU
Approval for use by FDA and last revision date	X	X	X

Packaging and Shipping Medications According to Manufacturers' Recommendations

Federal Restrictions on Shipping of Specific Medications and Supplies

Care should be taken to ensure that drug products remain at their correct storage temperature and humidity level throughout transit from manufacturer to end user. Refrigerated products may be kept cool using refrigeration units, ice boxes, and ice packs. Most medications survive short excursions; otherwise, it is imperative to avoid phase transitions: frozen medications like Varivax and Comirnaty® should remain frozen until ready to administer, and products containing liquids like Lovenox and Humira should be kept warm enough to remain liquid when transported through freezing conditions.

As with other electronics, the lithium-ion batteries found in diabetic testing supplies and blood pressure monitors must be declared for federal postage, and there is a national mail-order program sponsored by Medicare specifically for these testing supplies. Although lancets and insulin syringes are considered sharps, they may also be shipped federally or taken through TSA checks if they are declared with a valid prescription. Similarly, CGMs like Dexcom and injectables like Fiasp® may be defended as prescription products in these circumstances.

Although most medications may be shipped to customers through domestic mail, controlled substances typically require paperwork to maintain the chain of custody (e.g., DEA Forms 222, 106, and 41 for C-II orders, controlled substances loss/theft, and disposal). This formality may be waived for medications sent between DEA registrants, through a mail-back program, or to the patient directly as a prescription.

Prescription medications sent by mail must be secured within a plain outer package, and controlled substances must be issued with the relevant prescription number as well as the distributor's name and address. Prescription containers should never outwardly indicate their contents, but samples may be mailed in containers that display short, promotional blurbs about the product and the optional marking "Sample Enclosed."

If hazardous drugs and materials must be shipped, they should be sealed in containers that can prevent accidental exposure during the shipping process. Any notable flammability and volatility hazards should be indicated on the package along with markings that explain how to handle the product safely. Like other prescription drugs, hazardous drugs are typically only sent by mail from a manufacturer to a provider or from a pharmacy to a patient.

The Postal Service will not ship radioactive substances, so radiological diagnostic materials like Tc-99m lidofenin must be shipped through private distribution. There are no special requirements for the transport of radiotherapeutics besides NRC documentation and equipment like lead-lined pigs and ID-sealed cases which are used to shield personnel from the substances prior to use. Readings for the amounts of radiation detected within each syringe and on the outside of each shipping container must be documented to guard against accidental leak or contamination.

Selecting Appropriate OTC Product

OTC Medications

OTC medications, vitamins, minerals, and herbal supplements may be unsuitable for some people due to interactions with their prescription medications or disease states. The potential for toxicity of these substances is usually ignored by patients who assume that everything OTC is completely nontoxic. There is little difference in formulation between prescription and nonprescription drug products, although most prescription drugs are found in higher strengths, higher potencies, and extended durations of effect than their OTC counterparts. When discussing potential remedies with a patient, it may be worthwhile to suggest seeing a doctor for a prescription if the OTC products do not seem to have the desired effectiveness or duration.

The most important considerations when recommending a product are its active ingredients and whether it appropriately addresses the patient's concerns; however, other factors such as age and illness also inform the decision. OTC recommendations must always comply with the directions for use and age restrictions found on the packaging, regardless of personal experience. If a medication is not cleared for use in a pediatric age range, or if it cannot be taken in the patient's preferred way, then the patient must consult with their physician or pharmacist on whether it is appropriate for use.

Some product recommendations depend on the inactive ingredients rather than the active medication. For example, many syrups and oral solutions use sugar for flavoring, but these require large quantities of sugar that aren't healthy for diabetic and insulin-dependent patients. Other OTC syrups may be flavored with aspartame, an artificial sweetener, but these too may be problematic because some people cannot metabolize phenylalanine (a component of aspartame), which can build up to toxic or lethal quantities in the blood if not monitored. Many patients with diabetes and phenylketonuria are vigilant about the sugar and aspartame they consume, but not all patients think about dietary restrictions when choosing a medication; therefore, it is appropriate to warn them about such potential hazards.

Other medications may also affect a patient's blood chemistry (most noticeably, the electrolytes). While the kidneys usually maintain the body's electrolytes at a steady level by flushing out excess salt when levels are too high and retaining it when levels are too low, patients with poor renal function have difficulties keeping normal levels. This is of critical importance when considering the use of laxatives and diuretics, which bypass the kidney's gatekeeping role and may dump large amounts of sodium, potassium, and water, leading to sharp declines in blood volume. Alternatively, kidney failure patients may retain too much water when overhydrated, and they may develop toxicities when taking medications with high quantities of aluminum and magnesium salts like Maalox. Finally, NSAIDs like ibuprofen and naproxen directly reduce blood flow to the kidneys, which can reduce urine production, lower nutrient supply, and worsen renal health. Therefore, they should be avoided in patients with chronic kidney disease (CKD).

Vitamins, Minerals, and Herbal Supplements

Dietary supplements, unlike OTC medications, are not regulated by the FDA. The Dietary Health and Supplement Act of 1994 defines the guidelines that dietary supplements must meet, including those that:

- contain a vitamin, mineral, herb, botanical, and/or amino acid.
- are sold as a capsule, tablet, powder or liquid.
- are not purposefully marked to be the sole source of nutrition.
- have the labeling "dietary supplement."

The major vitamins are A, B, C, D, E, and K, and each of these is sold OTC. Some are also sold at prescription strengths, including B1 (thiamine), B3 (niacin), B6 (pyridoxine), B9 (folate), B12 (cyanocobalamin), C (ascorbic acid), D2 (ergocalciferol), and D3 (cholecalciferol). Vitamin K may also be administered in hospitals as a potential reversal agent for warfarin.

Some minerals may also be supplemented OTC. Calcium is found in carbonate and citrate salts as Tums, Oscal, and Citracal®; iron is found as ferrous sulfate in SlowFe®; and magnesium is found in citrate and oxide salts. Most multivitamins also contain these minerals as well as some electrolytes, but they may cater to specific age groups or special populations like prenatal or geriatric patients.

Some enzymes, hormones, and proteins naturally found in the human body may be sold OTC. Melatonin is produced by the pineal gland and maintains the circadian rhythms that control our day-and-night cycles. Although

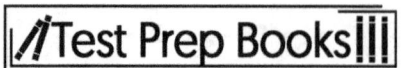

there is prescription-strength melatonin and melatonin analogues (like ramelteon), OTC melatonin may be used as a nonaddictive sleep aid. Coenzyme Q10 (CoQ10) may be used to aid cardiovascular health, and carnitine may help with neuropathy. Glucosamine and chondroitin are both protein-builders that can help with osteoarthritis by improving the body's ability to rebuild collagen in joints. Omega-3 fatty acids may also be found in OTC fish oil supplements, although these OTC supplements have not been proven to have the same cardiovascular and triglyceride-lowering benefits as prescription omega-3 acid (Lovaza®, Epanova®).

Most herbal supplements cannot be recommended as solutions or treatments to any particular disease or condition because they are neither regulated nor indicated by the FDA. They tend to have little data about their use, have large variation in their effectiveness, and can be touted as cure-alls for a wide range of illnesses. However, because patients may still choose to use supplements, pharmacy staff must be cognizant of possible interactions with other medications when making recommendations.

Supplement	Potentially Treats	Comments
Black cohosh	Hot flashes	Black cohosh is metabolized by the liver, so it may cause toxicity if taken with hepatotoxic drugs like APAP or alcohol.
Cranberry	Recurrent UTI	Cranberry is not useful to cure UTIs, but it may be useful to prevent recurrent UTIs. However, sugary drinks encourage bacterial growth, so patients should either take sugar-free cranberry juice or capsulated cranberry extract.
Echinacea	Common cold	Echinacea may increase side effects from caffeine use because it interferes with the breakdown of caffeine.
Garlic	High cholesterol, high blood sugar	Most garlic interactions are minor, but it may cause an increased risk of bleeding with warfarin use.
Ginger	Motion sickness, vertigo	Ginger is typically well-tolerated, but it may increase the risk of bleeding while on anticoagulants. It may also interfere with excretion of opioids, leading to potential overdose.
Ginkgo biloba	Anxiety, memory	Ginkgo may affect the blood levels of anti-seizure medications and may increase the risk of serotonin syndrome when combined with antidepressants.
Ginseng	Stress	Ginseng may affect vitamin K metabolism, so it should not be taken with warfarin. It may also increase the efficacy of antidiabetic medications, and interactions may lead to low blood sugar.
Green tea	Weight loss	Green tea leaves contain vitamin K, which will increase clotting and reduce the effectiveness of warfarin. It may also interfere with the metabolism of statins, leading to increased blood levels and potential rhabdomyolysis, or muscle breakdown.
Kava	Anxiety, insomnia	Kava may induce drowsiness and may affect liver function. It may cause increased sedation or hepatotoxicity when taken with APAP or alcohol.
Saw palmetto	Benign prostatic hypertrophy (BPH)	Saw palmetto may or may not be useful in mild BPH and may make oral hormones less effective.

Dispensing Process

Supplement	Potentially Treats	Comments
St. John's wort	Anxiety, depression	St. John's wort functions similarly to SSRIs, so it has many drug interactions. It should not be taken alongside any other antidepressants or migraine medications, and it may affect the metabolism of warfarin and oral hormones.
Valerian	Anxiety, insomnia	Valerian may induce drowsiness, so caution should be taken with other sedating drugs like muscle relaxants, pain medications, and alcohol.

Offering Pharmacist Consultation to Patients

All pharmacies are required by OBRA '90 to counsel Medicaid patients/caregivers and to provide written materials for further patient education. This is also required for pharmacies that dispense medications through delivery or post. Counseling may be accomplished through the advertisement of a toll-free number for consultation services hosted by the pharmacy. Each state is permitted to require and enforce this consultation requirement through its own state legislation, but most have implemented similar policies and require new prescription counseling for all applicable patients and medication orders, not just for Medicaid reimbursement. For example, Texas requires that new prescription counseling be completed and documented for every novel medication prescription, every prescription for a medication that has not been dispensed in the same strength and dosage form at the dispensing pharmacy within the last twelve months, all prescriptions transferred from another pharmacy, and inpatient discharge medication orders. Additionally, both law and standard operating procedures for outpatient pharmacies generally require that the offer to consult to come directly from the pharmacist or pharmacy intern. Patients and caregivers may refuse this consultation, and pharmacists are not criminally liable for adverse outcomes that could have been prevented through consultation if refusal is documented.

OBRA '90 also permitted each state to set up a Drug utilization review (DUR) board or Pharmaceutics & Therapeutics (P&T) committee, which enables the organization to identify substitutable drugs and create formularies of preferred drugs. These formularies may be quite large in the case of an outpatient or shipping pharmacy, or they may be quite small in the case of a hospital that requires its staff to restrict the amount and variety of medications from the same class of drugs. They may prefer and require specific brand or generic medications as reimbursement from an insurance company. If such a substitution occurs, the patient or caregiver must be notified upon dispensation.

OBRA '90 requires that pharmacists perform a DUR for each patient's medications, both prospective and retrospective. Pharmacists should ensure that all new prescriptions are safe and effective when combined with the patients' current list of medications and disease states while also ensuring that all existing recurrent prescriptions are each indicated, safe, and tolerated by the patient.

Forged, Copied, or Altered Prescriptions

Identifying a Forged Prescription
Individuals who falsify or change prescriptions frequently make common mistakes that are easy to recognize. It is important to review new prescriptions for these "tell signs" or mistakes:

- Personal information on the prescription is conflicting.
- The type of doctor who "wrote" the prescription would not usually prescribe the specified type of medication, for example, certain specialists or cardiologists. This "tell sign" could hint that the prescription blanks were stolen.

- Mistakes in the dosing instructions or abbreviations are hints, such as an unusual dose for the specified medication or mistakes using the codes.
- Glaring changes on quantity to be dispensed or number of refills. Sometimes erasing happens by the prescriber, but in such cases, the prescriber should be contacted to confirm the numbers.
- Varying types of ink on the prescription can indicate that changes have been made to a previously valid prescription.
- Usually, no refills are provided on Schedule II prescriptions; if there are refills requested, check with the prescriber to make sure it was not in error.
- Observe the quantity prescribed closely.

Security Features of Prescriptions

While electronic prescribing is preferable, many pharmacies continue to accept and fill physical and oral prescription orders. Most medications require very little legal evidence for proof of valid prescription, so the identification of forged, copied, and altered prescription orders relies heavily on common sense.

With handwritten prescriptions, red flags for invalid prescriptions may include handwriting that is too clearly legible or neat as well as directions and amounts that don't make sense considering the patient's age or indication. For example, omitting the quantity, writing a quantity of one when the drug doesn't come in unit-dose packaging, or writing out "three-month supply" for controlled substances may each indicate a forged prescription. If a prescription order is taken orally, listen for unnecessary pauses or unsure voices that may indicate fraud.

Prescriptions of controlled substances must include the prescriber's DEA number as well as that of the attending physician in the case of mid-level practitioners. Most companies also require that the quantity dispensed be written both long-form and numerically, but this is not a legal requirement. Some states have additional requirements for physical prescriptions of controlled substances; for example, Texas requires that all prescribers of controlled substance orders do so through e-scribing, writing orders on specially manufactured prescription pads, or submitting a waiver that indicates their lack of e-scribe capability. Prescription pads may also make use of thermochromic ink (which changes color when warmed by touch or breath), void pantographs (hidden text or figures that only become evident on facsimiles or copies of legitimate orders), serial control numbers for each unique prescription, light-translucent watermarks, holograms, and UV-fluorescent dyes.

Since the advent of the Opioid Epidemic, pharmacies have been encouraged to take fake and unnecessary sedative prescriptions more seriously, and state boards have attempted to introduce measures to curb excessive use and abuse of pain medication. Many states have introduced a Prescription Drug Monitoring Program (PDMP) whereby every pharmacy that fills controlled medications can report each prescription and check against the database to ensure that it has not already been filled elsewhere. Such measures protect the patient by preventing abusable medications from being filled too often, thus preventing potential misuse and overdose.

Calculations

Converting within and between the Systems of Measurement

Measurement Systems

Prescriptions usually come in metric measurements—grams, liters, etc.—, which the average American is not familiar with. Knowing the different measurement systems and their conversions are crucial to the success of any pharmacy employee.

Metric System

The metric measurement system consists of grams (g), liters (L), and meters (m). These measurements are based on a scale of 10, meaning that for each increase in most measurement units, it increases by 10, 100, 1000, etc. For example, 10 centigrams (cg) equals 1 gram and 1000 meters (m) equals 1 kilometer (km). The most common units seen in a pharmacy are milli-, micro-, kilo-, and no prefix. Milli- is 10^{-3}, or 0.001. 1 gram equals 1000 milligrams, 1 liter equals 1000 milliliters, and 1 kilometer equals 1000 meters. An easy approach to these conversions within the metric system is to just move the decimal point. If you are going from a smaller unit of measurement to a larger unit of measurement, you move the decimal point to the left. For example, to convert 1000 milligrams to grams, you would move the decimal point three places to the left: 1000. becomes 1.000, which is 1 gram. If you are going from a larger unit of measurement to a smaller unit of measurement, you would move the decimal to the right. For example, if you needed to go from 1 kilogram to grams, you would take the 1.0 kilogram and move the decimal right three places, which makes 1000.0 grams. In the metric system, kilo- is 10^3 (kg, km, kL), micro- is 10^{-6} (mcg, mcm, or mcL/ μg, μm, μL), milli- is 10^{-3} (mg, mm, mL), and no prefix means 10^1 (g, m, L). Common conversions are shown in the tables below:

1000 milligrams (mg)	1 gram (g)
10 centigrams (cg)	1 gram (g)
1000 grams (g)	1 kilogram (kg)

1000 millimeters (mm)	1 meter (m)
10 centimeters (cm)	1 meter (m)
1000 meters (m)	1 kilometer (km)

1000 milliliters (mL)	1 liter (L)
10 centiliters (cL)	1 liter (L)
1000 liters (L)	1 kiloliter (kL)

Household System

The household, or customary, system of measurement is mainly used in the U.S., and it does not have a pattern like the metric system does, so you have to memorize the conversions between units or use a conversion chart. The measurements most commonly seen in a pharmacy are listed in the table below:

Volume Measurement Conversions	
16 ounces (oz)	1 pound (lb)
12 inches (in)	1 foot (ft)
8 fluid ounces (fl oz)	1 cup (c)
2 cups (c)	1 pint (pt)
2 pints (pt)	1 quart (qt)
4 quarts (qt)	1 gallon (gal)

Distance Measurement Conversions	
12 inches (in or inch)	1 foot (ft)
3 feet (ft)	1 yard (yd)
5280 feet (ft)	1 mile (mi)
1760 yards (yd)	1 mile (mi)

A common way to remember the liquid household conversions is with something called "the Big G." It organizes in a drawing how many cups needed in a pint, etc. In the diagram below, C = cup, P = pint, Q = quart, and G = gallon:

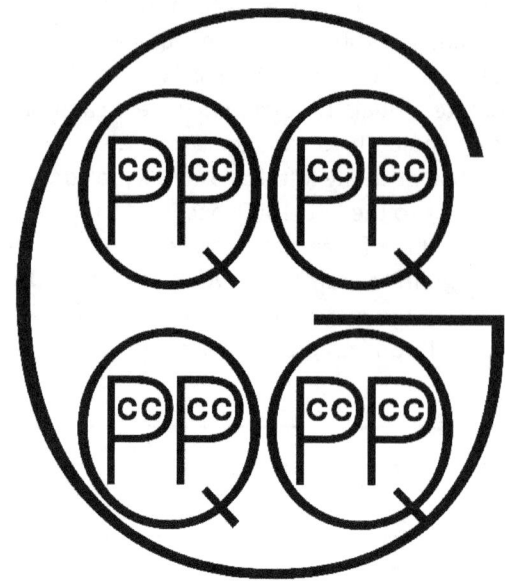

1 Gallon = 4 Quarts, 8 Pints, 16 Cups
1 Quart = 2 Pints, 4 Cups
1 Pint = 2 Cups

Other liquid measurements commonly seen are drops (gtt/gtts), teaspoons (tsp or t), and tablespoons (tbsp or T). 20 drops equals 1 mL, 1 teaspoon equals 5 mL, and 3 teaspoons equals 1 tablespoon.

Liquid Measurement Conversions	
3 teaspoons (tsp)	1 tablespoon (tbsp)
1 teaspoon (tsp)	5 milliliters (mL)
20 drops (gtts)	1 milliliter (mL)

Conversions between Systems

Often, you will be required to convert between the metric and customary measurement systems, either to convert a dosage for a patient or to understand and fill a prescription. This is most easily done using a technique called stoichiometry. It is used to convert simple and complex units to other units. First, 2.54 centimeters (cm) equals 1 inch. If you needed to convert 3 inches to centimeters, such as when filling a prescription for diclofenac gel that doses the cream by length, set up the stoichiometry equation like this:

$$\frac{3\ in}{1} \times \frac{2.54\ cm}{1\ in} = 7.62\ cm$$

Using the conversion above as an example, first note that writing any number over 1 does not change the value of the number. Second, make sure that the units that are the same (in this example, it is inches) are written diagonally from each other. The conversion value you are wanting to convert to, centimeters, goes on top of the inches to the right of the multiplication sign when writing the conversion value (in this case, inches to centimeters). For the conversion to work, the number on top of the conversion value must equal the number directly below it. This means that you must know or look up that 2.54 cm equals 1 in. Once the equation is properly set up, the inch units cancel each other out, leaving you with centimeters, the desired unit, as the only unit in the equation:

Dispensing Process

$$\frac{3}{1} \times \frac{2.54\ cm}{1} = 7.62\ cm$$

Once you have reached the desired unit, you multiply the top numbers horizontally together, 3 x 2.54, and divide the product by the bottom numbers multiplied together horizontally, 1 x 1:

$$\frac{3}{1} \times \frac{2.54\ cm}{1} = \frac{7.62\ cm}{1} = 7.62\ cm$$

So, 7.62 cm equals 3 inches. Remember that if you want to set up an equation like this but the first number, like this one, had no bottom unit, a placeholder "1" can be used since multiplying or dividing a number by 1 does not change the numerical value of the number. The table below lists other common conversions:

2.54 centimeters (cm)	1 inch (in or inch)
2.2 pounds (lb)	1 kilogram (kg)
29.6 milliliters (mL)	1 fluid ounce (fl oz)

Military Time

Another form of measurement used in the pharmacy is time, and for most prescriptions, time is dictated in military time due to ease of use and not needing to specify "AM" or "PM." Military time is written as one whole number without a colon to separate hours and minutes. For example, 1:00 AM would be 0100. All place values are always filled with a number, so if there is a time like the previous one, zeroes would be used in the empty places. If the time was 11:35 AM, you would write 1135. For AM, or morning times, the time is just translated straight without a colon. The appeal of military time is that it is based on a twenty-four-hour clock, not a twelve-hour clock like you may be used to. Therefore, PM times will look different. A simple trick is just to subtract 12 from the first two digits from the time given in PM, and that is the time in the twelve-hour clock. For example, 4:30 PM would be 1630 in military time. 16 minus 12 is 4, so the time is 4:30 PM.

Roman Numerals

Numbers can also be written in different systems, such as the Roman numeral system. Typically, we write our numbers in the Arabic numeral format, which includes 1, 3, 14, 3560, etc. The Roman numeral system uses I, V, X, L, C, D, and M.

I	One
V	Five
X	Ten
L	Fifty
C	One hundred
D	Five hundred
M	One thousand

To make all the numbers in between, combinations of these Roman numerals are created. The base Roman numeral is the largest Roman numeral. For example, if the number is 22, X would be the base Roman numeral, as X equals 10 and would be the base number. To continue to make the number 22, it would be XXII, which is X (10) + X (10) + I (1) + I (1) = 22. The lowest possible number of Roman numerals should be used to write out a number. XVVII would be incorrect because while V equals 5, and 5 plus 5 equals 10, an X should be used instead to use fewer numerals. To represent the number 4, the smaller Roman numeral goes in front of the other larger number it is subtracting from. If the number is 64, it would be LXIV, with the I in front of the V to indicate that the last digit is 1 less than 5, which is 4. Another example is 44, which would be XLIV. The X is in front of the L to demonstrate that it is 10 less than 50, which is 40, and the I is in front of the V to say that it is 1 less than 5, which is 4. This is done so that the Roman

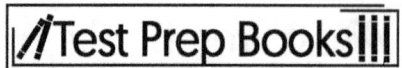

numerals do not end up being extremely long; if this rule did not exist, 44 would be XXXXIIII. For pharmacy, Roman numerals are commonly used in place of any Arabic number. For example, a prescription may say XXX tablets instead of 30 tablets.

Calculating Quantities of Prescriptions or Medication Orders

mEq

Milliequivalents, or mEq, are used for electrolytes, which are chemical elements that break down in water and have a positive (+) or negative (-) charge. An equivalent is the amount of the element it takes to combine/react with 1 mole of hydrogen atoms. A mole is how chemical elements are measured. 1 mole equals 6.022×10^{23} molecules of a chemical element, also known as Avogadro's number, and each chemical element's molecular weight in grams is equal to 1 mole. The molecular weight of an element is the element's atomic mass, found on the periodic table, in grams. For example, the atomic mass of oxygen is 16, so that means that the molecular weight of oxygen is 16 grams per 1 mole of atoms. The molecular weight of a compound can be calculated by adding the molecular weights of the individual ions together. For example, the molecular weight of nitrogen dioxide (NO_2) is:

$$\frac{14.01\ g}{1\ mol} + \frac{16\ g \times 2}{1\ mol} = \frac{46.01\ g}{1\ mol}$$

Note that, since mEq is used more frequently than Eq in pharmacy, mmol, or millimole, will also be more common than mole.

To find the mEq of an element, there are three possible equations:

$$grams\ equivalent\ to\ 1\ Eq = \frac{combined\ molecular\ weight\ of\ all\ ions}{|highest\ valence\ charge|}$$

$$mEq = mmols \times valence$$

$$mEq = \frac{mg\ of\ compound \times valence}{molecular\ weight\ of\ the\ compound}$$

The two vertical bars, | |, on the bottom of the first equation mean the absolute value. With absolute value, every number loses its charge and comes out positive. If the charge was -2, it would be 2. If the charge was +3, it would still be 3 because the absolute value only changes negative numbers to positive numbers. Valence is found on the periodic table for each element. It is found by looking at the column of the periodic table that the element is in. Elements from columns 1 and 2 are +1 and +2, respectively. To find the valence charge for elements from columns 15–18, subtract 18 from the column number (their charges are negative). Column 15's charge is -3, column 16's charge is -2, column 17's charge is -1, and column 18's charge is 0. The rest of the elements have various charges, and they should be provided to you on the exam:

Take sodium chloride (NaCl), for example: sodium has a charge of +1 and chloride has a charge of -1, which means that the valence charge will be 1. The molecular weight of sodium is 22.99 g/mol and the molecular weight of chloride is 35.45 g/mol; adding these together will give us the molecular weight of the compound:

$$x \, g \, NaCl = \frac{22.99 \, g/mol + 35.45 \, g/mol}{1} = 58.44 \, g \, NaCl$$

This means that 58.44 mg of sodium chloride is equivalent to 1 mEq of sodium chloride. Even though it says grams in this equation, because mEq has everything in milli- (millimoles, milligrams, milliequivalents), the units could all be converted to grams and they would still be the same numbers, because they are all an equal magnitude of measurement.

This equation can also be used to calculate the percent strength of a solution. As an example, let's calculate the concentration, or percent strength, of 10 mL of 380 mEq/L magnesium sulfate ($MgSO_4$). First, calculate the mEq (molecular weight = 120.366 g/mol, sulfate ion = -2 charge, magnesium ion = +2):

$$1 \, mEq = \frac{120.366 \, mg/mmol}{2}$$

$$1 \, mEq = \frac{120.366 \, mg/mmol}{2} = 60.18 \, mg$$

Because the valence charge of the magnesium ion is +2 and the valence charge of the sulfate is -2, +2 is the highest valence charge and should be used in the equation. Dividing the molecular weight of magnesium sulfate by 2 gives us 60.18 mg in 1 mEq of magnesium sulfate.

Dispensing Process

Next, multiply the total mEq/mL of this magnesium sulfate solution by 1 mEq of magnesium sulfate. Because the magnesium sulfate is given in mEq/L, it must first be converted to mEq/mL:

$$\frac{380 \; mEq}{1 \; L} \times \frac{0.001 \; L}{1 \; mL} = \frac{0.380 \; mEq}{1 \; mL}$$

Using this number, set up the rest of the equation:

$$\frac{60.18 \; mg}{1 \; mEq} \times \frac{0.380 \; mEq}{1 \; mL} = 22.87 \; mg/mL$$

Convert this back into grams to use the w/v% calculations:

$$\frac{22.64 \; mg}{1 \; mL} \times \frac{1 \; g}{1000 \; mg} = 0.02287 \; g/mL$$

Then convert to a scale of 100 to use the ratio calculation:

$$\frac{0.02287 \; g}{1 \; mL} \times \frac{100}{100} = 2.287 \; g/mL$$

2.287 g/100 mL, or 2.287% strength, is the concentration of 10 ml of 380 mEq/L.

Units

Several different medications and supplements use units as a measurement, instead of mL or mg. There is no direct calculation or conversion for units; it is based on bioavailability and other measures specific to the medication or organism. It can be written as "units," or "u," or "international units," or "IU." This measurement is most commonly seen with insulin, heparin (an anticoagulant injection), vitamins, and probiotics.

For insulin, it is written as units/mL. The most common insulin dosages are U100 (100 units/mL) and U500 (500 u/mL), but U200 (200 u/mL) and U300 (300 u/mL) are available as well.

Another medication that uses units is heparin, an anticoagulant injection. It is also called unfractionated heparin, or UFH.

Vitamins also use units. Each vitamin has a different conversion rate, usually from units to micrograms.

Probiotics also use units, but only for describing the amount of bacteria in the probiotic. Bacteria is measured in colony-forming units, or CFU. For probiotics specifically, CFU describes the number of live cells present in each dose, which is not the exact same way it is used for counting bacteria. As a pharmacy technician, you should not have to count bacteria colonies. Bacteria CFU means the number of bacterial cells that can multiply, which is the total number of bacteria that grew on an agar plate.

Body Surface Area

Body surface area (BSA) is a measure of a person's total body surface area. It is used to calculate drug dosages, most commonly for chemotherapy medications. The formula for BSA is:

$$BSA \; (m^2) = \sqrt{\frac{[height \; (cm) \times weight \; (kg)]}{3600}}$$

An example of this equation would be for a person who is 130 cm tall and weighs 70 kg:

$$BSA = \sqrt{\frac{[130\ cm \times 70\ kg]}{3600}}$$

$$1.59\ m^2 = \sqrt{\frac{[130\ cm \times 70\ kg]}{3600}}$$

This person's BSA is $1.59\ m^2$.

Pediatric Dosage Calculations

It is important to check and compare the dosage for children relative to that of adults, as the physician may request a dose that a manufacturer does not supply. The three general methods used to calculate pediatric doses are based on age, body weight, and body surface area.

Dose Calculation Related to Age

Young's Rule

This formula depends on age to calculate the dose and is preferably used for children between 1–12 years of age:

$$Child\ dose = Adult\ dose \times \frac{Age\ in\ years}{(Age + 12)}$$

Example: A child is 12 years old and the adult dose of the medicine is 500 mg:

$$Child\ dose = 500\ mg \times \frac{12}{(12 + 12)} = 250\ mg$$

Drilling's Rule

This formula uses the age of the child expressed in years:

$$Child\ dose = Adult\ dose \times \frac{Age\ in\ years}{(20)}$$

Example: A child is 10 years old and the adult dose of the medicine is 750 mg:

$$Child\ dose = 750\ mg \times \frac{10}{(20)} = 375\ mg$$

Fried's Rule

This formula is better to use in infants until 2 years of age, and the age of the child is expressed in months:

$$Child\ dose = Adult\ dose \times \frac{Age\ in\ months}{(150)}$$

Example: A child is 8 months old and the adult dose is 250 mg:

$$Child\ dose = 250\ mg \times \frac{8}{(150)} = 13.33\ mg$$

Dose Calculation Related to Body Weight

Clark's Rule

This is based on weight in pounds (not kg) and can be calculated with the formula below:

$$\text{Child dose} = \text{Adult dose} \times \frac{\text{Body weight in lb}}{(150)}$$

Example: A child weighs 80 pounds and the adult dose is 500 mg:

$$\text{Child dose} = 500 \text{ mg} \times \frac{80}{(150)} = 266.7 \text{ mg}$$

Dose Calculation Related to Body Surface Area

A child's dose can also be calculated relative to **body surface area (BSA)**. This approach is distinguished by obtaining a more representative measure of metabolic mass instead of body weight, as it is not affected as much by unusual amounts of fat. Note that an average adult with a weight of 70 kg and a height of 175 cm has a body surface area of approximately 1.85 m².

$$\text{Child dose} = \text{Adult dose} \times \frac{\text{Child's BSA}}{\text{Average adult's BSA}}$$

Body surface area (BSA) can be calculated using **Mosteller's equation** as follows:

$$\text{BSA } (m^2) = \sqrt{\frac{(\text{Height (cm)} \times \text{Weight (kg)})}{3600}}$$

For example, a prescription comes as 600 mg/m² of drug "X" for a 32-month-old boy. The boy weighs 30 lb (13.6 kg) and is 30 inches (76.2 cm) tall. What dosage should the boy receive?

$$\text{BSA } (m^2) = \sqrt{\frac{(76.2 \text{ cm} \times 13.6 \text{ kg})}{3600}} = \sqrt{.288} = 0.537 \text{ } m^2$$

Therefore, the calculation for the child's dose is:

$$600 \text{ mg} \times \frac{0.537 \text{ } m^2}{1.85 \text{ } m^2} = 600 \text{ mg} \times 0.290$$

$$600 \text{ mg} \times 0.290 = 174 \text{ mg}$$

W/W%, W/V%, V/V%

There are different ways that concentrations can be expressed: as a ratio of weight, volume, or percentage. The following ratios are used to present a concentration: W/W, W/V, and V/V. The unit for a **W/W** ratio is grams, as this represents a **weight/weight ratio**. The measurement unit for **W/V** is grams/mL, as this represents **weight/volume ratio**. The unit for a **V/V** ratio is mL, as this represents a **volume/volume ratio**.

Examples are:

- W/W = 5: 100 = 5 grams/100 grams = 5%
- W/V = 10/100 = 10 grams/100 mL = 10%
- V/V = 1: 500 = 1 mL/500 mL = 0.2%

Dispensing Process

Dilution and Concentration
Proportional Calculations
Proportional calculations are often used in the pharmacy to determine how much of a medication should be dispensed, to calculate a dose, or to measure the amount in compounding.

Proportional calculations are usually conducted as follows:

$$\frac{A}{B} = \frac{X}{C}$$

For example, the following prescription may be received: Amoxicillin suspension, 300 mg bid x 10 days. When checking the shelf, the only amoxicillin suspension concentration available is 5 mL/200 mg. To find the dose, the equation should be set up as:

$$\frac{5\ mL}{200\ mg} = \frac{X}{300\ mg}$$

$$X = \frac{5\ mL \times 300\ mg}{200\ mg} = 7.5\ mL$$

This set up allows you to apply the same concentration to a different quantity.

Proportion Technique for Dilution
The following steps should be used to solve a dilution problem while using the proportional technique:

- Set up the proportion equation
- Solve for x, which is the total number of units of active ingredient in the solution
- Use proportions to calculate the amount of diluted solution that should be made
- Calculate x to obtain the total amount of diluted solution that can be made

To find how much diluent to add, the technician needs to subtract the original amount of solution from the total amount of diluted solution.

Example: You have 1 L of 70% alcohol solution. How much sterile water and how much 70% solution will you need to get 1 L of 40% alcohol solution?

Set up the proportional equation and solve for x to get the amount of 70% alcohol solution you need:

$$\frac{70\%}{1000\ mL} = \frac{40\%}{X}$$

$$X = \frac{1000\ mL \times 40\%}{70\%} = 571.4\ mL$$

Subtract the amount of 70% solution from the desired total solution (1 L) to find the amount of diluent:

$$1000\ mL - 571.4\ mL = 428.6\ mL\ sterile\ water$$

Finally, add the total diluent to the total original solution to get the correct amount of the desired solution:

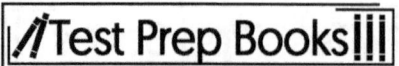

$$428.6 \, mL \, sterile \, water + 571.4 \, mL \, of \, 70\% \, solution = 1 \, L \, of \, 40\% \, alcohol \, solution$$

You will use 571.4 mL of 70% alcohol solution and 428.6 mL of sterile water to get 1L of 40% alcohol solution.

Intravenous Flow Rate

Intravenous (IV) flow rate is the rate at which an IV enters a person's veins. It is typically measured in mL/hr. Several equations are needed to find IV flow rate:

$$IV \, flow \, rate = \frac{total \, mL \, in \, the \, solution}{time}$$

For example, if a 1,000 mL bag of NS (normal saline, a common IV solution) is needed to be administered to a patient over 8 hours:

$$IV \, flow \, rate \, (\frac{mL}{hr}) = \frac{1000 \, mL}{8 \, hours}$$

$$125 \, mL/hr = \frac{1000 \, mL}{8 \, hours}$$

Therefore, the 1,000 mL solution should be administered over 8 hours at an IV flow rate of 125 mL/hr.

A prescription might also include a "bolus dose" or "loading dose" or say "push" in front of it, which means that it is a dose of this medication given at a specific rate, usually anywhere from 5 seconds to 30 minutes, to get the medication in quickly. Unless specified, this does not need to be included in the IV flow rate calculations because it is a quicker "push" of the medication into the patient's body rather than the slow, continuous/extended infusion like what was calculated above.

Alligation

This method is commonly called the **Tic-Tac-Toe method**, because it uses a grid that looks similar to a tic-tac-toe grid. The problem is set up by placing the desired concentration in the middle box, the higher concentration in the upper left-hand corner, and lower concentration in the lower left-hand corner. The process begins in the lower left-hand corner and moves towards the upper right-hand corner. The difference between the number in the lower left-hand corner and that in the middle box goes in the upper right-hand corner. Then, the difference between the upper left corner and the number in the middle is put in the lower right-hand corner. On the right, the number represents the parts of the concentration on the left that are used to make the needed concentration. By using proportion math, the volume of each can be calculated.

A figure and an example follow:

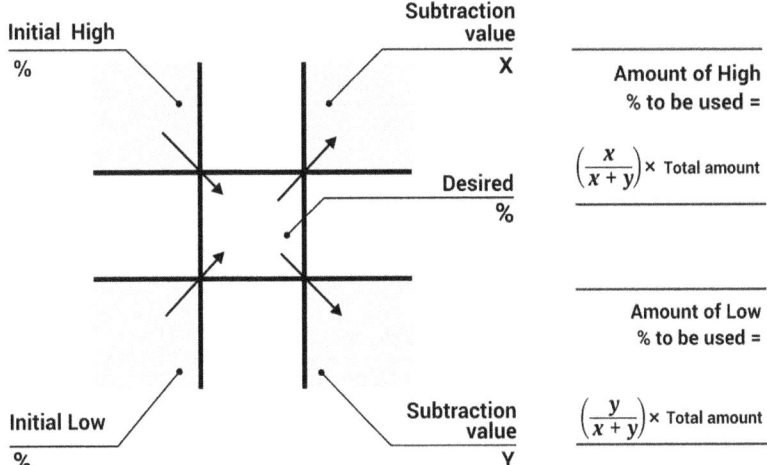

For example, how many grams of 1% hydrocortisone cream should be mixed with an appropriate quantity of 2.5% hydrocortisone cream to make 250 grams of 1.5% hydrocortisone cream?

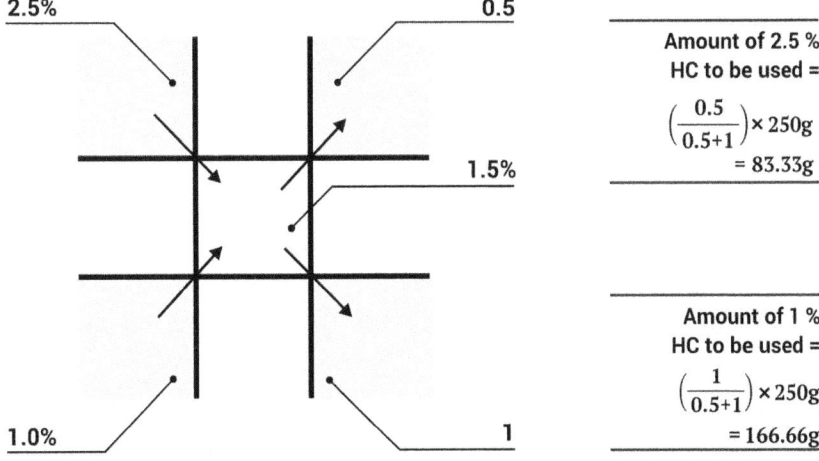

Therefore, 166.66 g of 1% hydrocortisone cream should be mixed with 83.33 g of 2.5% hydrocortisone cream to make 250 g of 1.5% hydrocortisone cream.

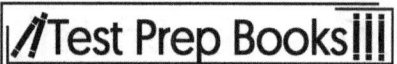

Calculating the Days' Supply for Prescriptions

Basic Algebra

Since physicians usually don't know how long a prescription will last, a pharmacy technician must be adept at an assortment of calculations. The first thing to master is the calculation of the days' supply of medication, which indicates how long a prescription will last. It must be calculated not only for tablets and capsules, but also for injectables, liquid medications, inhalers, and nasal sprays, as well as for PRN (as needed) lotions, ointments, creams, and drops. Other tasks requiring calculations are adjusting refills and short-fills.

Days' Supply for Tablets, Capsules, and Liquid Medications

The most straightforward calculations for days' supply are for tablets, capsules, and liquid medications.

Example: Calculate the days' supply for a prescription written for penicillin VK 500 mg tablets #40 i tab PO QID

$$Days'\ supply = \frac{Quantity\ Dispensed}{(Dose \times Frequency)}$$

$$Days'\ supply = \frac{40\ tabs}{(1\ tab \times 4\ times\ per\ day)} = 10\ days$$

Example: Calculate the days' supply for a prescription written for penicillin VK 500 mg/5 mL 200 mL i tsp PO QID

$$Days'\ supply = \frac{200\ mL}{(5\ mL \times 4\ times\ per\ day)} = 10\ days$$

Calculations for PRN (as needed) tablets, capsules, and liquid medications are more complicated due to the variability of doses and their frequencies. In general, the calculation should be made using the highest dose with the shortest interval.

Example: Calculate the days' supply for a prescription written for alprazolam (Xanax®) 0.5 mg #60 i-ii tabs PO q4-6h PRN anxiety.

$$Days'\ supply = \frac{60\ tabs}{2\ tabs \times \frac{24\ hours\ per\ day}{4\ hours}}$$

$$\frac{60\ tabs}{(2\ tabs \times 6\ per\ day)} = 5\ days$$

The results in the calculations above are even numbers. If the calculation yields a decimal, it's usually appropriate to drop the decimal.

Days' Supply for Insulins

The majority of insulins contain 100 units per mL, and insulin vials are typically packaged as either 10 mL vials or boxes of 5 syringes containing 3 mL per syringe for a total of 15 mL per box. Insulin vials should be kept no longer than 30 days after being opened.

Dispensing Process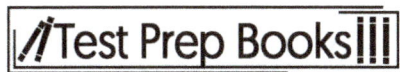

Example: Calculate the days' supply for a prescription written for insulin glargine (Lantus®) 10 mL 40 units SC daily.

$$Days'\ supply = \frac{10\ mL \times 100\ units}{40\ units\ per\ day} = 25\ days$$

This calculation does not account for the small amount lost per injection by priming a needle, however. If the wastage is accounted for, the calculated days' supply will be lower. In the case of insulin pens, up to approximately 2 units per injection may be lost by priming the needle before use.

Example: Calculate the days' supply for insulin glargine (Lantus®) 15 mL 50 units SC daily.

$$Days'\ supply = \frac{15\ mL \times 100\ units}{(50\ units\ per\ day) + (2\ units)} = 28.8\ days = 28\ days$$

Days' Supply for Inhalers and Sprays

With inhalers and sprays, it's important to observe on the packaging how many metered inhalations or sprays are actually in a container.

Example: Calculate the days' supply for a prescription written for a fluticasone (Flovent® HFA) 44 mcg inhaler ii puffs b.i.d. Each container is labeled as containing 200 metered inhalations.

$$Days'\ supply = \frac{200\ puffs}{(2\ puffs \times 2\ times\ a\ day)} = 50\ days$$

Days' Supply for Ointments and Creams

Calculations for ointments and creams are more complicated, because exactly how much is used per dose is unknown. Other complicating factors include the size of the area affected and the number of areas treated. In general, the directions are to use 1 gram (1000 mg) per dose per affected area.

Example: Calculate the days' supply for Kenalog® cream 15g apply b.i.d. to affected area(s).

$$Days'\ supply = \frac{15\ g}{(1\ g \times 2\ times\ per\ day)} = 7.5\ days = 7\ days\ (after\ dropping\ the\ decimal)$$

Days' Supply for Ophthalmic and Otic Medications

To determine the days' supply for ophthalmic and otic medications, use a conversion factor to convert milliliters (mL) to drops (gtt). The agreed-upon factor is 20 gtt/mL. For ophthalmic ointments, a dose equals 100 mg.

Example: Calculate the days' supply for pilocarpine 2% solution 15 mL ii gtt OU tid.

$$Days'\ supply = \frac{15\ mL \times \frac{20\ gtt}{mL}}{(4\ gtt \times 3\ doses\ per\ day)} = \frac{300\ gtt}{12\ gtt\ per\ day} = 25\ days$$

Example: Calculate the days' supply for Neosporin® ophthalmic ointment 3.5 g apply OU q3-4h while awake.

$$Days'\ supply = \frac{3.5\ g \times \frac{1000\ g}{mg}}{(200\ mg \times 5\ doses\ per\ day)} = 3.5\ days = 3\ days\ (after\ dropping\ the\ decimal)$$

The assumption, in this case, is that a patient sleeps 8 hours per day and is awake 16 hours per day. Using the shortest interval of dosing (every 3 hours while awake), the patient should apply approximately 5 doses per day.

Dispensing Process

Adjusting Refills and Short-Fills

Third-party prescription insurance providers often have dispensing limitations restricting the quantity of a medication that can be filled by a pharmacy. As a result, pharmacy technicians may have to adjust refills. The adjustment of refills oftentimes leads to short-filled prescriptions, or short-fills.

Example: A prescription is written for Celebrex® 100 mg caps #50 ȋ PO cap daily with 1 refill. The patient's insurance plan has a 30-day supply limitation. Calculate the number of refills and short-fills (if any) for the adjusted quantity.

First, calculate the total number of capsules over the life of the prescription:

$$50 \; capsules \times 2 \; total \; fills = 100 \; capsules$$

Next, calculate how many capsules needed per fill:

$$Capsules \; per \; fill = \frac{1 \; cap}{dose} \times \frac{1 \; dose}{day} \times \frac{30 \; days}{fill} = 30 \; caps/fill$$

Next, calculate how many fills are needed to dispense the quantity as specified by the prescriber:

$$Fills = \frac{100 \; caps}{(30 \; caps/fill)} = 3.333 \; fills$$

There will be at total of 2 refills after the initial fill by the pharmacy.

Now, calculate the quantity of the short-fill:

$$\frac{100 \; capsules}{3 \; fills \times (30 \; caps/fill)} = 10 \; capsules$$

There will be a short-fill of 10 capsules.

Example: A prescription is written for Lexapro® 20mg #50 ȋ PO cap daily with 3 refills. The patient's insurance plan has a 32-day supply limitation. Calculate the number of refills and short-fills (if any) for the adjusted quantity.

First, calculate the total number of capsules over the life of the prescription:

$$50 \; capsules \times 4 \; total \; fills = 200 \; capsules$$

Next, calculate how many capsules needed per fill:

$$Capsules \; per \; fill = \frac{1 \; cap}{dose} \times \frac{1 \; dose}{day} \times \frac{32 \; days}{fill} = 32 \; caps/fill$$

Next, calculate how many fills are needed to dispense the quantity as specified by the prescriber:

$$\frac{200 \; caps}{1} \times \frac{1 \; fill}{32 \; caps} = 6.25 \; fills$$

$$Fills = \frac{200 \; caps}{(32 \; caps/fill)} = 6.25 \; fills$$

There will be a total of *5 refills* after the initial fill by the pharmacy.

Dispensing Process

Now, calculate the quantity of the short-fill:

$$\frac{200 \ capsules}{6 \ fills \times (32 \ caps/fill)} = 8 \ capsules$$

There will be a short-fill of 8 capsules.

Caveat: Although pharmacy technicians are allowed to reduce the quantity dispensed in a fill, they cannot surpass the total prescribed quantity.

Calculating Individual and Total Daily Dosages

Units

The total daily dose (TDD) starting out is calculated with the formula 0.5 units/kg/day for insulin for type 1 diabetics (a basal and bolus dose), and 0.1 to 0.2 units/kg/day for type 2 diabetics (just a basal dose). For example, if a newly diagnosed type 1 diabetes mellitus patient weighs 30 kg, they would need 15 mg/day of insulin, as shown in this equation:

$$\frac{0.5 \ units \times 30 \ kg}{1 \ day} = x \ units/day$$

$$\frac{0.5 \ units \times 30 \ kg}{1 \ day} = 15 \ units/day$$

Type 1 diabetes mellitus patients are on a "basal/bolus regimen," which means that they take insulin at set times (basal) and before meals (bolus). Their daily doses are divided into these separate doses, to all equal the total daily dose of 15 units/day. To cover an entire month, it should cover 30 days. To calculate a monthly prescription:

$$\frac{15 \ units}{day} \times 30 \ days = \frac{x \ units}{month}$$

$$\frac{15 \ units}{day} \times 30 \ days = \frac{450 \ units}{month}$$

This patient would need 450 units every 30 days to have enough insulin. If the prescription is for U100 pens, the patient would need 5 pens:

$$\frac{450 \ units}{1 \ month} \div \frac{100 \ units}{1 \ insulin \ pen} = \frac{x \ pens}{1 \ month}$$

$$\frac{450 \ units}{1 \ month} \div \frac{100 \ units}{1 \ insulin \ pen} = \frac{4.5 \ pens}{1 \ month}$$

Even though it is more than the monthly dosage, there is no smaller dose, so you would want to give more insulin than needed to ensure that the patient has enough insulin to get through the month. Although insulin dosing is more complicated in how it breaks down for each meal and other adjustments, the prescription should indicate how much should be taken either per day or per dose.

Heparin is measured in 60 units/kg. Like insulin, it uses body weight to calculate the dose. For example, for a patient who weighs 70 kg:

$$\frac{70\ kg}{1} \times \frac{60\ units}{1\ kg} = x\ units/dose$$

$$\frac{70\ kg}{1} \times \frac{60\ units}{1\ kg} = 4200\ units/dose$$

If this patient needs 1 dose per day, the equation would be:

$$\frac{4200\ units}{day} \times 30\ days = x\ units$$

$$\frac{4200\ units}{day} \times 30\ days = 126{,}000\ units$$

If the heparin vials available were in 5,000 units/mL, and it came in a 10 mL vial, the patient would need:

$$\frac{5{,}000\ units}{1\ mL} \times \frac{10\ mL}{1\ vial} = x\ units/vial$$

$$\frac{5{,}000\ units}{1\ mL} \times \frac{10\ mL}{1\ vial} = 50{,}000\ units/vial$$

The patient would then need:

$$126{,}000\ units \div \frac{50{,}000\ units}{1\ vial} = x\ vials$$

$$126{,}000\ units \div \frac{50{,}000\ units}{1\ vial} = 2.52\ vials$$

Since, like with the insulin patient, you would not dispense part of a vial to a patient, the patient would receive 3 vials of 50,000 units/10 mL.

Pediatric Dosage Calculations

Pediatrics, children ages newborn to eighteen years old, usually use the same medications and therapies as adults, but their metabolism works differently, as their bodies are still developing. Therefore, different calculations are used to calculate dosages. The most common calculations are weight based, so you will most commonly see the Nomogram method (using body surface area [BSA]) and Clark's rule (using weight) used. Other methods of

Dispensing Process

calculating dosages include Fried's rule (using the child's age in months) and Young's rule (using the child's weight in pounds).

One of the most common calculations for pediatric dosing is with body surface area, which may also be called the Nomogram method. A nomogram is a chart that lists heights, weights, and BSA. You would take a patient's weight and height and draw a straight line between the two, and the BSA that is crossed by the line is a solid estimate of the patient's BSA.

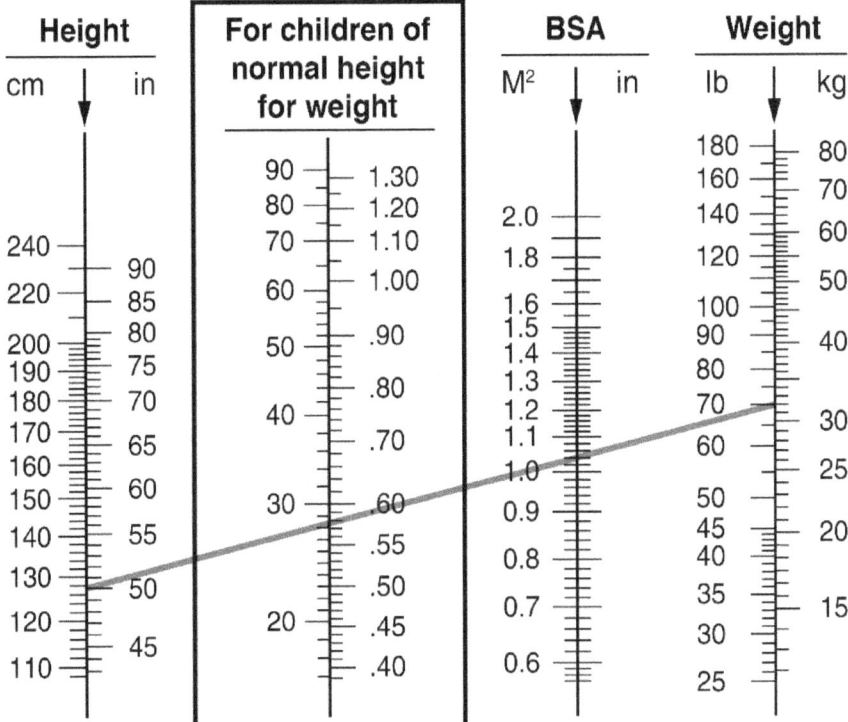

Another way of calculating the pediatric dose with BSA is by using the following formula:

$$Pediatric\ Dosage = \frac{child's\ BSA\ in\ m^2}{1.73\ m^2} \times adult\ dose\ (mg)$$

The adult dose used in the formula would be the typical adult dosage for that medication. For example, a 6-year-old patient named Bob weighs 50 lb (22.7 kg), is 45 inches (114.3 cm) tall, and needs a drug, CoughClear, which has a typical adult dose of 10 mg.

To calculate this, first calculate the BSA:

$$BSA\ (m^2) = \sqrt{\frac{[114.3\ cm \times 22.7\ kg]}{3600}}$$

$$0.85\ m^2 = \sqrt{\frac{[114.3\ cm \times 22.7\ kg]}{3600}}$$

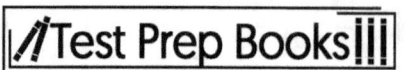

Then, use BSA to calculate the dosing for this patient:

$$dose\ (mg) = \frac{0.85\ m^2}{1.73\ m^2} \times 10\ mg$$

$$4.9\ mg = \frac{0.85\ m^2}{1.73\ m^2} \times 10\ mg$$

The dose Bob would need is 4.9 mg. The units are in mg because the units m^2 cancel out to leave mg.

Clark's rule uses the weight of the patient to adjust dosing. The formula using a child's weight in pounds is:

$$Pediatric\ Dosage = \frac{weight\ in\ lbs}{150\ lbs} \times adult\ dose\ (mg)$$

The formula using a child's weight in kilograms is:

$$Pediatric\ Dosage = \frac{weight\ in\ kg}{68\ kg} \times adult\ dose\ (mg)$$

For example, Bob, the same patient in the last example, needs a drug, PainRx, and the typical adult dosage is 100 mg. The calculation using his weight in pounds is:

$$\frac{50\ lbs}{150\ lbs} \times 100\ mg = dose\ (mg)$$

$$\frac{50\ lbs}{150\ lbs} \times 100\ mg = 33\ mg$$

The calculation using his weight in kilograms is:

$$\frac{22.7\ kg}{68\ kg} \times 100\ mg = dose\ (mg)$$

$$\frac{22.7\ kg}{68\ kg} \times 100\ mg = 33\ mg$$

The dosage for this specific patient would be 33 mg per dose. As shown above, it does not matter if pounds or kilograms are used for the weight measurement; both calculations end up being the same dose. The kg are divided, so they cancel out, which leaves the mg as the only unit.

Young's rule is based on age and recommended adult dosing. It is used for patients whose weight might not be available. The formula is:

$$pediatric\ dose = \frac{age}{(age + 12)} \times adult\ dose\ (mg)$$

Dispensing Process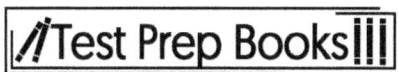

Using the same patient from earlier, we can calculate the dosage for PainRx again. As a reminder, Bob is 6 years old, and PainRx's recommended adult dosage is 100 mg:

$$\frac{6}{(6+12)} \times 100 \, mg = dose \, (mg)$$

$$\frac{6}{(6+12)} \times 100 \, mg = 33 \, mg$$

As seen above, using the patient's age gave the same dosing as using Clark's rule with the patient's weight. It does not always give as identical of a dosing recommendation, but it is accurate enough to use for dosing for most medications.

Fried's rule is similar to Young's rule, but it is personalized to infants. The equation is:

$$pediatric \, (infant) \, dose = \frac{infant's \, age \, in \, months}{150} \times adult \, dose \, (mg)$$

Sally is a 4-month-old who needs FeverBeGone, and the recommended adult dose is 50 mg:

$$\frac{4}{150} \times 50 \, mg = dose \, (mg)$$

$$\frac{4}{150} \times 50 \, mg = 1.3 \, mg$$

Sterile and Nonsterile Compounding Calculations

Basic Algebra

Besides the basic functions of addition, subtraction, multiplication, and division, understanding how to calculate percentages is crucial for pharmacy calculations. All percentages can be set up as two fractions that equal each other, like this:

$$\frac{part}{whole} = \frac{part's \, percentage}{100\%}$$

Using cross multiplication, you will be able to figure out any part of this equation that is missing, as long as you have the three other parts. The 100% will always be there. For example: What is 16% of 55? Fill in in the equation above:

$$\frac{16\% \, of \, 55}{55} = \frac{16\%}{100\%}$$

From here, multiply the two known values that are across from each other diagonally:

$$55 \times 16 = 880$$

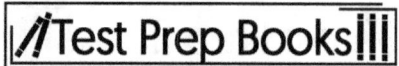

Another way of thinking about this step is that you can multiply both sides of the equation by 55 over 1 to remove the 55 from the left half of the equation. Remember, adding 1 under any number does not change the number's value:

$$\frac{\cancel{55}}{1} \times \frac{16\% \text{ of } 55}{\cancel{55}} = \frac{16\cancel{\%}}{100\cancel{\%}} \times \frac{55}{1}$$

This leaves:

$$16\% \text{ of } 55 = \frac{16 \times 55}{100} = \frac{880}{100}$$

From there, divide 880 by 100:

$$\frac{880}{100} = 8.8$$

Taking this number, 8.8, and substituting it back into the equation:

$$16\% \text{ of } 55 = 8.8$$

This gives us 8.8 as 16% of 55.

Another way to calculate percentages is by turning the percentage into a decimal and multiplying it by the original number:

$$original\ number \times \frac{percentage}{100} = percentage\ of\ the\ original\ number$$

Using the same example, 16% of 55:

$$55 \times \frac{16}{100} = 16\% \text{ of } 5.5$$

$$55 \times \frac{16}{100} = 8.8$$

Even though this second solution seems easier, knowing the cross-multiply method helps for many other equations, such as ratio strength and w/w% calculations.

Ratio Strength

Ratio strengths are usually used when there is a very low concentration of the active ingredient in the compound, so the percentage becomes harder to read, and ratios are used instead. A ratio shows the relationship between two objects, and in the pharmacy world, is usually 1:parts. For example, if you noticed you have 10 chicken nuggets to 7 fries left in your meal, it would be written as 10:7. For pharmacy, if the ratio was 1:150, that would mean 1 g or mL of the substance is in every 150 g or mL of the solution. Converting a percentage to a ratio is done using the following equation:

$$\frac{percent}{100\%} = \frac{1}{parts}$$

Dispensing Process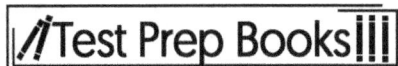

For example, converting 0.14% to a ratio:

$$\frac{0.14\%}{100\%} = \frac{1}{x\ parts}$$

$$\frac{x\ parts}{1} \times \frac{0.14\%}{100\%} = \frac{1}{x\ parts} \times \frac{x\ parts}{1}$$

$$x\ parts \times \frac{0.14}{100} = 1$$

$$x\ parts \times \frac{0.14}{100} \times \frac{100}{0.14} = 1 \times \frac{100}{0.14}$$

$$x\ parts = 714$$

$$\frac{0.14\%}{100\%} = \frac{1}{714\ parts}$$

The ratio would be 1:714. You can also use a simpler version where you would divide 100 by the percentage:

$$\frac{100\%}{percent\ strength} = parts$$

Then, this "parts" becomes the second number in the ratio, 1:parts. Using the same example, 0.14%:

$$\frac{100\%}{0.14\%} = x\ parts$$

$$\frac{100\%}{0.14\%} = 714\ parts, 1:714$$

When converting a ratio to a percentage, the same equation is used, but with different unknown variables:

$$\frac{percent}{100\%} = \frac{1}{parts}$$

For example, if the ratio strength of a diphenhydramine solution is 1:75:

$$\frac{x\%}{100\%} = \frac{1}{75}$$

$$\frac{100\%}{1} \times \frac{x\%}{100\%} = \frac{1}{75} \times \frac{100\%}{1}$$

$$x\% = \frac{100\%}{75} = 1.33\%$$

$$\frac{1.33\%}{100\%} = \frac{1}{75}$$

Therefore, the ratio 1:75 also means it is a 1.33% diphenhydramine solution.

W/W%, W/V%, V/V%

w/w% is short for percent weight-in-weight, which is the number of grams (g) of a substance in 100 g of a solution. This is used typically for semisolids, such as ointments, creams, and gels, where solid substances are added to a solid base. It is also used for very concentrated solutions, such as strong acid solutions. The basic equation for a 1% w/w solution is:

$$1\%\frac{w}{w} = \frac{1\ g\ substance}{100\ g\ solid\ preparation}$$

For example, if you wanted to find how many grams of zinc oxide go into a petroleum base compound of 300 g, which includes the petroleum base and the zinc oxide, of a 15% w/w solid compound, begin with the w/w% equation for 15%:

$$15\%\frac{w}{w} = \frac{x\ g\ zinc\ oxide}{100\ g\ solid\ compound}$$

$$\frac{100\ g\ solid\ compound}{1} \times 15\%\frac{w}{w} = \frac{x\ g\ zinc\ oxide}{100\ g\ solid\ compound} \times \frac{100\ g\ solid\ compound}{1}$$

$$15 = x\ g\ zinc\ oxide$$

$$15\%\frac{w}{w} = \frac{15\ g\ zinc\ oxide}{100\ g\ solid\ compound}$$

Dispensing Process

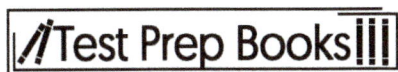

So, 15% w/w means that in 100 g of the solid compound, there would be 15 g of zinc oxide. We can then set it up as a ratio:

$$\frac{15 \text{ g zinc oxide}}{100 \text{ g solid compound}} = \frac{x \text{ g zinc oxide}}{300 \text{ g solid compound}}$$

$$\frac{300 \text{ g solid compound}}{1} \times \frac{15 \text{ g zinc oxide}}{100 \text{ g solid compound}} = \frac{x \text{ g zinc oxide}}{300 \text{ g solid compound}} \times \frac{300 \text{ g solid compound}}{1}$$

$$\frac{300 \times 15 \text{ g zinc oxide}}{100} = x \text{ g zinc oxide} = 45 \text{ g zinc oxide}$$

$$\frac{15 \text{ g zinc oxide}}{100 \text{ g solid compound}} = \frac{45 \text{ g zinc oxide}}{300 \text{ g solid compound}}$$

This means that in order to make a 15% w/w solid compound with a total weight of 300 g, 45 g of zinc oxide would be needed.

w/v% represents percent weight-in-volume, which has the same basic principles but is the number of grams of a substance in 100 mL of a liquid solution. This is used for solutions (nasal sprays, eye drops, etc.), lotions, and any type of solution or suspension. The basic equation for a 1% w/v solution is:

$$1\%\frac{w}{v} = \frac{1 \text{ g substance}}{100 \text{ mL solution}}$$

For example, if a 2.5% Augmentin solution is in a 200 mL bottle, the equation to find how many grams of Augmentin are in the bottle, 2.5% w/v, according to the w/v% equation, is:

$$2.5\%\frac{w}{v} = \frac{x \text{ g Augmentin}}{100 \text{ mL solution}}$$

$$\frac{100 \text{ mL solution}}{1} \times 2.5\%\frac{w}{v} = \frac{x \text{ g Augmentin}}{100 \text{ mL solution}} \times \frac{100 \text{ mL solution}}{1}$$

$$100 \text{ mL solution} \times 2.5\% = x \text{ g Augmentin} = 2.5 \text{ g Augmentin}$$

$$2.5\%\frac{w}{v} = \frac{2.5 \text{ g Augmentin}}{100 \text{ mL solution}}$$

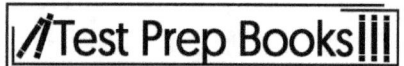

Dispensing Process

So, 2.5% w/v means that in a 100 mL of the solution, there would be 2.5 g of Augmentin. We can then set it up as a ratio:

$$\frac{2.5 \text{ g Augmentin}}{100 \text{ mL solution}} = \frac{5 \text{ g Augmentin}}{200 \text{ mL solution}}$$

This means that to make a 2.5% w/v solution with a total volume of 200 mL, 5 g of Augmentin would be needed to make this solution.

v/v% represents percent volume-in-volume, which also follows the same basic principles, but is the number of milliliters of a substance in 100 mL of a solution. It is used for when liquids are added to other liquids, such as emulsions, topical solutions, and other liquid-in-liquid solutions. The basic equation for a 1% v/v solution is:

$$1\% \frac{v}{v} = \frac{1 \text{ mL substance}}{100 \text{ mL solution}}$$

For example, if a 30% alcohol-in-water solution is in a 550 mL bottle, the equation to find how many milliliters are in the bottle, 30% v/v, according to the v/v% equation, is:

$$30\% \frac{v}{v} = \frac{x \text{ mL alcohol}}{100 \text{ mL water}}$$

$$30\% \frac{v}{v} = \frac{30 \text{ mL alcohol}}{100 \text{ mL water}}$$

So, 30% v/v means that in a 100 mL of the solution (water), there would be 30 mL of alcohol. We can then set it up as a ratio:

$$\frac{30 \text{ mL alcohol}}{100 \text{ mL solution}} = \frac{x \text{ mL alcohol}}{550 \text{ mL solution}}$$

$$\frac{550 \; \cancel{\text{mL solution}}}{1} \times \frac{30 \text{ mL alcohol}}{100 \; \cancel{\text{mL solution}}} = \frac{x \text{ mL alcohol}}{\cancel{550 \text{ mL solution}}} \times \frac{\cancel{550 \text{ mL solution}}}{1}$$

$$\frac{550 \times 30 \text{ mL alcohol}}{100} = x \text{ mL alcohol} = 165 \text{ mL alcohol}$$

$$\frac{30 \text{ mL alcohol}}{100 \text{ mL solution}} = \frac{165 \text{ mL alcohol}}{550 \text{ mL solution}}$$

This means that to make a 30% alcohol solution with a total volume of 550 mL, 165 mL of alcohol would be needed to make this solution. All of these types of percentage strengths work in the same way, but differ in what types of compounds (solid, liquid, semisolid, etc.) they represent.

Dispensing Process

Dilution/Concentration

Dilution is an amount that is put in a solution or compound to change the concentration, or makeup, of the solution. Concentration is the amount of an active ingredient or another aspect of the solution or base in comparison to the whole solution. To "concentrate" a solution is to increase the amount of active ingredient and decrease the amount of base and fillers, so that there is more drug per milliliter or milligram, etc. Diluent is the base or fillers added to decrease concentration of the active ingredients or provide a vehicle for the active ingredient to reside (otherwise the active ingredient may be too big, too small, not taste good, etc.). To "dilute" a solution is to decrease the amount of active ingredient and increase the amount of base and fillers. As verbs, concentrate and dilute are opposite words. As nouns, concentration and diluent work together. The formula for concentration and dilution is:

$$C_1 V_1 = C_2 V_2$$

C stands for concentration and V stands for volume in this equation. Since there is a C and a V on both sides, the units just have to be the same as the other side; there are no given units. This easy formula simplifies how do to these calculations. For example, what is the concentration of 500 mL of 150 mL of 12% dextromethorphan?

$$12\% \times 150\ mL = x\% \times 500\ mL$$

To solve this equation, multiply the 12% and 150 mL:

$$12\% \times 150\ mL = 18\ mL$$

Therefore,

$$18\ mL = x\% \times 500\ mL$$

Take the 18, and divide 500 mL from this number:

$$\frac{18\ mL}{500\ mL} = 0.036$$

$$0.036 \times 100\% = 3.6\%$$

The mL as units will cancel out when they are divided, and this leaves the final concentration of 0.036. We can multiply this number by 100 to get the concentration as a percent, which is 3.6%.

Since it is the same solution, but now in more base/dilution with the volume increase, the concentration decreases because the solution now has more parts base than it did before.

For another example, if you only have a 1.5-liter bottle of 16% magnesium hydroxide solution, but the prescription calls for 5% magnesium hydroxide, how much 16% magnesium hydroxide solution and diluent would be needed?

$$16\% \times 1500\ mL = 5\% \times V_2$$

Solving for V_2, it would equal 4,800 mL (milliliters are used because that is how percentages are read in pharmacy). This means that the final volume of the 16% magnesium solution should be 4,800 mL, or 4.8 L. However, this is the final volume of the solution, not the measurement of how much 16% magnesium hydroxide we used. Besides, the amount we started with is 1.5 L, so we could not account for what makes up the rest of this now 4.8 L solution. This is done by using the equation:

$$amount\ of\ base, or\ diluent, added = final\ volume - original\ amount\ of\ V_1\ added$$

Dispensing Process

In the case of the example above:

$$4.8\ L - 1.5\ L = 3.3\ L\ diluent\ added\ to\ 5\%\ solution$$

The final solution is that to get 4.8 L of a 5% magnesium hydroxide from a 16% magnesium hydroxide solution, use 1.5 L of 16% magnesium hydroxide solution and 3.3 L of diluent.

Alligation

Alligation is a calculation method used for mixing products with different strengths to find the desired intermediate strength. There are two different types of alligation problems: the first type involves mixing the same ingredient together with different strengths and amounts and finding the amount of the ingredient in the final product, and the second type involves knowing the final percentage but needing one of the ingredient's strengths or amounts. The first way is calculated by listing the quantity of each component, multiplying the quantity of each ingredient by its percentage in decimal form and adding up the products, dividing this value by the sum of the amount of each ingredient, and multiplying all of this by 100. Here it is in an equation:

$$\frac{part\ 1\ strength\ (\%)}{100} \times original\ part\ 1\ amount\ (g\ or\ mL) = equivalent\ amount\ of\ product\ 1\ (g\ or\ mL)$$

$$\frac{part\ 2\ strength\ (\%)}{100} \times original\ part\ 2\ amount\ (g\ or\ mL) = equivalent\ amount\ of\ product\ 2\ (g\ or\ mL)$$

$$\frac{part\ 3\ strength\ (\%)}{100} \times original\ part\ 3\ amount\ (g\ or\ mL) = equivalent\ amount\ of\ product\ 3\ (g\ or\ mL)$$

Then, these are added together:

$$equivalent\ amount\ of\ product\ 1 + equivalent\ amount\ of\ product\ 2 + equivalent\ amount\ of\ product\ 3 = total\ amount\ of\ all\ products$$

And these as well:

$$original\ part\ 1\ amount + original\ part\ 2\ amount + original\ part\ 3\ amount = total\ original\ amount\ of\ all\ parts$$

Similar to the ratios we did previously, set this up as a new ratio:

$$\frac{total\ amount\ of\ products\ in\ mixture}{total\ original\ amount\ of\ all\ parts} = \frac{amount\ of\ the\ product}{100}$$

Dispensing Process

This gives you the amount of the product, or the percentage of it, depending on what the question asks for. For example, if you are looking for the percentage of zinc oxide in the final product when mixing 50 g of 20% zinc oxide ointment, 75 g of 15% zinc oxide ointment, and 10 g of 30% zinc oxide ointment:

$$\frac{20\%}{100} \times 50\ g = 10\ g$$

$$\frac{15\%}{100} \times 75\ g = 11.25\ g$$

$$\frac{30\%}{100} \times 10\ g = 3\ g$$

Adding these together to get the new amount of zinc oxide in the ointment:

$$10\ g + 11.25\ g + 3\ g = x\ g\ zinc\ oxide$$

$$10\ g + 11.25\ g + 3\ g = 24.25\ g\ zinc\ oxide$$

Then, adding together the original amounts of the ointment itself to get the total weight of the ointment:

$$50\ g + 75\ g + 10\ g = x\ g\ ointment$$

$$50\ g + 75\ g + 10\ g = 135\ g\ ointment$$

Setting this up in the ratio:

$$\frac{24.25\ g\ zinc\ oxide}{135\ g\ ointment} = \frac{x\ g\ zinc\ oxide}{100\ g\ ointment}$$

$$\frac{100\ \cancel{g\ ointment}}{1} \times \frac{24.25\ g\ zinc\ oxide}{135\ \cancel{g\ ointment}} = \frac{x\ g\ zinc\ oxide}{\cancel{100\ g\ ointment}} \times \frac{\cancel{100\ g\ ointment}}{1}$$

$$\frac{100 \times 24.25\ g\ zinc\ oxide}{135} = x\ g\ zinc\ oxide = 18\ g\ zinc\ oxide$$

$$\frac{24.25\ g\ zinc\ oxide}{135\ g\ ointment} = \frac{18\ g\ zinc\ oxide}{100\ g\ ointment}$$

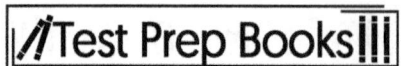

18 g is the new amount of zinc oxide in 100 g of the new solution, or 18% strength. The higher the strength, the more concentrated the ointment is, meaning that it is stronger.

The other form of alligation calculation is finding the ingredient amount or percentage strength from the other ingredients and total product. The easiest way to calculate this is by making a matrix:

Higher strength		Parts of higher
	Desired strength	
Lower strength		Parts of lower

Then, you subtract across the diagonals:

$$higher\ strength - desired\ strength = parts\ of\ lower$$

$$desired\ strength - lower\ strength = parts\ of\ higher$$

Add together the parts in the right-hand column:

$$parts\ of\ higher + parts\ of\ lower = total\ parts\ needed\ of\ the\ desired\ strength$$

This gives you the amount of parts per the percentage strength, which can help you find the ratio strength or proportion of parts of upper:parts of lower. You can also find the amount of grams of the higher or lower strength needed for this mixture by using the equation:

$$\frac{parts\ of\ higher}{higher\ strength\ amount\ in\ grams, mL, etc.} = \frac{parts\ of\ lower}{lower\ strength\ amount\ in\ grams, mL, etc.}$$

For example, how many mg of 10% WrinkleZap gel needs to be mixed with 3.3 mg of a 3% WrinkleZap gel to get a 7.5% WrinkleZap gel?

First, set up the table:

Higher strength: 10%		Parts of higher
	Desired strength: 7.5%	
Lower strength: 3%		Parts of lower

Then, subtract across the diagonals, with these equations:

$$higher\ strength - desired\ strength = parts\ of\ lower$$

$$desired\ strength - lower\ strength = parts\ of\ higher$$

Higher strength: 10%		Parts of higher: 4.5 parts
	Desired strength: 7.5%	
Lower strength: 3%		Parts of lower: 2.5 parts

You need 4.5 parts of the 10% gel and 2.5 parts of the 3% gel to achieve the desired strength of 7.5% gel. To find the amount in mg of how much 10% WrinkleGel is needed:

$$\frac{4.5\ parts\ higher}{x\ mg} = \frac{2.5\ parts\ lower}{3.3\ mg}$$

$$\frac{\cancel{x\ mg}}{1} \times \frac{4.5\ parts\ higher}{\cancel{x\ mg}} = \frac{2.5\ parts\ lower}{3.3\ \cancel{mg}} \times \frac{x\ \cancel{mg}}{1}$$

$$\frac{3.3}{2.5\ parts\ lower} \times 4.5\ parts\ higher = \frac{\cancel{2.5\ parts\ lower}}{\cancel{3.3}} \times \frac{\cancel{3.3}}{\cancel{2.5\ parts\ lower}} \times x$$

$$\frac{3.3}{2.5\ parts\ lower} \times 4.5\ parts\ higher = x = 5.94$$

Solving for x, x = 5.94 mg. Therefore, 5.94 mg of 10% WrinkleGel and 3.3 mg of 3% WrinkleGel would make a 9.24 mg mixture of 7.5% WrinkleGel.

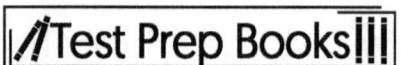

Basic Pharmacy Business Calculations

Types of Business Calculations

In addition to all of the pharmacy calculations, since the pharmacy is a business, a good grasp on how business calculations work is crucial to understanding profits, taking discounts at the register, and understanding what it takes to keep a business afloat.

Markup is the amount of money made off of a sale. To calculate this:

$$markup = selling\ price - cost\ of\ item$$

For example, if the pharmacy needed a bottle of Advil for a patient and it would cost them $2.50 to buy it from their distributor and they sold it to their patient for $8.75, the markup that the pharmacy makes from the selling of this bottle of Advil is $6.25:

$$\$6.25 = \$8.75 - \$2.50$$

This is not including any additional costs, but is simply based on the price the pharmacy had to buy it for and the price the customer paid the pharmacy for the Advil bottle.

Going along with markup, a markup percentage can be calculated:

$$\frac{cost\ the\ customer\ paid\ for\ the\ item}{cost\ the\ pharmacy\ paid\ for\ the\ item} = \frac{percent\ markup}{100\%}$$

If we use the same example:

$$\frac{\$8.75}{\$2.50} = \frac{x\%}{100\%}$$

$$\frac{100\%}{1} \times \frac{\$8.75}{\$2.50} = \frac{x\%}{\cancel{100\%}} \times \frac{\cancel{100\%}}{1}$$

$$\frac{100 \times 8.75}{2.50} = x\% = 350\%$$

$$\frac{\$8.75}{\$2.50} = \frac{350\%}{100\%}$$

This shows that the markup percentage is 350%. In other words, the pharmacy charged 350% above the price they paid for the Advil so that they could make a profit. If the pharmacy were to do what is called "break even," where they make the same exact money back that they paid for the item, the markup percentage would be 100%. Anything greater than 100% means that the business earned a profit, and if it is under 100%, the pharmacy lost money on the sale. Gross profit is the total revenue, or total income without subtracting any costs, minus manufacturing costs. Net profit is the profit the pharmacy will make after all of the costs of running the pharmacy have been taken out. It takes the markup and subtracts the other costs that the pharmacy pays to get the product, including employee salaries and the cost of the label and packaging, rent, utility bills, etc. These costs are usually

Dispensing Process

called overhead. You do not need to know how to calculate this cost for each prescription—just know that it exists and that it takes money from the profit made on each purchase. The equation is listed below:

$$net\ profit = markup - overhead$$

If we use the same example, but we add in a dispensing fee of $5.00, this would be calculated as:

$$\$x = \$6.25 - \$5.00$$

$$\$1.25 = \$6.25 - \$5.00$$

Another important pharmacy business calculation is taking discounts. Commonly, customers will come in with discount cards, coupons, and discounts on their account already for prescriptions, OTCs, and other items that the pharmacy may keep in stock. If the computer will not do it for you, this is the formula:

$$discounted\ price = price\ of\ the\ item - discount$$

For example, if a patient purchases a $10 bottle of Vitamin C 500 mg, and brings in a coupon he got in the mail for $3.00 off, this would be the equation:

$$\$x = \$10.00 - \$3.00$$

$$\$7.00 = \$10.00 - \$3.00$$

The price the customer would pay is $7.00 instead of the original price of $10.00.

Often, a discount will be represented as a percentage instead of a dollar amount. This would be calculated with this equation:

$$\frac{discount\ (\$)}{original\ price\ of\ the\ item} = \frac{discount\ (\%)}{100\%}$$

Then, you take the discount from this equation and subtract it from the original price:

$$discounted\ price = original\ price\ of\ the\ item - discount\ (\$)$$

If we use the same $10 bottle of Vitamin C, but the customer gets 20% off of all vitamins at this specific pharmacy:

$$\frac{discount = \$x}{\$10.00} = \frac{20\%}{100\%}$$

$$\frac{\$10.00}{1} \times \frac{discount = \$x}{\$10.00} = \frac{20\%}{100\%} \times \frac{\$10.00}{1}$$

$$discount = \$x = \frac{20 \times \$10.00}{100} = \$2.00$$

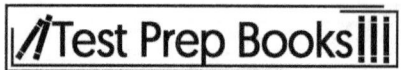

$$\frac{discount = \$2}{\$10.00} = \frac{20\%}{100\%}$$

Then:

$$\$final\ price = \$10.00\ (original\ price) - \$2.00\ (discount)$$

$$\$8.00 = \$10.00 - \$2.00$$

This means that with a 20% coupon, the patient will only pay $8.00 for the Vitamin C bottle instead of the original price of $10.00.

Turnover rate is the rate that measures how many employees are leaving the company. This includes employees that leave, employees that retire, or employees that are fired or let go. This is calculated by:

$$\frac{employees\ that\ leave\ (for\ any\ reason)}{average\ number\ of\ employees} \times 100 = \%\ employee\ turnover\ rate$$

For example, your pharmacy employs an average of 50 people over a year, and 7 leave for various reasons:

$$\frac{7\ employees\ leave}{50} \times 100 = \%\ turnover\ rate$$

$$\frac{7\ employees\ leave}{50} \times 100 = 14\%\ turnover\ rate$$

The turnover rate for this pharmacy is 14%. The higher the turnover rate, the more employees there are who are leaving. Businesses look at this number to determine what they need to work on—higher pay, more vacation days, better working conditions, better management, etc.—so that they do not have as many employees leave. It costs time and money to train new employees, and having more experienced employees promotes the success of a business.

Temperature Conversions

Temperature Scales

Celsius is the metric system unit of measurement for temperature. While it does not use any prefixes, it does use a system of tens for measurements based on the properties of water. Zero degrees Celsius (°C) is the temperature at which water freezes, and 100 °C is the temperature at which water boils. 37 °C is the average body temperature. 20 °C to 25 °C is the average room temperature, 2 °C to 8 °C is the range of refrigerator temperatures, and -18 °C is the typical freezer temperature. Room temperature, refrigerator temperature, and freezer temperature will be the most important measurements to remember, as many medications have specific temperature storage requirements.

Fahrenheit is the customary system's unit of measurement for temperature. It is also based on the properties of water, but again, it does not have a set pattern. 32 degrees Fahrenheit (°F) is the temperature at which water freezes, and 212 °F is the temperature at which water boils. An average normal body temperature is 98.6 °F, but it can fluctuate between 96 °F to 99 °F. Room temperature is defined as 68 °F to 77 °F, refrigerated temperature is typically defined as 36 °F to 46 °F, and freezer temperature is defined as around 5 °F or less.

Dispensing Process

To convert Celsius to Fahrenheit, this is the equation:

$$\frac{9}{5}(°C) + 32 = °F$$

The accuracy of this equation for the conversion from Celsius to Fahrenheit can be proven by using 37 °C and 98.6 °F (the normal body temperature for each of the measurement systems):

$$\frac{9}{5}(37°C) + 32 = x°F$$

$$\frac{9}{5}(37°C) + 32 = 98.6 °F$$

To convert Fahrenheit to Celsius, this is the same equation, but rearranged to make Celsius what the equation equals. This is the equation:

$$\frac{5}{9}(°F - 32) = °C$$

Taking the same body temperature conversion, 98.6 °F to 37 °C, here is the equation:

$$\frac{5}{9}(98.6°F - 32) = x°C$$

$$\frac{5}{9}(98.6°F - 32) = 37 °C$$

These two equations show the conversion between the two systems for body temperature.

The following table gives examples of temperature conversions:

32 °F	0 °C
40 °F	4.45 °C
20 °C	68 °F
60 °C	140 °F

Sterile and Nonsterile Products, Compounding, Unit Dose, and Repackaging

Universal Precautions

The Centers for Disease Control and Prevention (CDC) and the Occupational Safety and Health Administration (OSHA) created the universal precautions (UP) guidelines to help reduce infectious diseases in healthcare settings. The guidelines include precautions related to patients infected with specific pathogens like HIV, syphilis, or malaria. The guidelines also recommend using personal protective equipment (PPE) like gloves, masks, and eyewear (such as goggles) when handling potentially infectious materials that can be present in liquids (such as body fluids, plasma, or blood). In addition, those who work in health care and most other establishments (like the food or cosmetic industry) must wash their hands thoroughly before and after patient encounters. The guidelines apply to all healthcare providers, including hospitals, pharmacies, and long-term care facilities.

In addition to using PPE and hand washing, the UP guidelines recommend additional steps to help prevent the spread of infectious diseases. These include using disposable needles and syringes, avoiding recapping needles (potential for re-sticking), and making sure to dispose of used needles and other sharp objects into puncture-resistant containers (often called sharps containers). There are also recommendations outlining cleaning and disinfecting procedures for surfaces that have come into contact with blood or body fluids. Cleaning the surfaces and supplies using disinfectant registered by the EPA (Environmental Protection Agency) is one of the recommendations. Training is also an important aspect of UP. It outlines training for healthcare workers regarding the proper use of PPE, hand washing, and other infection control measures. Employers are typically responsible for providing this training and verifying that healthcare workers understand and follow the guidelines. The UP guidelines are followed to reduce the prevalence of infectious disease transmission, but there are some limitations to the guidelines which include the lack of consideration for non-blood borne pathogen transmission, e.g., respiratory diseases.

Infection Control

Hand Hygiene

Medical personnel should know the proper sequence for putting on and removing PPE. For example, pharmacy staff must adhere to guidelines set forth in USP <797>, a chapter on pharmaceutical sterile preparations in the USP National Formulary, when compounding sterile preparations. First, staff should remove all unnecessary outer garments and jewelry. Next, staff should put on shoe covers, facial and head hair covers, face masks, and optional face shields. Then, staff should perform mandatory hand hygiene. USP <797> specifies:

"...personnel perform a thorough hand-cleansing procedure by removing debris from under fingernails using a nail cleaner under running warm water followed by vigorous hand and arm washing to the elbows for at least 30 seconds with either nonantimicrobial or antimicrobial soap and water."

After performing hand hygiene, staff should put on a gown with sleeves fitting snugly around the wrists. Upon advancing to the buffer area (a clean, sterile area), a waterless alcohol-based scrub should be carried out. Lastly, sterile gloves should be put on prior to compounding sterile preparations.

USP <795> provides guidelines for infection control in nonsterile compounding to prevent the transmission of infectious agents and ensure safety for both compounders and patients. The guidelines recommend hand hygiene, PPE, cleaning, and disinfecting to minimize the risk of contamination. Proper disposal of waste products and regular testing and monitoring of compounded products for contamination and potency are also recommended. Nonsterile and sterile compounding areas should be separate and distinct.

Effective hand hygiene is crucial to prevent contamination and includes having proper water requirements for hand washing. These include a plumbing system that is free of defects, reliable hot and cold water, and readily available potable water which must meet standards defined by the EPA. Compounders must wash their hands with soap and water or use an alcohol-based hand sanitizer before and after compounding. PPE—such as gloves, gowns, and face masks—should also be worn during compounding. Cleaning and disinfecting surfaces and equipment using appropriate disinfectants, like 70% isopropyl alcohol, is critical to preventing contamination.

Proper waste disposal is necessary to minimize the risk of contamination and injury. Regular testing and monitoring of compounded products for contamination and potency can ensure safety and effectiveness.

Personal Protective Equipment

The pharmacy staff should use Personal Protective Equipment (PPE) appropriate to the nature of the contaminating agents. The PPE most commonly used in healthcare facilities are gloves, masks, gowns, head covers, shoe covers, and eye protection. Note that the use of PPE does not eliminate the need for proper hand washing. When used properly, PPE can significantly reduce the risk of infection spread; however, PPE cannot completely eliminate the risk. Staff should never share PPE. PPE should be completely changed after a task, and used PPE should be disposed of appropriately. Hand washing should be done every time after disposal of the PPE and before attending to another duty.

Gloves are routinely used in compounding practice to prevent contamination and the spread of infection. Their use also helps personnel reduce contamination while performing procedures.

The following considerations should be kept in mind for best use of gloves in practice:

- Gloves should be removed carefully to prevent skin contamination.
- Hands should be washed each time after removing gloves.
- Single-use gloves should not be reused and should be discarded.
- Gloves should be changed after contact with contaminated items, such as linens or wastes.
- Gloves should be purchased from manufacturers that meet the regulatory board standards.

Masks provide respiratory protection from airborne solid particles and droplets. Droplets refers to liquid particles larger than 5μm in size. The symbol μ means one millionth. So, 1 μm is equivalent to one millionth of a meter. Droplets do not stay suspended in air for very long. and instead fall on various surfaces. N-95 masks are widely used in health practice. The "N" means "not resistant to oil" and "95" indicates that it has 95% efficacy for filtering particles of 0.3 μm size. The National Institute for Occupational Safety and Health (NIOSH) in the U.S. certified that N-95 masks provide adequate protection against airborne particles, but not against gas or vapor. They also provide little protection against direct liquid splashes.

The following considerations need to be considered for proper use of masks in practice:

- Gloves should be removed first, and hands should be washed prior to removing the mask.
- The mask should be removed carefully to prevent contamination to airway or skin.
- Hold the mask, remove ties, and pull mask away from the face. Do not drag the mask over the face.
- Discard gloves and mask, and wash hands afterward.

Maintaining the Environment for the Sterile Product Compounding Area

Infection Control (USP <795> and <797>)

Infection control is crucial in any healthcare setting, particularly in the compounding of sterile products. USP <795> and <797> provide guidelines for the compounding of nonsterile and sterile preparations, respectively. Maintaining a clean and sterile environment is essential to prevent the contamination of sterile products during the compounding process. USP <797> outlines the requirements for maintaining the environment of the sterile product compounding area. This includes the use of HEPA (high-efficiency particulate air) filters to eliminate airborne pathogens as well as properly cleaning and disinfecting the compounding area. The compounding area should be in a separate room or area that is free from traffic and other sources of contamination. The area should be cleaned and disinfected before each use, including all surfaces, equipment, and supplies. USP <797> also recommends that the compounding area be equipped with laminar airflow workstations to provide a clean environment for the compounding of sterile products. The laminar airflow workstation provides a continuous flow of filtered air to

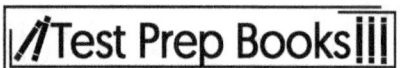

Dispensing Process

prevent the entry of contaminants into the sterile environment. These workstations should be properly maintained and serviced to ensure that they are functioning correctly.

In addition to maintaining a clean environment, USP <795> and <797> also provide guidelines for the proper handling and storage of supplies and equipment. Nonsterile supplies and equipment should be stored in a clean, dry area away from potential sources of contamination. Sterile supplies and equipment should be stored in a sterile environment, such as a laminar airflow workstation or a sterile storage area. USP <797> also requires that all personnel involved in the compounding of sterile preparations wear appropriate PPE, including gloves, gowns, masks, and eye protection. PPE should be changed between each step of the compounding process to prevent contamination. Proper hand hygiene is also essential for maintaining a clean and sterile environment.

Maintaining Sterile Environment (USP <797>)

USP <797> guidelines focus on maintaining an aseptic, or sterile, environment during the compounding of sterile preparations. Infection control is critical to preventing the introduction of microorganisms and other contaminants into the compounding area which could lead to the production of contaminated sterile products. Maintaining a sterile environment ensures the safety and efficacy of sterile preparations. USP <797> outlines requirements for the design and construction of the compounding area to maintain a sterile environment. The compounding area should be separate and designed to prevent the entry of contaminants, including the use of anterooms, HEPA filters, and laminar airflow workstations. These workstations should be properly maintained and serviced to ensure their functioning. USP <797> also provides guidelines for cleaning, disinfecting, and storing supplies and equipment to maintain a sterile environment. Personnel involved in the compounding of sterile preparations should follow proper gowning and gloving procedures to prevent the introduction of contaminants. USP <797> requires personnel involved in compounding to wear appropriate PPE and undergo regular training and competency assessments to ensure proper aseptic techniques.

Selecting Appropriate Equipment and Supplies

Needle Gauges and Types

Needles are medical devices that are used for a variety of medical procedures such as injections, blood draws, and infusions. The size and type of needle that is used depends on the medication being administered and the patient's condition. The gauge of a needle refers to the diameter of the needle's shaft. The higher the gauge number, the thinner the needle diameter. For example, a 30-gauge needle is thinner than a 27-gauge needle. A smaller gauge needle is typically used for thicker medications or when administering medications to children or patients with small veins. Thicker needles, such as an 18–20-gauge needle, are used for procedures such as blood transfusions and drawing blood for lab tests.

A filter needle is a specialized type of needle that is designed to remove any impurities or particles from medication before it is administered. These needles contain a filter inside the needle's hub that captures any unwanted particles that may be present in the medication. Filter needles are commonly used when administering medications that are reconstituted or have particulate matter, such as chemotherapy drugs.

Insulin needles are another type of needle that is specifically designed for administering insulin. These needles are much shorter and thinner compared to regular needles to reduce the patient's discomfort during the injection process. Insulin needles are available in different gauges, with the most common sizes being 28-gauge and 30-gauge.

Selecting the appropriate needle is important to ensure patient comfort and safety during a medical procedure. Using a needle that is too large can cause pain and discomfort for the patient and may also damage surrounding tissue or veins. A needle that is too small may result in difficulty administering the medication or drawing blood.

Types of Syringes

Syringes are medical devices used for a variety of purposes, including administering medications, drawing blood, and performing diagnostic tests. There are different types of syringes available, and selecting the appropriate syringe for a given medical procedure is important to ensure safe and effective patient care.

One of the most common types of syringes is the standard syringe. These syringes come in sizes ranging from 1 mL to 60 mL and are available in both Luer Lock and Slip Tip versions. Luer Lock syringes are designed to securely attach to needles and prevent accidental disconnection. Slip Tip syringes are designed for use with needles that slide onto the tip of the syringe.

Another type of syringe is the insulin syringe, which is specifically designed for administering insulin. These syringes are smaller than standard syringes, with sizes ranging from 0.3 mL to 1 mL. Insulin syringes have short, fine needles and are calibrated in units of insulin rather than milliliters.

There are also safety syringes, which are designed to minimize the risk of needlestick injuries. These syringes have a variety of safety features—such as retractable needles or needle shields—that help prevent accidental needlestick injuries during disposal.

Prefilled syringes are another type of syringe commonly used in healthcare settings. These syringes come prefilled with a specific medication and are ready to use. Prefilled syringes can help minimize the risk of medication errors and reduce the time needed for medication preparation.

Choosing the appropriate syringe for a given medical procedure is essential to ensure safe and effective patient care. For example, using a standard syringe instead of an insulin syringe to administer insulin can result in inaccurate dosing and potential harm to the patient. Similarly, using a syringe that is too large for a given procedure can result in discomfort or injury to the patient, while using a syringe that is too small can make it difficult to accurately measure and administer medications.

Diluents and Base Products

Diluents and base products are essential components of medications and are used to adjust the strength, viscosity, and stability of formulations. Diluents are utilized to decrease the concentration of active ingredients in a medication, but base products are utilized as a method, or vehicle, for delivering the medication. There are several factors to consider when selecting the appropriate diluent or base product for a given medication. These may include the physical and chemical properties of the active ingredient, the route of administration, and the characteristics of the final product.

A common diluent used is water for injection (WFI), which is a sterile, pyrogen-free water that is used to dissolve medications that are not stable in normal saline or other common diluents. Other common diluents include normal saline, dextrose, and alcohol.

Base products are used as the primary method for delivering medications and can be classified as aqueous or non-aqueous. Aqueous base products, such as water-based gels or creams, are commonly used for topical medications and intravenous (IV) medications. Non-aqueous base products, such as ointments or lipid-based formulations, are commonly used for topical medications and can be used to increase the stability and absorption of certain active ingredients.

It's important to consider the route, target site, and final concentration when choosing a base product. For example, a medication needed for intravenous administration may require an aqueous base product that is sterile and pyrogen-free, but a medication intended for topical use may require a non-aqueous base product that can be easily absorbed and can form a protective barrier for the skin. Compatibility considerations are also important (especially

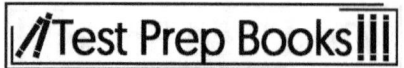

when adding other components such as preservatives, stabilizers, and flavoring agents) because they can affect the stability and efficacy of the final product and may need to be adjusted or eliminated depending on patient-specific factors.

Compounding Sterile Products Following Aseptic Technique

Pharmaceutical compounding refers to the formulation of a product in a pharmacy, distinct from one supplied by a commercial manufacturer, in order to meet the unique needs of a patient as specified by the physician. The reasons for pharmaceutical compounding vary:

- The product might not be available commercially.
- The product may be in short supply (e.g., a product on back-order).
- There may be a change in the dosage form (e.g., formulation of a liquid dosage form from solid tablets or capsules).
- The patient may have an allergy to an excipient (filler) in a product.
- There may be a need for large-scale intravenous or parenteral medications for hospital supply.
- There may be a need to improve compliance by altering the taste and texture of an otherwise unfavorable formulation.

Certain considerations should be considered to ensure the safety and efficacy of a pharmaceutical admixture:

- Personnel: It is crucial to delegate the responsibility of compounding a formulation to a person who has the requisite knowledge and expertise in pharmaceutical compounding. If a pharmacy is unable to compound an item, the patient should be referred to another pharmacy that has the ability to formulate it as specified. The designated personnel should have adequate knowledge in the following areas:
  - Physical and chemical properties of the ingredients
  - Physical and chemical compatibilities between ingredients and excipients (fillers)
  - Pharmaceutical calculations
  - Use of appropriate methods
  - Use of appropriate equipment
- Premises and environment: Compounding should be performed in a designated area that ensures an appropriate environment in terms of space, storage, and lighting. The assigned area for compounding should be clean, orderly, and sanitary. The compounding area might maintain a written protocol addressing various issues, such as hand washing, equipment cleaning, and managing staff injuries that result from compounding. The compounding area should have access to water for cleaning hands, equipment, floor, and surfaces.
- Equipment and supplies: The pharmacy should have appropriate equipment and supplies in order to formulate pharmaceutical admixtures per the specified standards. Equipment should be routinely cleaned and kept dry to minimize contamination with the formulation ingredients and extraneous materials. Pharmaceutical compounding generally requires the following equipment and auxiliary supplies, in addition to therapeutic ingredients, to formulate a compound:
  - Class A prescription balance or analytical balance to weigh the ingredients

- Weighing papers, wax papers, or measuring boats
- Spatula to transfer ingredients
- Mortar and pestle for grinding and mixing
- Graduated cylinders (10 mL and 100 mL)
- Ointment slab
- Cream or ointment base
- Wetting or levigating agent to reduce particle size
- Personal protective equipment (PPE)

- **Resources:** A compounding pharmacy should have adequate resources available to render the intended service. The pharmacist should gather information from peer-reviewed sources, such as academic journals, to formulate a product. If the formula is not available for the intended preparation, it should be prepared utilizing the knowledge of physical and chemical properties of the ingredients, pharmacology, and pharmaceutical science.

The following considerations should be considered when selecting tools and equipment for compounding practice:

- Equipment and utensils used in pharmaceutical compounding should have a suitable design and capacity that will allow for effective admixing. The type and size of the equipment to be utilized depends on the intended purpose of compounding, the dosage form, and the volume/amount to be compounded.

- The surface of the equipment should be chemically inert and should not alter the admixture through chemical reaction, addition, or absorption.

- Tools and equipment should be routinely cleaned and properly stored to avoid contamination.

- All electronic, automated, mechanical, and other instruments used in preparing or testing admixtures should be routinely calibrated and inspected.

- The cleaning of equipment should include extra care and caution when the preparation includes cytotoxic agents, antibiotics, and hazardous materials.

- When possible, equipment can be dedicated for a specific job that involves hazardous chemicals or requires high precision. Disposable equipment should be used to reduce the bio-burden and cross-contamination.

- The ingredients used in pharmaceutical compounding should be carefully selected to ensure acceptable strength, quality, purity, and stability in the final formulation. In the selection and use of ingredients, the following measures should be taken:

    - The compounding ingredients should be collected primarily from a preferred source that meets United States Pharmacopeia (USP) and National Formulary (NF) grades. If not available, another source that ensures high quality grade, e.g., Analytical Reagent (AR), American Chemical Society (ACS), and/or Food Chemicals Codex (FCC) can be used.

    - Components produced in an FDA-registered manufacturing facility should be used first. If that's not possible, the purity and safety of the ingredients should be ensured by reasonable means, which includes obtaining a Certificate of Analysis (C of A), determining the reputation of the manufacturer, and determining the reliability of the source. The C of A should be maintained in records for future reference.

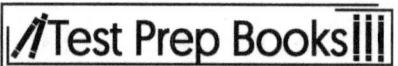

- o Pharmaceutical products such as tablets, capsules, and injectables are often used as sources for active ingredients. Staff should make sure that the pharmaceutical products used in compounding are collected from bottles labeled with a batch control number and expiration date.
- o If any of the ingredients do not carry an expiration date assigned by the manufacturer, then the container should be labeled with the date of receipt. A conservative expiration date should be assigned, based on the nature of the chemical, its degradation pattern, and the storage condition.
- o To ensure safety and avoid toxicity when compounding a formulation for human use, it is important to check that the required medication is not on the FDA list of drugs withdrawn from the market.
- o To ensure consistency and quality of the formulation, it is important to receive an ingredient from the same supplier every time. Ingredients from different suppliers may have a variation in physicochemical properties, resulting in an alternative drug response of the final formulation.

- Ingredients and excipients utilized in a particular formulation should be selected based the following criteria:
  - o Physical properties
  - o Compatibility
  - o Patient conditions (allergy, disease state, use of other medications)
  - o Intended use
  - o Possible duration of treatment
  - o Possible drug-drug and drug-excipient interactions
  - o Route and frequency of administration

There are several general considerations to take into account before initiating pharmaceutical compounding of non-sterile products (these also apply to sterile compounding):

- The physical and chemical properties of active ingredient(s)
- The pharmaceutical and therapeutic uses of active ingredient(s)
- Whether the admixture will provide adequate topical or systemic absorption
- Whether any components of the admixture will render unexpected allergic, toxic, or undesirable reactions
- Whether a dedicated clean and sanitized area is available for compounding
- Ensuring that compounds are performed one at a time in that dedicated area
- For orally-administered admixtures, what the possible effects of gastro-intestinal pH and hepatic metabolism on the bioavailability for active ingredient(s) would be

Dispensing Process

The compounding process (sterile and non-sterile) involves five distinct steps:

1. Preparing:
   - Review the prescription and determine whether the preparation would be safe and would fulfill the intended purpose
   - Make a list of chemical ingredients and excipients required for the formulation
   - Perform calculations to determine the amount of active ingredients and excipients required to compound the admixture
   - Select suitable equipment, ensuring that it is clean
   - Wash hands and wear appropriate PPE
   - Arrange necessary ingredients and equipment to perform compounding

2. Compounding:
   - Perform the admixing according to the formulary and directions in the prescription
   - Utilize the art and science of pharmaceutical compounding for admixing

3. Checking:
   - Check certain physical parameters of the admixture, including color, odor, consistency, and pH
   - Enter the information in the compounding log
   - Label the compound

4. Recording and signing: All information should be entered and signed by a pharmacist, confirming that the assigned procedure was carried out properly (to ensure quality and to serve the intended purpose) as specified in the prescription.

5. Cleaning:
   - Clean the equipment and compounding areas
   - Dispose of waste and PPE
   - Wash hands

Compounding sterile preparations requires strict adherence to aseptic techniques to ensure that the final product is free from contamination. Each step of the compounding process, from preparation to administration, can be conducted using the aseptic technique. The first step is to prepare the tools and materials needed for the compounding. They must be sterilized or disinfected before each use. This can be achieved through autoclaving, dry heat sterilization, or chemical disinfection. Sterile, single-use items can also be used to minimize the risk of contamination. Contact guidelines are protocols and procedures designed to prevent the contamination of sterile objects and maintain a sterile environment during compounding. This includes guidelines for handling equipment, tools, and materials as well as guidelines for hand hygiene, garbing, and cleaning. If a sterile object touches a nonsterile object, it is considered contaminated and should not be used. If this occurs, the compounding process should be stopped. Then, the contaminated object should be removed from the sterile field, and the area where the contamination occurred should be cleaned and disinfected. The sterile field should be re-established before continuing with the compounding process.

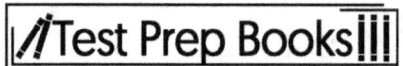

When using a laminar airflow hood, the compounder should position themselves so that they will not need to place their head into the hood. Any movement should be slow and deliberate to prevent the generation of airborne particles. All surfaces—including countertops, tools, and supplies—should be cleaned and disinfected before each use. A common disinfectant for compounding surfaces is 70% isopropyl alcohol. The alcohol should be allowed to dry completely before use to ensure that it is effective in killing microorganisms. Needles and syringes should be used only once and disposed of properly in a sharps container. Needles and syringes should never be reused or shared between patients since this increases the likelihood of infections. When transferring medications from one container to another, aseptic techniques should be used to prevent contamination. The use of sterile syringes and needles is recommended, and all needles and syringes should be labeled with the contents and the date of preparation.

Primary Engineering Controls

Laminar Flow Hood

A **laminar flow hood** is an air filtration system designed to ensure that the space in a pharmacy used for compounding sterile preparations does not have any contaminants or particulates. It pulls air through a **High Efficiency Particulate Arresting (HEPA) filter** and then blows it toward the person making the sterile compound, providing a constant stream of filtered air over all of the compounding materials and tools within the hood. Laminar flow hoods come in both vertical and horizontal designs, as well as additional airflow patterns needed for particular systems or uses. Manufacturers will provide specifications for maintenance; these must be followed carefully and the laminar flow hood must be thoroughly cleaned prior to each use to avoid spreading contaminants into sterile compounds.

Cleaning the laminar flow hood requires the use of a proper technique:

1. Collect your cleaning equipment: 70% ethanol or other disinfectant and sterile gauze or other laboratory grade wipes.

2. Dress in personal protective equipment, including gloves, mask, goggles, foot coverings, and a gown.

3. Turn the hood on, and allow the hood to run for five to twenty minutes before cleaning, depending on the hood manufacturer's manual. The hood should run for at least thirty minutes before use.

4. Remove any items that do not belong in the hood.

5. Spray the internal surfaces with the disinfectant, and clean with sterile wipes using a sweeping back and forth motion. Do not spray disinfectant into the HEPA filter.

6. Allow the hood to air dry.

Vertical Flow Hood

A vertical flow hood is a type of primary engineering control (PEC) used in sterile compounding to provide a clean environment for the preparation of sterile products. Its purpose is to create unidirectional laminar, or vertical, airflow that moves sterile air over the work surface and away from the operator. In a vertical flow hood, the laminar airflow moves downward from the top of the hood to the work surface. This downward airflow protects the work surface and the sterile product from contamination by airborne particles. The air is then filtered through a HEPA filter before being recirculated into the hood. Vertical flow hoods are preferred for compounding sterile products because they provide better protection against airborne contaminants than horizontal flow hoods. They are often used when compounding chemotherapeutics or hazardous medications.

Compounding Aseptic Isolators

Compounding aseptic isolators (CAIs) are PECs used in sterile compounding to create a barrier between the operator and the sterile product being compounded. CAIs are enclosed units that provide a high level of protection against microbial contamination during the compounding process. CAIs use unidirectional laminar airflow that moves sterile air over the work surface and away from the operator, like in vertical flow hoods. However, CAIs also use a physical barrier, such as a glove box or chamber, to separate the operator from the sterile product. Operators work inside the CAI through a pair of attached gloves or airtight sleeves. The operator's hands and arms are inserted into the gloves or sleeves. The sterile environment inside the CAI protects them from contamination. CAIs are commonly used in the compounding of hazardous drugs, as they provide an extra layer of protection against exposure to these drugs. They are also used in the compounding of sterile products that require a higher level of protection against contamination than can be provided by other PECs.

Compounding Aseptic Containment Isolators

Compounding aseptic containment isolators (CACIs) are PECs utilized in sterile compounding to provide greater levels of protection than other PECs, like CAIs. CACIs are intended to provide a fully contained environment for the preparation of hazardous drugs—such as antineoplastic and cytotoxic compounds—and other sterile products. CACIs use unidirectional laminar airflow similar to other PECs, but they also contain a physical barrier to separate the compounder from the sterile products. The CACI is a closed system with a negative pressure environment that prevents hazardous particles from leaking into the surrounding environment. Operators work inside the CACI through a pair of attached gloves or airtight sleeves, and all materials and components are passed through a transfer port to prevent contamination. CACIs also contain HEPA filtration systems that help ensure that the air inside remains sterile. They ensure the highest level of protection against exposure to these types of drugs and can be required by some regulatory agencies for certain compounding activities.

Compounding Non-Sterile Products

The following are techniques used in non-sterile compounding:

- **Blending**: mixing two substances together
- **Comminution**: making a substance into small, fine particles
- **Geometric dilution**: mixing two different ingredients together of unequal quantities, starting with the ingredient of smallest quantity and adding the same quantity of the other ingredient (of larger amount), continuing to repeat until all the ingredients are used
- **Levigation**: the use of water or another solvent to carry an insoluble drug powder through the process
    - Powder can turn into a thin paste with use of less water
- **Pulverization** by intervention: for powders that do not crush easily, a solvent (usually an alcohol) dissolves the powder can be used to intervene.
    - Mixing dissolved powder on an ointment slab or in a mortar helps the solvent evaporate, and the powder will come out in finer particles.

Emulsions and Enemas

Nonsterile emulsions are thermodynamically unstable mixtures composed of at least two liquids that are immiscible—liquids that are insoluble in one another and do not mix easily. The procedure for compounding these types of nonsterile formulations depends on the type of emulsion being prepared. Simple emulsions can either be oil in water or water in oil, while more complicated emulsions include water in oil in water and oil in water in oil. An emulsion consists of two phases; the dispersed liquid makes up the **internal phase**, while the medium which it is dispersed in composes the **external phase**. **Emulsifying agents**, which have chemical properties that make them both water and oil soluble, or amphiphilic, are used to stabilize the emulsion. The emulsifying agent acts by creating a barrier between the two phases. The **Dry Gum Method** and the **Wet Gum Method** of emulsion preparation involve the same ratio of 4:2:1, or four parts oil, two parts water, and one part emulsifying agent, but the order of application differs.

The nonsterile preparation of compounded enema solutions involves dissolving the active pharmaceutical ingredients in purified water, titrating to the necessary pH, and packaging the solution in individual bottles for dispensing. Referring to a master formulation, the procedure to compound would be to first weigh out the active pharmaceutical ingredient (API). The weighed API or solute is added to a solvent. When adding the API to a solvent, it is important to consider the displacement of the solvent by the API. It is generally best to add the API to a percentage of the final volume, which is typically specified in the master formula. A magnetic stirring rod should be used to thoroughly dissolve the API to achieve a homogenous mixture. The pH of the solution should be verified to make sure it is within the specified range for the specific enema being made. Then the solution should be brought to its final volume, and its pH checked again. If necessary, the pH can be adjusted to meet the specific range required in the quality assurance portion of the formula. The solution can then be poured into individual enema bottles and labeled appropriately.

Dry Gum Method

The dry gum method is a technique used in compounding preparations that involve emulsions or suspensions. It's an easy method that involves mixing an oil phase and a water phase with a gelling agent, such as gum acacia. First, mix the oil phase, which can include waxes and lipids, in a mortar with the gelling agent. Next, grind the mixture until a smooth paste is created. Transfer to a new container and mix in the water phase gradually while continuously mixing the paste. The water phase can include water, salts, and other aqueous ingredients. The mixture is then stirred until a uniform suspension or emulsion is formed. Often, a "clicking" noise will be heard when the process is properly completed. The dry gum method is particularly useful when compounding with lipids or insoluble substances, as the gelling agent helps to stabilize the emulsion and keep the ingredients in suspension. It is also a useful method for compounding substances that are sensitive to heat because, unlike other methods, this method does not require the use of heat.

One advantage of the dry gum method is that it does not require any special equipment or a high skill level. Also, it can be quickly and easily compounded in a pharmacy or other compounding setting with basic equipment, such as a mortar and pestle. However, the dry gum method does have some limitations. The gelling agent can affect the taste and texture of the final product which can be a concern when compounding products for oral administration. Additionally, the method may not be suitable for all types of suspensions or emulsions, particularly those that require a high degree of uniformity or stability.

Wet Gum Method

The wet gum method is another technique for emulsion or suspension preparations. It is an easy method that starts with mixing an oil phase and a water phase with the use of a gelling agent, such as gum acacia. Take note that the order is different from the dry gum method. First, start by mixing the water phase with the acacia. Then, add the oil phase in small increments to a mortar with the mixture. Next, grind until a smooth paste or emulsion is formed. This method can be used for compounds that require a high degree of accuracy in dosing since the use of a mortar and pestle allows for precise measurements.

One advantage of the wet gum method is that it can be performed quickly and with basic supplies, such as a mortar and pestle. It also allows for the easy incorporation of both aqueous and non-aqueous ingredients which can be important when compounding with a wide range of substances. However, the wet gum method also has some limitations that are similar to those of the dry gum method.

Diluent or Base Product Selection

Diluents and Base Products

When compounding medications, it's important to choose the appropriate diluent or base product to ensure that the medication is stable, effective, and safe for human or animal administration. Diluents and base products are considered inactive ingredients and can affect the solubility, stability, and compatibility of the active ingredients in the medication. Each manufacturer will have specific recommendations regarding their diluent or base product. These recommendations should be referenced prior to selecting and can include physical and chemical information. This information can be found in the product labeling and on the manufacturer's website. When selecting a diluent or base product, it is important to consider factors such as solubility, pH, compatibility with other ingredients, and stability of the final product. For example, some medications may require a specific pH range for optimal stability and effectiveness, while others may require a specific solvent for solubility. In addition to the manufacturer's recommendations, compounding pharmacists should also consider any patient-specific factors, such as allergies or sensitivities to specific ingredients. For example, some patients can have allergies to diluents or base products, like lactose, and will require different additives.

Sources of Information

Selecting an appropriate diluent or base product for compounding medications is a critical step in ensuring the safety and effectiveness of the final product. To make an informed decision, compounding pharmacists rely on various sources of information, including product package inserts, electronic resources, and reference books (such as Trissel's *Handbook on Injectable Drugs*).

Product package inserts are provided by the manufacturer of the active pharmaceutical ingredient and typically contain information about the product's physical and chemical properties, recommended diluents and base products, and stability and compatibility information. Package inserts are an important source of information for compounding pharmacists because they provide specific details about the product's characteristics and recommended use.

Electronic resources are also valuable tools for selecting appropriate diluents and base products. These may include online databases, such as the United States Pharmacopeia (USP) and the National Library of Medicine's DailyMed. These provide comprehensive information about pharmaceutical products, including diluent and base product recommendations. In addition, manufacturers often provide electronic resources that can be accessed online, such as product monographs and web-based reference tools.

Trissel's *Handbook on Injectable Drugs* is a widely recognized reference book that provides information about the compatibility, stability, and preparation of injectable drugs. The book contains detailed monographs for more than three hundred drugs, including recommended diluents and base products as well as compatibility and stability information.

Beyond-Use Dates for Both Compounded and Repackaged Products

Sources of Information

Determining beyond-use dates (BUDs) for compounded and repackaged products is an essential step in ensuring the safety and effectiveness of medications. BUDs are established based on published data or regulatory agency requirements, and compounding pharmacists rely on various sources of information to determine appropriate BUDs. Product package inserts, electronic resources, and reference books (such as Trissel's *Handbook on Injectable Drugs*) are valuable sources of information when determining BUDs. Product package inserts often provide guidance on the appropriate storage conditions and recommended BUDs based on stability studies conducted by the manufacturer. Electronic resources, such as the USP and the National Library of Medicine's DailyMed, provide information on regulatory agency requirements for BUDs, including USP <797> guidelines for sterile compounding. Trissel's *Handbook on Injectable Drugs* can help pharmacists determine appropriate BUDs for compounded medications.

When determining BUDs for compounded medications, pharmacists must consider several factors, including the chemical and physical properties of the active pharmaceutical ingredient, the final formulation, the route of administration, and the storage conditions. Stability studies conducted on the active pharmaceutical ingredient or final formulation can provide valuable information on the expected shelf life of the medication. The USP <797> guidelines provide recommendations for BUDs based on the risk level of the sterile compounding process, with shorter BUDs for higher-risk compounding activities. For repackaged products, BUDs are typically established based on regulatory agency requirements, such as the guidelines by the US Food and Drug Administration (FDA) for stability testing of repackaged drug products. The FDA requires that repackaged drug products have appropriate labeling that includes the expiration date or BUD, based on stability data. In some cases, the original product package insert may provide guidance on BUDs for repackaged products.

Labeling

BUDs are established based on published data or regulatory agency requirements, and labeling requirements for BUDs are outlined in the USP <795> and <797> guidelines. According to the USP <795> guidelines, compounded preparations should be labeled with the following information:

- The name of the preparation and strength
- The name of the prescriber or patient
- The date of preparation and BUD
- The storage requirements
- The directions for use

The BUD should be based on the stability of the preparation and the intended use. The label should also include any warnings or precautions, such as allergy information or potential adverse effects. For sterile compounding, the USP <797> guidelines provide specific labeling requirements for compounded preparations. These guidelines require that compounded sterile preparations (CSPs) be labeled with the following information:

- The name and strength of all components
- The name of the person who prepared the CSP
- The date of preparation and BUD
- The storage requirements
- The lot number or other unique identifier
- The route of administration
- Any other applicable warnings or precautions

The label should also include information on the compounding facility and the level of risk associated with the preparation. Repackaged products must also be labeled with the appropriate BUD based on stability data or regulatory agency requirements. The FDA requires that repackaged drug products be labeled with the following information:

- The name of the drug product
- The strength of the drug product
- The expiration date or BUD based on stability data
- The lot number or other unique identifier
- The name and address of the repackager
- The quantity of the contents

Dispensing Process

In addition, the label should include any warnings or precautions, such as potential adverse effects or allergy information.

Determining Beyond-Use Date

The **beyond-use date** refers to the date after which a compounded preparation should not be used and should be discarded. A beyond-use date should be assigned conservatively, utilizing professional judgement, and applying knowledge from pharmaceutical science and compounding experience. The beyond-use date should never be later than the expiration date of any of the ingredients.

These factors must be considered when specifying a beyond-use date:

- The chemical nature of the drug and its degradation kinetics
- The formulation dosage form and the ingredients
- Any possible microbial growth
- The packaging container
- The storage conditions
- The intended length of therapy
- Any information obtained from suppliers and published literature

In absence of stability information, the beyond-use date could be specified as illustrated in the following table:

Beyond-Use Date by the Type of Formulation	
Non-aqueous formulations	Not later than the time remaining until the earliest expiration date of any of the ingredients or 6 months
Aqueous oral formulations	Not later than 14 days since compounded and when stored at controlled cold temperatures
Aqueous topical/dermal and mucosal liquid and semisolid formulations	Not later than 30 days

USP <795> and <797> also contain methods for calculating beyond-use dates for nonsterile and sterile compounded pharmaceutical products, respectively, and should be referenced by pharmacy staff when making these determinations.

The beyond-use date (BUD) of a compounded medication refers to the time during which the medication retains its potency, purity, and stability under recommended storage conditions. Determining the appropriate BUD is an essential part of the compounding process and ensures that the patient receives safe and effective medication. Several methods can be used to determine the BUD of a compounded medication, including analytical testing, chemical stability testing, and microbial stability testing.

Analytical testing involves the use of various analytical techniques—such as high-performance liquid chromatography (HPLC), gas chromatography (GC), or spectrophotometry—to measure the potency or concentration of the active ingredients in the medication. This method is often used to determine the BUD of nonsterile preparations, such as creams, ointments, and oral liquids.

Chemical stability testing involves monitoring the physical and chemical changes that occur in a medication over time, such as changes in pH, color, or odor. This method is often used to determine the BUD of sterile preparations, such as injectable medications or ophthalmic solutions.

Microbial stability testing involves monitoring the growth of microorganisms, such as bacteria or fungi, in the medication over time. This method is often used to determine the BUD of sterile preparations, such as injectable medications or ophthalmic solutions.

In addition to these methods, compounding pharmacists may also consult published literature or regulatory agency requirements to determine the appropriate BUD for a particular medication. It is important to note that the BUD of a compounded medication is not the same as the expiration date of a commercially available medication. The expiration date is determined by the manufacturer based on the stability of the medication under specific storage conditions. The BUD of a compounded medication is based on the stability of the medication under specific compounding and storage conditions.

Final Inspection for Physical Incompatibilities

The preparation of compounds requires the consideration of potential incompatibilities that can affect the stability, effectiveness, and overall safety of the product. The two types of incompatibility that must be addressed when compounding are physical incompatibilities and chemical incompatibilities. **Physical incompatibilities** seen in compounds might result in the loss of product uniformity, change in odor, altered palatability, or an overall undesirable preparation. A **chemical incompatibility** is one in which the components in the compounded preparation undergo a chemical reaction resulting in the loss of potency and integrity of the active pharmaceutical ingredient.

A physical incompatibility often seen in topical emulsion preparations such as creams or lotions is immiscibility. **Immiscible liquids** do not mix easily with one another and tend to separate due to the differing polarity properties of the liquids. For example, oil-based liquids are hydrophobic, or nonpolar, whereas water-based liquids are hydrophilic, or polar. An **emulsifier**, or **surfactant**, is an agent used to stabilize immiscible preparations by forming a barrier and decreasing interfacial tension between the two liquids being mixed. Emulsifiers and surfactants are **amphiphilic**, meaning they have polar and nonpolar ends that act to create a barrier between the internal (dispersed) phase and the external (continuous) phase.

Using the incorrect type of emulsifying agent or the incorrect quantity of an emulsifier are two factors that can cause the phase separation of an emulsion. A disruption of interfacial tension breaks down the barriers between the internal and external phases of an emulsion, which can result in coalescence between the two phases. Coalescence can lead to the formation of larger droplet sizes and unequal distribution of the dispersed phase within the continuous phase. A cracked emulsion appears as a clear separation of the oil and water layers in a compounded medication. Coalescence is an irreversible process that can ultimately affect the therapeutic effectiveness of the compounded preparation, rendering it unusable.

Insolubility is a physical incompatibility in compounded medications that can be overcome with the addition of a wetting agent and by decreasing the particle size of the active ingredient. Wetting agents are a type of surfactant that can increase solubility of an active ingredient within a suspension by decreasing the surface tension. Reducing particle size increases the surface area of the solids, which allows the wetting agent to penetrate the molecules more easily. The wetting agent also lowers the surface tension of the liquid, allowing it to spread between the solid particles and increasing overall solubility. Two methods typically used to reduce particle size are trituration (a dry method) and levigation (a wet method). **Trituration** is the grinding of a solid ingredient, whether tablets or powders, into smaller particles using a mortar and pestle. **Levigation** is like trituration in that it involves the grinding of solids, but it is done in the presence of a wetting agent.

Liquification is an example of a physical incompatibility that can occur when certain solid ingredients with low melting points are combined, otherwise known as a eutectic mixture. While this may be useful in some preparations like fixed oil suspensions, it can be detrimental if a liquid preparation is not the desired dosage form.

Dispensing Process

Chemical incompatibility is a significant area of concern for intravenous and injectable medications that require reconstitution prior to administration. Using the incorrect diluent to reconstitute a medication can result in a chemical reaction between the active pharmaceutical ingredient and the diluent.

Precipitates and crystallization are examples of chemical incompatibilities that can occur in reconstituted intravenous medications when mixed incorrectly. Reconstituting with the incorrect diluent or at the incorrect concentration can cause the active ingredient to precipitate out of the solution causing the formation of solids or crystals within the solution. **Precipitates** and **crystal formation** are the result of a chemical reaction that changes the chemical properties of the active drug. The formation of a precipitate or crystals within the IV lines can have a range of consequences for the patient. The chemical reaction can result in the patient receiving a toxic medication, embolism due to crystallized particulates entering the body, irritated tissues at the IV site, and therapeutic failure.

It is not always evident whether a compounded preparation has lost stability due to chemical incompatibility issues. While color changes, precipitation formation, and changes in odor can be observed, chemical incompatibilities such as pH changes or product degradation are not necessarily detectable by visual inspection.

One specific form of incompatibility that needs to be inspected is osmolarity, which can affect the efficacy and safety of the final product. Osmolarity refers to the concentration of particles in a solution and is affected by freezing point depression and other colligative properties. When different components are combined in a compounded product, the osmolarity of the solution may change, leading to potential incompatibilities. For example, when two solutions with different osmolarities are mixed, the resulting solution may have a higher or lower osmolarity than either of the original solutions and could cause cell damage or hemolysis, which can be harmful to patients. Freezing point depression is a colligative property that can also affect the osmolarity of a solution. When a solute is added to a solvent, it lowers the freezing point of the solution. This can be problematic in compounded products that are meant to be frozen, such as some injectable medications. If the solution is not properly formulated to account for the freezing point depression, it may not freeze at the correct temperature or may freeze too quickly, potentially damaging the product.

To prevent incompatibilities related to osmolarity, it is essential to inspect all components for compatibility before compounding. It is also important to calculate the osmolarity of the final product to ensure that it falls within an acceptable range. This can be achieved using specialized software or manual calculations.

For example, to calculate the osmolarity of 2 grams of NaCl dissolved in 500 mL of water, follow the following steps:

1. Convert the mass of NaCl to moles by dividing by its molecular weight (58.44 g/mol):

$$2 \text{ g NaCl} \div 58.44 \text{ g/mol} = 0.0342 \text{ mol NaCl}$$

2. Calculate the total number of particles in the solution by multiplying the number of moles of NaCl by the number of ions it dissociates into (2):

$$0.0342 \text{ mol NaCl} \times 2 \text{ ions/mol} = 0.0684 \text{ osmoles}$$

3. Calculate the osmolarity of the solution by dividing the number of osmoles by the volume of the solution in liters:

$$0.0684 \text{ osmoles} \div 0.5 \text{ L} = 0.1368 \text{ osmol/L}$$

Answer: The osmolarity of the solution is 0.1368 osmol/L.

Several strategies can be used to minimize the risk of osmolarity incompatibility. One approach is to use pre-mixed components that have been prepared with a known osmolarity. Another strategy is to use an isotonic solution,

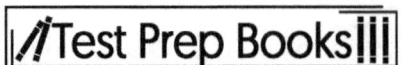

Dispensing Process

which has the same osmolarity as body fluids and is less likely to cause adverse effects. There are a variety of resources that can be used to verify incompatibilities, including Trissel's *Handbook* and third-source websites such as Lexicomp and Micromedex. In addition to visual inspection and the use of specialized equipment, it is important to consider the characteristics of the medications being prepared. For instance, medications that are known to have a short shelf life or are sensitive to light or heat should be prepared in smaller quantities to minimize the risk of degradation. Additionally, medications that are known to have a narrow therapeutic index should be prepared with caution to avoid under- or over-dosing.

Labeling Compounded Products

Labeling compounded products is important because it verifies pharmacist accuracy, ensures patient safety, facilitates proper use of the medication, and fulfills legal requirements. The labeling must have different types of information about the product, including its name, strength, dosage form, directions for use, and any potential hazards or side effects:

- Product name: The name of the product should be unique, clear, and easy to read. It should not be misleading and should not resemble the name of any other product.

- Strength and dosage form: The label should include the strength and dosage form of the medication, such as the concentration of the active ingredient, the amount per unit dose, and the type of dosage form (e.g., tablet, capsule, solution, cream).

- Directions for use: The label should provide clear instructions for use, including the route of administration, frequency of dosing, and any special instructions for storage or handling. It must match the prescribing information.

- Expiration date and beyond-use date: The label should include the expiration date, which is the date after which the product should not be used, as well as the beyond-use date, which is the date after which the product should not be used once it has been opened or prepared.

- Lot number: The label should include a unique lot number to help with product traceability and recall if necessary.

- Manufacturer or compounding pharmacy name: The label should include the name of the manufacturer or the compounding pharmacy that prepared the product.

- Patient information: The label should include the name of the patient, the prescribing healthcare provider, and any relevant information about the patient's condition.

Labels can and should also include any warnings or precautions, such as potential side effects, drug interactions, or other safety concerns. Compounded products may have additional labeling requirements depending on the state.

Repackaging and Labeling Unit Dose Products

Labeling

Repackaging and labeling unit dose products is important for medication safety. The USP <795> and <797> provide guidelines for ensuring proper repackaging and labeling of unit dose products. According to USP <795>, unit dose packaging should be labeled with the following information: drug name, strength, dosage form, expiration date, lot number, and quantity per package. The label should also include any special storage instructions or handling precautions as well as the name and address of the pharmacy repackaging the product.

Additionally, the label should include a unique identifier, such as a barcode or serial number, to ensure proper tracking and inventory management. USP <797> provides additional guidelines for labeling unit dose products when used in sterile compounding. The label should include the name and strength of the drug as well as the volume or weight of the product. The label should also include the date and time of preparation, the expiration date and time, and the lot number of the product.

Additionally, the label should include the name of the compounding pharmacist or technician as well as any special handling or storage instructions. Proper labeling of repackaged unit dose products is important to ensure patient safety and minimize medication errors. Pharmacists and technicians should be trained on the requirements for labeling unit dose products and should perform regular audits to ensure compliance with USP guidelines. Any deviations from the labeling requirements should be reported and investigated to determine the cause and prevent future occurrences. In addition to labeling requirements, USP <795> and <797> provide guidelines for ensuring the integrity and sterility of repackaged and compounded products. These guidelines include proper handling and storage procedures as well as quality control measures to ensure accurate and consistent dosing.

Components of a Unit Dose Label

A unit dose label is a critical component of medication administration in healthcare settings. It provides crucial information to ensure the safe and effective use of medication by the patient or caregiver. The following are the components of a unit dose label:

- Patient information: This includes the patient's name, medical record number, and other identifying information. This information ensures that the medication is administered to the correct patient.

- Medication name and strength: This identifies the medication being dispensed and the strength or concentration of the medication. This information ensures that the correct medication is administered in the appropriate dose.

- Route of administration: This specifies how the medication is to be administered, such as orally, intravenously, or topically.

- Administration time: This indicates when the medication is to be administered.

- Expiration date: This indicates the date beyond which the medication should not be used due to a decrease in potency or potential degradation.

- Lot number: This identifies the specific batch of medication that was dispensed and can be useful in tracking any potential issues or recalls.

- Barcode: This is a machine-readable code that contains information about the medication, such as the medication name, strength, lot number, and expiration date. Barcoding can be useful in reducing errors in medication administration.

- Storage instructions: This specifies any specific storage requirements for the medication, such as refrigeration or protection from light.

- Precautions/warnings: This includes any special precautions or warnings associated with the medication, such as potential side effects or interactions with other medications.

- Prescriber information: This includes the name of the prescribing healthcare provider, which can be useful in verifying the prescription or contacting the provider with any questions or concerns.

It is important to note that the components of a unit dose label may vary slightly depending on the type of medication and the facility's specific policies and procedures. However, ensuring that all necessary information is included on the label is essential for safe and effective medication administration.

Unit Dose Systems

Modern technology has allowed drugs or medications to be packaged in convenient and safe ways involving unit dose systems, which is when a medication is prepared in a labeled individual packet for convenience, safety, or monitoring. Unit dose packaging devices may be manual, semi-automatic, or automatic. The intent of a unit dose is to decrease administration error.

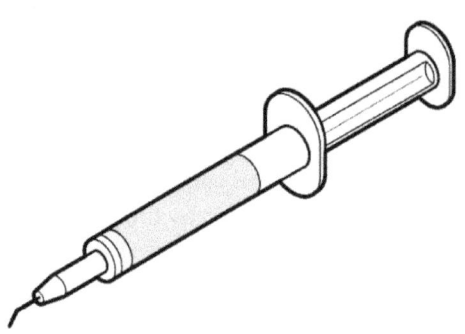

A Unit Dose System: A syringe as a final unit dose

A **modified unit dose system** is a drug delivery system that combines unit dose medications, which are blister packaged, into a multi-dose card instead of being placed loose in a box.

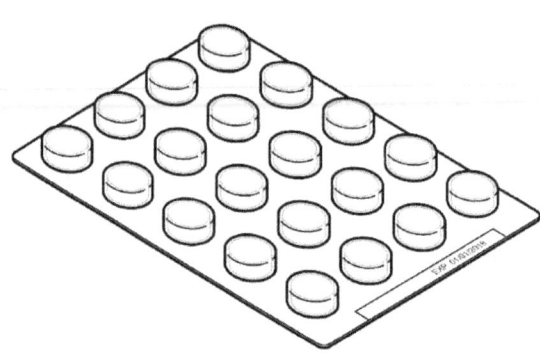

Pills in a Blister Pack

A **blended unit dose system** is a combination of the unit dose system and non-unit dose system. It may contain multiple medications packed in a cassette. An example is a compliance (or bubble or blister) pack, in which multiple medications are arranged in each bubble (or compartment) according to the time of administration in a day or week.

Maintaining Sterile and Nonsterile Compounding and Repackaging Equipment

Equipment Maintenance

Equipment maintenance is an important aspect of ensuring the safety and efficacy of compounded products, both sterile and nonsterile. USP <795> and <797> provide guidelines on equipment maintenance to minimize the risk of contamination and errors in compounding. For sterile compounding, primary engineering controls—such as laminar flow hoods and isolators—should be maintained and tested according to the manufacturer's instructions and USP guidelines. Regular maintenance and cleaning of equipment (including HEPA filters) are essential to maintain their integrity and effectiveness in providing a sterile environment.

Additionally, personnel performing maintenance and cleaning should follow appropriate aseptic techniques to minimize the risk of introducing contaminants. Nonsterile compounding equipment—such as balances, mixers, and grinders—should be calibrated and maintained according to the manufacturer's instructions and USP guidelines. Regular cleaning and disinfecting of equipment are essential to prevent cross-contamination between different products. Any damaged or malfunctioning equipment should be repaired or replaced promptly to ensure accuracy and consistency in compounding.

In sterile and nonsterile compounding, proper documentation of equipment maintenance is crucial to both demonstrate compliance with regulatory requirements and facilitate tracking of any issues or errors. This includes maintenance logs, calibration records, and documentation of any repairs or replacements. Furthermore, regular staff training and competency assessments in equipment maintenance and operation are essential to ensure that all personnel are proficient in using and maintaining equipment properly. This includes proper use of PPE when handling hazardous drugs or chemicals as well as appropriate disposal of contaminated materials and waste.

Manufacturers' Guidelines for Maintaining Repackaging Equipment

Maintenance of repackaging equipment is essential in sterile and nonsterile compounding to ensure the accuracy of medication doses, reduce medication errors, and enhance patient safety. This equipment includes, but is not limited to, electronic scales, capsule-filling machines, label printers, and tablet presses. Manufacturers provide guidelines for maintaining repackaging equipment to ensure the proper functioning and longevity of the equipment. The guidelines for maintaining repackaging equipment vary depending on the type of equipment and manufacturer. However, some general guidelines apply to most equipment. For instance, regular cleaning of the equipment is necessary to prevent contamination and ensure the accuracy of doses. Some equipment requires disassembly and thorough cleaning to reach all parts that contact the medication. Manufacturers provide specific instructions on how to clean each piece of equipment.

Lubrication is another maintenance requirement for repackaging equipment. Proper lubrication ensures the smooth operation of moving parts, which enhances the longevity of the equipment. Manufacturers provide instructions on which lubricants to use and how often to lubricate the equipment.

Calibration is also a crucial maintenance requirement for repackaging equipment. Calibration ensures that the equipment accurately measures medication doses. Calibration involves comparing the equipment's readings to a known standard and adjusting the equipment as necessary. Manufacturers provide specific instructions on how often to calibrate each piece of equipment and the calibration procedure.

Additionally, manufacturers provide guidelines for troubleshooting repackaging equipment. In case of equipment malfunction, the manufacturer's troubleshooting guide should be the first point of reference to identify and solve the problem. The manufacturer's technical support team can provide additional assistance if the problem persists. It is essential to follow the manufacturer's guidelines for maintaining repackaging equipment to ensure that the equipment functions correctly, to reduce the risk of contamination, and to prevent medication errors. It is also crucial to inspect and maintain equipment regularly, even if there are no apparent problems. Regular maintenance enhances the longevity of the equipment, reduces the need for repairs, and improves the accuracy of medication doses.

Required Documentation for Sterile, Nonsterile, and Repackaged Products

Documentation helps in systematically tracing, evaluating, and replicating the steps that were involved in a compounding process. Compounding pharmacies should maintain four sets of records:

1. Master formulation records

- Official name, strength, and dosage form of the compounded product
- Calculations used to determine and check quantities of components and doses
- Description of all ingredients and the individual quantities
- Compatibility and stability information (including available references)
- The equipment used/needed to make the preparation (when relevant)
- Instructions for mixing
- Order in which the ingredients were mixed
- Temperature during mixing or other environmental settings
- Amount of time of mixing
- Other relevant factors for repeating the preparation as compounded
- Sample label information, including legally required information as well as the following:
  - The generic name and the amount of each active ingredient
  - The beyond-use date (BUD) that was given
  - Required storage conditions
  - The number for the prescription
  - The container that was used to dispense the product
  - Requirements for packaging and storage of the product
  - Final preparation description
- Procedures used for quality control and expected results

2. Compounding records describe the process that occurred while the formulation was being compounded

3. Standard operating procedures (SOPs), including equipment maintenance records

4. Ingredients' records, including Certificates of Analysis (C of A) and Material Safety Data Sheets

Documentation should be preserved for the period of time specified by state laws. Records should be available in the pharmacy during the retention period for auditing purposes. Proper documentation is important to ensure consistency in batch-to-batch preparations. Records of complaints by patients and of serious harmful events due to compounded medications should be kept on record for at least two years from the day the prescription was dispensed. Follow-up investigations on the complaints should be included in the records. Calculations of the quantity of each component in the compounded medication should also be documented.

Dispensing Process

Master Formulation Record (Compound Formula)

Name of compound: _____

Strength: _____ **Dosage form:** _____ **Total quantity:** _____

Ingredients	Manufacturer	DIN	Quantity

Preparation instructions: _____

_____

_____

_____

Prepared by: _____

Reference: _____

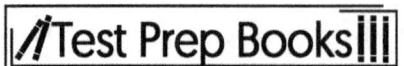

Compounding Record

Affix Rx label

Compound name: _____

Strength: _____

Dosage form: _____

Quantity: _____

Batch: _____

Date prepared: _____

Source of formula: _____

Beyond-use date: _____

Deviation from master formula: _____
_____
_____

Deviation approved by: _____

Ingredients	MFR	DIN	Lot#	EXP date	Quantity	Measured by	Verified by

Calculation: _____
_____
_____

Calculated by: _____ Verified by: _____

Formulation prepared by: _____

Signing off (Pharmacist): _____

Documentation Requirements (USP <795> and <797>)

Documentation is one of the most important aspects within the pharmacy profession, especially in sterile and nonsterile compounding and repackaging. Documentation requirements ensure that pharmacists maintain a record of all activities and procedures that occur in their practice, and these records can be utilized as a legal document in a court of law. USP <795> and <797> provide guidance on documentation requirements for sterile, nonsterile, and repackaged products. For sterile compounding, documentation must include the ingredients used, calculations performed, procedural steps, and results of tests performed to ensure that the product meets quality standards. The identification of the compounding personnel, the date and time of compounding, and any deviations from established procedures must also be included. This documentation is critical in ensuring accountability, traceability, and patient safety.

For nonsterile compounding, documentation must include the identity, strength, and quantity of all ingredients used; the name and address of the supplier; and the date of receipt. The documentation must also include the name and quantity of the final product, the name of the compounding personnel, and the date and time of compounding. Additionally, any changes from an established protocol must be documented to ensure that they are addressed and corrected.

Dispensing Process

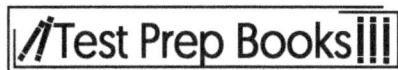

For repackaging, documentation must include the identity and strength of the drug product, the name and address of the manufacturer or distributor, the lot number, and the expiration date. All documentation must include the name and address of the pharmacy, the date of repackaging, the quantity of the drug repackaged, and the name and strength of the new package. It is important to note that documentation must be maintained in a manner that ensures confidentiality, security, and accessibility. This may include the use of electronic systems, logbooks, or other means of recordkeeping. Furthermore, all documentation must be available for review and inspection by regulatory agencies, such as the FDA and state boards of pharmacy.

Practice Quiz

1. Which medical professional CANNOT prescribe all forms of medication and medication classes, with or without physician supervision?
    a. Physician assistant
    b. Dentist
    c. Nurse practitioner
    d. Doctor of osteopathic medicine

2. A prescription states, "3 gtts AU TID." What does this mean?
    a. 3 milliliters in each ear two times daily
    b. 3 drops in each eye three times daily
    c. 3 ounces in each eye two times daily
    d. 3 drops in each ear three times daily

3. On an insurance card, what is the PCN, or the Processor Control Number?
    a. The employer's identification on the card
    b. The insurance provider's identification number
    c. The specific pharmacy benefit manager's identification
    d. The patient's identification number

4. Who could be insured by Medicare?
    a. A healthy fifty-five-year-old
    b. A healthy eighty-five-year-old
    c. A twenty-two-year-old with eczema
    d. A sixty-four-year-old who falls below the poverty line

5. What must be done to receive a prior authorization for a medication?
    a. Ask the pharmacist to call the insurance.
    b. Call the doctor's office to ask them to contact insurance.
    c. Call the patient to let them know their insurance will not cover this medication.
    d. Ask the patient for a written letter stating their need for the medication.

See answers on the next page.

Answer Explanations

1. B: Choice *B* is the correct answer; dentists can only prescribe mouth-related prescriptions. The other choices can all prescribe any medication classes.

2. D: Choice *D* is the correct answer. Gtts stands for drops, AU stands for each ear, and TID stands for three times daily.

3. C: Choice *C* is the correct answer; this is what a PCN identifies. Choice *A* is a group number; Choice *B* is a BIN, or bank identification number; and Choice *D* is an identification number.

4. B: Choice *B* is the correct answer; any American over sixty-five, a patient with end stage renal disease, and patients younger than sixty-five and disabled are eligible for Medicare. Choice *D* would be a patient eligible for Medicaid. Choices *A* and *C* fall out of the age criteria and could only receive Medicare if they had end stage renal disease or were disabled, which they are not.

5. B: Choice *B* is correct; a prior authorization must be given by a doctor to the patient's insurance company to prove that the patient has an accepted and therapeutic medical use for a medication that is not already on the insurance's approved formulary.

Medication Safety and Quality Assurance

Best Practices for Quality Assurance and Medication Safety

Best Practices for Quality Assurance during Entire Filling Process

Pharmacy personnel are responsible for providing dependable, safe, and effective care, which includes implementing strategies focused on the reduction of medication errors. **Risk management** refers to systems that identify, assess, and implement procedures aimed at reducing medication errors. Risk management has three components—quality control (QC), quality assurance (QA), and quality improvement. Pharmacies should include risk management guidelines and regulations in their SOPs. Risk management is an ongoing process and may require periodic adjustments.

Accuracy should be at the forefront of all prescription-filling activities. There are many medication error prevention strategies. Verification of patient information should be performed at every pharmacy visit. This practice is key in the reduction of allergic drug reactions and drug-drug interactions. There are various resources available on the Internet aimed at the prevention of medication errors. Pharmacies should also maintain an up-to-date library pertinent to the practice of pharmacy.

Advancements in pharmacy technology have made it possible to provide additional safety controls within the dispensing process. The order entry process can be automatically linked to the particular NDCs stocked on the pharmacy's shelves. As a result, the prescription label can be printed with a unique barcode linking it to a particular drug and patient profile. A barcode scanner can then be used to verify that the correct medication is being used to fill an individual patient's prescription. In the hospital setting, barcodes can be incorporated into patient hospital bracelets, allowing hospital personnel to verify that the correct medication is being administered to the right patient at the correct time. The automation of pharmacy dispensing equipment has reduced medication errors.

The separation of a pharmacy's inventory by drug categories is another medication error prevention strategy. TJC mandates that external and internal medications are stored separately. The commission also requires separate storage of oncology medications and volatile or flammable substances. Oncology medications should be stored in a sealed protective outer bag to prevent potential leakage. Volatile or flammable substances should be stored in a cool environment with adequate ventilation. The storage area must be designed to minimize fire and explosive potential. Common look-alike and sound-alike medications should be stored in different areas of the pharmacy. Lastly, insulin brands should be stored separately from one another.

The prescription label should be compared with the original prescription by at least two pharmacy personnel. Electronic prescribing is favored over writing, telephoning, or faxing prescriptions to a pharmacy. Other medication error prevention strategies include questioning illegible handwriting, ambiguous orders, and uncommon or unfamiliar abbreviations. Prescriptions should utilize the metric system. Prescribers should always position a leading zero in decimal values less than one. Likewise, a trailing zero to the right of a decimal point should never be used. Mistakes with both leading and trailing zeroes may result in a dosage error of between a tenth-fold and ten-fold. It is advisable to double-count prescriptions of narcotics. Overall, a prescription order should be reviewed a minimum of three times by pharmacy personnel.

Types of Prescription Errors

Medication dispensing errors are deviations in a medication dispensed to a patient from that which was written in a prescription order.

Medication Safety and Quality Assurance

An error might fall into one of these categories:

- Incorrect medication
- Incorrect dose
- Incorrect dosage form
- Incorrect quantity
- Incorrect or confusing direction
- Incorrect or inadequate labeling
- Incorrect patient
- Incorrect preparation etc.

Certain situations can increase the chance of medication dispensing errors:

- Unorganized work flow
- Work interruptions and distractions
- Poor handwriting and inadequate/incorrect information on prescriptions
- Excessive workload and stress
- Long shifts (fatigue)
- Ineffective communication with physicians and patients
- Lack of skilled personnel
- Inadequate staffing

Pharmacy technicians routinely handle refills of prescription medication. Some refill situations require special attention, including:

- **Early refill**: Medication dosage may have changed, or a patient may need a vacation fill. In some cases, insurance carriers have to be contacted.

- **No refills**: Generally, the prescriber must be contacted for a refill authorization. In some instances, the prescription may be greater than a year old, making it invalid.

- **Controlled substances**: Schedule II controlled substances cannot be refilled. Schedule III and IV controlled substances can only be refilled five times within a six-month period.

Medication error is a leading cause of death in the United States. Dispensing errors account for 21% of all medication errors.

There are many strategies to minimize dispensing errors:

- Correctly entering the prescription: Transcription errors (such as omissions and inaccuracies) account for approximately 15% of dispensing errors. These errors may be reduced by consistently using reliable methods of verification while entering a prescription order into the computer.

- Confirming that the prescription is accurate and complete: Pharmacy personnel should not second-guess ambiguous or illegible prescriptions. Other causes of medication error include the use of acronyms, nonstandard abbreviations, decimals, and call-in prescriptions. The prescriber should be contacted for clarification.

- Being aware of sound-alike and look-alike medications: Similar medication names account for 33% of medication errors. One example would be dispensing methadone instead of methylphenidate. Occasionally, these errors are fatal.

- Being careful with zeros and abbreviations: Misplaced decimal points or zeros and faulty units are frequent causes of medication error and are typically the result of misinterpretation. Misplacing a decimal point or zero may result in the patient receiving at least 10 times more medication than originally indicated. Stocking a single strength of a particular medication, computer alerts, and reviewing label instructions during patient medication counseling may reduce these errors.

- Keeping the workplace organized: In clinical trials, organization (e.g., work environment, workspace, and workflow) has been shown to markedly reduce medication dispensing errors. Examples of organization include adequate workspace and appropriate lighting. Pharmacy technicians should develop a routine for entering, filling, and checking pharmacy prescriptions.

- Reducing distractions: Distractions while working and multitasking are leading causes of dispensing errors. Automatic refill requests may reduce distractions. Factors that may influence work environments include window services, design of workflow, and automatic dispensing.

- Balancing heavy workloads and reducing stress: Increased workloads have often been noted as contributing to dispensing errors. Sufficient staffing with appropriate workload assignments may help to reduce dispensing errors. These measures should also reduce stress, which may limit medication errors.

- Storing drugs properly: Storing look-alike/sound-alike medications away from each other on the shelves can decrease dispensing errors. Always store stock medication with the container label facing forward. Locked storage for medications with a high potential for inducing errors is advisable.

- Thoroughly checking all prescriptions: Checks and counterchecks of medication labels may reduce dispensing errors. For instance, check the written prescription against the NDC in the computer, the printed medication label, and the drug being filled/dispensed.

- Always providing medication counseling to patients: The vast majority of dispensing errors (83%) are identified during medication counseling sessions between the patient and pharmacist. These errors may be corrected before the patient leaves the pharmacy. Directions for use of medications should be covered during the counseling session, as misunderstood directions for use account for a significant portion of dispensing errors.

Safe Dosage Ranges

Acetaminophen

The maximum daily dose of acetaminophen is 4,000 mg for people with a healthy liver. For those with compromised liver function, the maximum dose is only 2,000 mg per day. In some cases, people with liver disease cannot take acetaminophen at all. As acetaminophen is metabolized primarily in the liver, it is important to follow the dosing instructions to prevent liver damage. Consumption of excessive acetaminophen causes saturation of liver enzymes and buildup of acetaminophen. The metabolic by-products of acetaminophen damage liver cells (hepatocytes).

Controlled Substances

The following are the usual range of dosages, available forms, and routes of administration for controlled substances:

- **Hydrocodone/acetaminophen**: There are two dosage components: the hydrocodone can range in strength from 2.5 mg to 10 mg, and the acetaminophen can range from 325 mg to 650 mg. Depending on the severity of pain, doses are either one or two tablets, as needed for pain. It is important not to exceed 4,000 mg of acetaminophen each day with the dosing. The medicine is available in oral tablets of different strengths and as an oral solution.

Medication Safety and Quality Assurance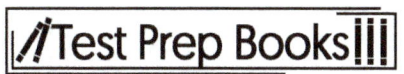

- **Lorazepam**: This drug is usually taken PRN or as needed, with up to a total of 6 mg each day in divided doses. This medication is available in two forms: oral tablet and injectable solution.
- **Methylphenidate**: This drug can be dosed up to 72 mg each day. Immediate release tablets can be taken once or twice a day, while extended-release formulations are only taken once a day. This medication is available in two forms: oral tablets and oral extended-release tablets.

Antibiotics

The following are the usual ranges for dosing and available forms for antibiotics:

- **Amoxicillin**: Usually dosed at 250 mg to 500 mg every 8 hours, or at a higher dose (500 mg to 875 mg) every 12 hours. This drug is available in a chewable tablet, a capsule, and a powder to make suspensions.
- **Penicillin VK**: This drug is usually dosed at 125 mg to 500 mg every 6–8 hours. It is available in either oral tablets or a powder to make suspensions.
- **Cephalexin**: The dose of this drug is 250 mg to 500 mg every 6–8 hours. It is available as oral capsules and powder for oral suspensions.
- **Cefuroxime**: The dose of this drug is usually 250 mg to 500 mg every 12 hours. The forms available are tablets and a powder for oral suspensions.
- **Azithromycin**: This drug can be taken in multiple combinations; the possibilities are as follows: a single dose of 1,000 mg, 500 mg for three days, or one dose of 500 mg followed by four days of 250 mg. This drug is available either in oral tablets or a powder for oral suspensions.

Antidepressants

The following are the typical dosages, form, and routes of administration for antidepressants:

- **Amitriptyline**: This medication can be started at a dose of 10 mg and can be increased to up to 300 mg per day. The dose can be taken at one time or divided over 2–3 occurrences. This drug comes in oral tablets and intramuscular injections.
- **Bupropion**: The usual daily adult dose for this drug is 150 mg to 300 mg, either in divided doses or in a single extended-release tablet. The maximum daily dose is 450 mg. This drug is available in standard or extended-release tablets.
- **Citalopram**: This drug is dosed at 20 mg to 40 mg daily; it is recommended not to exceed 40 mg per day. Citalopram can be taken in oral tablets or as an oral solution.
- **Mirtazapine**: This drug is usually dosed between 15 mg to 45 mg each day. It is available either in regular oral tablets or disintegrating oral tablets.

Antihypertensive Medications

The usual dosage range, forms, and routes of administration of common antihypertensive medications are outlined below:

- **Hydrochlorothiazide (HCTZ)**: The dosage for HCTZ can range from 25 mg to 100 mg per day, which can be taken once or in divided doses throughout the day. This medication is available as tablets, capsules, and as a solution.
- **Atenolol**: Based on the medical conditions, the usual dose of atenolol is 25 mg to 100 mg daily, with a maximum daily dose of 200 mg. This medication is available in oral tablets and as IV injections.

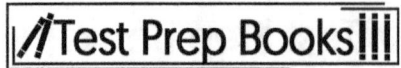

- **Amlodipine**: This drug can be prescribed from 2.5 mg to a maximum of 10 mg each day and is available as an oral tablet.
- **Losartan**: This medication is usually prescribed at 25 mg to 100 mg each day and can be taken all at once or divided into two doses. This drug is available as an oral tablet.

ISMP Guidelines

The Institute for Safe Medication Practices (ISMP) is an independent nonprofit that focuses on the prevention of medication errors. The ISMP guidelines are internationally followed to help prevent drug errors in pharmacies and medical settings. They include guidelines for specific areas of practice, such as in hospitals. For example, one of the hospital guidelines recommends "[using] a weekly dosage regimen default of oral methotrexate in electronic systems when medication orders are entered" to prevent incorrect dosing errors that have been widely documented in hospitals when providing oral methotrexate. The ISMP also provides a medication error reporting program, along with other resources for healthcare professionals to prevent and discuss medication warnings and errors, especially for error-prone drugs.

Black Box Warnings

A black box warning, or boxed warning, is required by the FDA if the medication poses a serious (but usually rare) risk or side effect. This is the highest level of warning a drug can receive besides being banned from the market. A black box warning can also contain safe handling instructions or correct use of the drug (specific instructions) if mishandling or misusing the drug could cause significant harm. Additionally, it can include information about increased or decreased safety and/or efficacy in certain populations, such as in the elderly or in children.

A black box warning can be added to a drug when it is first released or later if a serious adverse event occurs after its release onto the market. The black box warning must be placed on the medication packaging and on the medication insert, which is the information provided with a medication to explain what it is used for, how to store the drug, potential side effects, and other pertinent information.

For example, ibuprofen has two black box warnings: one for serious cardiovascular thrombotic events and another for serious gastrointestinal bleeding, ulceration, and perforation. For the cardiovascular warning, the black box warning states that there is a higher risk of myocardial infarction (heart attack) and stroke for patients who take ibuprofen on a regular basis and continue to take it for a long period of time. It also states that ibuprofen is contraindicated (should not be used) before, during, or immediately after coronary artery bypass graft (CABG) surgery. This black box warning not only includes a general statement, but also elaborates on the duration of therapy and the point during therapy at which someone would be at a higher risk for a serious side effect. This black box warning includes what this medicine can increase the risk of, the duration of therapy that increases the risk, and which patient population it affects the most.

As a reminder, if a drug is still FDA approved even with several black box warnings, the FDA has decided that the benefits of patients taking this medication outweigh the risks. Each doctor and patient must decide on an individualized basis whether the benefits outweigh the risks for them personally.

Adverse Drug Events

An adverse drug event (ADE) is an overall term to describe any adverse event that occurs because of a medication, including adverse drug reactions (ADRs) and medication errors, and that could cause injury to the patient. Medication errors can be prescribing errors (by the provider), dispensing errors (by the pharmacy), or administration errors (for example, giving a medicine intramuscularly instead of subcutaneously or giving the wrong medicine to the wrong patient).

An ADE can result from augmented pharmacological effects, which are mostly dose-dependent. It is more prevalent with medications that have a narrow therapeutic index (i.e., dose margin). For example, warfarin is an anticoagulant that has a narrow therapeutic index. The dose of warfarin is determined and adjusted based on routine blood work. An augmented effect of warfarin from a high dose or interaction with other medications can cause an internal hemorrhage—an ADE. If untreated, an ADE could lead to organ damage, disability, hospitalization, and even fatality. A pharmacist should appropriately intervene in a situation of an ADE to ensure the best patient outcome.

An ADR is an adverse, or unwanted, event that occurs at a normal therapeutic dose, such as drowsiness with Benadryl or an allergic reaction to penicillin. ADRs do not occur in every patient, but each medication has its own ADR (or side effect) profile that contains ADRs that occur more frequently than other ADRs.

Expanding on the examples of Benadryl and penicillin, Benadryl is well known for causing drowsiness at normal therapeutic doses, but it does not cause drowsiness in everyone. Penicillin is an antibiotic that is well known for causing allergic reactions (rash, itching, hives, shortness of breath, anaphylactic shock) at normal therapeutic doses, but this does not occur in every patient who takes penicillin. If a patient approaches a pharmacy technician with a question about whether a medication is causing a specific ADR, ask the pharmacist to consult with the patient. Pharmacy technicians cannot legally counsel patients on even minor questions such as whether Benadryl causes drowsiness, even if they do know the answer. However, it is good to know the general signs of ADRs for medications when conversing with a patient while ringing them up in case they mention a potential ADR or medication error that the pharmacist should address.

MedWatch

MedWatch is the FDA program that allows healthcare professionals and consumers to report adverse reactions to and safety concerns regarding products regulated by the FDA. These products include medications, medical devices and supplies, and dietary supplements.

Event Reporting Procedures

Medication error documentation may be accomplished with incident reports. Medication errors are numerous and varied and include issues in filling the quantity or type of medication prescribed, errors reading a prescription or label, failing to verify a patient's medical conditions and any contraindications for a prescription, or dispensing a different patient's prescription to the wrong recipient. The individual staff member observing or initially informed of the incident should complete the incident report and turn it in to the supervisor on duty. Incident reports should contain specifics of the individuals involved in the incident (name, contact information, whether employee or patient); the date, time, and location of the incident; a description of the occurrence; the type of injury; the treatment provided (if applicable); the name and signature of the individual filing the report; and the date the report was filed. The MedWatch Program is overseen by the FDA and provides an online voluntary reporting form. MedWatch also furnishes safety alerts for drugs, medical devices, biologics, cosmetics, and nutritional supplements. It is the FDA's "gateway for clinically important safety information and reporting serious problems with human medical products." The FDA also administers the Adverse Event Reporting System (FAERS) containing information on medication error reports and adverse events. The FDA also oversees the **Vaccine Adverse Reporting System (VAERS)**, which is a national vaccine safety surveillance database.

The **Institute of Safe Medication Practices (ISMP)** provides impartial, timely, and accurate drug safety information. The ISMP provides pharmacy resources such as "do not crush" lists, black box warnings, error-prone abbreviations lists, confused drug names lists, high alert medications, and tall man letters. The ISMP also manages the **National Medication Errors Reporting Program (MERP)** and the National **Vaccine Errors Reporting Program (VERP)**. Currently, the ISMP is the only national nonprofit body concentrating on the prevention of medication errors.

An adverse effect or reaction to a medication is usually an unexpected event and can often be harmful. An allergic reaction to a medication such as a severe rash is an example of an adverse effect. It is important to report adverse events to MedWatch when they happen. The Food and Drug Administration's **Adverse Event Reporting System**, or **FAERS**, is an information database that compiles incident reports that have been submitted to MedWatch regarding adverse medication effects, product integrity, and medication errors. The reports in the database are evaluated to identify possible safety concerns that have arisen after products have gone to market. MedWatch is a useful tool used by clinicians to look for trends regarding product safety and provide the FDA with information for issuing safety warnings when necessary. Anyone can voluntarily submit a report to the FDA concerning an adverse event. The FDA, however, requires the manufacturer of a product to forward any adverse effects that are reported directly to them by a healthcare professional or consumer.

Product integrity concerns might include an adulterated product, misbranded drugs, counterfeit products, or an improperly labeled product. The sudden increase in the number of recalled counterfeit medications entering the market led to legislation to protect supply chains. In 2013, the **Drug Supply Chain Security Act (DSCSA)** was enacted to help establish guidelines for the tracing of prescription medications within the supply chain. The DSCSA requires wholesale distributors and their third-party logistic providers to obtain national licensure with the FDA in order to ensure a prescription medication's chain of custody remains unbroken within the supply chain.

Most medication errors are reported and reviewed internally utilizing established pharmacy or hospital protocols. Internal medication reporting practices allow for the immediate review of an error within the environment in which it occurred. MedWatch can be used to report all types of medication errors in addition to reporting adverse events and product integrity concerns. A **near miss** is a type of medication error that has the potential to do harm but does not because it does not reach the patient, or the medication does reach the patient, but, by mere chance, no harm was done. Reporting medication errors is important because it allows a systemic procedural review to determine how the error occurred. Knowing what led to the error can be useful in creating an action plan to prevent it from happening again.

REMS

A Risk Evaluation and Mitigation Strategy (REMS) is a drug safety program implemented by the FDA to monitor specific drugs with safety concerns. A REMS focuses on ensuring that healthcare providers prescribe, administer, and store the medication safely based on potential safety concerns for the provider or the patient. All this information can be found on the FDA's website under Drug Databases, then REMS. Each drug has its own REMS, as each drug has its own risks and monitoring strategies. A typical REMS warning includes a list of goals, the specific products (formulations/manufacturers) included, what each party needs to know and follow, and a history of the updates for the drug. To prescribe a REMS medication, providers must also be registered with the REMS program for that specific medication.

For example, clozapine is a REMS drug with thirteen different formulations. Clozapine (ANDA203039) by Teva Pharmaceuticals USA and FazaClo® ODT (clozapine, NDA021590) by Jazz Pharmaceuticals are two specific formulations that are included under the REMS. (ANDA stands for abbreviated new drug application, and NDA stands for new drug application. These are applications submitted by pharmaceutical companies to get FDA approval for their medications.) The major safety concern with clozapine is neutropenia in a patient; the prescriber must counsel each patient on the signs and risks of neutropenia and also monitor the absolute neutrophil count (ANC) throughout treatment. The patient is responsible for getting regular blood tests as suggested by the provider. An outpatient pharmacy has to have REMS certification and train staff on clozapine and neutropenia, and an inpatient pharmacy must also dispense no more than a seven-day supply. Wholesalers/distributors have to keep accurate records on clozapine and their distribution of it.

This REMS focuses on the major safety concern for the patient and how each participating party can help mitigate the risk. Currently, there are seventy-three REMS medications, and the frequency of dispensing them in a specific practice location depends on the patient population and healthcare setting. Some REMS are meant to ensure the safety of the healthcare worker dispensing or administering the medication, as some medications can cause adverse

Medication Safety and Quality Assurance

reactions even for people who touch the medication. For medications that have REMS, pharmacy technicians should be trained on how to handle each medication appropriately.

Pregnancy and Lactation Warnings

Pregnancy and lactation warnings are mostly focused on the risk to an unborn fetus or a breastfeeding child. Most medications with pregnancy and/or lactation warnings are generally safe in nonpregnant and nonbreastfeeding women; there are special considerations with pregnancy and breastfeeding because a medication or dose proven safe for an adult is not always safe for a growing fetus or infant. However, one cannot assume that because a medication has a pregnancy warning, it also has a warning for breastfeeding. Usually, if there is a risk associated with a medication in pregnancy, there will be a similar risk with breastfeeding, but this is not always the case. Not all medications have the same labeling system for pregnancy and lactation warnings. The Pregnancy and Lactation Labeling Rule (PLLR) required all drugs approved after June 30, 2001 to include the pregnancy registry; clinical considerations; a risk summary; and supporting data for pregnancy, labor/delivery, lactation, and reproductive potential in males and females. However, the PLLR did not apply to OTCs, so some OTC products may still follow the old FDA pregnancy categories—A, B, C, D, and X—where A is the safest in pregnancy and X is the greatest risk for pregnancy.

There are many resources out there to look up pregnancy/breastfeeding information if one is unsure, and one can always ask the pharmacist for insight as well. Some resources include *Briggs's Drugs in Pregnancy and Lactation*, the InfantRisk Center, and the American Academy of Pediatrics. A common resource for breastfeeding is Hale's Lactation Risk Categories, which ranks drugs on a scale of L1 to L5. L1 is the safest, with numerous studies done on the drug; L2 is safe but has limited studies; L3 is moderately safe with no real studies, and a provider must compare risk versus benefit; L4 is possibly hazardous, and there is documented risk, but risk versus benefit must still be discussed; L5 is contraindicated in breastfeeding, meaning that the drug exhibits significant and proven risk to breastfeeding infants. Again, if the pharmacy technician is unsure or a patient who is pregnant/breastfeeding asks a question about the safety of a medication, the technician should always consult the pharmacist.

Drugs that are considered teratogenic, or agents that cause fetal abnormalities or death, are the antiepileptics phenytoin (Dilantin), phenobarbital (primidone/Mysoline®), and topiramate (Topamax); blood pressure medications such as ACE inhibitors (ending in -pril, i.e., lisinopril [Prinivil, Qbrelis, Zestril], captopril, etc.), angiotensin II receptor blockers (ending in -sartan, i.e., losartan [Cozaar], candesartan [Atacand], etc.); renin inhibitors (aliskiren [Tekturna]); spironolactone (Aldactone); and atenolol (Tenormin). Oral anticoagulants, such as warfarin and apixaban (Eliquis), are also teratogenic. Propylthiouracil is teratogenic in the second and third trimesters of pregnancy. The GI OTC drugs bisacodyl (Dulcolax, Fleet), senna, and any products containing magnesium, castor oil, sodium bicarbonate, or aluminum, such as Pepto Bismol, are also all teratogenic.

Some important medications to remember that are dangerous to infants with breastfeeding mothers are estrogen (birth control or other hormonal medications); tetracycline antibiotics (doxycycline, minocycline); antiepileptics like valproic acid, phenytoin, and phenobarbital (primidone/Mysoline); topiramate; pseudoephedrine (Sudafed); benzonatate (prescription cough medication); and Pepto Bismol.

Even though a pharmacy technician is not verifying orders or prescribing medications, and legally, they cannot give medical or prescription advice, knowing what signs to look for if the drug is teratogenic or harmful is still crucial. Most pharmacies will have either a warning printed on the patient's prescription label or a sticker that must be added to the bottle or packaging. The sticker on the prescription bottle will usually have a picture of a baby and a mother and/or a pregnant woman; it will say something like "Warning: do not take if pregnant, trying to become pregnant, or breastfeeding."

If the pharmacy technician knows that a medication is dangerous for pregnancy OR breastfeeding, they should ask the pharmacist whether it is a danger to both conditions or just to pregnancy or breastfeeding. For example,

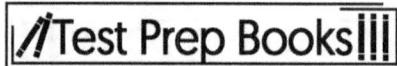

Medication Safety and Quality Assurance

bisacodyl is contraindicated in pregnancy but not in breastfeeding. A patient can safely take bisacodyl after they are no longer pregnant. A pharmacy technician is the frontline support for patient care. If a drug has a pregnancy and/or breastfeeding contraindication or risk, to ensure safety for the mother and baby, the technician should ask the patient if they are pregnant, are trying to become pregnant, have a chance of becoming pregnant, or are breastfeeding.

Assisting Pharmacist in Identifying Patient Medication Adherence Issues

Medication Adherence

Compliance with a medication refers to adherence of the patient to the prescribed medication as directed by the prescriber. Non-compliance is one of the major causes for discontinuation of a medication.

The following are examples of non-compliance:

- Not taking the full dose of the medication (i.e., taking a smaller dose than what was prescribed)
- Not taking medication for the full length of time (i.e., stopping early)
- Not adhering to the time of day to take the medication (i.e., night vs. morning)
- Discontinuation of treatment
- Taking expired medications

Non-compliance with a medication can impose significant harm to the patient. There are many reasons for non-compliance, such as physical issues, cognitive problems, misunderstandings, and fear of or experience with side effects. Pharmacies have systems to help keep track of refills and reminders (calls, texts, and emails) for patients to promote compliance. The pharmacy can send notifications to the patient and their physician when the patient is not compliant with treatment.

Health Literacy

Health literacy is defined as an individual's ability to understand and use medical information. Health literacy is an important aspect of patient education, as most patients who are starting a new medication either have never heard of it before or know only a small amount of information about it. It is important to always ask a patient whether they have any questions for the pharmacist. This makes the patient feel welcome to ask questions they may have felt embarrassed to ask otherwise. A technician cannot legally counsel a patient, but knowing what patients are confused by and understanding health literacy will help them provide better care and know when the pharmacist should intervene. One of the most important aspects of health literacy is using layman's terms. Instead of using words that only medical professionals are likely to know, use words and explanations that all people should understand. For example, instead of using the phrase "anaphylactic shock," saying "an allergic reaction, such as swelling, itching, hives, or trouble breathing" helps the patient understand in layman's terms what anaphylactic shock is and what they should look out for. Depending on the patient, explaining insurance terms in layman's terms might be beneficial. For example, if a patient does not understand the word *copay*, saying "the part you pay after insurance pays their part" will clear up the meaning of the word *copay* to them.

Knowing the routes of administration for most medications is helpful as well. For tablets and capsules, most patients will understand how to take them. However, for inhalers, injections, nebulizers, creams, suppositories, patches, dissolving tablets, etc., it may be the first time the patient has ever had this route of administration with a medication before. Each medication will have special instructions, which can differ even with the same route of administration (like two different inhalers), so being able to identify new prescriptions for different routes of administration can help prevent medication usage errors.

Safety Strategies to Prevent Mix Ups

Error Prevention Strategies

Medication dispensing errors can be prevented or minimized by adopting systematic approaches in workflow. A pharmacy should adopt and implement suitable strategies to prevent medication dispensing errors. The following are some examples that can minimize medication dispensing errors in a pharmacy:

- Collect adequate information about the patient and the prescription:
    - Verify the patient's information with the information written on the prescription (e.g., name, address, and date of birth). In the case of a patient with hearing or visual impairment, find an alternative means to communicate with the patient to verify the information.
    - For existing patients, find the patient's profile by entering the patient's date of birth, and then verify by matching two unique identifiers on the pharmacy profile and the prescription.
    - For new patients, verify two unique identifiers (e.g., date of birth and address) between the prescription and the newly-entered pharmacy profile before entering the prescription.
    - If any part of the prescription information is missing, incomplete, or unclear, contact the corresponding physician to reconfirm the information.
    - Be cautious when dispensing look-alike or sound-alike drugs. It's important to be careful about zeros, decimal points, and abbreviations.
    - Incorporate an IVR (interactive voice response) that prompts physicians to leave thorough details about the prescription. The message should require that they provide details about the prescriber (prescriber's name, license number, phone number), details about the patient (patient's name, date of birth, phone number), and details about the medication (name, strength, direction of use, duration of treatment, and number of repeats/refills).
    - Verify the "therapeutic use of the medication" with the patient to confirm that the treatment is appropriate for the patient's condition.
    - If a verbal prescription is received through an IVR or direct communication, collect all necessary information and always reconfirm by reading back the prescription.
    - Pharmacy prescription entry load can be reduced through electronic prescriptions.
- Provide an environment that reinforces accurate prescription entry.
- Provide supportive measures that assist in accurate information entry for filling out the prescription. Consider integrating the following at the prescription entry/drop-off station/counter:
    - A scanner with a re-sizable prescription imaging system on the screen
    - A stand to hold the prescription at eye level
    - Image magnification and zooming software
    - Adequate light and counter space
- Allow entry of only one patient's prescriptions at a time. Keep other prescriptions away to avoid possible mix-ups. Distractions should be reduced as much as possible.
- Always use "baskets" to keep individual patient's prescriptions separate. This strategy significantly decreases dispensing errors and allows better tracking of patients to be served (in order according to drop-off or requested pick-up time).

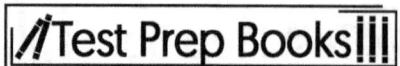

- Provide entry during peak hours for facilities that allow remote prescription.
- Patients should be encouraged to place orders in advance through the IVR, online, or by email to reduce the workload at peak hours.
- The technicians' shifts should be planned efficiently so that adequate staff is available during busy hours (or predicted busy days).
- Employ additional staff and/or utilize automated processes to identify and correct errors:
  - If feasible, provide additional employees to cross-check the prescription entry before it reaches the pharmacist for the final check.
  - Design the pharmacy software in a way that requires action by the staff to enter a patient's information completely prior to processing the prescription.
  - Keep the hard copy and/or scanned image of the prescription available for the pharmacist for the final check.

Separating Inventory

Dispensing errors can happen from mix-ups of the medications that are LASA or from medications that are packaged in similar ways. Mix-up errors can also happen from a medication with different strengths.

The following inventory management strategies can be implemented to minimize such errors:

- Labeling medications with both the brand name and generic name
- Using separate shelving for LASA medications
- Tagging warning labels on high-alert medications
- Incorporating provisions in pharmacy software to alert users of LASA or high-alert medications

Look-Alike/Sound-Alike Drugs

Some drug names look like or sound like other drug names. These include both generic and brand names of medications. Look-Alike and Sound-Alike **(LASA) medications** are a common cause of medication errors. With the presence of thousands of medications on the market, errors due to confusing drug names are possible and can be significant.

Consider the following examples:

LASA Medications	
Drug name	Often confused with
amlodipine	aMILoride
acetazolamide	acetoHEXAMIDE
ARIPiprazole	RABEprazole
chlorpropamide	chlorproMAZINE
ClobaZAM	ClonazePAM

Pharmacies can adopt the following strategies to prevent or reduce errors associated with LASA medications:

- Printing both the brand name and the generic name on prescriptions and pharmacy labels
- Adding the indication of each medication on a prescription

- Designing clinic-office/pharmacy software in a way that prevents LASA medications from appearing concurrently
- Changing the appearance of LASA medications to attract attention to their dissimilarities
- Implementing independent double-checks throughout the entire pharmacy workflow
- Storing LASA medications in separate locations on the shelves
- Reading back prescriptions, spelling out the name of medications, and providing the indication of the medication when receiving a verbal prescription from the prescriber
- Emphasizing the use of methods such as "tall man lettering" to differentiate drug names

Tall Man Lettering

Tall man lettering refers to the practice of using mixed case letters (uppercase and lowercase) to bring attention to the dissimilarities in LASA medication names. The **Institute for Safe Medication Practices (ISMP)** and the FDA encourage use of tall man lettering to decrease possible mix-ups of LASA medications.

Examples of Tall Man Lettering	
acetaZOLAMIDE	acetoHEXAMIDE
Chlorpromazine	chlorproPAMIDE
DAUNOrubicin	DOXOrubicin
Dimenhydrinate	diphenhydrAMINE
DOBUTamine	DOPamine

High-Alert/High-Risk Medications

High-alert/high-risk medications are those medications that can cause significant harm to the patient when administered incorrectly or used in error. These medications generally have a narrow window of safety. Errors associated with high-risk medications result in devastating consequences to the patient and cause practitioners to suffer immense anxiety and guilt.

Here are some examples of high-alert medications:

- **Benzodiazepines**, primarily **midazolam**: used for sedation
- **Chemotherapeutic agents**: used for cancer treatment
- **Intravenous digoxin**: used to treat cardiac arrhythmia and heart failure
- **Dopamine, dobutamine**: used to treat depressed cardiac function
- **Heparin, warfarin**: used to prevent blood clots
- **Insulin**: used to control blood sugar
- **Lidocaine**: used to induce anesthesia
- **Opiate narcotics**: used for pain management
- **Neuromuscular blocking agents**: used as a muscle-relaxant or paralyzing agent
- **Electrolyte solutions**, e.g., intravenous sodium chloride, potassium chloride (or potassium phosphate), and magnesium sulphate

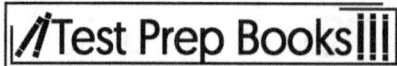

Medication Safety and Quality Assurance

Pharmacies can use the following strategies to aid in avoiding errors associated with high-alert medications:

- Remove high concentration electrolytes from dispensing areas
- Use a leading "0" before the decimal place
- Avoid using risky abbreviations like "u" for unit or a trailing "0" on the dosage (e.g., 1.0 mg)
- Review LASA medications
- Use "tall man" letters for LASA medications
- Use colored warning labels
- Double-check dosage calculation independently

It is also necessary to pay attention to medications that should not be crushed as doing so could lead to high-risk situations. There are several reasons why certain medications should not be crushed:

- Dosage form is slow-release
- Dosage form is extended-release
- Dosage form is enteric-coated
- Mucous membrane could be irritated
- Possible increased rate of absorption
- Tablet coating could release the drug over a set period of time
- Taste
- Can irritate the skin
- Medication is liquid filled
- Dosage form is sublingual
- Dosage form is coated with a film
- Tablet is effervescent
- Potential for birth defects, teratogenic effect
- Acts as local anesthetic on the oral mucosa

A few examples of some medications that should not be crushed are *Cymbalta, Depakote, Prilosec,* and *Wellbutrin (SR, XL)*.

Matching Patient Information to Prescription or Medication Order

The best practice for matching patient information to their prescription is to use two identifiers—usually this is the name and date of birth, but it can also include the phone number or address. Commonly, patient names, birthdays, phone numbers, and addresses will be in the pharmacy's system multiple times for multiple different patients, so asking the patient for two different identifying markers is crucial. For example, say a mother, Mary Smith, came in for a prescription for her two-year-old daughter, Jane Smith. If the technician just asked for the phone number, most likely, the phone number would show up on both Mary's and Jane's profiles. Asking for the daughter's full name and phone number would narrow this down further to Jane. A special case would be a retail pharmacy or other pharmacy that dispenses veterinary medications. Commonly, either the animal is on the owner's chart and the owner and animal's medications are mixed together, or the pet just has a filler date of birth. Asking for the full name and phone number or address would be the best idea in this scenario.

Assuring Delivery of the Correct Prescriptions to Patients

Besides safety measures for LASA drugs, high-alert/high-risk drugs, and common medication errors already discussed, there are other best practices for filling prescriptions. If any part of a prescription is unclear or does not make sense—for example, albuterol #60 tablets (it does not come in tablet form)—, always call the provider's office to clarify. The pharmacy would also be held liable for any adverse reactions or consequences, and the technician would harm the patient by potentially dispensing the wrong dose, quantity, or medication.

During the filling process, always ensure that the label includes all of the necessary information. For noncontrolled substances, this could mean the name, address, and phone number of the pharmacy; the unique identification number of the prescription (Rx #); the initials or identification code of the dispensing pharmacist; the date the prescription is dispensed; the name of the prescribing practitioner; the patient's name; instructions for use; the quantity dispensed; the name and strength of the drug; and appropriate auxiliary instructions. This is a general example of what might be required in a state for prescription labels. Different states will have different requirements for prescription label information; always follow the stricter law between federal and state, which is usually the state's law. If any of the required information is missing or unclear on the label, refer back to the original prescription. If it is still not clear, contact the provider to clarify. The label must be clear and easy to read as well, and make sure not to cover up any crucial information, such as storage instructions on a box or measurement markers on a liquid bottle.

To ensure accuracy in the counting process, if the pharmacy technician is distracted and has to leave the pills in the middle of counting or if they drop a pill, they should always recount. Patients depend on an exact count for their medications so that they have enough to last until the next refill, so if there is a possibility that the technician may not have an accurate count, they should recount.

Corrective Action after Detecting Potential Medication Errors or Near Misses

Record-Keeping Requirements

The FDA has an adverse event reporting program called MedWatch where healthcare professionals and patients can report medication errors or adverse events. If it is serious enough and happens often enough (as determined by the FDA), the FDA will post a public service announcement.

Reporting of medication errors should be done on an internal level and an external level. If the error is on a hard-copy prescription, the original copy needs to be kept and not altered in any way to fix the mistake. If there is an electronic drug order with a mistake, the order should not be deleted and can only be changed if the change is documented properly in the system. The error should also be voided in the system to avoid dispensing a medication incorrectly or twice if a new drug order was already inputted. Depending on the facility, they may also have other record keeping requirements or other error reporting systems in place.

If it is a **near miss**, a medication error that was caught before it occurred, the same procedure is followed for prescriptions and reporting. An error on a prescription caught before it is dispensed is considered a near miss. Once the medicine is dispensed to the patient, then it becomes an actual medication error.

Continuous Quality Improvement

Continuous quality improvement is the act of retrospectively evaluating errors to make prospective changes in a process. For pharmacy technicians, it is specifically reducing medication errors and improving patient satisfaction. Always look at what stage the medication error occurred in—prescribing, dispensing, or administration. Prescribing errors are mistakes made when writing the prescription; this is when most medication errors are made. They can include prescribing the wrong dose, the wrong medication, etc. Dispensing errors are errors made by the pharmacy when processing the prescription or during filling, such as prescribing to the wrong patient or prescribing the wrong quantity of the drug. Administration errors are errors made by the patient when taking the medication, such as not taking the correct dose or not priming an inhaler. Pharmacies can continually help with all areas of medication errors—reading prescriptions to make sure they are logical and contacting the prescriber if they are not, double-checking that it is the right medication when filling, and counseling patients on new prescriptions. Continually recognizing errors, even minor errors, and identifying the source of the error is crucial to lowering the incidence of medication errors.

Root Cause Analysis

Root cause analysis is a method of reviewing the underlying factors that can lead to a medication error rather than seeking to place blame on an individual or individuals. Root cause analysis examines the current pharmacy procedures and helps to identify systemic failures that led to the error. Conducting a root cause analysis requires establishing an investigation team, collecting data, analyzing the incident, and identifying risk factors and causal pathways. After evaluating all the information, the team will create an action plan for corrections, finalize the report, and share the action plan with the entire pharmaceutical team.

Maintaining Clean Drug Dispensing and Patient Care Environments

Best Practices for Quality Assurance during Entire Filling Process

In a pharmaceutical compounding practice, personnel are accountable for providing safe and ethical services to patients by strictly following the guidelines of infection control and hygiene and cleaning standards. It is recommended that all personnel adhere to the current infection control programs.

The infection control guidelines should be practiced in the following terms:

- Personal safety and prevention of spreading disease
- Prevention of an infection being spread from compounding tools and equipment
- Prevention of an infection being spread from materials and sources in the compounding environment

To prevent infections, the following routine practices must be employed:

- Hand washing or hand hygiene
- Use of additional barrier precautions, i.e., use of Personal Protective Equipment (PPE)
- Appropriate handling of workplace equipment
- Cleaning of the premises, equipment, and environment
- Appropriate methods for handling waste
- Personal care for disease prevention, e.g., immunization

Each institution will have different and specific rules for these routine practices; follow the guidelines that apply to that institution, and do not assume that they are the same between different pharmacies or facilities. Some overall guidelines are set by state or national governing boards and some by the facility; the strictest policy should be followed.

Procedures to Avoid Cross-Contamination

Cleaning Items and Equipment Used to Count Medication

Throughout the pharmacy, there are tools and equipment used in the preparation of medications (measuring, counting and pouring) that become dirty or tainted with dust from the medications. At least once a day, these tools and equipment (counting trays and spatulas, etc.) should be washed with hot soapy water. It is also recommended to keep cleaning wipes readily accessible to wipe down counting trays throughout the day. Most pharmacies have separate tools for preparing prescriptions that are often known to cause allergies (sulfa antibiotics and penicillin are examples). In theory, the powder from these medications can be transferred to other medications if counted on the same trays and equipment, leading to an allergic reaction. Any tools used to pour or scoop liquid and cream medications should be cleaned directly after use.

Medication Safety and Quality Assurance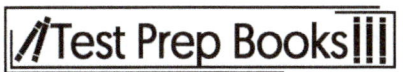

When counting pills, the pharmacy technician should clean the pill counter or counting tray and spatula (or tool they are using to push the pills on the counter) before starting. Some pills will leave a residue, which could lead to cross-contamination. If a pill leaves behind a residue, after the technician is done with that prescription, they should clean the pill counter/counting tray and spatula again. If the technician uses their hands to touch the pills, they should wash their hands following proper handwashing techniques and put on gloves. The drug could interact with something that was on the technician's hands, such as lotion, or the drug could affect the technician if they touch the loose powder and it is a REMS drug or a drug with a black box warning for healthcare providers.

Areas of the Pharmacy To Be Cleaned Each Day

Pharmacy technicians are responsible for keeping the pharmacy as clean as possible on a daily basis. In order to keep the pharmacy clean, dusting should be performed regularly. Below are the daily cleaning tasks that a pharmacy technician should perform:

- Washing off the counter and all surface areas
- Rinsing all tools from medication dispensing
- Washing off keyboards and all phone surfaces
- Taking out the trash from the pharmacy
- Cleaning the floor of the pharmacy using a broom or a vacuum
- Using a wet mop with disinfectant on the pharmacy floor
- Disinfecting the waiting area or lobby of the pharmacy

Sanitization Processes

Environmental surfaces should be cleaned daily and when visibly dirty. These surfaces generally need a low level of disinfectant similar to general housekeeping. The places requiring cleaning include tables, counter tops, floors, bathrooms, doorknobs, sinks, and waiting room chairs. Disinfectants used in daily cleaning are toxic and hazardous and, therefore, should be properly labeled, handled, and stored. The most common disinfectants include alcohols, 3% hydrogen peroxide-based products, phenolic compounds, and household bleach.

The type of disinfectants to be used for cleaning tools and equipment depends on the purpose and level of disinfection required. Here are some examples of routinely-used disinfectants in clinical practice:

- Low-level disinfectants:
    - Phenolic compounds
    - Quaternary ammonium compounds
    - 3% hydrogen peroxide
    - Hypochlorite household bleach
- Intermediate-level disinfectants:
    - Alcohols (70–90%)
    - Hypochlorite household bleach
    - Iodine and iodophor (e.g., povidone-iodine)
    - Boiling item for more than 20 minutes
    - Ortho-phthalaldehyde
    - Glutaraldehyde for 20 minutes
    - 6% hydrogen peroxide soak for 5 minutes
- High-level disinfectants:
    - Sterilization
    - Exposure to steam at a high temperature and pressure (autoclave)
    - Glutaraldehyde for 10 hours
    - Gas sterilization (ethylene oxide)

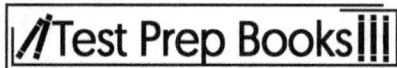

Medication Safety and Quality Assurance

o Dry heat sterilization

Low-level disinfectants are used for typical cleaning of keyboards, chairs, and other commonly touched areas. Intermediate-level disinfectants are used for a mix of critical and noncritical items, such as scrubs or operation tables that had the potential to come into contact with bacteria, infectious material, or bloodborne pathogens. High-level disinfectants are reserved for areas that would come in contact with mucous membranes or nonintact skin, with a high risk of bacteria, infectious material, or bloodborne pathogen contamination. Pharmacy technicians mostly use low-level and intermediate-level disinfectants, but it is good to know the differences and when to use which disinfectant. The goal of infection control is the prevention of healthcare-associated infections. These types of infections may be acquired in hospitals, outpatient clinics, rehabilitation facilities, nursing homes, or other clinical settings. The infections may spread from medical staff to patients, from patients to medical staff, from patient-to-patient, or among medical staff.

Quality Assurance Checks of Floor Stock

Best Practices for Quality Assurance during Entire Filling Process

While filling medications or stocking the shelves, continually checking that products are not expired and that medication and/or packaging is not damaged or tampered with is important for quality assurance. Unsecured medication, medication that is not behind the counter or locked, is especially important to check. Additionally, alerting the pharmacist/purchaser if a medication is running low ensures that the floor stock is still safe and that the counts are accurate compared to the inventory count. Floor stock includes unsecured medications, emergency medications, and all over-the-counter items.

Continuous Quality Improvement

Even though a complete inventory of the pharmacy is only done biennially, ensuring that the inventory is always correct is important. If a medication is prescribed and promised to be filled by a certain time because the inventory says it is in stock, but it actually is not in stock, then the prescription will not be filled by the promised time for the patient. Some ways to prevent inaccurate inventories are to check for expired medications on a regular basis, letting the pharmacist/inventory technician know that more of a medication is needed soon if it is running low, and ensuring that the pharmacy is organized with an easy-to-read organizational system. In addition, checking medications for damage, especially ones that are on the floor stock and open to the public, helps ensure that each drug will be ready to be dispensed or sold when it is requested.

Practice Quiz

1. What is the safe maximum daily dose for acetaminophen without decreased liver function?
   a. 1,000 mg
   b. 2,000 mg
   c. 3,000 mg
   d. 4,000 mg

2. What would be considered a normal daily dose of mirtazapine?
   a. 5 mg
   b. 15 mg
   c. 50 mg
   d. 100 mg

3. Why would a medication warrant a black box warning?
   a. A medication is found to cause stroke in 0.1 percent of patients.
   b. A medication is found to cause headaches in 25 percent of patients.
   c. A medication now has a new adverse reaction: itching.
   d. A medication is approved for a new indication: treatment of severe hypotension.

4. To which system would a patient report an adverse reaction to a vaccine?
   a. VAERS
   b. MedWatch
   c. REMS
   d. InfantRisk

5. As a patient is picking up the antidepressants that they have been on for years, they state that they recently became pregnant. What should be the technician's next step?
   a. Tell the patient congratulations and give them their medication.
   b. Alert the pharmacist so that they can check for any interactions in their medications with pregnancy.
   c. Stop and call the prescriber to make sure the medication is still okay now that the patient is pregnant.
   d. Look up the medication themself and let the patient know what they have found.

See answers on the next page.

Answer Explanations

1. D: Choice *D* is the correct answer; the maximum daily dose of acetaminophen is 4 grams, or 4,000 mg. With decreased liver function, the maximum daily dose would be 2 grams, or 2,000 mg.

2. B: Choice *B* is the correct answer; a normal daily dose of mirtazapine is between 15 mg to 45 mg.

3. A: Choice *A* is the correct answer. A black box warning is issued by the FDA if the medication can cause a serious, but usually rare, adverse reaction. Choices *B* and *C* would not be considered severe adverse reactions, and Choice *D* is adding a new indication for the use of the medication and not discussing an adverse drug reaction.

4. A: Choice *A* is the correct answer; VAERS stands for Vaccine Adverse Event Reporting System and is open to the general public to report any adverse reactions that could have been a result of a vaccination. MedWatch is for all medications and medical devices, REMS is for specific high-risk drugs, and InfantRisk is a resource for pregnant and breastfeeding women and medication.

5. B: Choice *B* is correct; medications that a person has taken prior to being pregnant could now be harmful to the fetus or the mom. It is best practice to bring this up to a pharmacist so they can counsel the patient on medications now that they are pregnant.

ExCPT Practice Test #1

1. Why are drug utilization reviews an integral part of the pharmacy process?
    a. They help alert the pharmacist when the prescriber has an inactive license.
    b. They are used by the financial office to see which drugs are utilized the most.
    c. They help prevent medication errors.
    d. They can only prevent drug allergy and drug-drug interactions.

2. Which of the following pieces of information is NOT included in the inscription?
    a. Medication name and strength
    b. Instructions for the pharmacist
    c. Quantity to dispense
    d. Dosage form

3. Which of the following is true regarding dietary supplements?
    a. The Dietary Supplement Health and Education Act of 1994 states dietary supplements must be labeled as such.
    b. Dietary supplements undergo the same rigorous FDA evaluation processes as legend drugs.
    c. Dietary supplements are deemed safe and effective by the FDA.
    d. Any product claims for a dietary supplement made by its manufacturer must be substantiated.

4. What is the primary reason for selecting the appropriate needle gauge and type?
    a. To prevent contamination
    b. To ensure accuracy of dosage
    c. To reduce pain during administration
    d. To save time and resources

5. What is an example of an administration error?
    a. A provider writing a prescription for amoxicillin but meaning to prescribe amlodipine
    b. A pharmacy technician dispensing hydroxyzine instead of hydralazine
    c. A patient using an estrogen product as a topical cream when it is an intravaginal cream
    d. A delivery service delivering a prescription to the wrong address

6. Which of the following statements is correct regarding ASAP and STAT prescription medication orders?
    a. ASAP orders, but not STAT orders, are only encountered in a hospital.
    b. ASAP orders need to be filled within 15 minutes of receiving them, whereas there is more leniency with STAT orders.
    c. STAT orders need to be filled within 15 minutes of receiving them, whereas there is more leniency with ASAP orders.
    d. STAT orders, but not ASAP orders, are only encountered in a hospital.

7. Which of the following is NOT considered Protected Health Information?
    a. Date of Death
    b. Vehicle ID Number (VIN)
    c. Email Address
    d. Employee Records

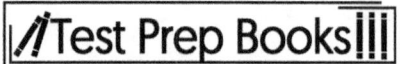

8. Which class of medications is NOT allowed to have refills?
    a. Non-controlled
    b. CIII
    c. CV
    d. CII

9. Which of the following is LEAST LIKELY to be a transmission method that could contribute to infection spread in a compounding pharmacy?
    a. Droplet transmission
    b. Contact transmission
    c. Airborne transmission
    d. Waterborne transmission

10. Which drug class is used to treat acute and chronic pain without loss of consciousness?
    a. Anesthetic
    b. Analgesic
    c. Anticonvulsants
    d. Antiarrhythmics

11. A common abbreviation used by pharmacies is the letter q, which stands for the Latin word *quaque*. What does this abbreviation mean?
    a. Every
    b. Quickly
    c. As needed
    d. Before

12. Which of the following statements is more appropriate for an OTC label than an Rx label?
    a. A barrier method should be used in addition to this product.
    b. This medication's mechanism of action works by blocking histamine receptors.
    c. This concurs with the findings of Elisset et al, indicating a nearly fourfold increase in hemoglobin over the course of treatment.
    d. This drug is contraindicated in patients with underlying chronic kidney disease.

13. What is NOT typically included in a REMS program?
    a. A list of goals to prevent the abuse/misuse of a drug and severe ADRs
    b. Specific drugs that are included
    c. An update history on the drug/program
    d. A comprehensive adverse drug reaction list for each medication

14. Which of the following is NOT a demographic piece of information essential for the patient's profile?
    a. Date of birth
    b. Drug allergy
    c. Address
    d. Phone number

15. What class of medication is used for the treatment of seizures?
    a. Antipsychotics
    b. SSRIs
    c. NSAIDs
    d. Anticonvulsants

16. A patient needs 20 units of insulin glargine in the morning and at bedtime, and 10 units of insulin aspart at each meal. What would her prescription say, and what would be the total monthly dose?
    a. 20 units insulin glargine, 30 units insulin aspart daily; 600 units insulin glargine, 900 units insulin aspart monthly
    b. 20 units insulin glargine, 10 units insulin aspart daily; 600 units insulin glargine, 300 units insulin aspart monthly
    c. 40 units insulin glargine, 10 units insulin aspart daily; 1200 units insulin glargine, 300 units insulin aspart monthly
    d. 40 units insulin glargine, 30 units insulin aspart daily; 1200 units insulin glargine, 900 units insulin aspart monthly

17. A patient returns a partially full bottle of their medication to a pharmacy technician. What should the pharmacy technician do?
    a. Refuse to accept the medication.
    b. Accept the medication and return it directly to the manufacturer.
    c. Accept the medication and put it back into the pharmacy's inventory.
    d. Accept the medication and place it in a secure location so it may be disposed of later.

18. Which of the following statements is correct regarding the difference between creams and ointments?
    a. Ointments are preferred for dry skin, whereas creams are preferred for wet skin.
    b. Ointments are preferred because they have a spreadable consistency, whereas creams   are greasy.
    c. Ointments contain more oil, whereas creams contain more water.
    d. Ointments cannot be used for rectal use, whereas creams can.

19. Which of the following is a sign that a prescription might be forged?
    a. The number of refills appears to have been altered
    b. The patient is a first-time customer of the pharmacy
    c. No refills are given for a Schedule II medication
    d. The prescription is phoned in by the physician

20. RM is a thirty-four-year-old female who has come to the pharmacy to pick up her new medication after leaving the local urgent care. She presented to the clinic seizing, was diagnosed with hyperglycemia, and was given a prescription for an injectable. She knows it is an insulin that is taken only once a day because she routinely has long shifts at work and cannot take multiple doses, but she's not sure whether it will need to be stored in the refrigerator or not. Her prescription may be which of the following injectables?
    a. Levemir
    b. Lovenox
    c. Humalog
    d. Trulicity

21. "Ibuprofen may cause constipation." What level of risk is this warning considered to be?
    a. Black box warning
    b. Warning statement
    c. Adverse drug reaction
    d. Side effect

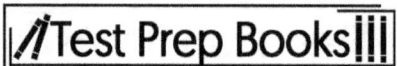

22. Which inventory control system ensures that a consistent supply of a medication is always available?
    a. PAR
    b. Rotating inventory
    c. Just-in-time ordering
    d. Online ordering

23. Which of the following is true regarding lot numbers?
    a. They have the same digits as the expiration date.
    b. They have a distinct number for each drug manufactured and supplied by the manufacturer.
    c. They contain only numbers and no letters.
    d. They can be used interchangeably among different drugs from the same manufacturer.

24. Which of the following people or organizations may never have access to information on a specific patient's prescriptions?
    a. Pharmacist
    b. A legal guardian or parent of a minor patient
    c. Law enforcement
    d. Pharmaceutical manufacturer

25. Which of the following numbers is used to identify the employer on an insurance card?
    a. BIN
    b. PCN
    c. Group number
    d. Person code

26. Which act protects health data integrity, confidentiality, and availability?
    a. Kefauver-Harris Amendment
    b. Durham-Humphrey Amendment
    c. Health Insurance Portability and Accountability Act
    d. Medicare Modernization Act

27. Why is documentation for sterile and nonsterile compounding important?
    a. To ensure accurate billing and payment for services rendered
    b. To comply with regulatory agency requirements
    c. To provide information on drug interactions
    d. To track inventory levels of compounded products

28. What does the term reverse distributor refer to?
    a. A company who collects and appropriately disposes of hazardous waste.
    b. A pharmacy or pharmacist that sells unused drugs to the manufacturer.
    c. A private firm that dispenses unexpired medications from a pharmacy at a discount.
    d. A third party that facilitates the granting of credits for controlled substances.

29. Which of the following medications is NOT used to treat hyperlipidemia?
    a. Zocor
    b. Norvasc
    c. Vytorin
    d. Simvastatin

ExCPT Practice Test #1

30. What is the purpose of an SDS in the pharmaceutical industry?
    a. To provide comprehensive information on a controlled product
    b. To provide the accurate price of a medication
    c. To secure a controlled product safely
    d. To enable proper medication labeling

31. Which of the following medications would be most appropriate to dispense in the manufacturer's original packaging?
    a. NitroStat
    b. Lidoderm
    c. Coumadin
    d. Dilantin solution

32. What is the purpose of a beyond-use date (BUD) for compounded or repackaged products?
    a. To indicate the date the product should be discarded after opening
    b. To provide information about the product's expiration date
    c. To establish a period during which the product is expected to maintain its stability and potency
    d. To indicate the date on which the product was packaged

33. What is needed to order Schedule II narcotics from a wholesale warehouse?
    a. Approval from the FDA
    b. A prescription from a physician
    c. Form 222 must be filled out on paper or electronically.
    d. The perpetual inventory must show that the Schedule II narcotics are fully stocked.

34. The prescription reads "Ibuprofen 200 mg; Daily Dose: 1.8 g; Take 3 pills at 0800, at 1400, and at 2000," and the patient asks you to explain what these weird numbers on the instructions are, what would you tell them?
    a. "Take 3 pills at 8 AM, 3 pills at 2 PM, and 3 pills at 8 PM."
    b. "Take 3 pills at 8 AM, 3 pills at 4 PM, and 3 pills at 10 PM."
    c. "Take 1 pill at 8 AM, 1 pill at 2 PM, and 1 pill at 10 PM."
    d. "Take 3 pills 3 times a day whenever you want to."

35. Which of the following was NOT considered a major shortcoming of the Food and Drug Act in 1906?
    a. It did not require the label to list ingredients or directions for use.
    b. It did not include cosmetic products.
    c. It did not require warnings to be stated on the products.
    d. It did not prohibit misbranded food.

36. A pharmacy technician notices that a patient's list of medications contains two prescriptions for the same medication from separate prescribers. What should they do?
    a. Remove the duplication.
    b. Contact the prescribing physicians.
    c. Alert the pharmacist.
    d. Leave it; it must be there for a specific reason.

37. Which body system is affected in Crohn's disease?
    a. Digestive
    b. Respiratory
    c. Lymphatic
    d. Skeletal

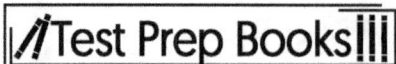

38. A physician called the pharmacy to give a verbal order of ZyPREXA® 10 (olanzapine 10 mg). However, the order was misinterpreted, and the prescription was filled for ZyrTEC® 10 (cetirizine 10 mg). Which of the following strategies would NOT help to prevent such dispensing errors associated with LASA medications?
    a. The pharmacist reading back the prescription, including spelling the medication name
    b. The physician's office calling the patient and informing him/her that a prescription order has been placed at the pharmacy
    c. Counseling the patient about the medication, including the purpose of the treatment
    d. Storing ZyPREXA and ZyrTEC on separate shelves

39. A patient in the ICU needs a 4.5 g bolus dose of Zosyn, then 4.5 g in 500 mL D5W over 4 hours every 8 hours. What is the patient's total daily dose (not including the bolus dose), and what is the infusion rate?
    a. 13.5 g daily; 100 mL/hr
    b. 4.5 g daily; 125 mL/hr
    c. 4.5 g daily; 100 mL/hr
    d. 13.5 g daily; 125 mL/hr

40. What action should you prioritize upon discovering the theft of a controlled substance from the pharmacy?
    a. Alert local law enforcement authorities to the theft.
    b. Engage the pharmacy's lawyers to communicate with the DEA.
    c. File a Form 222 electronically or in hard copy within one day.
    d. Notify the local DEA Diversion Field Office immediately by phone.

41. What is the correct interpretation of the following prescription directions: "1 capsule po QID"?
    a. Take one capsule by mouth every other day
    b. Take one capsule by mouth at night
    c. Take one capsule by mouth four times a day
    d. Take one capsule by mouth three times a day

42. What was one result of the Hatch-Waxman Act?
    a. It allowed the FDA to approve generic medications after completing efficacy and safety studies.
    b. It established the abbreviated new drug application (ANDA).
    c. It removed the need to demonstrate bioequivalence.
    d. It required that brand name manufacturers have a shorter patent.

43. A patient is just starting her insulin regimen for type 1 diabetes. If she weighs 100 kg, what is her daily insulin dosage?
    a. 30 units/day
    b. 45 units/day
    c. 50 units/day
    d. 100 units/day

44. Which of the following is NOT a controlled-released dosage form?
    a. Buccal tablets
    b. Enteric-coated tablets
    c. Vaginal tablets
    d. Sublingual tablets

45. Which of the following are NOT packaged in blister packs?
    a. Pills
    b. Topicals
    c. Encapsulated liquid pills
    d. Solid dosages

46. Which of the following is TRUE regarding the Omnibus Budget Reconciliation Act of 1990 (OBRA '90)?
    a. The federal government regulates pharmacist practice.
    b. It requires pharmacists to counsel patients with Medicaid in order to receive funding.
    c. Prescribers must counsel every time a prescription is written for a Medicaid patient.
    d. It allows prescribers to authorize off-label use for a medication if deemed necessary.

47. What system encompasses a centralized system in using barcode technology with conveyors capable of choosing drugs from a patient's file as well as putting the medication in the right drawer for the patient?
    a. Automated pump system
    b. Automated dispensing systems
    c. Robotic dispensing
    d. Automated tracking

48. Identify the situation that would prevent you from refilling a prescription.
    a. A refill on a medication that a practitioner changed the dosage for
    b. A refill on a prescription that is greater than one month old
    c. A refill on a Schedule II substance for the second time in two months
    d. A refill on a Schedule IV substance for the fifth time in six months

49. A medicine is dosed by 0.25 mg/kg, taken once daily. The patient weighs 138 lb; how many mg will the patient need daily of this medication (rounded to the nearest whole number)? If the pills only came in increments of 5 mg, how many pills would this patient need daily?
    a. 16 mg, 3 pills
    b. 20 mg, 4 pills
    c. 13 mg, 3 pills
    d. 16 mg, 2 pills

50. Which of the following personnel is permitted to select and dispense an over-the-counter medication for a patient?
    a. Pharmacy technician and pharmacist
    b. Pharmacist and prescribing physician
    c. Pharmacy technician only
    d. Pharmacist only

51. Who is the last person of defense to prevent a medication error?
    a. Physician
    b. Pharmacist
    c. Nurse
    d. Patient

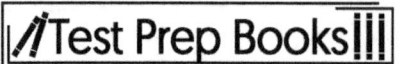

52. What is the correct temperature for a pharmacy drug storage refrigerator?
    a. 34–36° F
    b. 36–46° F
    c. 32° F only
    d. 42–45° F

53. JR is a seventy-five-year-old male who calls the pharmacy complaining of shortness of breath. He recently suffered a heart attack and was discharged from the hospital two days ago. His wife picked up a new list of medications on the same day for him. Although this does not seem like an emergency situation, he reports feeling weak and being unable to breathe as deeply as he would like since returning home and starting the new medications. He has not had any infection or other respiratory illnesses. Which of the following from his drug list is most likely to adversely affect his breathing?
    a. Proair Respiclick, every 8 hours as needed
    b. Duragesic 25 mcg/hour, applied once every 72 hours
    c. Tadalafil 10 mg, once every 12 hours as needed
    d. Mevacor® 40 mg, once daily

54. Which of the following does NOT contain information about the pharmacology of a medication?
    a. PPI
    b. Product monograph
    c. Prescription label
    d. Master formulation record

55. If a doctor writes a prescription for "XLV tablets fluoxetine," how many tablets is this?
    a. 65 tablets
    b. 45 tablets
    c. 35 tablets
    d. 10 tablets

56. What event occurred that led to the passing of the Food, Drug, and Cosmetic Act of 1938?
    a. A sulfa drug was combined with an untested solvent that caused the death of over one hundred individuals.
    b. A horse antitoxin was used to treat diphtheria patients, but the patients contracted tetanus, resulting in the death of thirteen children.
    c. Thalidomide, a commonly used sedative, was found to be teratogenic.
    d. Rare disease research was not being funded, so the act was passed to provide incentives for manufacturers to deliver medications for rare diseases or conditions.

57. Which act below designates five controlled drug classes (Schedules I-V) and specifies the type of medications that are controlled under each class?
    a. Prescription Drug Marketing Act
    b. Controlled Substances Act
    c. Federal Food, Drug, and Cosmetic Act
    d. Poison Prevention Packaging Act

58. When the laws differ between the state and federal level, which laws should be followed?
    a. The most lenient law should be followed
    b. Both sets of laws should be followed to the fullest extent possible
    c. Neither set of laws should be followed because they are different
    d. The strictest law should be followed

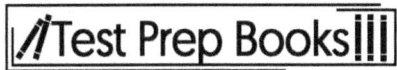

59. Which of the following is an example in which the prescriber does NOT have prescribing authority?
    a. A nurse practitioner prescribes antibiotics for a six-year-old.
    b. A veterinarian prescribes ibuprofen for their daughter.
    c. A dentist prescribes an antibiotic rinse for a fifty-year-old before a root canal.
    d. A Doctor of Medicine prescribes opioids to a cancer patient.

60. What is the highest level of warning for a medication?
    a. Black box warning
    b. White box warning
    c. Adverse drug reaction
    d. Warning statement

61. What can be done with expired medications in a pharmacy's inventory?
    a. They can be given to a reverse distributor.
    b. They should be sold immediately.
    c. They can be given directly back to the manufacturer.
    d. They can be given to the DEA.

62. Which of the following agencies oversees the National Medication Errors Reporting Program (MERP)?
    a. Drug Enforcement Administration (DEA)
    b. The Institute of Safe Medication Practices (ISMP)
    c. Occupational Safety and Health Administration (OSHA)
    d. The Joint Commission (TJC)

63. Which of the following is the target for non-opioid analgesics?
    a. Cyclooxygenase enzyme
    b. Nerve cells of the brain
    c. Stratum corneum
    d. Dopamine receptors

64. Which of the following pairs correctly associates the brand name to its generic counterpart?
    a. Zytrim® and allopurinol
    b. Zyprexa and olanzapine
    c. Zyban and tolterodine
    d. Zyrtec and loratadine

65. Which of the following drugs requires a lead-shielded pig in the shipping and handling process?
    a. Trastuzumab
    b. T99m lidofenin
    c. Uracil mustard
    d. Docetaxel

66. How long should dispensed prescriptions be kept on file and should Schedule II prescriptions be kept with other medications that have been dispensed?
    a. Forever; keep everything together
    b. 2 years; keep Schedule II prescriptions separate from other medications
    c. 5 years; keep Schedule II prescriptions separate from other medications
    d. Until the prescription is filled; keep everything together

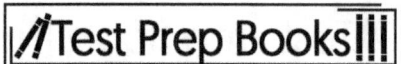

67. Which of the following is true regarding NPIs?
   a. They are a specific set of numbers that identify a healthcare professional and their prescribing authority.
   b. NPIs are recommended by the HIPAA administrative standard.
   c. NPIs are only for individual healthcare providers and not for organizational providers.
   d. NPIs are required to be documented on all insurance claims.

68. In which of the following cases is the corresponding auxiliary label most appropriate?
   a. A 35-year-old male receiving a three-day prescription of fluconazole: Do not take while pregnant.
   b. A 47-year-old female receiving a month prescription of phendimetrazine: May cause drowsiness.
   c. A 21-year-old female receiving a seven-day prescription of Augmentin solution: Refrigerate.
   d. A 73-year-old male receiving a ninety-day prescription of ezetimibe: Do not drive while under the effects of this medication.

69. What is the name of the nonprofit organization that focuses on the prevention of medication errors?
   a. Food and Drug Administration
   b. Drug Enforcement Agency
   c. Institute for Safe Medication Practices
   d. Centers for Disease Control

70. Which of the following is NOT a mechanism for disintegrating agents used for immediate-release products?
   a. Swelling
   b. Lyophilized
   c. Wicking
   d. Deformation

71. If a prescription says "3 drops of amoxicillin 2 times daily," what would the patient's prescription be in mL for the month?
   a. 7.5 mL
   b. 9 mL
   c. 12 mL
   d. 18 mL

72. Why do we focus on continuous quality improvement?
   a. To call people out for their past mistakes
   b. To recognize what mistakes have already been made so the same mistakes don't get made again
   c. To continue to note how we can improve as a team whether mistakes are made or not
   d. To fulfill the company's quality metrics

73. A pharmacy technician receives a counterfeit medication in an order. What should they do?
   a. Inform the local police.
   b. Notify the pharmacist so they can dispose of the counterfeit medication.
   c. Notify the pharmacist so they can contact the FDA, the manufacturer, and their distributor.
   d. Put the medication into stock and sell it.

74. There are three segments to the NDC number. Which segment identifies who manufactured a drug?
   a. Packaging code
   b. Product code
   c. Labeler code
   d. NDC

75. A woman brings a scribbled list of medications to the pharmacy counter, saying these are all the medications she could find in her mother's pill cabinet. Her mother has dementia, and she doesn't know which medications she should be taking anymore. The woman asks the pharmacist to tell her which ones are current. The pharmacist cannot find the patient's information in the software system, and the woman now recalls that her mother usually uses a different pharmacy in another state. However, even without her dispensing history, the pharmacist notices that several medications are duplicates, whereas others seem to interact and probably shouldn't be taken together. Which of the following pairs of medications should the woman follow up on with her doctor or pharmacy before taking them?
    a. Aricept and Imitrex
    b. Nystatin and Simvastatin
    c. Qbrelis and Zestoretic
    d. Glucophage and Invokana

76. What is the difference between a vertical flow hood and a compounding aseptic isolator?
    a. The type of airflow
    b. The size of the equipment
    c. Decontamination method
    d. The level of containment

77. What is the purpose of USP <797>?
    a. To provide guidelines for sterile compounding
    b. To provide guidelines for nonsterile compounding
    c. To provide guidelines for labeling
    d. To provide guidelines for equipment maintenance

78. Which of the following government organizations oversees the MedWatch program?
    a. Drug Enforcement Administration (DEA)
    b. Occupational Safety and Health Administration (OSHA)
    c. United States Food and Drug Administration (FDA)
    d. The Joint Commission (TJC)

79. Which information does NOT need to be collected to ensure safe medication dispensing for a pediatric patient?
    a. Age and allergies
    b. Body weight
    c. Indication for the prescription
    d. Height

80. The following is a DEA registration number: BJ6125341. What is the check digit and is the number valid?
    a. 1 and yes
    b. 4 and yes
    c. 1 and no
    d. 4 and no

81. What is the difference between a laminar flow hood and a compounding aseptic isolator (CAI)?
    a. Laminar flow hoods use HEPA filters, while CAIs do not.
    b. Laminar flow hoods are designed for sterile compounding, while CAIs are designed for nonsterile compounding.
    c. Laminar flow hoods provide horizontal airflow, while CAIs provide vertical airflow.
    d. CAIs provide a physical barrier between the compounding area and the operator, while laminar flow hoods do not.

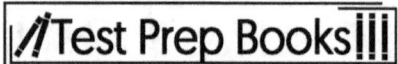

82. ES is a fifteen-year-old male who recently picked up an atomoxetine prescription from the outpatient pharmacy. His mother is calling and asking if her son could have an allergy to the medication. Which of these may indicate an allergy instead of a side effect or unrelated condition?
    a. Urticaria
    b. Tinnitus
    c. Borborygmi
    d. Bruxism

83. To prevent a mix-up between chlorpromazine and chlorpropamide, all EXCEPT which of the following strategies will be applicable?
    a. Tall man lettering
    b. A computer alert for LASA medications
    c. Bar-code scanning of bottles at the filling station
    d. Better lighting on the shelves

84. Which of the following methods of communication can NOT be used for controlled II medications?
    a. Fax
    b. Electronic
    c. Written
    d. Telephone

85. Which of the following statements best describes the purpose of REMS programs?
    a. To reduce the likelihood of unknown medication interactions
    b. To ensure the safety of workers against occupational hazards
    c. To mitigate drug-caused fetal malformations through structured therapy
    d. To avoid or prevent known dangers through proactive monitoring

86. Which is NOT an effective strategy for preventing errors when receiving a verbal prescription?
    a. Collecting the treatment indication
    b. Reading back the prescription
    c. Spelling the drug's name
    d. Using abbreviations

87. Which disease state is a genetic and environmental disease that causes insulin resistance?
    a. Type 1 diabetes
    b. Type 2 diabetes
    c. Hyperinsulinemia
    d. Chronic kidney disease

88. TJ drops off a prescription for a pair of hazardous drugs. One of the drugs is considered carcinogenic by NIOSH, but the other is not. Which of the following pairs could be on this prescription?
    a. Bleomycin and vinblastine
    b. Dutasteride and daunomycin
    c. Mitomycin and methotrexate
    d. Sirolimus and streptomycin

89. What level of disinfectant is usually used for scrubs for sterile compounding?
    a. Low-level disinfectant
    b. Intermediate-level disinfectant
    c. High-level disinfectant
    d. No disinfectant needed

90. Which of the following, upon inspection of a reconstituted or mixed medication, would warrant dispensation and administration to the patient?
    a. Augmentin solution using tap water with brown particulates
    b. First-Omeprazole with a cherry-red coloration
    c. Clindamycin paste with dry, gray cracking from oxidation
    d. Milky-white lipid-and-dextrose total parenteral nutrition (TPN) with noticeable clumping

91. What is the purpose of equipment maintenance in compounding?
    a. To ensure the equipment lasts longer
    b. To maintain quality and safety of compounded products
    c. To save money on repairs
    d. To comply with regulations

92. A pharmacy technician is helping an elderly patient who has had issues complying with their medication schedule. What should the pharmacy technician do?
    a. Personally administer the patient's medications.
    b. Suggest a compliance device.
    c. Write the patient a note to remind them.
    d. Inform the patient's family or caregivers that they must force the patient to take their medication.

93. Why is it important to collect the patient's medical history before filling a prescription?
    a. It is not usually important, unless the patient is elderly.
    b. It can provide an allergy history and prevent dangerous drug reactions.
    c. It can help the pharmacist predict the next medical condition.
    d. It can make it easier to provide refills.

94. Which of the following is NOT an organization that influences quality assurance (QA) in the pharmacy setting?
    a. United States Pharmacopeia (USP)
    b. Occupational Safety and Health Administration (OSHA)
    c. American Board of Internal Medicine (ABIM)
    d. American Pharmacy Association (APhA)

95. What is a medication error?
    a. An unwanted side effect associated with a drug
    b. An error in prescribing, dispensing, or administration
    c. A medication being recalled due to incorrect labeling
    d. Manufacturers producing the medication with the wrong ingredients

96. Which of the following medications should be stored in glass rather than plastic?
    a. Doxycycline
    b. Sublingual nitroglycerin
    c. Linezolid
    d. Acetazolamide

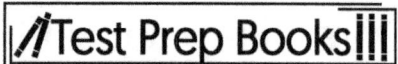

97. What is Trissel's *Handbook on Injectable Drugs* used for?
    a. To provide information on drug side effects
    b. To provide information on drug pricing
    c. To provide information on drug stability and compatibility
    d. To provide information on drug dosing

98. Which of the following numbers is used to identify insurance providers on an insurance card?
    a. BIN
    b. PCN
    c. Group number
    d. Person code

99. Which of the following is true regarding formularies?
    a. There are open and closed formularies, but open formularies are the most utilized.
    b. Open formularies will pay for all medications including those for cosmetic purposes.
    c. A patient/provider will not get reimbursed if they purchased a medication not in a closed formulary.
    d. Formularies are private information and cannot be accessed by the patients.

100. The strength of a medication in a prescription is written as 1%. The pharmacy technician feels that it might be too high of a dose and that it should probably be 0.1%. Which of the following would be an appropriate action for the technician to take?
    a. Ask the patient about the strength
    b. Fill the prescription as written
    c. Inform the pharmacist
    d. Call the physician's office to check the strength

Answer Explanations #1

1. C: Drug utilization review (DUR) is a verification step utilized by pharmacies, providers, and insurance companies to help prevent medication errors, therefore answer Choices A and B are incorrect. Choice D is incorrect because DURs can be utilized to catch a variety of errors including abuse, therapeutic duplication, drug allergies, and drug-drug interactions.

2. B: The inscription should include the name of the medication, the strength and dosage form, and the quantity to dispense. The instructions for the pharmacist are part of the subscription. Both the inscription and subscription should be part of the prescription, along with information such as the number of refills, the prescriber's information and signature, and patient information.

3. A: The FDA regulates dietary supplements under the Dietary Supplement Health and Education Act of 1994 guidelines, which means Choice A is correct because it states "Dietary Supplements" must be present on the product labeling. Manufacturers and distributers are required to verify that their products are safe and effective and that their products meet FDA and DSHEA regulations. The FDA does not require manufacturers of dietary supplements to adopt the same practices as drug manufacturers. In addition, manufacturers cannot make claims that dietary supplements can be used for the treatment or cure of a condition or ailment; therefore, Choices B, C, and D are incorrect.

4. B: Selecting the appropriate needle gauge and type is important to ensure the accuracy of dosage, Choice B. Choices A and C are incorrect. Even though preventing contamination and reducing pain during administration may also be important, the primary reason for selecting the appropriate needle gauge and type is to ensure the accuracy of the dosage. Choice D is incorrect because saving time does not correlate with why specific needles are chosen.

5. C: An administration error occurs after the prescription has been dispensed and it is now up to the patient to take the medication correctly. This example involved the wrong route of administration, a common source of confusion with estrogen creams. Choice A is a prescribing error, Choice B is a dispensing error, and Choice D does not technically fit in any of these categories, but it would fall under dispensing error if anything since the prescription has not yet reached the patient.

6. C: There are several types of prescription medication orders. Both STAT and ASAP are relatively urgent orders that are received in hospital settings. STAT refers to a medication order that should be filled within 15 minutes of its receipt. ASAP orders need to be processed as soon as possible, but they are of lower priority than STAT orders. In contrast, PRN and standing orders are of much lower priority.

7. D: Choice D is correct. Employee records do not qualify as Protected Health Information. Choices A, B, and C are all key identifiers defined by the U.S. Department of Health and Human Services.

8. D: Controlled II prescriptions are not allowed to have refills, and a new prescription must be written each time. However, the prescription can be written for either a thirty-day or ninety-day supply. Choice A is incorrect because non-controlled medications can technically have an unlimited number of refills; however, non-controlled medication orders are only valid for one year, therefore most 30-day prescription orders have twelve refills if intended to provide a one-year supply. Choices B and C are incorrect because CIII and CV medications can have a maximum of five refills and cannot be refilled more than six months after the date that the prescription was written. This means a 30-day tramadol prescription order can be filled six times in total or a 90-day order filled two times in total.

9. D: While it is possible to transmit diseases through contaminated water, this is unlikely to be an issue in a compounding pharmacy. All of the other choices are likely causes of transmission.

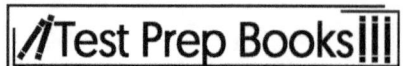

Answer Explanations #1

10. B: The correct answer is analgesics. Analgesics are medications used to treat acute and chronic pain. They provide pain relief and partial loss of physical sensation without loss of consciousness, whereas anesthetics provide pain relief through complete loss of physical sensation with or without consciousness. Therefore, Choice *A* is incorrect. Choice *C* is incorrect because anticonvulsants are used to treat seizure disorders. Choice *D* is incorrect because antiarrhythmics are used to treat disorders related to heart rhythm.

11. A: *Every* is the correct answer because the Latin word *quaque* means "every." The letter *q* is commonly used in pharmaceutical abbreviations to refer to the frequency with which a medication should be taken. Choice *B*, quickly, is incorrect because no abbreviation exists that tells a patient to take a medication quickly. *STAT* is used in medication situations to mean "immediately," but this would not be included in prescription information for a patient. Choice *C*, as needed, is incorrect because it is abbreviated by *PRN*, which stands for the Latin phrase "pro re nata." Choice *D*, before, is incorrect because it is abbreviated by the letter *a*, which stands for the Latin word "ante."

12. A: OTC nonoxynol spermicide products are mandated to recommend a closed barrier method such as a condom because, while the product is successful at preventing pregnancy, it does not protect against HIV and STIs. Choices *B* and *C* are incorrect because a drug's mechanism of action and related clinical studies are more appropriate for a prescription label or for a product insert. Choice *D* is incorrect because contraindications are included on both OTC and prescription labels.

13. D: A REMS program details only the most crucial information for a specific drug with a safety concern; it does not have programs to report all adverse drug reactions or medication errors. For example, clozapine is a REMS drug due to the chance of neutropenia. Clozapine can also cause high blood pressure, dizziness, nausea, and many other adverse drug reactions. Since these are not necessarily life-threatening, they are not included in the REMS patient monitoring program. The other three choices are included in the REMS for each drug listed.

14. B: Demographic information includes all non-clinical pieces of information, and drug allergy information is considered clinical data. Choices *A*, *C*, and *D* are incorrect because non-clinical information like the patient's full name, date of birth, updated address, contact information (phone number, email, fax number, etc.), age, biological sex, ethnicity, and insurance information are all important demographic information to include in a patient's profile. Broader information such as patient occupation, marital status, etc., may also be included.

15. D: Choice *D*, anticonvulsants, is the class of medication used to treat seizure disorders, such as epilepsy. Some examples of anticonvulsants include Dilantin and Phenobarbital. Antipsychotics, Choice *A*, are used to treat mental health disorders, such as schizophrenia or bipolar disorder. Choice *B* is incorrect because SSRIs are used to treat anxiety and depression. Non-steroidal anti-inflammatory drugs, or NSAIDs, are used to treat pain and inflammation; therefore, Choice *C* is also incorrect.

16. D: Choice *D* is correct. This patient is on a basal/bolus dose regimen, so they take insulin at set times and before or when they eat. The basal doses are at set times, and the bolus doses are for meals. The basal dose here must be taken twice a day, so:

$$20 \text{ units} \times 2 = x \text{ units insulin glargine}$$

$$20 \text{ units} \times 2 = 40 \text{ units insulin glargine}$$

Therefore, Choices *A* and *B* are not correct, because they only account for one of the doses, not both. Although it can be argued that this prescription was written to say 20 units insulin glargine BETWEEN two doses, morning and night, this question states that they need 20 units in the morning AND at bedtime. Prescriptions and orders may not

Answer Explanations #1

always have the clearest language, so if you are unsure in practice, be sure to check with a coworker, pharmacist, or even the prescriber who called it in to ensure the correct dosing—not just for insulin, but for any medication.

The bolus doses are for meals. Unless stated otherwise, every patient's insulin is divided into 3 assumed meals: breakfast, lunch, and dinner. Since this says they need 10 units at each meal:

$$10 \text{ units} \times 3 = x \text{ units insulin aspart}$$

$$10 \text{ units} \times 3 = 30 \text{ units insulin aspart}$$

30 units of insulin aspart should be taken daily if three meals are eaten. However, some patients may skip a dose or a meal or have "correctional dosing" where they have specific ratios. As a technician, this is not necessary to worry about; you just have to fill the amount that the prescription says because we want to ensure that the patient does not run out of insulin or medication. No new answer choices are eliminated with this answer.

Now that we have the daily dosages, we can calculate the amount of each type of insulin needed for a 30-day prescription:

$$\frac{40 \text{ units}}{1 \text{ day}} \times \frac{30 \text{ days}}{1 \text{ month}} = x \text{ units insulin glargine}$$

$$\frac{40 \text{ units}}{1 \text{ day}} \times \frac{30 \text{ days}}{1 \text{ month}} = 1200 \text{ units insulin glargine/month}$$

$$\frac{30 \text{ units}}{1 \text{ day}} \times \frac{30 \text{ days}}{1 \text{ month}} = x \text{ units insulin aspart}$$

$$\frac{30 \text{ units}}{1 \text{ day}} \times \frac{30 \text{ days}}{1 \text{ month}} = 900 \text{ units insulin aspart/month}$$

The patient needs 1200 units insulin glargine and 900 units insulin aspart each month, which eliminates Choice C. Therefore, Choice D is correct.

17. D: Choice D is the correct answer. All unused medications must be disposed of in a manner compliant with DEA regulations. The medication must be removed from its container and isolated so it will not be put into inventory accidentally. The medication may then be collected by a reverse distributor to be disposed of properly. Choice A, refuse to accept the medication, is incorrect because unused medications should be returned to pharmacies. Pharmacies in many states have drop boxes that securely accept any unused medication so they can be disposed of safely. Choice B, accept the medication and return it directly to the manufacturer, is incorrect because dispensed medications that have been returned to a pharmacy are given to a reverse distributor who then corresponds with the manufacturer. The pharmacy will not return medications directly to the manufacturer. Choice C, accept the medication and put it back into the pharmacy's inventory, is incorrect because the FDA prohibits returning drugs to stock after they have left a pharmacist's possession.

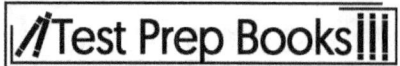

Answer Explanations #1

18. C: Choice C is correct because the biggest difference between creams and ointments is the amount of oil and water they contain. Creams contain more water, which makes for a smoother application, whereas ointments contain more oil and can feel greasy after application. Choice A is incorrect because creams are best used on dry skin or wet, weeping lesions, whereas ointments are preferred on normal to oily skin types and dry, thick lesions. Choice B is incorrect because creams are described as spreadable, and Choice D is incorrect because both dosage forms can be used rectally.

19. A: It's possible that the doctor made a mistake or changed their mind when writing the number of refills; however, it's still suspicious if the number of refills has been altered. You should contact the physician by looking up the number to their office (rather than using the number on the prescription pad), and ask them to confirm the number of refills they are prescribing. People must be a first-time customer of a pharmacy at some point, and people often relocate, so it's not necessarily suspicious. Schedule II medications typically do not have refills associated with the prescription. In emergency situations, a physician can call in a prescription as a verbal order, which must then be followed up with a paper version within seven days.

20. A: Levemir (insulin detemir) is the only basal or long-acting insulin presented as a potential answer. Humalog (insulin lispro) is an insulin, but it is a bolus or short-acting insulin and would likely be dosed multiple times per day. Lovenox (enoxaparin) is okay to be stored at room temperature and is dosed once per day, but it is an anticoagulant that can affect blood sugar. Once insulins are dispensed to the patient and their seal is broken, they are okay to keep at room temperature for twenty-eight days. Trulicity (dulaglutide) is an antidiabetic drug, but it is not an insulin and is dosed once per week.

21. C: An adverse drug reaction (ADR) is any unintended effect of a medication. Constipation is one such effect worth noting, especially for patients who already have a GI dysfunction, so it is listed as an adverse drug reaction. However, it is not life-threatening enough to be listed as a black box warning, so Choice A is incorrect. Choices B and D are not used as official terms to describe any adverse drug reactions. *Side effect* is the general, layman's term for adverse drug reactions, and ADR covers side effects, along with patient error while taking the medication. If presented with this question, ADR will be the correct answer.

22. A: *PAR*, which stands for Periodic Automatic Replenishment, is the correct answer. It is an inventory management and ordering system that establishes a minimum and maximum level of an item in inventory. If the item's stock gets near the minimum level, more must be ordered. Choice B, rotating inventory, is incorrect because it is an inventory management technique that ensures that older items are sold before newer items. Choice C, just-in-time ordering, is incorrect because it is an ordering technique in which items that are not in constant demand are only ordered when needed. Choice D, online ordering, is incorrect because it is not an inventory management technique.

23. B: A lot number has a distinct number for each drug manufactured that is supplied by the manufacturer. It is important to note that drug manufacturers have their own system for numbering. A Lot number could, for example, be expressed as B11907. The B represents the initial of the company's name followed by in-house numbering. Unlike an expiration date, it typically has the month and year expressed, for example as 06/2016, 06/16, or June 2016.

24. D: Choice D is the correct answer because, under HIPAA, pharmaceutical manufacturers are not permitted to view any patient's medical information without the patient's consent. Choice A, pharmacist, is incorrect because a patient's pharmacist must be permitted to view their prescriptions to do their job properly. Choice B, a legal guardian or parent of a minor patient, is incorrect because parents of minors and legal caregivers are permitted to view medical history of their children or the people for whom they are responsible. Choice C, law enforcement, is incorrect because, although law enforcement may not normally see a person's medical history, they may access it with a proper warrant.

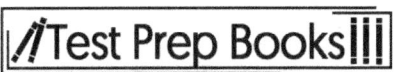

25. C: Most patients have insurance coverage through an employer, and the group number is specific to that employer. The employers are also capable of picking specific plans, coverages, and prices for the employee's insurance. Choices *A*, *B*, and *D* are incorrect.

26. C: Choice *C* is correct. The Health Insurance Portability and Accountability Act of 1996, also known as HIPAA, was passed to protect an individual's health information and to make health insurance coverage portable for workers who changed or lost jobs. Choice *A* is incorrect because this amendment required the establishment of drug efficacy. Choice *B* is incorrect because this amendment led to the differentiation between prescription and non-prescription medications. Choice *D* is incorrect because this act established prescription coverage within the Medicare program.

27. B: Documentation requirements are established by regulatory agencies (such as the FDA) and are intended to ensure the safety, efficacy, and quality of compounded products. Choice *A* is incorrect because billing and payment are not directly related to the documentation of compounding. Choice *C* is incorrect because drug interactions are typically documented in patient medical records, not in compounding documentation. Choice *D* is incorrect because tracking inventory levels of compounded products is important, but it is not the primary purpose of documentation for sterile and nonsterile compounding.

28. D: A reverse distributor registered with the DEA evaluates unused or expired controlled substances transferred from a pharmacy to determine if credit may be granted. Choice *A* is incorrect because reverse distributors may dispose of controlled substances if necessary but not other forms of hazardous wastes. Choice *B* is incorrect because reverse distributors act as a go-between between pharmacies and manufacturers. Choice *C* is incorrect because reverse distributors do not dispense medications.

29. B: Choice *B* is correct because Norvasc, a calcium channel blocker, is used to control hypertension. Choices *A* and *D* are incorrect because not only are they both statins, but they are the same medication. Simvastatin is the generic equivalent to the brand medication Zocor; both are used to treat hyperlipidemia. Choice *C*, Vytorin, is a combination medication used to treat hyperlipidemia that includes the absorption inhibitor Ezetimibe and the statin Simvastatin.

30. A: Choice *A* is the correct answer because an SDS (safety data sheet) exists to provide technical information on a controlled product so that it may be safely handled. Choice *B*, to provide the accurate price of a medication, is incorrect because an SDS provides safety information, whereas the Red Book lists medication prices. Choice *C*, to secure a controlled product safely, is incorrect because controlled substance security is done by tracking all controlled substances, physically securing a pharmacy, and other techniques. Choice *D*, to enable proper medication labeling, is incorrect because an SDS is not used to label medications because they should already be properly labeled before the pharmacy receives them.

31. A: NitroStat (sublingual nitroglycerin) is shipped in a photoprotective, amber-colored glass vial that prevents ambient humidity from degrading the medication. Nitroglycerin should always be dispensed in such a vial, and few pharmacies keep a steady supply of them for repackaging. Each Lidoderm patch (transdermal lidocaine) should remain in the individual sleeve in which it is received, but the thirty-count box is not necessary for dispensation; therefore, Choice *B* is incorrect. While both Coumadin (warfarin) and Dilantin (phenytoin) are hazardous drugs that should be handled and disposed of with respect to USP <800>, neither necessitates use of the original packaging. Therefore, Choices *C* and *D* are incorrect.

32. C: The beyond-use date is a critical element in ensuring the safety and efficacy of compounded or repackaged products. It is based on the stability and potency of the product and considers factors such as the ingredients used, the storage conditions, and the intended use of the product. Choice *A* is incorrect because it refers to the expiration date after opening, which is not the same as the beyond-use date. Choice *B* is incorrect because the beyond-use

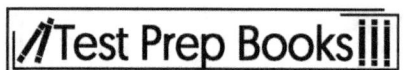

date and the expiration date are not the same. The expiration date is provided by the manufacturer and is based on stability and potency. Choice D is incorrect because the date on which the product was packaged is not the same as the beyond-use date, which is based on the product's stability and potency and is specific to the product and the conditions under which it was prepared.

33. C: Form 222 from the DEA must be filled out on paper or electronically to order Schedule II medications from a wholesale warehouse, to transfer Schedule II medications between locations, or to return Schedule II medications to the wholesaler. Approval from the FDA is required for a medication to be marketed. A prescription from the physician is required for the patient to obtain the medication. The perpetual inventory needs to be maintained at all times. However, if all of the Schedule II medications are fully stocked, it is unlikely that the pharmacy will need to order more.

34. A: Choice A is correct. The tablet that was prescribed is a 200 mg tablet, and the daily dose is 1.8 g. To find the total number of pills needed daily:

$$\frac{1.8 \; g}{1} \times \frac{1000 \; mg}{1 \; g} \times \frac{1 \; pill}{200 \; mg} = x \; pills$$

$$\frac{1.8 \; g}{1} \times \frac{1000 \; mg}{1 \; g} \times \frac{1 \; pill}{200 \; mg} = 9 \; pills$$

With all the units canceled out after conversion from g to mg (what the tablet is measured in), that leaves you with the unit "pills," which means 9 pills are needed daily. The instructions for administration are to "take 3 pills at 0800, at 1400, and at 2000," and now that we know the patient takes 9 pills daily, we know that the patient has to take 3 pills at each dose to split it up evenly. (Prescriptions will not always be split evenly; they may say "take two in the morning and one at night" or something along those lines, but if it is not spelled out, assume the dose should be split evenly between each time it is taken.) This rules out Choice C because the total number of pills daily in this option is 3 pills, not 9 pills. Choice D should be ruled out because there are exact times given for administration of the drug, so it would not be whenever the patient felt like it. This leaves Choice A and Choice B, which only differ by how military time is measured. 0000 is midnight, 0100 to 1259 is 1:00 AM to 12:59 PM, and 1300 to 2359 is 1:00 PM to 11:59 PM. Therefore: 0800 is 8:00 AM, and the other two times:

$$1400 - 1200 = x$$

$$2000 - 1200 = x$$

$$1400 - 1200 = 200$$

$$2000 - 1200 = 800$$

Put a colon after the first number, meaning 2:00 PM and 8:00 PM. You only have to subtract 12 for the numbers above 1259, or add 12 starting at 1:00 PM. Therefore, with the times 8:00 AM, 2:00 PM, and 8:00 PM, Choice A is correct.

35. D: The Food and Drug Act of 1906, previously known as the Pure Food and Drug Act, was passed due to poor regulations within the food and drug industries. Prior to the act, there were no laws requiring the inspection of meat products or drugs before they reached the consumer. The act only prohibited the misbranding of food or drugs, but it did not include cosmetic products. The act also neglected to require companies to state ingredients, directions of use, or any known warnings on the product. Therefore, Choices A, B, and C are incorrect because these were major shortcomings of the Food and Drug Act. Therefore, Choice D is the correct answer.

Answer Explanations #1

36. C: Choice C is the correct answer because a pharmacist must be notified of any errors, such as a duplication. Choice A, remove the duplication, is incorrect because a pharmacy technician is not permitted to alter prescriptions. Choice B, contact the prescribing physicians, is incorrect because a pharmacist should handle an issue like this. Choice D, leave it, is incorrect because any possible errors in a patient's medications must be reported in case there is an actual issue.

37. A: Choice A is correct because Crohn's is an inflammatory bowel disease that causes swelling in the intestinal area. Therefore, Choices B, C, and D are incorrect.

38. B: Choice B is correct because the physician's office did not inform the patient about the name of the medication and, thus, the patient cannot help prevent a medication error. Choices A, C, and D are all strategies that would help prevent LASA medication dispensing errors.

39. D: Choice D is correct. The bolus dose would not be included in the total daily dose, as it only occurred once at the beginning of treatment. The prescription calls for 4.5 g in 500 mL D5W over 4 hours every 8 hours, and you can ignore the 500 mL and over 4 hours for now—these will be used to calculate the IV flow rate but not the TDD, as that is in grams/day:

$$4.5\ g \times \left(\frac{24\ hours}{8\ hours}\right) = TDD\ \left(\frac{g}{day}\right)$$

$$4.5\ g \times \left(\frac{24\ hours}{8\ hours}\right) = 13.5\ g/day$$

24 is divided by 8 to get the number of doses, 3, given in a 1-day period. Therefore, Choices B and C can be eliminated, because they just represent the amount in each dose, not for the entire 24-hour period.

The bolus dose would not be factored into the flow rate equation here, so the prescription calls for 4.5 g in 500 mL D5W over 4 hours every 8 hours. For calculating this flow rate, you can ignore the 4.5 g and every 8 hours, we only need the amount of liquid going into the person and the time it should take to administer, which is the 500 mL and over 4 hours:

$$\frac{500\ mL}{4\ hours} = x\ mL/hr$$

$$\frac{500\ mL}{4\ hours} = 125\ mL/hr$$

The flow rate is 125 mL/hr of the Zosyn D5W solution. Therefore, Choice D is correct.

40. A: Though not required by federal law or policies, it is important to notify local law enforcement and state regulatory agencies of the theft because it is a crime. Choice B is incorrect because the notice to the DEA should come directly from the registrant or authorized individual of the registrant; intermediaries should not be engaged. Choice C is incorrect because the correct form in this instance is a DEA Form 106 (Report of Theft or Loss of Controlled Substances); Form 222 documents the transfer, order, or return of Schedule II substances. Choice D is incorrect because the DEA Diversion Field Office must be notified in writing.

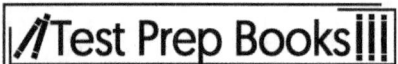

41. C: The abbreviation "po" indicates a prescription should be taken orally. The abbreviation "QID" means four times a day. The other answer choices incorrectly direct how often to take the capsule.

42. B: Choice *B* is the correct answer. The FDA allowed generic applications without repeating safety or efficacy studies and created a new form specifically for generics called the abbreviated new drug application. The manufacturers of generic medications were still required to demonstrate bioequivalence. Thus, Choices *A* and *C* are incorrect. Choice *D* is incorrect because brand name medication manufacturers apply for a specific length of patent of their choosing, which is typically the maximum of twenty years.

43. C: Choice *C* is correct. The formula for type 1 diabetics when first starting insulin treatment is 0.5 units/kg/day:

$$\frac{100 \text{ kg}}{1} \times \frac{0.5 \text{ units}}{1 \text{ kg}} = x \text{ units daily}$$

$$\frac{100 \text{ kg}}{1} \times \frac{0.5 \text{ units}}{1 \text{ kg}} = 50 \text{ units daily}$$

This patient would need 50 units of insulin for her total daily dose (TDD). A faster way to do this is to just divide the patient's weight in kg in half, since 0.5 equals ½:

$$\frac{100 \text{ kg}}{2} = x \text{ units daily}$$

$$\frac{100 \text{ kg}}{2} = 50 \text{ units daily}$$

This way will not work for basal doses (0.1 to 0.2 u/kg/day), but it works for 0.5 u/kg/day.

44. D: Sublingual tablets, Choice *D*, are an immediate-release dosage form meant to be placed under the tongue for rapid absorption. Choice *A* is incorrect because buccal tablets are designed to be placed between the cheek and gingiva and dissolve slowly so that the drug can be gradually absorbed through the oral mucosa and into the blood. Choice *B* is incorrect because enteric-coated tablets are compressed with a polymer that prevents them from dissolving in acidic conditions, like in the stomach, instead disintegrating in a more basic pH, like the small intestine. Choice *C* is incorrect because vaginal tablets are meant to dissolve slowly in that area.

45. B: There are various drugs packaged in blister packs from pills to encapsulated liquid pills (e.g., liquid Nyquil capsules), but topical ointments or medications do not come in blister packs. Only pills or solid dosages.

46. B: Choice *B* is correct. OBRA '90 requires pharmacists to offer counseling to Medicaid patients in order to receive Medicaid funding. The federal government is unable to regulate professional practice directly; therefore, the individual states impose this responsibility on the pharmacist. Therefore, Choice *A* is incorrect. Choice *C* is incorrect because this act is specifically for pharmacists. Choice *D* is incorrect because this allowance comes from section 510 of the Federal Drug and Cosmetics Act.

47. C: Robotic dispensing systems use barcode technology to choose drugs from a patient's file and can even put the medicine in the right drawer for the patient. Choice *A* is incorrect because automated pump systems are computerized infusion pumps that provide controlled flow rates. Choices *B* and *D* are incorrect because automated dispensing systems and automated tracking are tools that are used to save time and reduce human errors by automatically recording inventory data.

48. C: Schedule II controlled substances cannot be refilled. Choice A is incorrect because a patient may need an early refill if the prescriber updated the medication dosage. Choice B is incorrect because prescriptions do not become invalid until they are one year old. Choice D is incorrect because Schedule III and IV controlled substances may be filled five times within a six-month period.

49. A: Choice A is correct. First, the weight of the person in kg needs to be calculated, then multiplied times the amount of medication (mg) per kg:

$$\frac{138 \ lbs}{1} \times \frac{1 \ kg}{2.2 \ lb} \times \frac{0.25 \ mg}{1 \ kg} = x \ mg \ daily$$

$$\frac{138 \ lbs}{1} \times \frac{1 \ kg}{2.2 \ lb} \times \frac{0.25 \ mg}{1 \ kg} = 16 \ mg \ daily$$

Multiplying 138 lb x 1 kg x 0.25 mg and then dividing that number by the product of the bottom numbers (1 x 2.2 lb x 1 kg) equals 16 mg. Next, we must calculate how many pills the patient would need, especially since pills only come in specific strengths:

$$\frac{16 \ mg}{1} \times \frac{1 \ pill}{5 \ mg} = x \ pills$$

$$\frac{16 \ mg}{1} \times \frac{1 \ pill}{5 \ mg} = 3.2 \ pills$$

Depending on the medication and on the hospital's or office's procedures, you may be asked to split the pill accordingly (rarely), or round up or down. For most medications except antibiotics, rounding down is preferred so we do not give too high of a dose to a patient, especially when only 1 mg out of 16 mg will be taken out (6.25%, or 0.2 only equals 20% of the 5 mg pill). Therefore, only 3 pills would be dispensed to the patient. Again, ensure that you are following the company policy and medication-specific guidelines before assuming rounding rules. Choice A is correct.

50. D: Choice D is the correct answer because only a pharmacist is permitted to give medical advice and dispense medication. Choices A and C are incorrect because only a pharmacist is permitted to give advice on medication within a pharmacy. Choice B, pharmacist and prescribing physician, is incorrect because although both may provide medical advice regarding medications, only a pharmacist is permitted to dispense a medication.

51. D: Patients are an integral part of the medication safety team. Patients should be educated about their medications and treatment objectives so that they can effectively contribute to preventing medication errors. It is recommended that pharmacists show medications to the patient at the time of dispensing, as this approach significantly decreases dispensing errors.

52. B: "36–46° F" is the correct answer. Pharmacy refrigerators used for drug storage are required to maintain a temperature between 36° F and 46° F. This ensures that temperature sensitive medications remain active and safe. All other answer choices are incorrect.

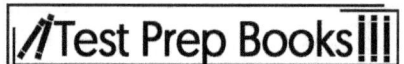

Answer Explanations #1

53. B: Duragesic (fentanyl) is an extremely potent opioid and has the potential for significant respiratory depression in new patients. Proair (albuterol) is a rescue anti-asthmatic medication and would instead assist his breathing. Tadalafil (Cialis) is better known for its use for the treatment of erectile dysfunction, but it also can be used to lower blood pressure in the lungs and increase respiratory capacity, depending on the patient's other health conditions. This may assist with his breathing or have little effect on it, but it is unlikely to make it more difficult for him to breathe. Mevacor (lovastatin) is an anti-cholesterol medication and does not have any typical side effects that would affect breathing.

54. C: The prescription label does not provide pharmacology information. Choice A, the PPI (patient package insert), is incorrect because it carries detailed information about the medication including the pharmacology. Choice B, the product monograph (product insert [PI] or prescribing information [PI]), is incorrect because it carries various details of the medication including pharmacology, toxicology, and clinical studies. Choice D, the master formulation record, is incorrect because it provides information about a compounded medication, including expected results and other pharmacology information.

55. B: Choice B is correct. The Roman number given is XLV. X means 10, L means 50, and V means 5. L is the base Roman numeral, since it is the largest one with a value of 50. Next is the X, which is front of the L. Since it is in front of a Roman numeral that has a higher value (50), it is subtracted from 50, which gives us 40. Choices C and Choice D are now incorrect, since they are less than 40. The V is on the very right end of the Roman numeral, so you would just add it to the number you already have:

$$40\ (XL) + 5\ (V) = x\ (XLV)$$

$$40\ (XL) + 5\ (V) = 45\ (XLV)$$

Choice B is the correct answer of 45 tablets of fluoxetine.

56. A: The correct answer is Choice A. In 1937, a liquid form of sulfanilamide was marketed to pediatric patients, but it contained diethylene glycol as the solvent, which is similar to antifreeze. Choice B is incorrect because the event described led to the passing of the 1902 Biologics Control Act. Choice C is incorrect because this occurrence led to the passing of the 1963 Kefauver-Harris Amendment. Choice D is incorrect because it led to the passing of the Orphan Drug Act of 1983.

57. B: The Controlled Substances Act classifies drugs into five controlled categories. The Prescription Drug Marketing Act ensures that all drugs marketed to the public are safe and effective and do not introduce risk from alterations. The Federal Food, Drug, and Cosmetic Act grants the FDA oversight of the safety of the food, drug, and cosmetic industries. The Poison Prevention Packaging Act requires the use of child-resistant caps on medication bottles.

58. D: The strictest law should be followed. If the state has more requirements than the federal government, then the state laws and requirements should be followed. Due diligence should be given to understanding both state and federal laws pertaining to the pharmacy and, if there are questions, follow-up with the appropriate agencies and authorities is required.

59. B: Veterinarians can only prescribe medication classes that are approved for animal use. Choice A is incorrect because nurse practitioners can prescribe all medications under the supervision of a physician. Choice C is incorrect because dentists, including all specialties within dentistry, can only prescribe medications used to treat mouth-related diseases. They can prescribe non-controlled and controlled medications. Choice D is incorrect because Doctors of Medicine (MDs) are the most common healthcare provider with the broadest spectrum of prescribing power.

Answer Explanations #1

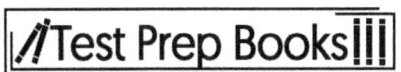

60. A: A black box warning is a warning that indicates that the medicine poses a serious threat to the preparer or user of the drug if given incorrectly or warns of severe adverse drug reactions associated with the medication. Choices B and D are made-up terms, and Choice C is a general term that applies to any side effects associated with a medication, no matter how rare, common, severe, or nonsevere. A black box warning indicates an adverse drug reaction (ADR), but specifically the most severe type of reaction, and the FDA requires black box warning labeling.

61. A: The correct answer is Choice A because reverse distributors accept expired and unidentified medications to dispose of them in a safe and legal manner. Choice B, they should be sold immediately, is incorrect because an expired medication should never be sold. Choice C, they can be given directly back to the manufacturer, is incorrect because expired medications should be given to a reverse distributor who will then communicate with the manufacturer if necessary. The pharmacy does not correspond directly with the manufacturer regarding expired medications. Choice D, they can be given to the DEA, is incorrect because the DEA does not deal with expired medications.

62. B: The Institute of Safe Medication Practices (ISMP) oversees the MERP. The service provides for confidential and voluntary reporting of medication errors. The MERP performs analyses of the errors reported and circulates recommendations for their prevention to drug manufacturers and regulatory organizations. The ISMP also manages the National Vaccine Errors Reporting Program (VERP).

63. A: Non-opioid analgesics target the cyclooxygenase enzyme, Choice A, and inhibit its action to prevent the production of prostaglandins known to play a large role in increasing sensitivity to pain and in creating signs of inflammation, pain, and fever. Choice B is incorrect because the nerve cells of the brain are the target of opioid analgesics. Choice C is incorrect because the stratum corneum is the target for most topical medications. Choice D is incorrect because dopamine receptors are the target for antidepressant medications.

64. B: Zyprexa and olanzapine are the same antipsychotic, and this is the only pair that is correctly coupled. Zytrim (orlistat) is a cholesterol medication, whereas allopurinol's brand is Zyloprim. Zyban is an anti-smoking formulation of bupropion, and Zyrtec's generic is cetirizine.

65. B: Lead-lined storage containers are required for radioactive materials like Tc-99m or T99m lidofenin. While the other drugs listed are hazardous and carcinogenic, they are not radiopharmaceuticals that would require a lead-shielded pig for transportation.

66. B: Prescriptions should be kept on file for a minimum of two years, and Schedule II medication prescriptions must be filed separately from other prescriptions. All prescriptions that were filled, need to be readily accessible during an inspection or visit from authorities. The other answer options are not correct due to not maintaining the prescription file for the appropriate length of time, not separating controlled substance prescriptions from regular prescriptions, or discarding the prescription after it has been filled.

67. A: The National Provider Identifier is a unique and specific set of numbers that identify a healthcare professional and their prescribing authority. Choice B is incorrect because it is required by the Health Insurance Portability and Accountability Act (HIPAA) standard and is utilized to find providers in various electronic healthcare systems. Choice C is incorrect because there are two types of NPI categories: NPIs for individual providers and NPIs for organizational providers. Choice D is incorrect because NPIs are required to be documented on all Medicare Part D claims, but not necessarily all insurance claims.

68. C: Augmentin (amoxicillin and clavulanate) solutions should be refrigerated during storage after reconstitution. Choice A is incorrect because, while fluconazole is teratogenic and should be avoided by pregnant females, this is not a concern for male patients. Choice B is incorrect because phendimetrazine (Bontril®) is a stimulant and is therefore unlikely to cause sedation. Choice D is incorrect because ezetimibe (Zetia) has no significant effects on

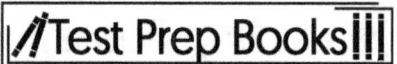

Answer Explanations #1

cognition or sedation, and it does not cause dizziness or mental disturbance; therefore, using it should not prevent a patient from manipulating heavy machinery.

69. C: The Institute for Safe Medication Practices (ISMP) is an independent nonprofit organization that focuses on the prevention of medication errors by providing guidelines, hosting medication error reporting programs, and giving out free resources on medication safety. The Food and Drug Administration (FDA), the Drug Enforcement Agency (DEA), and the Centers for Disease Control (CDC) are not directly involved with ISMP, although they all work together.

70. B: The correct answer is Choice *B* because this method is used to make orally dissolving tablets. Choice *A* is incorrect because the swelling mechanism occurs when the disintegrating agents encounter an aqueous fluid and begin to expand to the point where the tablet falls apart. Choice *C* is incorrect because the wicking mechanism occurs when disintegrating agents create pores in the tablet that draw liquid through and rupture the inter-particulate bonds inside and cause the tablet to fall apart. Choice *D* is incorrect because deformation occurs when starch grains are compressed into the tablet and expel energy once in contact with water.

71. B: Choice *B* is correct. First, calculate the total daily dosage of this prescription. If 3 drops of amoxicillin are needed twice daily:

$$3 \; drops \; \times 2 \; times \; a \; day = x \; drops$$

$$3 \; drops \; \times 2 \; times \; a \; day = 6 \; drops$$

If 6 drops are needed daily, and a month is considered 30 days:

$$6 \; drops \; daily \; \times 30 \; days = x \; drops \; monthly$$

$$6 \; drops \; daily \; \times 30 \; days = 180 \; drops \; monthly$$

Then, convert this to mL, where 1 mL equals 20 drops:

$$\frac{180 \; drops}{1} \times \frac{1 \; mL}{20 \; drops} = x \; mL$$

$$\frac{180 \; drops}{1} \times \frac{1 \; mL}{20 \; drops} = 9 \; mL$$

The monthly dosage would be 9 mL of amoxicillin. This is just one way to work this problem; you can also start by converting it to milliliters in the beginning. Converting the units at the end is more foolproof because if the unit is converted incorrectly in the beginning, the rest of the problem will be wrong, whereas if it is converted at the end, only the last step would be wrong, and you may be able to deduce when you get it wrong because it may just look wrong. Therefore, Choice *B* is correct.

72. C: We do not want to harp on people's past mistakes, as this will make them feel undervalued and belittled, so Choice *A* is incorrect. Choice *B* implies that if we know what mistakes we made in the past, we will not make them again, which is also incorrect. Choice *D* should not be the goal of improving; the goal should be patient care. Choice *C* is correct because it focuses on continually improving the quality of the pharmacy.

73. C: Choice *C* is the correct answer. According to the Drug Supply Chain Security Act, the FDA must be contacted within 24 hours of receiving counterfeit medication. Additionally, the manufacturer and distributor must be contacted to ensure that it was not their mistake. Choice *A*, inform the local police, is incorrect because the FDA has authority over counterfeit medications, and local police do not have jurisdiction. Choice *B*, notify the pharmacist so they can dispose of the counterfeit medication, is incorrect because even though the pharmacist should be notified and the counterfeit medication will ultimately be disposed of, the FDA must also be involved. Choice *D*, put the received medication into stock and sell it, is incorrect because unidentified medications may not be sold; they could be extremely unsafe for patients.

74. C: The labeler code is the first segment that reveals the manufacturer who produced the drug.

75. C: Qbrelis (lisinopril) and Zestoretic (lisinopril + hydrochlorothiazide [HCTZ]) are both blood pressure medications; however, the lisinopril is duplicated between the two medications, and it is unlikely the physician intended for both to be taken together. On the other hand, some combinations of medications are used for synergistic effect, as in the case of Choice *D*, in which Glucophage (metformin) is added to Invokana (canagliflozin) therapy in order to reduce blood sugar through both mechanisms. Aricept (donepezil) is an anti-Alzheimer's drug, and Imitrex (sumatriptan) is taken to treat migraines; there are no significant interactions here. Nystatin (mupirocin) is a topical antibiotic, whereas simvastatin works to lower cholesterol; these are also okay to take concurrently.

76. A: Choice *A*, the type of airflow, is correct. A vertical flow hood uses vertical laminar airflow, while a compounding aseptic isolator (CAI) uses unidirectional or recirculating airflow. Choices *B*, *C*, and *D* are incorrect. While size, decontamination method, and level of containment may vary between different equipment, the main difference between a vertical flow hood and a CAI is the type of airflow used.

77. A: USP <797> provides guidelines for sterile compounding, including procedures, practices, and quality standards. Choices *B*, *C*, and *D* are incorrect because USP <797> specifically pertains to sterile compounding, not nonsterile compounding, labeling, or equipment maintenance. While other USP chapters provide guidance for nonsterile compounding (such as USP <795>) and labeling (such as USP <1163>), USP <797> specifically addresses the unique challenges and requirements for maintaining a sterile environment during the compounding of sterile preparations.

78. C: The FDA oversees the MedWatch program, which is a safety information and adverse event reporting service (AERS). MedWatch focuses on drugs and medical devices. MedWatch is a voluntary reporting system and allows the information to be shared amongst healthcare professionals and the lay public. Reports are submitted via the Internet.

79. D: Height is the only piece of information that is not necessary to ensure safe medication dispensing for a pediatric patient. Confirming age and allergy are the primary requirements prior to prescription entry. Body weight is important because drug dose is based on weight. The indication of medication helps verify whether the intention of the treatment matches with the prescribed medication.

80. A: The DEA number formula should be used to validate the check digit. The formula is to add digits 1, 3, and 5 which is SUM1, and then add digits 2, 4, and 6, which is SUM2. Then, SUM2 is multiplied by 2, resulting in Product 1. Next, SUM1 and Product 1 are added together. The check digit should be the same as the second digit in the answer.

81. D: CAIs provide a physical barrier between the compounding area and the operator while laminar flow hoods do not. While both laminar flow hoods and CAIs are primary engineering controls used for sterile compounding, CAIs provide a physical barrier between the operator and the compounding area to prevent contamination. Laminar flow hoods use a glove system to maintain a sterile environment. Both controls use HEPA filters and can be used for all

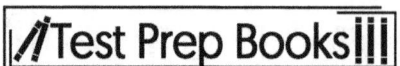

types of compounding; therefore, Choices A and B are incorrect. Choice C is incorrect because laminar flow hoods can be horizontal or vertical airflow, and CAIs use a recirculating airflow.

82. A: Urticaria (hives) is a classic example of an allergic reaction and tends to present alongside swelling (inflammation), reddened skin (erythema), and itching (pruritus). Tinnitus (a ringing sensation in the ears) may be a side effect of high doses of IV inpatient antibiotics, but this does not constitute an allergy. Borborygmi (stomach growling) and bruxism (teeth grinding) are likely unrelated to the medication.

83. D: Better lighting will NOT prevent LASA medication mix-up as they are still next to each other on the shelf. Physical separation of LASA medications on the shelves, however, can reduce the possibility of mix-up.

84. D: Telephone orders can be utilized for non-controlled and controlled (CIII-V) medications; however, the prescriber's DEA number and the patient's address must also be documented. Schedule II medications cannot be prescribed via this method. Choices A, B, and C are incorrect because these are legitimate methods to order CII medications.

85. D: REMS programs aim to prevent known medication interactions and mitigate known risks through proactive monitoring. REMS programs are followed to prevent teratogenic and reproductive mutations and to lessen the impact of unexpected side effects. Choice A is incorrect because REMS programs address known medication interactions not unknown interactions. NIOSH, OSHA, and USP <800> are responsible for workers' occupational safety, making Choice B incorrect. Choice C is incorrect because REMS programs do not involve structured therapy; instead, they use proactive monitoring to avoid or prevent dangers.

86. D: Using abbreviations increases the chance of errors due to misinterpretation. For example, some abbreviations are particularly risky, like writing "u" for unit or adding a trailing "0" on the dosage (e.g., 1.0 mg).

87. B: The correct answer is Choice B because type 2 diabetes is a genetic and environmental disease that leads to insulin resistance, often caused by obesity, family history, and physical inactivity. Choice A is incorrect because type 1 diabetes is an autoimmune disease that causes destruction of beta cells in the pancreas that results in a complete deficiency of insulin. Choice C is incorrect because hyperinsulinemia is a condition characterized by excessive insulin. Choice D is incorrect because chronic kidney disease is the progressive loss of kidney function.

88. B: This is the only option that represents a pair of carcinogenic (daunomycin or daunorubicin) and noncarcinogenic (dutasteride) hazardous drugs. Bleomycin, methotrexate, mitomycin, and vinblastine are all considered carcinogenic; therefore, Choices A and C are incorrect. Choice D is incorrect because, while sirolimus is considered noncarcinogenic and hazardous, streptomycin is a common antibiotic and isn't considered hazardous.

89. B: Scrubs are usually considered an intermediate risk because they could come into contact with bacteria, so Choice B is the correct answer.

90. B: Pediatric proton pump inhibitors (PPIs) are typically red once mixed with their respective dye-containing solutions. Antibiotic solutions should always be mixed with distilled water, and neither the off-color particulates of an oral solution nor noticeable clumping of an injectable sterile product (as in the case of Choice D) would be acceptable for administration. Pastes and creams should not appear cracked or dry before use, as it may potentially represent the loss of water and concentration of the medication or the degradation of the active drug ingredient.

91. B: Equipment maintenance is essential in compounding to maintain the quality and safety of compounded products. Choices A, C, and D are incorrect. Even though saving money on repairs and complying with regulations may be desired outcomes, the primary purpose of equipment maintenance in compounding is to maintain the quality and safety of compounded products.

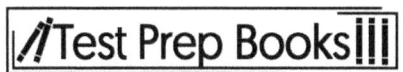

Answer Explanations #1

92. B: The pharmacy technician should suggest a compliance device. Pharmacy technicians are permitted to give advice on compliance aids, and one might help the patient remember to take their medication. Choice A, personally administer the patient's medications, is incorrect because it is not the pharmacy technician's responsibility to make a patient take their prescribed medications. They can suggest ways to help with compliance, but they cannot force a patient to take medication. Choice C, write the patient a note to remind them, is incorrect because a pharmacy technician is not permitted to give medical advice. Choice D, inform the patient's family or caregivers that they must force the patient to take their medication, is incorrect because without consent from a patient, nobody can forcibly administer medical care.

93. B: Collecting the patient's history can help identify allergic reactions or drug-drug interactions. Although in some cases having the patient's history can help track which medications may need to be refilled, it's not the primary intent.

94. C: The ABIM is a nonprofit organization that certifies physicians who practice internal medicine and its subspecialties. Only physicians who demonstrate the knowledge, skills, and aptitude to engage in the health care of adults are certified. Choices A, B, and C are all organizations that play a role in molding QA practices in the pharmacy setting.

95. B: A medication error is an error in the prescribing, dispensing, or administration of a medicine. Choice A describes an ADR, and Choices C and D are not considered medication errors because they are not part of any of the above three processes.

96. B: According to the United States Food and Drug Administration's specifications for tamper-evident packaging, sublingual nitroglycerin should not be stored in plastic containers. The medication can bond with the PVC in plastic containers, which can alter the structure and eventually harm the efficacy of the medication. Glass is a great alternative because it is inert (nonreactive). The other medications are light-sensitive, which means they should be dispensed in amber-colored containers, but they can be plastic.

97. C: Trissel's *Handbook on Injectable Drugs* is a reference book used in pharmacy practice to provide information on the compatibility, stability, and storage requirements of injectable medications. Choice A, providing information on drug side effects, is incorrect as Trissel's *Handbook* is not primarily used for this purpose. It may contain some limited information on side effects, but this is not its primary focus. Choice B, providing information on drug pricing, is also incorrect as the book is not designed to provide pricing information. Choice D, providing information on drug dosing, is incorrect as Trissel's *Handbook* primarily focuses on drug stability and compatibility rather than dosing information.

98. A: The Bank Identification Number has no association with a bank when used in the healthcare industry context. It is the number that identifies the insurance providers. For example, United Health, Aetna, Blue Cross Blue Shield, etc. will all have a specific number that identifies them from other companies. Therefore, Choices B, C, and D are incorrect.

99. C: A closed formulary describes a specific set of medications that are covered, and if a medication is not in the formulary, the patient or provider will not be reimbursed if the medication is purchased. Choices A and B are incorrect because open formularies are the least used because it states that the payer, or insurance company, will pay for all prescriptions unless they are for cosmetic purposes or can be purchased over the counter. Choice D is incorrect because formularies are public information.

100. C: The appropriate action is to inform the pharmacist. Choices A and B are inappropriate. Choice D is incorrect because communication with the physician is a pharmacist's responsibility.

ExCPT Practice Test #2

1. How many locks, at a minimum, should controlled substances be behind?
    a. One
    b. Two
    c. Three
    d. Four

2. A customer asks for your help in finding a medication, and soon there are several people asking various questions about OTC medications. Which of the following should merit a consultation with the pharmacist?
    a. WF, a 75-year-old male who takes lisinopril and atenolol for high blood pressure and warfarin for his recent valve transplant, asks how many doses per day he can take of Sudafed PE.
    b. TR, a 35-year-old male with a penicillin allergy, has recently run into a patch of poison ivy and asks whether he can take his normal bedtime Benadryl early to reduce the itching.
    c. AP, a 20-year-old female, comes to the pharmacy and requests one bottle of Pepto-Bismol and two bottles of Pedialyte.
    d. AC, a 43-year-old female with a history of type 2 diabetes and insomnia, asks whether it would be worth it to get a prescription for Freestyle Libre 2 so she can run it on her insurance, or if she should get it OTC and pay for it out-of-pocket.

3. Which of the following is true regarding narrow therapeutic index medications?
    a. Patients taking these medications require minimal monitoring.
    b. Achieving an optimal therapeutic dose can be difficult.
    c. These types of medications must always be administered intravenously.
    d. They are generally considered safer than medications with a higher therapeutic index value.

4. Which of the following pieces of information is NOT required on the prescription when transferring a controlled (CIII-CV) substance?
    a. Patient's name
    b. Pharmacy's DEA number
    c. Patient's allergies
    d. Remaining refills

5. If a patient is receiving two medications within the same drug class, what type of third-party rejection might you receive?
    a. High dose
    b. Prior authorization
    c. Missing diagnosis code
    d. Duplicate therapy

6. A pharmacy technician notices that one medication newly prescribed to a patient is harmful when taken with a medication for which that patient already has a prescription. What is this an example of?
    a. Duplication
    b. Omission
    c. Dosing error
    d. Drug interactions

7. What should a pharmacy technician do if a prescription is missing crucial information, such as the quantity and the dosing?
    a. Call the doctor for clarification
    b. Look on the patient's chart to see if they have filled this medicine in the past and copy that information onto the new prescription
    c. Throw the prescription away because it is invalid
    d. Call the patient to ask what dose and how many days' supply they need

8. Which over-the-counter vitamin is used to increase blood clot formation?
    a. Vitamin A
    b. Vitamin C
    c. Vitamin D
    d. Vitamin K

9. According to the FDA, which of these is approved as tamper-evident packaging?
    a. All metal tubes
    b. Bottles with childproof caps
    c. Bubble packs
    d. Injection needles

10. What level of disinfectant is 3 percent hydrogen peroxide?
    a. Low-level disinfectant
    b. Intermediate disinfectant
    c. High-level disinfectant
    d. It is not a disinfectant.

11. Among all the people and organizations involved in the prescribing process, which one does NOT need to have licensure with the DEA?
    a. The provider writing the prescription for a controlled substance
    b. The manufacturer making the controlled substance
    c. The patient picking up their Schedule II controlled substance
    d. The pharmacist receiving and filling a Schedule IV controlled substance

12. What is the wet gum method used for in compounding?
    a. To ensure that the final product is free of particulate matter
    b. To mix ingredients together evenly
    c. To ensure the sterility of the final product
    d. To provide a uniform suspension of insoluble particles in a liquid

13. What is the name of the FDA's program to monitor adverse events?
    a. Institute for Safe Medication Practices
    b. Risk Evaluation and Mitigation Strategies
    c. MedWatch
    d. Prescription Monitoring Program

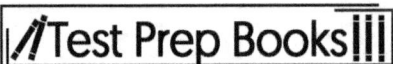

14. A pharmacist wishes to know if a new medication has been approved by the FDA. Which resource should they use?
    a. The Red Book
    b. The Orange Book
    c. *United States Pharmacopeia*
    d. Micromedex

15. Which body system plays a main role in hormonal regulation, sleep, mood, and metabolism?
    a. Endocrine
    b. Digestive
    c. Cardiovascular
    d. Nervous system

16. What does teratogenic mean?
    a. The medicine causes cancer.
    b. The medicine contains radiation that it can transmit to people.
    c. The medicine is poisonous.
    d. The medicine is harmful to a fetus.

17. What is the DAW code for the phrase "substitution to generic is unauthorized by the pharmacy, and prescriber requires brand name be dispensed"?
    a. DAW 0
    b. DAW 1
    c. DAW 2
    d. DAW 3

18. AB is a thirty-four-year-old female who recently received her first dose of the bivalent Moderna coronavirus disease 2019 (COVID-19) vaccine three and a half weeks ago. A dose of which of the following would be appropriate to administer today in order to complete her series?
    a. Spikevax
    b. Comirnaty
    c. Vaxneuvance®
    d. None of the above are appropriate at this time.

19. Which prescription should most likely be reviewed by a pharmacist to ensure its accuracy?
    a. Ms. Smith has been taking sertraline 50 mg and is now switching to sertraline 100 mg.
    b. A prescription for one thousand tablets of oxycontin
    c. A prescription for amoxicillin indicated for a viral infection
    d. Mr. Jones's propranolol has decreased from 60 mg to 20 mg.

20. A pharmacy technician notices that one of their orders containing a controlled substance is incomplete. What must they do immediately upon noticing?
    a. Contact the manufacturer.
    b. Contact the distributor for a refund.
    c. Contact local law enforcement in case the medication was stolen.
    d. Contact the DEA and fill out Form 222.

21. What is the maximum number of refills allowed for CIII-CV medications?
    a. Zero
    b. 1
    c. 5
    d. 12

22. A 3 mL preparation of 16% Hiccupazine needs to be made into 5% Hiccupazine. What is the amount of diluent added to the 5% Hiccupazine to achieve the desired concentration?
    a. 4.8 mL
    b. 5.5 mL
    c. 5.9 mL
    d. 6.6 mL

23. What are the two BEST identifiers a pharmacy technician can use to identify patients?
    a. First and last name, date of birth
    b. First name, date of birth
    c. Full name, Social Security number
    d. First name, phone number

24. What is the Purple Book used for?
    a. To determine bioequivalence of biologic products
    b. To compare therapeutic equivalents of generic medications
    c. To obtain accurate pricing of medications
    d. To find information regarding the CDC's health advisements for international travel

25. Which of the following describes the difference between over-the-counter (OTC) and behind-the-counter (BTC) products?
    a. OTC products do not require pharmacist or store employee intervention, whereas BTC products do.
    b. BTC products do not require pharmacist or store employee intervention, whereas OTC products do.
    c. OTC products are not available as prescription products, whereas BTC products are prescription only.
    d. BTC products are not available as prescription products, whereas OTC products are prescription only.

26. Which of the following statements are true?
    a. All drugs that are dangerous for pregnancy are dangerous for breastfeeding.
    b. Drugs that are safe in pregnancy are not always safe in breastfeeding, and vice versa.
    c. All medications that are unsafe in pregnancy and lactation are considered unsafe because they will harm the fetus/child.
    d. The PLLR has five categories for rating the safety of medications in pregnancy: A, B, C, D, and X.

27. Which of the following statements is correct about workers' compensation claims?
    a. The pharmacist fills out the initial claim for the patient.
    b. The prescription must indicate that it is for workers' compensation.
    c. The insurance will cover all medical expenses even if it does not relate directly to the claim.
    d. Workers' compensation insurance is part of the patient's private insurance.

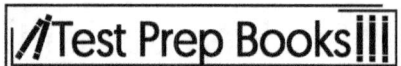

28. Which of the following scenarios is an example of misbranding?
    a. A multivitamin product claims to contain only vitamins A, D, E, and K, but it was found to have vitamins B and C also.
    b. A bottle of hair growth tablets claims to contain one hundred tablets but only has ninety-five.
    c. A manufacturer dilutes a drug suspension to save money but does not inform the consumers.
    d. A manufacturing company falsifies documents and values to pass quality standard expectations.

29. What is the SIG code for the phrase *as needed*?
    a. PO
    b. BC
    c. QID
    d. PRN

30. In which of the following cases would a DEA Form 106 be required?
    a. A patient sends an expired phendimetrazine prescription through a mail-back program.
    b. A pharmacy mails a 30-day supply of triazolam to a patient.
    c. A shipping agent delivers five bottles of Restall to the pharmacy.
    d. A pharmacist reports that two bottles of tapentadol still haven't been delivered by the shippers.

31. Which of the following is NOT required by the Pregnancy and Lactation Labeling Rule?
    a. Risk summary
    b. Data on reproductive potential in both males and females
    c. Clinical considerations
    d. Whether a child can take this medication

32. Which class of antiarrhythmic medications are sodium channel blockers used to slow electrical impulses?
    a. Class I
    b. Class II
    c. Class III
    d. Class IV

33. Which of the following statements would be LEAST necessary to include on an OTC label?
    a. After administration, subjects were allowed to rest for fifteen minutes.
    b. Medication for ophthalmic use only
    c. Contains aspartame
    d. Please call us with questions at 1-800-377-7884.

34. What is an example of a near miss?
    a. A patient develops dizziness after taking medication for three days before realizing it was the wrong medication.
    b. A patient takes triple the dose of a medication but does not have any severe adverse reactions.
    c. A technician incorrectly counts controlled substances for inventory.
    d. A technician catches a prescription that was inputted into the computer for a 900-day supply instead of a 90-day supply.

35. If a pharmacy intern is transferring a prescription for metformin (a non-controlled medication) to another pharmacy via phone, who is authorized to receive the transfer?
    a. Pharmacy intern
    b. Pharmacy technician intern

c. Pharmacist
d. Prescriptions may not be transferred over the phone.

36. Which part of Medicare covers prescriptions?
    a. Part A
    b. Part B
    c. Part C
    d. Part D

37. Which of the following is not a prescription drug?
    a. Acetaminophen
    b. Hydrocodone
    c. Penicillin
    d. Metformin

38. What is the resource most commonly used to determine the safety of prescriptions in breastfeeding?
    a. Hale's Lactation Risk Categories
    b. Breastfeeding Mothers Guide to Medication
    c. A Mother's Milk and Your Baby
    d. Smith's Lactation Categories

39. Which of the following statements on an OTC label would likely cause the product to be misbranded?
    a. Caution in those over the age of 65; may cause sedation.
    b. Box contains twelve packets, each of which contains one dissolvable tablet.
    c. This product contains asparaginase.
    d. Directions for infants less than 2 years old: Give 2.5 mL by mouth every twelve hours as needed.

40. Which of the following medications should NOT be taken in combination with nitroglycerin and what would be the result if they were taken together?
    a. Warfarin, excessive blood thinning
    b. Sildenafil, irreversible hypotension
    c. Allegra®, increased heart rate
    d. Sertraline, increased depression

41. A patient comes in to purchase a $15.99 cough syrup and gives you a 20% off coupon, and the pharmacy paid $3.75 to purchase the cough syrup to sell, what is the net profit? Assume the overhead cost is $5.00.
    a. $7.24
    b. $4.04
    c. $9.04
    d. $7.79

42. Which of the following is NOT a requirement within pharmacies?
    a. The pharmacy must close when no pharmacist is present.
    b. Pharmacists must provide medication counseling to all patients.
    c. Areas where controlled medications are stored must remain locked.
    d. Pharmacy technicians must never provide any medical advice.

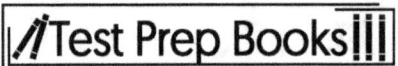

43. RL is a nineteen-year-old female who calls the pharmacy for assistance. She is currently in the second trimester of her first pregnancy and was advised by her pediatrician that there are some vaccinations she and her close family members should receive before the due date. She is otherwise healthy and has no other known pertinent health conditions. Which of the following vaccinations may be appropriate for her to receive at this time?
    a. Twinrix
    b. FluMist Quadrivalent
    c. M-M-R II
    d. Shingrix

44. Which of the following DEA numbers is correct for Dr. Drake?
    a. AD123334590
    b. BD9374957
    c. DM5784930
    d. FD4342793

45. What is a situation in which a pharmacy technician can help improve patient health literacy?
    a. Counseling patients on the prescription they are picking up
    b. Using medical terms that the patient will not understand
    c. Ignoring a patient's question on how to take their medication because the pharmacist is in a bad mood and will not want to answer questions from customers
    d. Recognizing when a new medication has a different route of administration, such as an inhaler, and asking the pharmacist to come and counsel the patient

46. A new trainee begins to fill an Effient prescription. He takes the order leaflet from the printer, immediately opens a new bottle, and pours a handful of pills onto a nearby counting tray. What advice should be given to the trainee?
    a. Effient is considered a hazardous medication and should only be counted on a tray designated as "hazardous."
    b. Effient's manufacturer has indicated that it should be sold only in the original packaging.
    c. Effient has a REMS program that requires the pharmacist to ensure that the patient's bloodwork is in order. Since Effient is such an expensive medication, the trainee should wait for the pharmacist to verify that the prescription is fillable before proceeding.
    d. The trainee's actions were completely appropriate in this scenario.

47. What is the difference between USP <797> and USP <800>?
    a. USP <797> contains the standards for sterile compounding, whereas USP <800> contains the standards for hazardous material handling.
    b. USP <797> contains guidelines for non-sterile compounding, whereas USP <800> contains guidelines for sterile compounding.
    c. USP <797> establishes standards for sterile compounding within hospital pharmacies, whereas USP <800> establishes standards for hazardous material handling at pharmaceutical manufacturing sites.
    d. USP <797> is regulated by the United States Pharmacopeia, whereas USP <800> is regulated by The National Institute for Occupational Safety and Health (NIOSH).

48. Which of the following statements is true regarding non-controlled medications?
    a. They have a maximum of five refills within six months.
    b. They have an unlimited number of refills, and the same prescription can be used for two years.
    c. They have an unlimited number of refills, but the prescriptions expire after one year.
    d. No refills are allowed for prescriptions written for a ninety-day supply.

49. What is the purpose of a laminar flow hood?
    a. To provide containment for hazardous drugs
    b. To provide a sterile environment for compounding
    c. To mix ingredients for compounding
    d. To measure drug concentrations

50. What would NOT be considered a best practice for quality assurance?
    a. Drinking water while counting pills
    b. Washing one's hands before touching medication
    c. Verifying that the prescription one is dispensing is the correct prescription by reading the label
    d. Cleaning surfaces at the end of the day

51. Which class of patients has different partial filling requirements for Schedule II controlled substances?
    a. Children
    b. Terminally ill or LTCF patients
    c. Prisoners
    d. Older people

52. Which of the following is an approved medication disposal method?
    a. Flushing it down a drain with excess water
    b. Sending it to a landfill
    c. Sending it to a reverse distributor to be resold
    d. Giving it to an approved waste management company

53. In which of the following situations is the corresponding vaccination indicated and safe?
    a. A nineteen-year-old female requesting a dose of MenB in order to fulfill requirements for first-year college housing
    b. A dose of measles, mumps, and rubella (MMR) that appears to have a yellow tint after reconstitution for a twenty-three-year-old male
    c. A dose of Varivax (VAR) for a thirty-five-year-old male who is in the store today picking up his new prescriptions for a Z-pak and prednisone
    d. A dose of hepatitis C (HepC) for a forty-seven-year-old female nursing student to satisfy her blood-borne pathogens requirement

54. Which of the following most likely indicates a forged or manipulated prescription?
    a. A single script with new three-month prescriptions and refills for lisinopril, metoprolol, clonidine, atorvastatin, and escitalopram
    b. A prescription written from a doctor's general prescription pad with the DEA number BW6675435 handwritten above the signature
    c. A Xanax prescription written with the instructions "tk 1 t po 3 h prior to procedure and g other to staff at check-in" and quantity of #20
    d. A fax for a ninety-day supply of eszopiclone written by a mid-level practitioner including both her and her supervising physician's DEA number

55. Which of the following is NOT an observable sign of physical incompatibility?
    a. Cracking
    b. Coalescence
    c. pH change
    d. Liquification

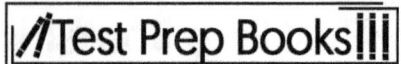

56. Which controlled substances are considered "exempt narcotics?"
    a. Schedule I
    b. Schedule II
    c. Schedule III
    d. Schedule V

57. What does the SIG code *BID* stand for?
    a. Twice a day
    b. Three times a day
    c. Four times a day
    d. Before meals

58. Who is held liable for prescription errors once the prescription is received by the pharmacy?
    a. The provider
    b. The receptionist who sent the prescription over
    c. The pharmacy
    d. The patient

59. A pharmacy technician tells the pharmacy cashier about which medications they think a patient should take after viewing their medical history. What mistake did the pharmacy technician make?
    a. They violated the rules of HIPAA by telling patient information to a coworker.
    b. They gave medical advice.
    c. They viewed a patient's medical history.
    d. They communicated with a pharmacy cashier.

60. Which organs/body parts compose the excretory system?
    a. Bones, joints, and cartilages
    b. Kidney, ureters, and urinary bladder
    c. Oral cavity, stomach, and anus
    d. Pancreas, thyroid, and adrenal gland

61. While filling the following prescriptions, in which scenario would the pharmacist NOT be legally required to counsel the patient?
    a. The pharmacist receives a pioglitazone transfer. It was first filled three months ago for a ninety-day supply, and there are nine months' worth of refills left on the prescription.
    b. A patient drops off two new prescriptions for amlodipine and lisinopril. The pharmacist recognizes that these were the same strengths and frequencies the patient took before they moved away three years ago.
    c. A patient requests a three-month refill of Estarylla®. They have only two months of medication remaining on the prescription, but the pharmacist will dispense both today.
    d. The pharmacist receives a set of new prescriptions from the county hospital. It seems to be a respiratory infection cocktail, and the patient recently picked up a similar set of medications when discharged from the same hospital two weeks ago.

62. Which compounding technique requires a wetting agent to increase solubility?
    a. Pulverization
    b. Levigation
    c. Geometric dilution
    d. Trituration

63. What is the name of the over-the-counter drug class used to treat nausea and vomiting?
    a. Antacids
    b. Antiemetics
    c. Anti-inflammatories
    d. Antipyretics

64. The Controlled Substances Act is enforced by which of the following organizations?
    a. The EPA
    b. The FDA
    c. The DEA
    d. The USDA

65. How long must all controlled substance records be kept by the pharmacy?
    a. Six months
    b. One year
    c. Two years
    d. Five years

66. A patient sets a box of insulin aspart on the counter, and the medication's label bears the following instructions:

    inj 37u sc tid ac

He says that he needs enough syringes for a month. Which of the following box contents is most appropriate, considering his prescription?
    a. 0.3 mL syringes with attached 5/8" 29 G needles in a quantity of 100
    b. 0.3 mL syringes with attached 1.5" 31 G needles in a quantity of 75
    c. 0.5 mL syringes with attached 12.7 mm 30 G needles in a quantity of 100
    d. 0.5 mL syringes with attached 38.1 mm 28 G needles in a quantity of 100

67. Which law is usually stricter and therefore supersedes any other laws in place?
    a. State law
    b. Federal law
    c. Local law
    d. International law

68. Which abbreviation refers to a medication that needs to be taken after meals?
    a. BID
    b. A.C.
    c. PRN
    d. P.C.

69. Tricyclic medications like amitriptyline and doxepin are a part of which drug class?
    a. Antiarrhythmics
    b. Anticonvulsants
    c. Antidepressants
    d. Diuretics

70. Which of the following is true regarding patient assistance programs?
    a. They can be utilized by uninsured and insured patients.
    b. They can only be utilized by patients with insurance who need help with high copays.
    c. They are supplied only by non-profit organizations.

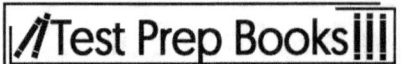

d. They can help cover 100 percent of the cost of medications for a monthly fee.

71. Which of the following auxiliary labels is the most appropriate?
    a. A label on a bottle of Septra® solution indicating a beta-lactam cross-allergy
    b. A label on a bottle of levocetirizine tablets indicating potential thyroid overdose
    c. A label on a box of cyclosporine eyedrops indicating that the product must be refrigerated
    d. A label on a bottle of modafinil tablets indicating that the product is regulated as a controlled substance

72. After opening, which of the following brands of insulin would be stable when refrigerated or at room temperature for greater than 28 days?
    a. Lantus vials
    b. Tresiba FlexTouch insulin pen
    c. Humalog vials
    d. Humulin 70/30 insulin pen

73. Who would NOT qualify for Medicare?
    a. A fifty-year-old with diabetes.
    b. A twenty-year-old with end-stage renal disease
    c. A sixty-seven-year-old with high blood pressure
    d. A forty-year-old with disabilities.

74. A nasal solution, Allergide, has a w/v% of 1:250. What is the amount of the active ingredient, mucusaline, in this preparation in oz?
    a. 0.5 oz
    b. 1.1 oz
    c. 1.4 oz
    d. 1.9 oz

75. Which of the following information will NOT be included on a medication bottle's barcode?
    a. Recommended dosage
    b. Prescribing physician
    c. Strength
    d. Medication name

76. Which of the following accurately describes the prescribing authority of pharmacists?
    a. They can prescribe all non-controlled medications, depending on the state.
    b. They cannot prescribe medications in any situation.
    c. They can prescribe under a collaborative practice agreement with a physician.
    d. They can only prescribe medications within their specialty.

77. If Amanda, a 9-year-old, 80 lb, 4'0" girl needed the medication Funolol, and the recommended adult dosage is 60 mg, what dose should Amanda receive?
    a. 60 mg
    b. 45.3 mg
    c. 38.5 mg
    d. 25.8 mg

78. For which of the following types of medication must INR values be closely monitored?
    a. Blood thinners
    b. Statins
    c. Antibiotics

d. Anticonvulsants

79. Which of the following is the main purpose of enteric coating on tablets?
    a. It ensures that the drug is dissolved in the stomach.
    b. It ensures that the drug is dissolved in the small intestine.
    c. It prevents the tablet from disintegrating in the oral cavity.
    d. It prevents extended release of the active ingredient.

80. Why are beyond-use dates (BUDs) used for compounded products?
    a. To ensure that the product is sterile
    b. To ensure that the product is potent
    c. To ensure that the product is labeled correctly
    d. To ensure that the product is cost-effective

81. Which of the following contributed to the passing of the Anabolic Steroid Act of 1990?
    a. The price of steroids was increasing, and the legislation allowed for tighter cost control.
    b. More frequent illegal steroid use led to an increase in disabilities and mortality.
    c. Steroids were being advertised to children, and the act forbade marketing ploys.
    d. There was an increase in illegal trafficking of steroids, and the act approved only over-the-counter steroids to be sold to decrease the quantity of steroids sold on the streets.

82. ML is a twenty-three-year-old male who is calling the pharmacy to update his patient information in the system. He asks to add an allergy to an antibiotic that he picked up five days ago but had since quit taking. After being asked what side effects he had been having, he clarifies that he had suffered diarrhea since taking the medication and yesterday began to notice a small rash on his chest. He hadn't completed the medication regimen but stopped taking it today. What would be the most appropriate advice for the patient?
    a. This does not constitute an allergy. He should continue taking the medication in order to fully get rid of his illness.
    b. This may be an allergy. In order to maximize safety, he should stop taking the medication. If he still feels sick, he can contact his doctor to prescribe a different medication, but if he feels fine, there is no need.
    c. This may be an allergy. In order to maximize safety, he should stop taking the medication. Because he was unable to finish the regimen, he should contact his doctor to prescribe a different medication.
    d. This is definitely an allergy. His profile should be updated, and his doctor should be alerted to never prescribe him any medications from that class of antibiotics. Because he was unable to finish the regimen, he should contact his doctor to prescribe a different medication.

83. Which of the following categories best applies to epinephrine inhalers?
    a. OTC
    b. Legend
    c. BTC
    d. CGM

84. Which of the following is NOT a common base for ointments?
    a. Oleaginous
    b. Absorption
    c. Water-soluble
    d. Vanishing

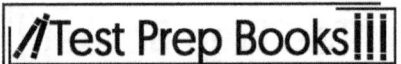

85. What should the pharmacist do when receiving a prior authorization rejection from a third party?
    a. Override, as it is only a suggestion.
    b. File the prior authorization claim.
    c. Let the prescriber's office know to file the claim.
    d. Tell the patient that the medication will never be covered as it is not in the formulary.

86. Which of the following is true regarding oral antibiotic suspensions reconstituted with water?
    a. All oral antibiotic suspensions must be refrigerated after mixing.
    b. Clarithromycin oral suspension must be refrigerated after mixing with water.
    c. Amoxicillin oral suspension is stable for 14 days after mixing with water.
    d. Reconstitution of oral antibiotic suspensions reduces the risk of microbial contamination.

87. Which of the following is NOT legally required to be listed on a prescription label?
    a. Patient's name
    b. Prescriber's name
    c. Name of medication
    d. Patient's date of birth

88. Which of the following is NOT a characteristic of a stable suspension?
    a. An internal phase that is uniformly dispersed in the external phase
    b. Small particle size
    c. Insoluble particles that are easily redistributed after settling
    d. Sedimentation or caking of particles

89. Which of the following is correct regarding OSHA's requirements for proper sharps disposal?
    a. Only the top of the container is required to be leak-proof.
    b. The container must be appropriately labeled and must be red.
    c. Reusable sharps containers must be cleaned between each empty cycle.
    d. The container should be upright, but it does not have to be.

90. What is the correct meaning behind DAW 4?
    a. The provider has not indicated that the drug needs to be anything specific, and the pharmacy can choose any manufacturer that is in stock or preferred by the patient's insurance company.
    b. Substitution is allowed by all parties; however, the generic drug was not in stock so the brand-name medication was dispensed.
    c. In some states, laws require the brand-name medication to be dispensed for a certain indication.
    d. All parties allow substitution, but there is no substitution available; therefore, the brand-name medication was dispensed.

91. Convert 78 °F to °C.
    a. 172.4 °C
    b. 46.0 °C
    c. 32.3 °C
    d. 25.6 °C

92. Which tier is most likely to include preferred brand-name medications in a four-tier system?
    a. Tier 1
    b. Tier 2
    c. Tier 3
    d. Tier 4

93. If the pharmacist asks you to make a 2.3 L 15% PainRx solution, but you only have 3% and 20% concentrations, how much of each would you need (in mL)?
    a. 1,624 mL of 20% PainRx and 677 mL of 3% PainRx
    b. 1,658 mL of 20% PainRx and 710 mL of 3% PainRx
    c. 1,675 mL of 20% PainRx and 720 mL of 3% PainRx
    d. 1,684 mL of 20% PainRx and 650 mL of 3% PainRx

94. Which of these categories are a potential risk to both a pregnant mother and her fetus and a breastfeeding mother and her baby?
    a. Antidepressants
    b. Oral anticoagulants
    c. Antiepileptics
    d. Antihistamines

95. Which of the following TPN mixes and intravenous (IV) drug admixtures would NOT be safe?
    a. Furosemide added to a dextrose 5% in water (D5W) solution
    b. Amino acid solution added to a lipid emulsion
    c. Levofloxacin added to a lactated Ringer's (LR) solution
    d. Vitamins added to a normal saline (NS) solution

96. In which case below is the dispensed medication correctly paired with its associated REMS specifications?
    a. A 27-year-old male asks for a 24-count of Allegra-D. He must be able to supply a valid photo ID, and the sale information must be logged in the pharmacy's records.
    b. A 17-year-old female submits a prescription for Amnesteem. She must complete a pregnancy test monthly and attest to her use of two types of birth control through the iPledge system.
    c. A 35-year-old female is prescribed thalidomide for Hansen's disease. She must be at least three months into the use of an intrauterine device (IUD), and she must use condoms regularly.
    d. A 56-year-old female approaches the pharmacy with a refill prescription of methimazole to counter her Hashimoto's disease. Her blood must be tested every month to ensure that her thyroid stimulating hormone (TSH) is within appropriate levels.

97. Which form is used to order Schedule II controlled substances?
    a. DEA Form 41
    b. DEA Form 106
    c. DEA Form 222
    d. DEA Form 300

98. Which type of third-party rejection does NOT require prescriber intervention?
    a. Prior authorization
    b. High dose
    c. Duplicate therapy
    d. Plan limits exceeded

99. Calculate 1 mEq of $Ca(OH)_2$ (mw = 74.093 g/mol).
    a. 74.09 mg
    b. 58.44 mg
    c. 37.05 mg
    d. 24.7 mg

100. A 27-year-old woman approaches the outpatient pharmacy and requests to purchase syringes for an injectable medication. For which of the following drugs might the patient need these syringes?
   a. Trulicity
   b. Lovenox
   c. Zovirax oral solution
   d. Depo-Provera

Answer Explanations #2

1. B: Choice B is correct. The DEA states that controlled substances must be behind at least two locks, such as a safe with a keypad in a locked room. Choice A is incorrect because one lock is not enough. Choices C and D are incorrect because, although the substances *can* be behind three or four locks, they *must* be behind at least two.

2. A: Since this elderly patient has hypertension, use of stimulants like Sudafed PE (phenylephrine) should be cautioned; this is particularly worrisome with the addition of the patient's anticoagulant, which increases the risk for aneurysm and stroke. The pharmacist should counsel WF on whether he can take phenylephrine depending on how well-controlled his high blood pressure is and whether he's tried other remedies. Since TR already takes Benadryl routinely, there should be no immediate problem beyond daytime drowsiness if he takes his nighttime dose early; therefore, Choice B is incorrect. AP is likely suffering from a hangover or food poisoning; for young adults who otherwise present with no other medical conditions, simple self-medication is likely benign; therefore, Choice C is incorrect. AC should be instructed that CGMs like Libre 2 cannot be bought OTC and require a prescription for sale, but this short explanation can be given in the pharmacist's absence; therefore, Choice D is incorrect.

3. B: Choice B is the correct choice because narrow therapeutic index medications require close, frequent monitoring and have several risk factors associated with their administration. Choices A and D are therefore incorrect. Choice C is incorrect because narrow therapeutic index medications are available in various dosage forms, including intravenously, oral tablets or capsules, injectables, suspensions, etc.

4. C: Choice C is the correct answer. When transferring a controlled medication, the patient's name and address must be documented along with the contents of the prescription (name, quantity, original and remaining refills, and original date written). Specific to controlled medications, the DEA number of the transferring pharmacy must also be documented. Although a patient's allergy history should be documented, it is not required when transferring medications.

5. D: If the insurance company notices active prescriptions for two medications in the same drug class, they will reject the prescription order and require the pharmacy to address the duplication, usually through inactivation of one of the orders. This can also occur if a patient filled the same medication in two different pharmacies. Choice A is incorrect because for each medication, there is a maximum dose allowed for human consumption, and these values are placed within the insurance company database to catch a potential error in prescription or prescriber entry. Choice B is incorrect because this occurs when medications are not covered, and the prescriber must fill out a prior authorization form to inform the insurance company why that specific medication is required and not the one that the insurance company normally covers. Choice C is incorrect because an ICD-10 code informs the insurance company what the indication for the prescriptions is.

6. D: Drug interactions occur when one medication reacts with a different medication to produce an undesirable outcome. Choice A, duplication, is incorrect because it is when one medication is prescribed multiple times for the same patient when it should only be prescribed once. Choice B, omission, is incorrect because it is when a necessary drug is not prescribed or dispensed. Choice C, dosing error, is incorrect because it is when an incorrect dosage of a medication is prescribed or dispensed.

7. A: Calling the prescriber to clarify when the pharmacy technician is unsure of a prescription is always the best practice. Choice B assumes that the prescription information stayed the same, Choice C is incorrect because the patient still needs the correct prescription and all errors must be documented, and Choice D is incorrect because the patient may not know and/or may tell the technician something incorrect to receive more of the medication.

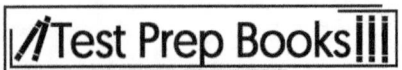

Answer Explanations #2

8. D: The correct answer is Choice *D* because vitamin K is needed to make pro-coagulant factors in the body. Choice *A* is incorrect because vitamin A is used for eye health. Choice *B* is incorrect because vitamin C is used to boost the immune system. Choice *C* is incorrect because vitamin D is used for bone health.

9. C: The FDA specifies 11 technologies capable of fulfilling the definition of tamper-evident packaging including blister and bubble packs, film wrappers, heat-shrink wrappers or bands, bottles equipped with inner-mouth seals, plastic packs or paper foil, breakable cap-ring systems, sealed tubes, tape seals, plastic blind-end heat-sealed tubes, sealed cartons, all metal and composite cans, and aerosol containers. This list excludes the packaging listed in Choices *A*, *B,* and *D*.

10. A: Three percent hydrogen peroxide is considered a low-level disinfectant because it will not kill all pathogens it comes into contact with.

11. C: Choice *C* is correct because every individual and company that is part of the controlled substance process—the manufacturer (Choice *B*), the distributor, the prescriber (Choice *A*), the pharmacy, and the pharmacist (Choice *D*)—needs licensure with the DEA. However, the patient does not need to be registered with the DEA because patients are considered the "ultimate users." However, patients are still subject to DEA-enforced laws on abuse and misuse.

12. D: The wet gum method is used to provide a uniform suspension of insoluble particles in a liquid. This method involves mixing the insoluble particles with a small amount of a liquid—typically a thickening agent like glycerin or tragacanth—to form a paste-like substance called a wet gum. Choice *A* is incorrect as ensuring that the final product is free of particulate matter typically involves filtration or other methods of particle removal, not the wet gum method. Choice *B* is incorrect as mixing ingredients together evenly can be achieved through various methods, and the wet gum method is specific to creating a uniform suspension of insoluble particles in a liquid. Choice *C* is incorrect as ensuring the sterility of the final product typically involves following aseptic techniques and using sterile components. The wet gum method does not necessarily contribute to the sterility of the final product.

13. C: The FDA runs MedWatch to monitor medications and adverse events to know whether it needs to recall a drug, add a black box warning, etc., for medications. Choice *A* is run by a nonprofit, Choice *B* is used for the specific drugs that are enlisted in the REMS program, and Choice *D* is for controlled substances or REMS medications.

14. B: "Orange Book" is the correct answer because it lists all FDA-approved medications. Choice *A*, Red Book, is incorrect because it lists the actual prices of all medications. Choice *C*, *United States Pharmacopeia*, is incorrect because it is a publication from USP that describes USP standards. Choice *D*, Micromedex, is incorrect because it is a division of IBM that produces the Red Book of drug pricing.

15. A: The correct answer is Choice *A* because the endocrine system is made of a variety of organs (pancreas, ovaries) and glands (thyroid, pituitary, adrenal) that play a role in hormonal regulation, sleep, mood, metabolism, and more. Choice *B* is incorrect because the digestive system involves the stomach, intestines, and esophagus and plays a role in the breakdown and absorption of food. Choice *C* is incorrect because the cardiovascular system contains the heart and blood vessels that supply the body with oxygen. Choice *D* is incorrect because the nervous system regulates the brain, spinal cord, and nerves.

16. D: Teratogenic means that the substance can be harmful to a fetus. Choice *A* is a carcinogen, Choice *B* is not a specific term, and Choice *C* would just be poisonous or toxic.

17. B: DAW 1 means that substitution by the pharmacy is unauthorized per the prescriber. Generally, the prescription is written for the brand-name medication and DAW 1 indicates that the pharmacy may not switch to the generic version. This can be for a variety of reasons including patient preference, allergies, etc. Choice *A* is incorrect because DAW 0 indicates that the provider has not specified that the drug needs to be a brand name and the pharmacy can choose any manufacturer that is in stock or preferred by the patient's insurance company. Choice C is incorrect because DAW 2 indicates that the provider allows substitution, but the patient prefers the brand-name medication. This may or may not be covered by the insurance. Choice D is incorrect because DAW 3 indicates that the provider and the patient allow substitution, but the pharmacist chooses the specific product that is dispensed.

18. D: As the patient received her primary dose of the Moderna vaccine less than twenty-eight days ago, she is not indicated to receive her second dose yet. After the full twenty-eight days have passed, it would be best if she received the Spikevax as her second dose. Comirnaty (Pfizer) may be administered if Spikevax is unavailable and the patient refuses to wait, but this is not generally advised by the Centers for Disease Control and Prevention (CDC). Vaxneuvance is the 15-valent pneumococcal conjugate vaccine (PCV15) and is not indicated in this patient with the available information.

19. B: A controlled substance, or any medication, would not be prescribed for one thousand tablets for one fill of a prescription. This is a simple mistake with writing/typing too many zeroes and is something a technician can catch and bring to the attention of a pharmacist. Choices A and D are incorrect because they are both typical courses of treatment. Choice C is incorrect because, although the medicine will not be effective in curing the viral infection, one does not need to worry about therapeutic uses unless it is completely mismatched, such as hydralazine and hydroxyzine.

20. D: It is a legal requirement to inform the DEA about missing or incomplete orders containing controlled substances and to fill out DEA Form 222. Choice A, contact the manufacturer, is incorrect because pharmacies buy medications through distributors, not directly from manufacturers. Choice B, contact the distributor for a refund, is incorrect because they need to complete the legal requirements before worrying about getting refunded for missing orders. Choice C, contact local law enforcement in case the medication was stolen, is incorrect because missing controlled substances are under the jurisdiction of the DEA.

21. C: If a prescriber writes ten refills for a controlled medication, it's important to relay to the patient that the maximum number of CIII-CV medications is five and that all remaining refills will be voided. Therefore, Choices A, B, and D are incorrect.

22. D: Choice D is correct. This is a dilution question, so we will use $C_1V_1=C_2V_2$ to find our answer:

$$3\ mL \times 16\% = 5\% \times V_2$$

V_2 equals 9.6 mL, which is the FINAL volume needed of the 5% Hiccupazine. To get the diluent added to make the solution:

$$9.6\ mL - 3\ mL = 6.6\ mL\ diluent\ added$$

Choice D is the correct answer with 6.6 mL diluent added to 3 mL of 16% Hiccupazine to make 9.6 mL of 5% Hiccupazine.

23. A: Using two patient identifiers when picking up prescriptions is crucial to ensure that the right prescription is going to the right patient. The best identifiers include the patient's first and last name along with either a birthday, phone number, or address. Choice B is incorrect because it only says the first name, which could bring up hundreds of patients. Choice C is incorrect because the patient may feel uncomfortable sharing their Social Security number in public. Choice D is incorrect because if the pharmacy technician just checked for a patient's first name and phone number, multiple people could potentially pick up that patient's prescription. Choice A is correct because it includes the first and last name and the date of birth.

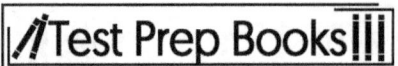

24. A: Choice *A* is the correct answer. The Purple Book is used to determine interchangeability between biologic products. Choice *B* is incorrect because this information can be found in the Orange Book. Choice *C* is incorrect because this information can be found in the Red Book. Choice *D* is incorrect because this information can be found in the Yellow Book.

25. A: The correct answer is Choice *A* because BTC medications are available for purchase without a prescription but require intervention from either a pharmacist or store employee. OTC medications can be purchased freely. Therefore, Choice *B* is incorrect. Choices *C* and *D* are incorrect because neither OTC nor BTC medications require a prescription.

26. B: Even though there is some overlap, drugs that are safe in pregnancy may not be safe for breastfeeding, and vice versa. This rules out Choice *A*. Choice *C* is incorrect because it says ALL medications unsafe in pregnancy are considered dangerous because of the risk to a fetus/child, and that is the case for most of the medications but not all; medications can be dangerous because of changes in the health of the mother due to changing hormones and other factors. Choice *D* represents the old FDA pregnancy labeling system, not the new system after the PLLR was instated.

27. B: If a patient is injured at work, their employer may offer workers' compensation to help cover the medical costs. Considerable documentation must be written on the prescription including ICD codes (diagnosis codes), and it must be written on the prescription order that the medication is related to a workers' compensation claim. Choices *A, C,* and *D* are incorrect because workers' compensation is a separate insurance that will only cover medical and prescription expenses directly related to the claim.

28. B: Choice *B* is the correct answer. Misbranding occurs when a label contains false information that leads to consumer confusion, like claiming there are one hundred tablets when there's only ninety-five. Adulteration is when the quality, purity, or strength listed on the bottle is different than its contents. Choice *A* is incorrect because this is an example of sophistication adulteration: the additional vitamins were added intentionally but were not reported. Choice *C* is incorrect because this is an example of admixture adulteration, which occurs when there is an addition of an unreported ingredient. Choice *D* is incorrect because this is an example of deterioration adulteration, which involves impairment of quality.

29. D: *PRN* means as needed, making Choice *D* the correct answer. *PO* means by mouth, *BC* means after meals, and *QID* means four times a day, which means that Choices *A, B,* and *C* are incorrect.

30. D: Tapentadol (Nucynta) is a CII substance, and the pharmacist should fill out Form 106 to alert the DEA that there are two bottles of controlled medication unaccounted for. Mail-back programs and medications mailed to patients do not require declarations of loss, making Choices *A* and *B* incorrect. Restall (hydroxyzine injection) is not a controlled medication, so Choice *C* is incorrect.

31. D: A child's ability to take a specific medication is not noted by the Pregnancy and Lactation Labeling Rule (PLLR); most medications have pregnancy/breastfeeding warnings because of a potential risk to an unborn child/infant. The other choices are all requirements to be included with a medication.

32. A: The correct answer is Choice *A.* Class I medications like flecainide and propafenone are sodium channel blockers used to slow electrical impulses. Choice *B* is incorrect because class II medications include metoprolol and propranolol, which are beta blockers that slow down the heart rate. Choice *C* is incorrect because class III medications include amiodarone and sotalol, which are potassium channel blockers that help slow electrical impulses. Choice *D* is incorrect because class IV medications include diltiazem and verapamil, which are non-dihydropyridine calcium channel blockers that are used to slow the heart rate and contractility.

Answer Explanations #2

33. A: This statement represents an excerpt from a clinical trial, which is not required for OTC labels. Directions for use, notices for those with dietary restrictions (e.g., cannot consume the artificial sweetener aspartame), and a method of contact must be included on all OTC labels.

34. D: When someone catches a mistake before it impacts anyone else, that is a near miss. Choices A and B are medication errors that were not caught, so they must be fully reported as a dispensing error for Choice A and an administration error for Choice B. Choice C can be detrimental to the pharmacy for inventory purposes, but it is not considered a medication error, so it cannot be a near miss.

35. C: Choice C is the correct answer. If a pharmacy intern is giving the prescription, only a pharmacist can receive the transfer. However, if a pharmacist were giving the prescription, a pharmacist or pharmacy intern could receive the transfer; therefore, Choice A is incorrect. Choice B is incorrect because pharmacy technician interns are not authorized to receive or give transfers. Choice D is incorrect because non-controlled prescriptions are authorized to be transferred over the phone.

36. D: Only patients with Medicare Part D have prescription insurance and will have a specific prescription card indicating that. If the patient only has a Medicare Part A or B card, it's important to inform them that medications will not be covered, and they may need to utilize a prescription discount service, like GoodRx, or a patient assistance program to help pay for their medications. Therefore, Choices A, B, and C are incorrect.

37. A: Acetaminophen is an over-the-counter drug. Choice B, hydrocodone, is incorrect because it is an intensely controlled substance that requires a prescription. Choices C and D, penicillin and metformin, are incorrect because they are prescription drugs.

38. A: Hale's Lactation Risk Categories, which ranks drugs on a scale of L1 to L5, is the most commonly used resource for determining the safety of medications during lactation. The other three answers are made-up sources.

39. C: Asparaginase is a chemotherapeutic drug that is not found OTC; a product claiming to sell it OTC would either be misbranded or illegal. Cautions about side effects, descriptions of the container's contents, and directions specific to patients within certain age ranges are each appropriate items to find on an OTC label.

40. B: Sildenafil and nitroglycerin should not be taken together, as both cause blood vessel dilation, leading to the potential of irreversible hypotension. The other listed combinations do not have documented direct effects when taken in combination with nitroglycerin.

41. B: Choice B is correct. This requires several of the business calculations we learned. First, take the 20% discount off of the selling price:

$$\frac{discount}{\$15.99} = \frac{20\%}{100\%}$$

$$\frac{\$15.99}{1} \times \frac{discount}{\$15.99} = \frac{20\%}{100\%} \times \frac{\$15.99}{1}$$

$$discount = \frac{20 \times \$15.99}{100} = \$3.20$$

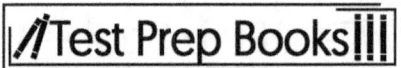

Answer Explanations #2

$$15.99 - \$3.20 = \$12.79 \ discounted \ price$$

If the pharmacy paid $3.75 to purchase this from their supplier to sell, and overhead costs are $5.00:

$$\$12.79 - \$3.75 - \$5.00 = \$4.04 \ net \ profit$$

The net profit the pharmacy makes is $4.04. If the discount was not taken out before the net profit was calculated, Choice A would have been correct. Since this asked for net profit, the overhead costs for the item were subtracted. If the question had asked for markup, the overhead costs would not have been taken out, and Choice C would have been correct. If just the overhead costs were subtracted, and not the actual price the pharmacy paid as well, Choice D would have been correct.

42. B: Pharmacists are only required to *offer* medication counseling to patients; they are not required to actually provide the counseling if the patient does not want it. The remaining choices are incorrect because they all describe situations that ARE requirements within pharmacies. Choice A, the pharmacy must close when no pharmacist is present, is incorrect because a pharmacy must be closed if there is no pharmacist working. Pharmacy technicians and other pharmacy employees cannot work when there is no pharmacist. Choice C, areas where controlled medications are stored must remain locked, is incorrect because places where controlled drugs are kept must remain locked and only approved pharmacy employees are allowed to enter. Choice D, pharmacy technicians must never provide any medical advice, is incorrect because it is a requirement that pharmacy technicians never provide medical advice.

43. A: Twinrix (HepA-HepB) is indicated and recommended for pregnant patients. Although it is more common for pregnant patients to receive Boostrix (HepB), Twinrix is also allowed, and it is the only available choice that is both safe and indicated for her. FluMist Quadrivalent (live attenuated influenza vaccine [LAIV]) and the M-M-R II are both live vaccines; both are contraindicated in pregnant patients. Because the CDC does recommend an annual flu shot, she may be indicated to receive an inactivated (IIV4) or recombinant (RIV4) version such as Flucelvax or FluBlok instead. Although not contraindicated, Shingrix (zoster recombinant vaccine [ZRV]) is only indicated for patients older than fifty and those older than nineteen with a compromised immune system, so she does not require a dose at this time.

44. D: Choice D is the correct answer. When determining whether a DEA number is valid, you will need to utilize an equation. The first thing to look at is the first two letters. The first letter describes the registrant type. "A/B/F" describe practitioners, and "M" describes a mid-level practitioner. The second letter is the first letter of the doctor's last name. Therefore, Choice C can be ruled out immediately. There should be seven digits following the two letters. Therefore, Choice A is incorrect since it has nine digits. Next, add the first, third, and fifth numbers together. Then add the second, fourth, and sixth numbers together and multiply that value by two. Add the first sum to the second. The last digit of this sum should correspond to the last digit of the DEA. View the step-by-step calculation below for Choice D:

1. (4 + 4 + 7) = 15

2. (3 + 2 + 9) = 14

3. 14 x 2 = 28

4. 15 + 28 = 43 <--- the last digit is 3, which corresponds to the last digit of the DEA number in Choice D.

Answer Explanations #2

45. D: Helping patients improve their health literacy includes understanding what they might not understand about their medications. Choice *D* involves making sure a patient can take their medication correctly. Choice *A* is incorrect because technicians cannot counsel. Choices *B* and *C* would hurt patient health literacy and not help the patient.

46. B: Effient is neither a hazardous medication under USP <800> nor a medication requiring a REMS program. However, its manufacturer considers it to be easily damaged by ambient humidity and advises that it be sold only in its original packaging to ensure stability.

47. A: Choice *A* is the correct answer. The USP <797> is updated consistently to establish new standards regarding sterile compounding to prevent any adverse drug events, and USP <800> establishes the standards for hazardous material handling to decrease safety-related incidents. Choice *B* is incorrect because USP <797> is specific to sterile compounding. Choice *C* is incorrect because both USP <797> and USP <800> are applied within all hospital and community pharmacies. Choice *D* is incorrect because the United States Pharmacopeia does not regulate USP <797> or USP <800>, and The National Institute for Occupational Safety and Health (NIOSH) defines and categorizes hazardous materials and drugs.

48. C: Non-controlled medications can technically have an unlimited number of refills; however, non-controlled medication orders are only valid for one year. Therefore, most thirty-day prescription orders have twelve refills if intended to provide a one-year supply. CIII-CV medications can have a maximum number of five refills within six months; therefore, Choice *A* is incorrect. Choice *B* is incorrect because non-controlled prescriptions expire after one year. Choice *D* is incorrect because only CII prescriptions do not have refills.

49. B: A laminar flow hood provides a sterile environment for compounding by directing a flow of filtered air over the work surface and minimizing contamination from the surrounding environment. It protects both the compounder and the patient. Choice *A* is incorrect because a laminar flow hood is not specifically designed for the containment of hazardous drugs. There are specific guidelines and requirements for handling hazardous drugs, including the use of proper PPE and designated areas for preparation. Choice *C* is incorrect because a laminar flow hood is not used for mixing ingredients. It is designed to provide a sterile environment by filtering air and removing particles and microorganisms that could contaminate the preparation. Choice *D* is incorrect because a laminar flow hood is not used to measure drug concentrations. The device is designed to provide a controlled environment for compounding, not analytical testing.

50. A: No food or drink should be consumed in the area of the pharmacy where drugs are compounded and/or filled. Many medications can be contaminated or destroyed by water, and if the water were to spill, it would ruin the medication. Choices *B*, *C*, and *D* are all considered best practices when filling medications.

51. B: Choice *B* is correct. Terminally ill or LTCF patients can receive partial fills up to the total quantity of the Schedule II controlled substance written on the prescription. Choices *A*, *C*, and *D* are incorrect because the other groups—children, prisoners, and older people—are not included in a special group. However, as individuals, any of these patients could also develop an illness that places them in the terminally ill or LTCF patient category.

52. D: Most waste management companies have specialists that can dispose of medications in a manner approved by the EPA. Choice *A*, flushing it down a drain with excess water, is incorrect because this action was made illegal in 2019 because it is an environmental hazard. Choice *B*, sending it to a landfill, is incorrect because controlled medications must be disposed of by professionals in a manner approved by the EPA. They cannot be dumped in a landfill. Choice *C*, sending it to a reverse distributor to be resold, is incorrect because reselling is not disposal. Reverse distributors are an option to dispose of medications, but they will never resell them.

53. B: The reconstituted MMR vaccine does appear yellow upon inspection and may be given to adults with unknown immune history or as a catch-up dose for the original series. New college students require the MenACWY vaccine, not the MenB, and the VAR vaccine is a live vaccine, so it should not be given to patients who are currently

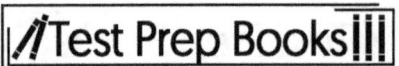

Answer Explanations #2

sick (as evidenced by his new antibiotic). Although healthcare workers are often required to maintain immunization against hepatitis A (HepA) and hepatitis B (HepB), there is currently no available vaccine for HepC.

54. C: With instructions indicating "to take 1 tablet by mouth three hours prior to procedure and give remaining tablet to staff upon check-in," this Xanax prescription appears to require a quantity of #2 tablets. However, it is written as #20. Unless the prescription was written for enough tablets for ten different procedures, this quantity is likely incorrect and is the most likely to have been forged or contain an error. If the quantity had been written out long-form (as "two" or "twenty") or the prescription been sent electronically, there would be fewer chances for mistakes, although it is always advisable to contact the prescriber to verify unclear directions and quantities. There are no blatant problems with a three-month prescription for maintenance of non-controlled medications, even if they all appear on the same document. As long as the DEA number is valid, it may be handwritten on the prescription; considering the prescription is on the physician's personal pad and their DEA number cannot be easily researched, it is unlikely that this prescription is a forgery. Mid-level practitioners may prescribe controlled substances while under the supervision of a physician, and faxes remain a viable (if not preferable) medium for transmitting controlled prescriptions as long as they contain the providers' DEA numbers.

55. C: Cracking and coalescence occur in emulsions and are visible signs of instability; therefore, Choices A and B are incorrect. Choice D, liquification, is incorrect because it is a near instantaneous reaction of two solids with low melting points physically changing in structure during the mixing process. Therefore, Choice C, the change in pH of a medication, is correct because this sign cannot be visualized and must be determined using litmus paper or a pH meter.

56. D: Choice D is correct because Schedule V drugs are considered "exempt narcotics." They are exempt because they contain lower quantities of controlled substances than drugs in the other four classes.

57. A: BID means twice a day, making Choice A the correct answer. TID means three times a day, QID means four times a day, and AC means before meals, which means that Choices B, C, and D are incorrect.

58. C: Once the prescription is received and processing has begun, the pharmacy is responsible for medication errors until the patient starts to administer the medication. Even then, if the wrong medication was dispensed, it would still be the pharmacy's fault. Choice A is only responsible if they write the prescription incorrectly, and the pharmacy is still responsible for making sure the prescription makes sense. Choice B is just relaying information, and Choice D is only at fault if the patient is properly counseled and they still administer the medication incorrectly.

59. A: HIPAA, the Health Insurance Portability and Accountability Act, prohibits the sharing of medical information with any person who is not permitted to view it. Choice B, they gave medical advice, is incorrect because they did not give medical advice to a patient. Choice C, they viewed a patient's medical history, is incorrect because pharmacy technicians can view medical history if a pharmacist assigns them to help with a patient. Choice D, they communicated with a pharmacy cashier, is incorrect because they are not prohibited from speaking to their coworkers.

60. B: The correct answer is Choice B because the excretory system is composed of the kidney, ureters, and urinary bladder and is responsible for elimination of unnecessary biological components like body fluids, microorganisms, and cellular waste products. Choice A is incorrect because these components make up the skeletal system. Choice C is incorrect because these components make up the digestive system. Choice D is incorrect because these components make up the endocrine system.

61. C: While OCs require the pharmacist to provide a PPI with every dispensation, regardless of refill status, this does not apply to counseling. Choices A, B, and D are incorrect because pharmacists must counsel on every transferred medication, on every new prescription that has not been dispensed at the same strength and frequency in the last year, and on every prescription sent after an inpatient is discharged. Considering the patient in Choice D is receiving the same medications from a similar discharge situation twice in the same month, it is very likely that the pharmacist should counsel them, answer any questions they may have, and see if they have any difficulties with taking the medication properly.

62. B: Pulverization and trituration are both dry methods used to break down tablets and powders for use in compounded drugs; therefore, Choices A and D are incorrect. Choice C, geometric dilution, is a process of mixing unequal ingredients in a manner that forms a homogenous mixture. It is achieved by diluting the ingredient with a smaller quantity with an ingredient with a larger quantity until it is thoroughly mixed. Choice B, levigation, is the correct choice because it involves the grinding of the active ingredient in a wetting agent.

63. B: The correct answer is Choice B because antiemetic medications like bismuth subsalicylate and Dramamine are for preventing or treating nausea and vomiting. Choice A is incorrect because antacids are used to prevent or slow down heartburn. Choice C is incorrect because anti-inflammatories are used to decreased redness, heat, and swelling associated with inflammation. Choice D is incorrect because antipyretics are used to treat fever.

64. C: The Drug Enforcement Agency (DEA) enforces all laws on controlled substances. The Controlled Substances Act regulates drugs that may be potentially abused, and the DEA enacts and enforces rules to prevent drug abuse. Choice A, the EPA, is incorrect because the EPA enforces proper handling and disposal of hazardous medications. Choice B, the FDA, is incorrect because the FDA ensures that drugs are safe to consume. Choice D, the USDA, is incorrect because it has nothing to do with pharmaceuticals; it is the U.S. Department of Agriculture.

65. C: Choice C is correct. The files related to controlled substances must be kept at the pharmacy for two years per DEA regulations.

66. C: Insulin should be given subcutaneously into the layer of fat between skin and muscle, which typically requires a needle of length 1/2" to 5/8" (12.7 mm to 15.9 mm), although some patients with larger fat deposits may comfortably use a longer 1" needle if available. Since the patient's prescription is for injections given three times daily, a month's supply would require 90 syringes, so a box of 100 would be appropriate. The prescription was written for 37 units per injection of a U-100 insulin, so each injection will require 0.37 mL of insulin. Therefore, the 0.5 mL syringes would be best.

67. A: The state law regulating pharmacies is usually stricter than the federal guidelines and therefore is the one that is followed. Choice B is usually less strict, and Choices C and D are not (usually) involved in pharmacy regulations.

68. D: "P.C." is the correct answer. It stands for the Latin phrase *post cibum*, which means "after meals." Choice A, BID, is incorrect because it stands for the Latin phrase *bis in die*, which means "twice a day." Choice B, A.C., is incorrect because it stands for *ante cibum*, which means "before meals." Choice C, PRN, is incorrect because it stands for *pro re nata*, which means "as needed."

69. C: The correct answer is Choice C because tricyclics, along with serotonin selective reuptake inhibitors and norepinephrine reuptake inhibitors, are examples of antidepressants. Choice A is incorrect because antiarrhythmics are used to control heart rate. Choice B is incorrect because anticonvulsants are used to prevent epileptic seizures. Choice D is incorrect because diuretics are used to decrease reabsorption of fluids and cause an increase in urine production.

70. A: Patient assistance programs are offered for patients who don't have insurance or for patients with insurance that does not cover the medication they need under their plan. Choice B is incorrect because patient assistance programs do not help cover copay costs. Choice C is incorrect because these programs can be sourced from pharmaceutical or insurance companies, government agencies, and non-profit organizations. Choice D is incorrect

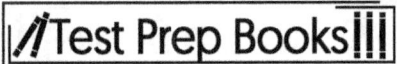

Answer Explanations #2

because they can be utilized to cover the entire cost of the medication or a portion of the cost and can be used multiple times or once.

71. D: Modafinil is considered a Schedule IV controlled substance, so the associated auxiliary label is appropriate. Choice A is incorrect because Septra (sulfamethoxazole and trimethoprim) has no cross-allergenicity with beta-lactam drugs like penicillin and cephalosporin. Choice B is incorrect because levocetirizine (Xyzal) is an antihistamine and has no special relationship with thyroid hormones. Choice C is incorrect because cyclosporine eyedrops (Restasis) may be kept at room temperature without need for refrigeration.

72. B: Tresiba FlexTouch insulin pens can remain stable at room temperature or when refrigerated for up to 56 days after opening. Lantus and Humalog vials maintain stability under these same conditions for up to 28 days; therefore, Choices A and C are incorrect. Humulin 70/30 insulin pens are stable only at room temperature or when refrigerated for up to 10 days; therefore, Choice D is incorrect.

73. A: Medicare is available to those over the age of 65, those younger than 65 years old and disabled, and anyone with end-stage renal disease. Therefore, Choices B, C, and D are incorrect.

74. C: Choice C is correct. This question requires converting a ratio to a percentage and w/v% calculations. First, calculate the ratio, 1:250, as a percentage:

$$\frac{1}{250} = \frac{x\%}{100\%}$$

x% would equal 0.4, so 1:250 to percentage is 0.4%. Now that we know the w/v% percentage, calculate how much, in grams, of the active ingredient, mucusaline, is present in the solution?

$$0.4\% \frac{w}{v} = \frac{x \text{ g mucusaline}}{100 \text{ mL solution}}$$

Solving for x, we get 40 grams mucusaline for every 100 mL solution. The last step is converting this to ounces as the question asked:

$$\frac{40 \text{ g}}{1} \times \frac{1 \text{ kg}}{1000 \text{ g}} \times \frac{2.2 \text{ lb}}{1 \text{ kg}} \times \frac{16 \text{ oz}}{1 \text{ lb}} = x \text{ oz}$$

$$\frac{40 \text{ g}}{1} \times \frac{1 \text{ kg}}{1000 \text{ g}} \times \frac{2.2 \text{ lb}}{1 \text{ kg}} \times \frac{16 \text{ oz}}{1 \text{ lb}} = 1.4 \text{ oz}$$

Since we only know the conversion for kilograms to pounds (2.2 lb = 1 kg), we converted the g to kg before converting over to pounds. 1.4 oz of mucusaline is present in 0.4%, or 1:250, w/v% preparation of Allergide. Choice C is correct.

75. B: The information on a medication's barcode will only be relevant to the medication, not the prescriber. All other choices are incorrect because medication barcodes will always include the recommended dosage form, the strength, and the name of the medication.

76. C: Pharmacists can work under a collaborative practice agreement and can prescribe medications that the provider authorizes, depending on the specialty. For example, an oncologist may authorize an oncology pharmacist to prescribe cancer medications, but they would not be able to prescribe medications for a foot infection. They are limited to the specific agreement's terms. Therefore, Choices A, B, and D are incorrect.

Answer Explanations #2

77. C: Choice C is correct. First, convert Amanda's weight to kg:

$$\frac{80 \text{ lb}}{1} \times \frac{1 \text{ kg}}{2.2 \text{ lb}} = x \text{ kg}$$

$$\frac{80 \text{ lb}}{1} \times \frac{1 \text{ kg}}{2.2 \text{ lb}} = 36.4 \text{ kg}$$

Next, convert Amanda's height to cm:

$$\frac{4 \text{ ft}}{1} \times \frac{12 \text{ in}}{1 \text{ ft}} \times \frac{2.54 \text{ cm}}{1 \text{ in}} = x \text{ cm}$$

$$\frac{4 \text{ ft}}{1} \times \frac{12 \text{ in}}{1 \text{ ft}} \times \frac{2.54 \text{ cm}}{1 \text{ in}} = 121.92 \text{ cm}$$

Now, insert these two values into the BSA equation:

$$BSA\ (m^2) = \sqrt{\frac{[121.92 \text{ cm} \times 36.4 \text{ kg}]}{3600}}$$

$$1.11 \text{ m}^2 = \sqrt{\frac{[121.92 \text{ cm} \times 36.4 \text{ kg}]}{3600}}$$

Using the equation from BSA Pediatric Dosing/Nomogram method:

$$dose\ (mg) = \frac{1.11 \text{ m}^2}{1.73 \text{ m}^2} \times 60 \text{ mg}$$

$$38.5 \text{ mg} = \frac{1.11 \text{ m}^2}{1.73 \text{ m}^2} \times 60 \text{ mg}$$

Amanda should take 38.5 mg Funolol based on her BSA. Therefore, Choice C is correct.

78. A: Choice A is correct because monitoring INR values is the standard method for determining whether blood thinners have reached a therapeutic level. Choice B is incorrect because statins are not monitored via INR values but instead require annual bloodwork to screen cholesterol values. Antibiotics do not typically require monitoring, so Choice C is incorrect. Anticonvulsants require monitoring of bloodwork, but INR values do not apply here, so Choice D is incorrect.

79. B: The correct answer is Choice B because enteric-coated tablets are compressed with a polymer that prevents them from dissolving in acidic conditions, like in the stomach, but instead lets them dissolve in a more basic pH, like

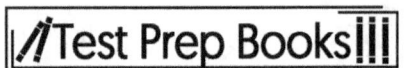

the small intestine. Therefore, Choice *A* is incorrect. Choice *C* is incorrect because prevention from disintegrating in the oral cavity is not the main purpose. Choice *D* is incorrect because enteric coating is a method of ensuring extended release and preventing immediate release.

80. B: The primary purpose of a beyond-use date for compounded products is to ensure that the product remains potent over a specified time. It does not relate to sterility, labeling, or cost. BUDs are based on the chemical and physical stability of the compounded preparation, the intended storage conditions, and the likelihood of microbial growth or contamination. They are established by the compounding pharmacist and are specific to each individual compounded product. The BUDs are used to ensure that the compounded product is still safe and effective when used by the patient. Choice *A* is incorrect because sterility is maintained through proper compounding techniques and aseptic procedures, not through BUDs. Choice *C* is incorrect because labeling accuracy is ensured through proper labeling procedures, not BUDs. Choice *D* is incorrect because BUDs are based on the product's stability and potency, not its cost-effectiveness.

81. B: Choice *B* is the correct answer. The Anabolic Steroid Act of 1990 was passed in response to an increase in illegal trafficking of steroids that were being used to improve athletic performance and personal appearance. Choice *A* is incorrect because the price of steroids had nothing to do with the act. Choice *C* is incorrect because steroids were not being marketed to children. Choice *D* is incorrect because although there was an increase in illegal trafficking, the act banned over-the-counter use of steroids and steroid precursors.

82. C: This may be an allergy; although diarrhea is a common side effect of antibiotics, the rash is a potential indicator of a new allergy. However, it is not certain due to its small size and the potential to mistake a rash for topical dermatitis. Because he had not completed his antibiotic regimen, his doctor should be contacted for advice on whether he should be prescribed a new medication. He should not restart the medication due to the possibility that it is an allergy. Immune systems may take multiple administrations before their white blood cells are familiar enough with the medication to present with maximal severity. It is safer to discontinue the medication and encourage him to contact his physician.

83. A: Epinephrine inhalers like Primatene Mist are regulated as OTC products, as they may be sold without a pharmacy consult. BTC medications require a pharmacy consult and are typically kept behind the counter or locked up, while legend drugs and continuous glucose monitors (CGMs) each require a prescription for dispensation.

84. D: The correct answer is Choice *D* because a vanishing base is an example of a cream dosage form. There are four common bases for ointments: oleaginous, absorption, water-removable, and water-soluble. Therefore, Choices *A*, *B,* and *C* are incorrect.

85. C: Prior authorization can only be completed by the prescriber and then, once approved, they will let the pharmacy know to reprocess the claim. Some medications are not covered and will require the prescriber to fill out a prior authorization form to inform the insurance company why that specific medication is required rather than the medication that the insurance company normally covers. The pharmacy will get this rejection and is responsible for relaying it to the prescriber's office. Therefore Choices, *A*, *B,* and *D* are incorrect.

86. C: Not all antibiotics require refrigeration after reconstitution. Refrigeration decreases the stability of reconstituted Clarithromycin oral suspension by altering the viscosity or pourability of the suspension as well as affecting the taste; therefore, Choices *A* and *B* are incorrect. Choice *D* is incorrect because reconstitution of any oral antibiotic increases the risk of microbial growth. Therefore, the correct answer is Choice *C*.

87. D: The patient's date of birth is not required on a prescription label. All other choices are incorrect because the patient's name, the prescriber's name, and the name of the medication are always required on prescription labels. Although some states vary slightly on what they require to be included on a prescription label, these aspects are always mandatory.

88. D: Choices *A*, *B*, and *C* are incorrect because even distribution of small particles within a suspension vehicle that easily redistributes with moderate shaking are classic characteristics of a stable suspension. The insoluble particles should be able to separate from each other and flow easily in the external phase. Choice *D* is correct because even distribution of the internal phase is lost when the particles adhere to one another, forming large caking clumps within the suspension that can affect accurate dosing of the medication.

89. B: Choice *B* is the correct answer. Per OSHA guidelines, sharps containers must be accurately labeled and must be red. Hazardous waste containers often have different colors indicating the type of material within them. Choice *A* is incorrect because the sides and bottom of the container must be leak-proof to prevent contamination. Choice *C* is incorrect because patients with reusable containers are advised against opening and cleaning the containers to reduce the risk of contamination. Choice *D* is incorrect because sharps containers should always be upright to prevent leakage.

90. B: DAW 4 is used when the generic medication is out of stock, and the pharmacy must dispense the brand name. Choice *A* describes DAW 0, Choice *C* describes DAW 7, and Choice *D* describes DAW 8.

91. D: Choice *D* is correct. The equation to go from Fahrenheit to Celsius is:

$$\frac{5}{9}(°F - 32) = °C$$

Inputting 78 °F:

$$\frac{5}{9}(78 °F - 32) = 25.6 °C$$

Choice *D* is correct, as 78 °F equals 25.6 °C. Choice *A* is if you used the °C to °F equation and plugged in 78 °F as 78 °C.

92. B: Under a four-tier system, Tier 1 usually includes only preferred generic drugs, although some systems may include both low-cost generic drugs and low-cost brand-name drugs in this tier. Tier 2 includes more expensive, generally nonpreferred generic drugs and preferred brand-name drugs, both of which have a higher cost than Tier 1 drugs. Tier 3 includes high-cost drugs, usually brand name and often with a cheaper generic version available. Tier 4 includes the highest cost drugs, also usually brand name and frequently known as specialty drugs. Therefore, Choices *A*, *C*, and *D* are incorrect.

93. A: Choice *A* is correct. This is an alligation question, where you have two concentrations and need to make a middle, desired concentration. First, start by filling out the table with what we know:

Higher strength: 20%		Parts of higher:
	Desired strength: 15%	
Lower strength: 3%		Parts of lower:

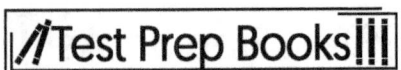

Then subtract across the diagonals:

Higher strength: 20%		Parts of higher: 12 p
	Desired strength: 15%	
Lower strength: 3%		Parts of lower: 5 p

This means that you need 12 parts of 20% PainRx and 5 parts of 3% PainRx. To solve for the separate amounts, add the total number of parts:

$$12\,p + 5\,p = 17\,p\ total$$

Then use this equation to set up a proportion:

$$\frac{total\ amount}{total\ parts} = \frac{amount\ of\ higher/lower\ solution}{parts\ of\ higher/lower\ solution}$$

To find the amount of the 20% solution:

$$\frac{2.3\ L\ total}{17\ p\ total} = \frac{x\ L\ 20\%}{12\ p\ 20\%} = 1.624\ L$$

To find the amount of the 3% solution:

$$\frac{2.3\ L\ total}{17\ p\ total} = \frac{y\ L\ 3\%}{5\ p\ 3\%} = 0.677\ L$$

This means that x equals 1.624 L and y equals 0.677 L. Converting these to mL, you need 1,624 mL of 20% PainRx and 677 mL of 3% PainRx to make 2.3 L of 15% PainRx. Choice A is the correct answer.

94. C: Antiepileptics are a drug class that requires extreme caution in both pregnant and breastfeeding mothers. Select medications are tolerated in both, but their medication regimen should always be reviewed. Choice A as a class is not dangerous to either group, Choice B is only contraindicated in pregnancy for every drug in the class, and Choice D is not dangerous to either group.

95. C: Levofloxacin is a fluoroquinolone that will chelate in the LR solution due to its calcium content. Furosemide may safely be added to D5W, and vitamins may safely be added to NS. A simple mixture of amino acids into a lipid emulsion is also acceptable. With TPN directions, it is advisable to first mix amino acids and dextrose together before adding to the lipid emulsion; this TPN consists of only two solutions, and the emulsion in the final bag, so this would be fine.

96. B: Amnesteem (isotretinoin) is a REMS drug that requires the pledged use of two birth control methods in addition to monthly pregnancy tests for females of childbearing age. While thalidomide also has a REMS program, it does not specify which kinds of birth control must be used, nor does it require a time frame before allowable use; therefore, Choice C is incorrect. Choice A is incorrect because although Allegra-D is subordinate to the CMEA and indeed may only be purchased with a valid photo ID, this is not a REMS program. Choice D is incorrect because although testing thyroid hormones like T3, T4, TRH, and TSH may be useful for physicians to gauge the success of a thyroid treatment, it is not a REMS program and typically does not happen monthly.

97. C: Choice C is correct because DEA Form 222 is the order form and transfer form for Schedule II controlled substances. Choice A is incorrect because DEA Form 41 is used to provide a record of destroyed controlled substances. Choice B is incorrect because DEA Form 106 is for theft or significant loss, and Choice D is incorrect because DEA Form 300 does not exist.

98. D: *Plan limits exceeded* means that an insurance company only allows a thirty-day supply rather than a ninety-day supply, and this will require a change in the pharmacy system and a call to the patient informing them of the change. Choices A, B, and C all require prescriber clarification to proceed with the claim.

99. C: Choice C is correct. Using the equation for mEq:

$$\text{grams equivalent to 1 Eq} = \frac{\text{combined molecular mass of all ions}}{|\text{highest valence charge}|}$$

The valence charge of Ca is +2, the valence charge of OH is -1, so 2 will be used in this equation. Because OH represents hydroxide, you take the valence of hydroxide, not O and H. Even if you used them all separately, +2 would still be the highest, as O is -2 and H is +1. This is the correct equation:

$$x \text{ grams} = \frac{74.093 \text{ g/mol}}{2} = 37.05 \text{ g}$$

37.05 g of Ca(OH)$_2$ is equal to 1 Eq based on mol, so 37.05 mg is equal to 1 mEq based on mmol; therefore, Choice C is correct. Choice A is incorrect because it uses -1 as the valence charge. Choice D is incorrect because it adds the absolute value of both charges together to create a valence of 3. Choice B is the mEq of NaCl, a commonly used mEq value.

100. D: While Trulicity (dulaglutide) and Lovenox (enoxaparin) are both injectables, they each come with their own needles and do not require individual syringes. Therefore, Choices A and B are incorrect. No oral solutions (including Zovirax, or acyclovir) should be injected under normal circumstances because they do not necessarily have the sterile qualifications for direct administration to the bloodstream. Therefore, Choice C is incorrect. Depo-Provera (medroxyprogesterone) is the only medication listed that comes in a vial and could require an outpatient syringe, although some medroxyprogesterone shots come in pre-filled syringes. Alternatively, enoxaparin may be supplied to nursing units or hospitals as a multi-dose vial, but this is uncommon for most outpatient concerns.

ExCPT Practice Test #3

To keep the size of this book manageable, save paper, and provide a digital test-taking experience, the 3rd practice test can be found online. Scan the QR code or go to this link to access it:

testprepbooks.com/bonus/excpt

The first time you access the tests, you will need to register as a "new user" and verify your email address.

If you have any issues, please email support@testprepbooks.com.

Dear ExCPT Test Taker,

Thank you again for purchasing this study guide for your ExCPT exam. We hope that we exceeded your expectations.

Our goal in creating this study guide was to cover all of the topics that you will see on the test. We also strove to make our practice questions as similar as possible to what you will encounter on test day. With that being said, if you found something that you feel was not up to your standards, please send us an email and let us know.

We have study guides in a wide variety of fields. If the one you are looking for isn't listed above, then try searching for it on Amazon or send us an email.

Thanks Again and Happy Testing!
Product Development Team
info@studyguideteam.com

FREE Test Taking Tips Video/DVD Offer

To better serve you, we created videos covering test taking tips that we want to give you for FREE. **These videos cover world-class tips that will help you succeed on your test.**

We just ask that you send us feedback about this product. Please let us know what you thought about it—whether good, bad, or indifferent.

To get your **FREE videos**, you can use the QR code below or email freevideos@studyguideteam.com with "Free Videos" in the subject line and the following information in the body of the email:

    a. The title of your product

    b. Your product rating on a scale of 1-5, with 5 being the highest

    c. Your feedback about the product

If you have any questions or concerns, please don't hesitate to contact us at info@studyguideteam.com.

Thank you!

www.ingramcontent.com/pod-product-compliance
Lightning Source LLC
Chambersburg PA
CBHW080730300426
44114CB00019B/2537